Anthropological Papers
Museum of Anthropology, University of Michigan
No. 89

Caciques and Their People

A Volume in Honor of Ronald Spores

edited by
Joyce Marcus and Judith Francis Zeitlin

Ann Arbor, Michigan
1994

Printed in the United States of America

ISBN 0-915703-37-8

The University of Michigan Museum of Anthropology currently publishes three monograph series: Anthropological Papers, Memoirs, and Technical Reports. We have over seventy titles in print. For a complete catalog, write to Museum of Anthropology Publications, 4009 Museums Bldg., Ann Arbor, MI 48109-1079, or call (313) 764-0485.

Library of Congress Cataloging-in-Publication Data

Caciques and their people : a volume in honor of Ronald Spores /
edited by Joyce Marcus and Judith Francis Zeitlin.
p. cm.—(Anthropological papers / Museum of Anthropology, University of Michigan ; no. 89
Includes bibliographical references.
ISBN 0-915703-37-8 (alk. paper)
1. Caciques (Indian leaders)—Mexico. 2. Indians of Mexico—Kings and rulers. 3. Indians of Mexico—History—Sources. 4. Ethnohistory—Mexico. 5. Spores, Ronald. I. Marcus, Joyce. II. Zeitlin, Judith Francis. III. Spores, Ronald. IV. Series: Anthropological papers (University of Michigan. Museum of Anhthropology) ; no. 89.
GN2.M5 no. 89
[F1219.3.K55]
306 s—dc20
[972′.01] 94-34805

The paper used in this publication meets the requirements of the ANSI Standard Z39.48-1984 (Permanence of Paper)

Contents

Figures

Tables

Preface

JOYCE MARCUS AND JUDITH FRANCIS ZEITLIN

RONALD M. SPORES—ethnohistorian, archaeologist, ethnologist—taught at Vanderbilt University from 1965 to 1993. In 1989 the editors began planning this volume so that it would be ready to present to Spores upon his retirement from Vanderbilt. Many of his friends and colleagues felt strongly that his intellectual contributions to the field should be much more widely known, and his unfailing generosity to other scholars should be acknowledged. All the contributors to this volume know Spores well, and we hope that the book leads others to his work.

Although no single book could include articles from *all* the scholars who have been influenced and inspired by Spores' ethnohistoric and archaeological studies, this volume does bring together the work of fourteen of his friends, all of whom have learned and benefitted from his careful scholarship.

Like Spores' own publications, the contributions in this volume range from ethnological to archaeological to ethnohistoric, and from theoretical to empirical and substantive. Many contributors integrate multiple lines of evidence, and some compare different ethnic groups as "case studies." In this volume one can see examples of the comparative approach, the direct historical approach, and the evaluation of "degree of fit" between different lines of evidence. Those are the kinds of approaches that typify Spores' work.

This volume, then, is both a tribute to Ronald Spores as well as a contribution to the anthropology, ethnohistory, and archaeology of Mesoamerica.

CONTRIBUTORS

John Chance
Department of Anthropology
Arizona State University
Tempe, Arizona 85287–2402

Gary Feinman
Department of Anthropology
1180 Observatory Drive
University of Wisconsin
Madison, Wisconsin 53706–1393

Kent V. Flannery
Museum of Anthropology
University of Michigan
Ann Arbor, Michigan 48109–1079

Frederic Hicks
Department of Anthropology
University of Louisville
Louisville, Kentucky 40292

Robert C. Hunt
Department of Anthropology
Brandeis University
Waltham, Massachusetts 02254

Michael Lind
1910 North Greenbriar Street
Santa Ana, California 92706

Joyce Marcus
Museum of Anthropology
University of Michigan
Ann Arbor, Michigan 48109–1079

John Monaghan
Department of Anthropology
P.O. Box 6050, Station B
Vanderbilt University
Nashville, Tennessee 37235

John Paddock
Instituto de Estudios Oaxaqueños
Apartado 464
Oaxaca, Oaxaca, Mexico

Elsa M. Redmond
Department of Anthropology
American Museum of Natural History
Central Park West at 79th Street
New York, New York 10024–5192

Dra. María de los Angeles Romero Frizzi
Centro Regional de Oaxaca, INAH
Pino Suárez 715
Oaxaca, Oaxaca 68000, Mexico

Mary Elizabeth Smith
417 Sycamore St., N.E.
Albuquerque, NM 87106

Charles S. Spencer
Department of Anthropology
American Museum of Natural History
Central Park West at 79th Street
New York, New York 10024–5192

Judith F. Zeitlin
Department of Anthropology
University of Massachusetts, Boston
Boston, Massachusetts 02125-3393

CHAPTER 1

Retired? You Must Be Kidding!

A Tribute to Ronald Spores

JOYCE MARCUS AND KENT V. FLANNERY

UNIVERSITY OF MICHIGAN

SO THE UNTHINKABLE has happened: Ron Spores has retired. No, not from thinking, or writing, or doing ethnology and ethnohistory and archaeology. Just from teaching at Vanderbilt, even though he still looks younger than most of his graduate students.

This unthinkable news has prompted us to look back over Spores' three decades of research and publication (pardon us, we mean his *first* three decades of research and publication). Since the moment that he was chosen, while still a student at Harvard, to write a definitive article for the *Handbook of Middle American Indians* (1965), Spores has been a generalist whose work spanned more than one discipline. He has done archaeological survey and excavation, has established a chronology for the Mixteca, has done ethnology, and has excelled at ethnohistoric research. His enduring interests span prehistory; political and legal anthropology; ethnohistoric sources and methods; the origins of social stratification; indigenous religion, social organization, and settlement patterns; and Spanish Colonial law and government.

Beginnings

Ron Spores received his Bachelor of Science in 1953 from the University of Oregon. After graduation he served in the military, then worked in the insurance business in Los Angeles. In search of a more satisfying career, he eventually left business to pursue a Master's degree in Anthropology from Mexico City College (now University of the Americas). After receiving his M.A. in 1960 he enrolled at Harvard University, where he earned a second Master's degree (1963) and a Ph.D. (1964) in Anthropology. He was hired by the University of Massachusetts in 1964 and lectured there for one year; from 1965 to 1993 he taught at Vanderbilt University. Spores retired from Vanderbilt in April, 1993.

Spores' experience in Mexico was to shape the rest of his career: he went on to use the Mixtec as the source for many of his best contributions, a kind of long-term case study. Spores' work spans the early villages of the Mixteca Alta (1300 B.C.) to the rise of the Classic cities (A.D. 500–900), to the Postclassic and Colonial *cacicazgos* of A.D. 1500–1600. He then covered the historic period from early Colonial times to the nineteenth-century presidency of Porfirio Díaz, and then went on to the market towns and pottery-making villages of the late twentieth-century Mixteca (Fig. 1.1). We have no doubt that he will still be making contributions to Mixtec anthropology in the twenty-first century.

Ethnohistoric Contributions

Armed with anthropological data, comparative methods, and political theory, Spores began his career working with the archives of Mexico and Spain, using Colonial documents as if they were "informants" (Spores 1964, 1973b). He was doing "documentary ethnography," focusing on anthropological issues that could be addressed with the data in the wills, marriage records, censuses, and court cases (Figs. 1.2, 1.3). Spores often credited France V. Scholes for a lot of his inspiration; other scholars who influenced him include Ralph Roys, Alfonso Caso, Wigberto Jiménez Moreno, Jorge Acosta, Ignacio Bernal, and John Paddock.

Spores' first article, "The Genealogy of Tlazultepec: A Sixteenth-century Mixtec Manuscript," was an ethnohistoric study (Spores 1964). He focused on a 1597 document submitted to the Spanish court in support of the claim of succession by doña Juana de Rojas of Tlazultepec (a small community now known as San Agustín Tlacotepec). Spores was intrigued by the fact that this document retained so many prehispanic features (e.g., Mixtec "hill glyphs" and other signs for place names; footprints to show travel and places of origin of individuals) even after 70 years of Spanish influence. The genealogical drawing was used by doña Juana to show that her grandfather and grandmother had been *caciques* of Tlazultepec, as was her father, even though he chose not to reside in his hometown and allowed his sister to rule Tlazultepec. Contesting doña Juana's claim was don Juan de Guzmán y Velasco, who had married doña Juana's cousin, another ruler of Tlazultepec. Since that cousin had left no offspring, doña Juana argued that the title should revert back to the principal trunk of the lineage, i.e. the one passing through her own grandfather and father. The courts set aside an earlier decision which had found in favor of don Juan, and decided in favor of doña Juana. She was formally installed as *cacica* of Tlazultepec on February 12, 1599.

In another influential ethnohistoric article, "Marital Alliance in the Political Integration of Mixtec Kingdoms," Spores (1974b) showed convincingly that one

Figure 1.1. The ethnographer Ronald Spores (right) takes to the field with a twentieth-century informant.

Figure 1.2. Ronald Spores the ethnohistorian examines Colonial documents in the State Archives of Oaxaca.

of the mechanisms maintaining the sixteenth-century *cacicazgos* was a complex network of arranged marriage alliances. He demonstrated that the significant corporate group for the Mixtec was not the lineage but the localized ruling family. He also concluded that the "ideal" marriage alliance resulted in the joining of two or more kingdoms. A family who could draw on the labor and tribute of two or more kingdoms would be in an advantageous position to meet other kinds of economic and political goals. Spores' evidence suggested that marriage alliances, along with other voluntaristic strategies (e.g., political confederation) and coercive strategies (war, conquest), should be the subject of future investigation, since they were important in the maintenance, formation, and expansion of states.

Archaeological Contributions

After working with sixteenth-century and seventeenth-century archival documents for twenty-one Mixtec *cacicazgos,* Spores set out to uncover the antecedent prehispanic patterns. From Colonial documents he had gained a detailed picture of Mixtec life at the time of the Conquest (Spores 1964, 1965, 1967) and had

Figure 1.3. Ronald Spores (left) with Dr. Manuel Esparza, Director of the Oaxaca archives.

developed a set of expectations and testable models for Mixtec "community kingdoms." To find the social, economic, and political *antecedents* for the patterns he had documented in the archives, however, he knew that he had to turn to the archaeological record (Fig. 1.4). In so doing, Spores (1972:2) consciously employed the "direct historical approach" pioneered by Waldo Wedel (1938), Julian Steward (1942), and William Duncan Strong (1940, 1953). That is, he worked back from the *known* (the historically identified patterns) to the *unknown* (the patterns to be revealed in the archaeological record).

In 1966 Spores undertook the first systematic settlement pattern survey of the Nochixtlán Valley, a region he regarded as an ideal "test unit for intensive study" (Spores 1972:2).

> The Nochixtlan Project has attempted to determine 1) if the material manifestations of community patterns, macrosettlements, or settlement systems can be identified archaeologically, first for the European contact period, then for protohistoric and prehistoric times, 2) how far back in time such patterns can be projected, and 3) if material manifestations can be identified, to determine if sixteenth century community patterns and intercommunity relations can be utilized to explain changing patterns of settlement and intersite relations in prehistoric times. [Spores 1972:4]

Figure 1.4. Ronald Spores, the archaeologist, oversees an excavation into Mixtec prehistory.

Another major goal of the Nochixtlán Valley Project was:

> to trace the origins and developments of social stratification and the Mixtec kingdom as inferred from the archaeological and documentary record of cultural development in the Nochixtlan Valley. Such processual considerations reflect two of anthropology's most perplexing and persisting problems, the origins of systems of stratification and the state. [Spores 1972:6]

To publish his settlement pattern results, Spores established a new publication series called Vanderbilt University Publications in Anthropology (VUPA). The first volume of the series, published in 1972, was entitled *An Archaeological Settlement Survey of the Nochixtlán Valley*. As of 1993, more than forty monographs have been published in the VUPA series.

In his 1972 monograph, Spores established a ceramic-based chronological sequence for the Nochixtlán Valley and used survey and excavation to document intercommunity relations and settlement systems as they evolved from the Formative villages of 1300 B.C. to the "community kingdoms" of A.D. 1600.

The oldest period defined by Spores was the Cruz phase (Early Cruz 1300–700 B.C.; Late Cruz, 700–200 B.C.). This period was detected by surface survey at 18 of the 176 sites in the Nochixtlán Valley. Spores also recovered Cruz ceramics in his excavations at Yucuita, Initiyu, Etlatongo, and Iglesia Vieja de Chachoapan.

Cruz phase sites tended to be small and were found in three typical locations: (1) on the lower ends of piedmont spurs near the river; (2) at stream confluences; and (3) on low rises in the center of the valley. Cruz phase farmers were apparently concerned with being near water and good alluvium, away from areas that flooded.

Spores called his second phase Ramos (200 B.C.–A.D. 600). During this time the site of Yucuita became a major center, covering perhaps 1.5 km^2; surrounding Yucuita were at least five satellite communities. Yucuita served as the economic and political center for the valley and had a centripetal effect on settlement patterns. Not only were Ramos phase sites much larger and more complex than those of the Cruz phase, there were twice as many of them (35), suggesting at least a doubling of the population (Spores 1972:176). There were three levels to the site-size hierarchy at this time: (1) the main center of Yucuita, alone at the top; (2) ten "town-size" sites; and (3) twenty "rancho-size" settlements. Yucuita was associated with the richest alluvial deposits in the valley, while another cluster of important Ramos phase sites lay in the Etlatongo-Jaltepec region. Spores noted that both Yucuita and Etlatongo were among a handful of sites occupied continuously from Cruz to Ramos times.

Spores found pottery of the Las Flores phase (A.D. 500–1000) at 113 sites; during this period one of these (Yucuñudahui) became the political and economic successor to Yucuita. Other large centers of the Las Flores phase included Etlatongo, Cerro Jazmín, La Palmita, Jaltepec, and Topiltepec. Yucuita continued to be occupied, but it did not appear to have functioned as the main political center for the valley at this time.

Spores' Natividad phase (A.D. 1000–1530) represents the period of maximum population density for the ancient Nochixtlán Valley; a total of 159 sites could be assigned to this period. Significantly, the Natividad phase showed a marked decline in monumental architecture; furthermore, houses were generally smaller and more widely spaced than they had been during Ramos and Las Flores times. Just as the political center of the valley had shifted from Yucuita to Yucuñudahui during the Las Flores phase, it shifted to ancient Yanhuitlán during the Natividad phase. At this time Yanhuitlán controlled at least fifteen other settlements; less powerful *cacicazgos* were centered at Etlatongo, Nochixtlán, Chachoapan, Soyaltepec, Jaltepec, and Tiltepec. Spores showed that although Etlatongo was never the valley's main capital, it was occupied and significant throughout the entire prehispanic sequence.

Spores' final phase was designated Convento (post-A.D. 1530). Although many settlements remained in their prehispanic locations, others (such as Nochixtlán and Chachoapan) were deliberately relocated by the Spaniards. This phase was late enough in time to allow Spores to compare and contrast the archaeological and ethnohistoric records.

The Integration of Ethnohistory and Archaeology

To integrate his various and growing bodies of information—settlement pattern data, excavation data, and archival data from many towns—Spores sat down to write an overview of Mixtec civilization and culture. He ended up writing a book that has become a Mesoamerican classic. That overview—*The Mixtec Kings and Their People*—was published by the University of Oklahoma Press in both hardback (1967) and paperback (1973).

By 1984, however, so much new information had been recovered by Spores and his colleagues in Oaxaca that he then undertook the writing of a second major book, *The Mixtecs of Oaxaca in Ancient and Colonial Times* (published in 1984 by University of Oklahoma Press). Together, his two University of Oklahoma books constitute excellent syntheses of his own contributions to Mixtec studies. They both add to our understanding of the cultural evolution of civilizations in general.

The Career and the Man

Spores' unique combination of ethnohistoric, ethnographic, and archaeological research demonstrates the importance of attacking anthropological problems by integrating many lines of evidence (e.g., Spores 1983j, 1984c). Take, for example, the case of the five major *cacicazgos* that existed in the Nochixtlán Valley at the time of the Spanish Conquest: Yanhuitlán, Nochixtlán, Etlatongo, Chachoapan, and Jaltepec. Using excavations and settlement pattern surveys, Spores showed how these *cacicazgos* had come into being, using the data to construct a model for the origins of the "Mixtec system of social stratification" (Spores 1983j). As they came into focus in the Spanish documents of the sixteenth century, he then showed in detail how the form and composition of these *cacicazgos* could change with every royal death, every change in title, and every royal marriage alliance. What might have been viewed, on the basis of limited archaeological evidence, as a monolithic political unit was revealed to be a very flexible system whose size and composition varied over time.

Despite the high quality and significance of his work, Spores has remained an underutilized resource because of his own unassuming nature. In an age when it is becoming the norm for Mesoamericanists to spend half their time beating their own drum, Spores has followed the pattern of a kinder and gentler time: he has preferred to let his work speak for itself. Working quietly in the dusty corners of a local archive, in the back room of an archaeological field laboratory, or in the adobe houses of a Mixtec village, he has labored to increase our knowledge rather than his own notoriety.

His colleagues who have put together this volume, however, know and appreciate his research, and they invite everyone to sample his publications (many of which are listed below). In much the same way that Sir Eric Thompson loved everything Maya—archaeology, epigraphy, ethnography, ethnohistory—Ron Spores has loved everything Mixtec. If it is true that wisdom and generosity were important characteristics of the Mixtec ruler, then for us Ron Spores is the last *tay toho*.

Selected Bibliography of Ronald Spores

1964 The genealogy of Tlazultepec: A sixteenth-century Mixtec manuscript. Southwestern Journal of Anthropology 20:15–31.

1965 The Zapotec and Mixtec at Spanish contact. In: Handbook of Middle American Indians, edited by Robert Wauchope. Vol. 3: Archaeology of Southern Mesoamerica, edited by Gordon R. Willey, pt 2, pp. 962–87. Austin: University of Texas Press.

1967 The Mixtec Kings and Their People. Norman: University of Oklahoma Press.

1969a Settlement, farming technology, and environment in the Nochixtlán Valley. Science 166:557–69.

1969b Reconocimiento arqueológico del Valle de Nochixtlán. Boletín del Instituto Nacional de Antropología (October 1969), pp. 35–43. Mexico.

1972 An Archaeological Settlement Survey of the Nochixtlán Valley, Oaxaca. Vanderbilt University Publications in Anthropology, no. 1. Nashville.

1973a Documentos para la etnohistoria del estado de Oaxaca: Indice del Ramo de Mercedes del Archivo General de la Nación, México (co-authored with Miguel Saldaña). Vanderbilt University Publications in Anthropology, no. 5. Nashville.

1973b Ethnohistorical Research in Mexico. In: Research in Mexican History, edited by Richard Greenleaf and M. Meyer, pp. 25–48. Lincoln: University of Nebraska Press.

1974a Stratigraphic Excavations in the Nochixtlán Valley, Oaxaca. Vanderbilt University Publications in Anthropology, no. 11. Nashville.

1974b Marital alliances in the political integration of Mixtec kingdoms. American Anthropologist 76:297–311.

1975 Documentos para la etnohistoria del estado de Oaxaca: Indice del Ramo de Indios del Archivo General de la Nación, México (co-authored with Miguel Saldaña). Vanderbilt University Publications in Anthropology, no. 13. Nashville.

1976a La estratificación social de la antigua sociedad Mixteca. In: Estratificación social en la Mesoamérica prehispánica, edited by Pedro Carrasco, Johanna Broda, et al., pp. 207–20. Centro de Investigaciones Superiores, Instituto Nacional de Antropología e Historia. Mexico City.

1976b Documentos para la etnohistoria del estado de Oaxaca: Indice del Ramo de Tributos, Archivo General de la Nación, México (co-authored with Miguel Saldaña). Vanderbilt University Publications in Anthropology, no. 17. Nashville.

1976c Indice del Archivo del Juzgado de Teposcolula, Oaxaca, Epoca Colonial (co-authored with María de los Angeles Romero). Cuadernos de los Centros Regionales, Instituto Nacional de Antropología e Historia. Mexico City.

1978 The Handbook of Middle American Indians: A Retrospective Look (co-authored with Joyce Marcus). American Anthropologist 80:85–100.

1980a Ethnohistory in middle age: An assessment and a call for action. Ethnohistory 25:199–205.

1980b New World ethnohistory and archaeology, 1970–1980. Annual Review of Anthropology 9:575–603. Palo Alto, California: Annual Reviews, Inc.

1982 Indice del Archivo del Gobierno del Estado de Oaxaca (co-authored with María de la Luz Topete). Instituto Nacional de Antropología e Historia. Oaxaca.

1983a Excavated sites of the Oaxaca Preceramic (co-authored with Kent V. Flannery). In: The Cloud People: Divergent Evolution of the Zapotec and Mixtec Civilizations, edited by Kent V. Flannery and Joyce Marcus, pp. 20–26. San Diego: Academic Press.

1983b The cultural legacy of the Oaxacan Preceramic (co-authored with Joyce Marcus and Kent V. Flannery). In: The Cloud People: Divergent Evolution of the Zapotec and Mixtec Civilizations, edited by Kent V. Flannery and Joyce Marcus, pp. 36–39. San Diego: Academic Press.

1983c Origins of the village in the Mixteca (Early Cruz Phase). In: The Cloud People: Divergent Evolution of the Zapotec and Mixtec Civilizations, edited by Kent V. Flannery and Joyce Marcus, p. 46. San Diego: Academic Press.

1983d Middle and Late Formative settlement patterns in the Mixteca Alta. In: The Cloud People: Divergent Evolution of the Zapotec and Mixtec Civilizations, edited by Kent V. Flannery and Joyce Marcus, pp. 72–74. San Diego: Academic Press.

1983e Divergence of the Mixteca and the Valley of Oaxaca, 1330–500 B.C. In: The Cloud People: Divergent Evolution of the Zapotec and Mixtec Civilizations, edited by Kent V. Flannery and Joyce Marcus, p. 77. San Diego: Academic Press.

1983f Ramos Phase Urbanization in the Mixteca Alta. In: The Cloud People: Divergent Evolution of the Zapotec and Mixtec Civilizations, edited by Kent V. Flannery and Joyce Marcus, pp. 120–23. San Diego: Academic Press.

1983g Las Flores Phase Settlement Patterns in the Nochixtlán Valley. In: The Cloud People: Divergent Evolution of the Zapotec and Mixtec Civilizations, edited by Kent V. Flannery and Joyce Marcus, pp. 152–55. San Diego: Academic Press.

1983h Yucuñudahui. In: The Cloud People: Divergent Evolution of the Zapotec and Mixtec Civilizations, edited by Kent V. Flannery and Joyce Marcus, pp. 155–58. San Diego: Academic Press.

1983i The Mixteca Alta at the end of Las Flores. In: The Cloud People: Divergent Evolution of the Zapotec and Mixtec Civilizations, edited by Kent V. Flannery and Joyce Marcus, p. 207. San Diego: Academic Press.

1983j The origin and evolution of the Mixtec system of social stratification. In: The Cloud People: Divergent Evolution of the Zapotec and Mixtec Civilizations, edited by Kent V. Flannery and Joyce Marcus, pp. 227–38. San Diego: Academic Press.

1983k Postclassic settlement patterns in the Nochixtlán Valley. In: The Cloud People: Divergent Evolution of the Zapotec and Mixtec Civilizations, edited by Kent V. Flannery and Joyce Marcus, pp. 246–48. San Diego: Academic Press.

1983l Postclassic Mixtec Kingdoms: Ethnohistoric and archaeological evidence. In: The Cloud People: Divergent Evolution of the Zapotec and Mixtec Civilizations, edited by Kent V. Flannery and Joyce Marcus, pp. 255–60. San Diego: Academic Press.

1983m Sixteenth-century kinship and social organization (co-authored with Kent V. Flannery). In: The Cloud People: Divergent Evolution of the Zapotec and Mixtec Civilizations, edited by Kent V. Flannery and Joyce Marcus, pp. 339–42. San Diego: Academic Press.

1983n Mixtec religion. In: The Cloud People: Divergent Evolution of the Zapotec and Mixtec Civilizations, edited by Kent V. Flannery and Joyce Marcus, pp. 342–45. San Diego: Academic Press.

1984a Five Centuries of Law and Politics in Central Mexico (co-edited with Ross Hassig). Vanderbilt Univerity Publications in Anthropology, no. 30. Nashville.

1984b Multi-level government in nineteenth-century Oaxaca. In: Five Centuries of Law and Politics in Central Mexico, pp. 145–71. Vanderbilt Univerity Publications in Anthropology, no. 30. Nashville.

1984c The Mixtecs of Oaxaca in Ancient and Colonial Times. Norman: University of Oklahoma Press.

1986a Benito Juárez, Gobernador de Oaxaca: Documentos de su mandato y servicio público. Conservados en el Archivo General del Estado de Oaxaca. Oaxaca: Gobierno del Estado de Oaxaca.

1986b Handbook of Middle American Indians, Supplement 2: Ethnohistory (vol. ed.). Austin: University of Texas Press.

1986c Los reyes de la Mixteca en la Epoca colonial. In: Lecturas Históricas del Estado de Oaxaca, Epoca Colonial, edited by María de los Angeles Romero. Instituto Nacional de Antropología e Historia. México.

1988 El Handbook of Middle American Indians (co-authored with Joyce Marcus). Anuario de Etnología y Antropología Social, vol. I:75–97. Mexico.

1990a Relaciones gubernamentales y judiciales entre los pueblos, los distritos y el estado de Oaxaca (siglo XIX). In: Lecturas Históricas del Estado de Oaxaca, vol. III (siglo XIX), edited by María de los Angeles Romero, pp. 239–90. Instituto Nacional de Antropología e Historia. Mexico City.

1990b Los caciques de la Mixteca Alta, siglo XVI. In: Lecturas Históricas del Estado de Oaxaca, vol. II (Epoca Colonial), edited by María de los Angeles Romero, pp. 101–49. Instituto Nacional de Antropología e Historia. Mexico City.

1990c La situación económica de la Mixteca en la primera decada de la independencia. In: Lecturas Históricas del Estado de Oaxaca, vol. III (siglo XIX), edited by María de los Angeles Romero, pp. 129–86. Instituto Nacional de Antropología e Historia. Mexico City.

1992 Colección de documentos del Archivo General de la Nación para la etnohistoria de la Mixteca de Oaxaca en el siglo XVI. Vanderbilt University Publications in Anthropology, no. 41. Nashville.

in press Los Mixtecos de Oaxaca. Mexico: Editorial Leyenda.

in press Differential response to Colonial control among Mixtecs and Zapotecs of Oaxaca. In: Native Resistance in New Spain, edited by Susan Schroeder. Lincoln: University of Nebraska Press.

Acknowledgments

We thank Laura Junker and Mary Thieme for supplying the photographs in this paper, and for doing so without letting Ron know we were assembling a book to honor him.

References Cited

Steward, Julian H.
1942 The direct historical approach to archaeology. American Antiquity 7:337–43.

Strong, William Duncan
1940 From history to prehistory in the Northern Great Plains. Miscellaneous Collection, Smithsonian Institution, vol. 100:353–94. Washington, D.C.
1953 Historical approach in anthropology. In: Anthropology Today, edited by Alfred L. Kroeber, pp. 386–97. Chicago: University of Chicago Press.

Wedel, Waldo R.
1938 The Direct-Historical Approach in Pawnee Archaeology. Miscellaneous Publications, Smithsonian Institution, vol. 97, no. 7. Washington, D.C.

CHAPTER 2

Toward an Archaeology without Polarization

Comments on Contemporary Theory

GARY M. FEINMAN

UNIVERSITY OF WISCONSIN

DECADES AFTER THE DAWN of the New Archaeology, the discipline in the 1980s was said to be at a "crossroads" (Trigger 1984) or even "slumbering" (Shanks and Tilley 1989). One archaeologist went so far as to suggest that the field was afraid to examine what it does (Dunnell 1982) and that it was in "considerable theoretical disarray" (Dunnell 1979:440). In the social sciences, self-doubt extended beyond archaeology; for example, the *American Journal of Sociology* featured an article entitled "Is 1980s Sociology in the Doldrums?" (Collins 1986). Although the problems may not be as serious as portrayed, few could disagree with Trigger's (1989a:369) recent assessment that archaeology is once again, after almost three decades, embroiled in a familiar theoretical discourse between particularizing idealism, on the one hand, and generalizing materialism, on the other.

As the Processual-Postprocessual rhetoric heated up in the late 1980s, some scholars seemed to suggest that we had to choose sides. Several articles appeared with two-column tables like the menus at some Chinese restaurants, listing attributes such as science, objectivity, deduction, determinism, materialism in Column A, and critique, subjectivity, induction, eclecticism, idealism in Column B (e.g., Shanks and Tilley 1989). Is a radical swing to Shanks and Tilley's archaeology for the 1990s in order? Or must we retreat to a doctrinaire, arch-empiricist Processualism of the kind that Flannery (1973) warned us of twenty years ago? For me, the answer is "no" to both queries, and it is the potential, polarizing destructiveness of these extreme positions that requires reflection.

A consideration of contemporary archaeological theory and its recent history raises several troublesome questions. Why are we faced repeatedly with polarizing position papers? Why does the pendulum of interpretive opinion swing so frequently from one extreme to another? Is it constructive that theoretical debates in archaeology (such as between Processualists and Postprocessualists) often are conducted without presenting case studies, empirical data, or regional prehistories? How much does contemporary rancor and divisiveness owe to conflicting expectations regarding the nature of scientific inquiry and strategies for archaeological interpretation?

The Dangers of Extremes and Polarization

Archaeology is not the only science plagued by destructive extremes (Gould 1987a:8–10). For example, in "Pretty Pebbles" Stephen J. Gould (1988:16) writes that "the enemy of resolution, here as nearly always, is that old devil Dichotomy. We take a subtle and interesting issue, with a real resolution embracing aspects of all basic positions, and we divide ourselves into two holy armies, each with a brightly colored cardboard mythology as its flag of struggle." Earlier, in an essay discussing the vitalist-mechanist debate in biology, Gould (1985a:379) recognized a reality of contemporary science that fostered polarization. "The extremes make good copy, and a convenient (if simplistic) theme for discussion."

Randall Collins' (1986) analysis of perceived doldrums in contemporary sociology raises a demographic consideration that seems to parallel recent trends in anthropology and archaeology. Collins argues that a fourfold to fivefold increase in sociologists over the last decades has led to increased specialization and fragmentation. He reasons that

> instead of seeking recognition in the larger field, one opts for a smaller arena within which the discourse and the search for originality and for allies can go on (see also Berger 1990). But this in itself creates a certain degree of malaise. Grander conceptions are remembered from the days when the whole field had fewer members and hence theories and models seemed to have wider relevance. Furthermore, since knowledge is defined in a universalistic way, the feeling of fragmentation undermines our belief that we are actually achieving much. [Collins 1986:1339–1340]

While disciplinary trends to growth and specialization may have many positive effects, they also carry the danger of giving false credibility to only those few overarching messages and approaches that are so familiar, simple, and straightforward that they seem to appeal to a wide array of fragmented subpopulations (Fagan 1989:447). At a time when personality and rhetoric have greater importance on our national political scene than does the complexity of issues (e.g., Wicker 1990), we should bypass such potential pitfalls in archaeology by resisting the construction of false dichotomies, by rejecting extreme positions that already have been placed before us, and by avoiding the polar frameworks for contemporary archaeology that have been advanced in recent years.

I now will evaluate several dichotomies central to contemporary archaeological debate. First, the issue of archaeological paradigms is raised. Then the Processual-Postprocessual debate is addressed. I suggest that aspects of each framework are valuable; however, both polar extremes are flawed. In evaluating this debate, I reject the long-standing dichotomy of history versus science.

On Paradigms in Archaeology

More than a decade ago, Meltzer (1979) reviewed the nature of paradigms in archaeology. He critiqued Kuhn's (1970) model of scientific revolutions for imprecise use of the paradigm concept. In addition, following Masterman's (1970) multitiered definitions for "paradigm," Meltzer questioned whether the changes in 1960s' archaeology represented a paradigm shift in the overarching or metaphysical sense, as Custer (1981), Martin (1971), and others implied. Furthermore, Meltzer (1979:654) persuasively argued that recent changes in archaeological thought were more incremental than revolutionary. Yet, after carefully rejecting the notion that changes in archaeology represented a Kuhnian revolution or a shift in metaphysical paradigms, Meltzer (1979:650–51) suggested a rather extreme alternative by implying that recent (1960–1979) changes in archaeology were little more than shifts in methodology.

Meltzer's stance is surprising, because after having questioned the Kuhnian paradigm and its archaeological application, he seems to argue that almost anything short of such a metaphysical revolution is simply a methodological change. For example, according to Meltzer (1979:651), post-1960 examinations of past social formations and the consideration of their role in long-term change constituted only a methodological shift in archaeology. A similar position was advanced by Dunnell (1982), who asserted that the archaeology of the 1970s was no more scientific than traditional archaeology, and that the former had made little (if any) contribution to systematic archaeological knowledge (world prehistory).

I concur with Meltzer that the strict expectations of the Kuhnian revolutionary model are not appropriate for contemporary archaeology (see also Clark 1987; Blanton 1990), and this point is central to my upcoming discussion of the Processual-Postprocessual debate. Yet, the polar opposite, which suggests that recent changes in archaeology are largely methodological if they are not metaphysical represents the first of several dichotomies that I challenge. As Clark (1987:56) has suggested, "the classic Kuhnian notion of revolutionary change works best in disciplines characterized by cohesive, well-established metaphysical paradigms (that often have a major experimental component or are exercises in pure logic)." Trigger (1989a:6) amplifies this position, noting that the social sciences, because of the complexity of their subject matter, have more competing schools and paradigms than do the natural sciences. Giddens (1987:29–32) makes a similar point for modern sociology. Consequently, individual theoretical approaches in archaeology (and in the other human or social sciences) tend to coexist and replace each other slowly. An independent and completely homogeneous body of archaeological theory at the level of metaphysical paradigm has never existed (and may not in the near future).

Rather, archaeological theory is eclectic and related to selected aspects of social anthropological thought, as well as theories in other social, historical, and natural sciences (Clark 1987:31). In other words, significant theoretical changes in archaeology (or other social science) may never be acknowledged if the sole expectation is for an all-encompassing Kuhnian revolution. As Searle (1984:75) stated, "I think we need to abandon . . . the idea that the social sciences are like physics before Newton, and that what we are waiting for is a set of Newtonian laws of mind and society." Nevertheless, as noted by Giddens (1987:31), the sole alternative is not a deliberately cultivated diversity of theoretical standpoints. Different interpretive frameworks can be evaluated in terms of their fruitfulness and accuracy, and theories can always to some degree be assessed in terms of observations generated by empirical research (see also Blanton 1990).

The main argument here is that theoretical change and development in archaeology should not be expected to follow the natural science model nor should the lack of conformance with such notions necessarily relegate archaeology to immaturity or inferiority. As Mayr (1982:14) has reminded us: "Most general histories of 'science' have been written by historians of physics who have never quite gotten over the parochial attitude that anything that is not applicable to physics is not science."

Given modifications more appropriate for a human science, changes in archaeological thought and practice over the last half-century should be recognized for both their theoretical and methodological significance (Spaulding 1988; Trigger 1989a:312). Dunnell (1985) may well be correct in suggesting that recent methodological advances in archaeology have outstripped theoretical progress (a trend incidentally fostered by recent NSF funding priorities toward instrumentation and laboratory analysis, see Cordes 1990). Yet the theoretical changes in the field over the last three decades are nevertheless significant. Archaeology in the 1940s and early 1950s was primarily a matter of framing questions about cultural traits, ethnicity, mental templates, migration, and diffusion, as well as temporal control. There was relatively little concern with intrasite or intraregional variability, or with the role of sociopolitical organization in change. Archaeological data rarely were examined in a spatial or relational fashion, except to define "ethnic groups" or "culture areas" (for the role of relational analyses in contemporary archaeology, see Earle and Preucel 1987:503–4; Kowalewski 1990; Trigger 1989a:287–88; Wilcox 1988).

The growing collection and use of spatial and relational data in contemporary archaeology is not just a product of computers and an arsenal of geographic techniques (although these methodological advances have hastened the process), but owes as much or more to changes in the nature of the larger questions we are asking about how social systems (and their component parts) function and change. Certainly there were innovators in the 1940s and 1950s, and people out of step with their scholarly cohort, just as there are today. But that is not unexpected in a social science characterized by competing frameworks and more gradual, incremental theoretical transitions. Nevertheless, in suggesting that conceptual shifts need not be revolutionary to be significant, I do not mean to imply that theoretical transitions always occur at a constant or glacial pace (e.g., Sterud 1978).

When one looks at specific segments of the archaeological literature, the magnitude of theoretical changes and empirical achievements over the last decades is evident (Trigger 1989a:396; Fagan 1989). They extend beyond the statement of "pie-in-the-sky" goals and methodological advances (cf. Meltzer 1981). Unfortunately, this firmer foundation for world prehistory (and its recasting from traits and artifacts to social relations and economic activities) are points that were underplayed in the volume marking the fiftieth anniversary of the Society for American Archaeology (Meltzer, Fowler, and Sabloff [eds.] 1986).

Recently, I reread the regional syntheses prepared on Oaxaca prehistory three decades ago by Bernal (1965) and Paddock (1966), and compared them to more recent overviews both by Flannery and Marcus (Flannery [ed.] 1976; Flannery and Marcus [eds.] 1983; Flannery, Marcus, and Kowalewski 1981; Marcus and Flannery 1990) and by my colleagues on the regional survey (Blanton and Kowalewski 1981; Blanton et al. 1982, 1983; Kowalewski et al. 1989). I did this not to diminish the contributions of Caso, Bernal, Acosta, Paddock, or their predecessors. One cannot help but recognize that these early studies were not only far ahead of their time (e.g., Caso, Bernal, and Acosta 1967; Willey [ed.] 1965), but also invaluable empirical foundations for so much of our contemporary research.

Yet the last thirty years of research also have yielded impressive substantive gains. Empirical achievements lie not simply in the number of sites reported or features excavated, but in the recognition and interpretation of a pre-Monte Albán occupation in the Valley of Oaxaca (Flannery [ed.] 1976; Flannery and Marcus [eds.] 1983). Prior to the 1960s, the question of agricultural origins was barely touched—a significant realization when one considers the recent contributions of Flannery's Prehistory and Human Ecology Project.

Yet the expansion of the empirical record for Oaxaca was no more dramatic than the marked change in how these two sets of syntheses approached the past. The earlier 1960s overviews were mostly concerned with delineating temporal change in material culture. Consistent with contemporary conceptual approaches, the 1960s overviews usually described artifactual shifts as the product of changing patterns of outside influence (whether Olmec, Maya, Teotihuacán, Toltec, or Mixtec). Relatively little attention was given to intraregional variation of any kind, except for the Late Postclassic period when an effort was made to distinguish the nature of the Mixtec presence in different parts of the valley (Bernal 1965, 1966;

Paddock 1966). The 1960s syntheses did not address the rise of Monte Albán as a sociopolitical phenomenon, the nature of economic specialization, nor make in-depth comparisons of Monte Albán's rise and the Valley of Oaxaca's settlement history to that of other regions. These issues represent dominant themes in contemporary writings and debate. Significant methodological and theoretical advances have been made in Oaxaca archaeology over the last two to three decades, and these changes have enabled us to contribute to conceptual debates in the social and historical sciences that extend well beyond both Oaxaca and the discipline of archaeology.

Kuhnian Expectations and Theoretical Change in Archaeology

A central theme of this paper is that Processual-Postprocessual debate should not be framed as a simple dichotomy, forcing archaeologists to select one framework, like contestants choosing curtains on a TV game show. Yet, before getting to some of the substantive points of this debate, it is appropriate to ask why the discussion has been framed in this manner to begin with. Maybe, as Gould said, extremes just make "good copy." More likely, this tack is fostered by the false expectation that archaeology should conform to the Kuhnian model or a related view of scientific revolution. For example, Dunnell (1985:599) has asserted that the absence of theoretical consensus in archaeology is a major impediment to the growth of knowledge and ultimately a threat to the discipline as a whole.

Yet, possibly, the structure of the contemporary debate also is an unfortunate product of recent history in American archaeology, which has seen radical swings in the polemic pendulum before (Marcus 1983a; Trigger 1989a:369). As the 1980s witnessed an increasing drift away from the growing orthodoxy of certain Processual positions (see Flannery 1982; Hodder 1984:27; Renfrew 1982), it became opportune for those at the conceptual extremes to encourage a drastic swing again, either to the arch-empiricism, scientism, and materialist determinism of the right or to the anti-science relativism of the left. The point taken here is not simply to decry the use of the "strawman" as a tool for argumentation, but also to challenge the notion that there are really only a few coherent conceptual positions to select from, and if a student or practitioner does not adhere to one extreme position then the only viable alternative is 180 degrees away.

In the remainder of this section, I examine episodes of archaeological transition. The prime focus is the contemporary debate, but to provide context I briefly delve into the practice and rhetoric of the 1960s. To illustrate the dangers of dichotomy, I focus on three key aspects of current discussion: (1) the false distinction between history versus science; (2) the claims made about scientific method versus relativism; and (3) the materialist versus idealist schism. In each instance, my argument is that the Postprocessualist critique has some degree of legitimacy, and that, in fact, parallel criticisms *already* had been raised within the Processualist camp itself. Often, the Postprocessual critiques seem more appropriate for Processual archaeology as it was practiced by a few in the 1960s, or perhaps as it is currently practiced by orthodox factions of contemporary Processualism (but not by the majority of Processualists). In each case, however, Postprocessualists simplify and distort the extant heterogeneity in the discipline (Renfrew 1989; Trigger 1989b:3) and then offer overstated alternatives.

Before proceeding, it is necessary to acknowledge that due to space limits, I, too, have had to minimize the diversity of views, even at the polar extremes. Several strands of Postprocessualism already exist (Leone 1986; Mithen 1989; Patterson 1989; Shanks and Tilley 1989), and the reactionary wing of contemporary Processual archaeology includes several distinct intellectual camps, including strict Hempelians, rigid material determinists, and arch-empiricists of various ilks. In general, I have directed my comments at only those positions that have been most vocal and extreme.

History vs. Science

In anthropology, the false dichotomy between history and science (or empiricism versus generalization) was not born with the New Archaeology (see Kluckhohn 1940; Taylor 1948). Yet its long-standing acceptance (and indeed fostering) in the rhetoric of New Archaeology is peculiar, given the general and comparative questions posed by such historians as Marc Bloch (1970) and Fernand Braudel (1980). To them, history is much more than diplomatic events and charismatic leaders. The false duality, adhered to by some archaeologists, becomes all the more paradoxical if one follows the writings of the evolutionary biologist, Stephen J. Gould. Gould (1985b:408, 1986) recognizes his field as a historical science that must account for unique situations and immensely complex historical accidents on the one hand, and for more general processes on the other.

Archaeology, too, is a historical science, meaning we must wind our way through particulars and specific sequences, while not losing sight of general, comparative, and theoretical questions concerning cultural differences, similarities, and change (Clark 1987:45; Schiffer 1975:844; Trigger 1984:293). We cannot explain classes of events or sequences of societal transition without reference to generalizations about human behavior and cultural process. Yet conversely, even if we were able to develop a body of general theory analogous to the synthetic theory of biological evolution, we (like paleontologists) could not blindly predict or retrodict the course of specific sequences of change in living systems (Gould 1987b:12–13; Mayr 1961; Trigger 1989a:374). As Cowgill (1988:249) recently wrote, to accomplish our aims "we urgently need studies . . . that deal with particulars but do not assume that the facts speak for themselves."

Although Hodder (1986; see also Shanks and Tilley 1989:7) critiques the New Archaeology for denying the discipline's distinctly historical character (Hassan

1989), he does little to change our field's misconception of what a historical discipline is and can be. Like those he challenges (e.g., Binford 1962), Hodder (1986: Ch. 5) associates history with an idealist or idiosyncratic approach that eschews generalization. This is certainly not the same sense of history that one gets from Gould, Trigger, or even Braudel and many other historians (e.g., Hodges 1986; Knapp 1987; Upham 1990; Wolf 1990). All these approaches integrate the scientific and the historical to emphasize: (1) the study and comparison of particular sequences (see also Kirch 1984); (2) the recognition of change as a historical process in which pre-existent structures (and their internal and scalar contradictions) play a role, along with new perturbations and opportunities (see also Ellen 1982:61–65; Trigger 1982:39–40); and (3) the general inappropriateness for historical disciplines of entirely mechanistic explanations (see also Mayr 1961). Yet, they do not seem to view change in their respective fields as purely mentalist in nature, nor do they seem to see their fields as exclusively context-specific, non-comparative and anti-generalizing (Trigger 1989b:4). As Eric Wolf (1982:21) noted: "theoretically informed history and historically informed theory must be joined together to account for populations specifiable in time and space, both as outcomes of significant processes and as their carriers."

On Scientific Method

I have argued that historical disciplines need not deny their historical component to make generalizations and unravel process, and that scientific procedures and reasoning should not be considered inappropriate in such endeavors. Obviously, these positions might be contested if one adheres to a narrow definition of science. Clearly, there is no scientific consensus about the essence of "science," as vividly illustrated by contemporary debate in archaeology. While some (e.g., Dunnell 1982:1) have questioned whether our discipline is any more scientific than it was two decades ago, others (Shanks and Tilley 1989:1–2) have attacked Processual archaeology for its application of scientific methods. Once again, I take a middle ground in which contemporary archaeology is argued to be generally more scientific than it was three or four decades ago. Furthermore, archaeology should aspire self-consciously to scientific principles. Yet, having said that, I do not equate science with the application of universal laws (Flannery 1973; Mayr 1982:37–43; Renfrew 1982:8, 1989:38; Sherratt 1988; cf. Binford 1968:27), a commitment to rigid determinism or reductionism (Renfrew 1989:34; Spaulding 1988:263), or an adherence to the false notion that scientists or their data can be absolutely objective (Binford 1986:460; Earle and Preucel 1987:509; Hull 1988:26; Renfrew 1989:38). In a sense, both the arch-empiricists and the radical relativists (Shanks and Tilley 1989:4–5) share extremely narrow and inaccurate visions of science, just as they do of history.

What then is fundamental to "science"? Here, I rely primarily on the writings of both Gould and the philosopher of science, David L. Hull. Hull's even-handed analysis, *Science as a Process* (1988), is particularly valuable for establishing an intermediate position between those who see science as an isolated, internal enterprise in which the weight of the evidence is never fettered by outside factors, and others who view it as an endeavor completely determined by external or relativistic forces. Furthermore, Hull (1988:357) cogently emphasizes the collective nature of science. Scientists are not infallible, but as long as they are explicit, mutual use and checking should eventually move a field towards greater understanding. As Hull (1988:455) notes, "the most important testing that occurs in science is one scientist testing the views of another."

Gould (1985b:408, 1987b:13) stresses that the Cartesian, or "big science," tradition is not necessarily appropriate for all scientific research. He points out that styles of science are as varied as their subject matters, and that the explanation of complex historical processes does not lend itself to the kinds of classical determinism and complete predictability that prevails in high school physics experiments (see also Mayr 1961; Spaulding 1988:268). Gould does not deny the power or past successes of Cartesianism, nor does he appeal to mysticism or intractability. Rather, he argues (Gould 1987b:14) "that equally powerful (but different) techniques of historical *sciences*—with their themes of irreducible interaction, hierarchy, and resolvable contingency—must be embraced to break the hegemony of what, in our parochialism, we call *the* scientific method." Cartesian tradition narrowly equates this method with experiment, laboratory control, repetition, and reduction.

Significantly, both Hull (1988:357) and Gould see testability as a fundamental principle of science (see also Wylie 1982:373). Hull (1988:356) remarks that "scientific hypotheses must be testable, but such testing is frequently quite indirect and never easy." Gould (1985c:417) notes that "science works with testable proposals." If we accept this vision of science, then it becomes increasingly difficult to deny that archaeology has become more scientific in orientation over the last decades. Few archaeologists could question that over the last thirty years we have witnessed a greater emphasis on explicit research designs, problem orientations, and the testing of interpretations with empirical observations (Spaulding 1988:267). Quantification, the presentation of observations, and the collective effort to recognize and correct for sources of bias also are part of this process, although I certainly recognize that steps in this direction were present long before 1960 and that such trends cannot be detected in all current work.

Of course, the mere application of scientific methods does not offer any assurance that ultimate truth can or will be achieved (Spaulding 1988:264). Yet, if the alternative is literary criticism (as Shanks and Tilley [1989:4–5] imply), how then are we to verify and evaluate interpretations except by the power, authority, or the political stance of the proponent (Schiffer 1988:468). And the long-term danger is who determines which political ideas are correct? As Hull (1988:26; see also Trigger 1989a:408) thoughtfully reminds us: "science is not a perfect machine for grinding out true claims about the world . . . , but it is the best of all the imperfect machines developed to date."

The Postprocessualist challenge should remind the rest of us that neither rigid scientism, the application of technical gadgets, nor the promise of a "right" or "correct" methodology (Kaplan 1984:25) are suitable substitutes (in themselves) for thoughtful science. Archaeology does not have one way of knowing, or a single fruitful approach (Renfrew 1980). There is more than one appropriate sampling design, more than one way to classify artifacts, and more than one scale on which to engage in research (Flannery [ed.] 1976; Kowalewski and Fish 1990:262–263; Trigger 1989a:330–337). As in most sciences, when designing our investigations, we must balance specific *and* general goals, while considering research constraints (money, time, environment).

In the absence of a careful evaluation of empirical findings with specific research questions in mind, the blanket rejection of certain research strategies in the name of "science" merely leaves the door open to those of anti-science mentality at the opposite pole. The excesses and zeal of some practitioners of the New Archaeology (e.g., rigid advocation of Hempelian logic, the equation of correlation with causality and prediction with explanation, the rejection of inductive science, and the unbending acceptance of environmental and demographic determinism) have lent a certain credibility to Postprocessualist claims (Gilman 1987; Renfrew 1989; Spaulding 1988; Trigger 1984, 1989a; Watson 1986; Zeitlin 1987). As Gould (1987b:14–15) has noted, "complex, contingent, interactive, and hierarchical do not mean unknowable—quite the reverse, for these are tools of a different kind of rational understanding."

Materialism vs. Idealism

The methodological and logical rhetoric from the "young fogeys" camp (Flannery 1973) of Processual archaeology often has sounded more like simple scientism rather than science. Frequently, we see articles (even books) with little or no mention of past human behavior, process, or history. Rather, we are left with hardly anything beyond methodological jargon and self-evident "laws" that imply the essence of "real" science. Nevertheless, the greatest excesses committed by segments of the Processualist school are evident in early doctrinaire and narrow interpretations of the materialist tradition. Conceptual positions with causal frameworks broader than technological, demographic, or environmental determinism were dismissed as eclectic, unscientific, particularistic, and even threatened with Occam's Razor as if it were the Sword of Damocles.

As late as 1979, Sanders, Parsons, and Santley (1979:360) boldly claimed that four or five major variables should be able to account for 80 percent of the cultural similarities and differences visible in the archaeological record. Yet, more than a decade later, they have neither demonstrated the causal links, nor named the crucial variables and how they are articulated (see Trigger 1984:280). Even today, one can see a single one-shot correlation between settlement changes and greater precipitation presented as a simple (yet necessary and sufficient) explanation for aggregation, while elsewhere, other archaeologists trot out comparable correlations and proclaim that wet cycles account for episodes of dispersion. Unfortunately, the climatic determinists in each region are rarely bothered by the obvious cross-cultural inconsistencies, or by the challenge of unraveling the various possible linkages between water, settlement patterns, and social behaviors (Plog and Hantman 1990).

Still at present, a shrinking (but still significant) number of determinists continue to search for that small and largely exogenous suite of food-related variables that they believe can explain the course of human history (Blanton 1983). Yet, these reductionists neglect the diversity of coping strategies that humans employ in reaction to similar perturbations (e.g., De Garine and Harrison 1988:469; Eisenstadt 1988:238–9; Orlove 1980:242). As Ellen (1982:262) has written, "responses to environmental variables, or the actions made on environmental variables, to a large extent depend on how they are mediated by the structure of social relations."

But leaving aside anthropological archaeology, how many substantive, universal laws do we have in any social, historical, or even biological science (Mayr 1982:37–38; Renfrew 1989:38; Searle 1984:71–85; Trigger 1982:33)? After centuries, how many narrow deterministic links have we been able to forge convincingly? Are such laws even a reasonable goal for a historical human science? There is only one universal law in biology according to Mayr (1982:37–38): "All biological laws have exceptions."

On a positive note, the late 1970s, 1980s, and early 1990s have witnessed an ever-growing segment of Processual archaeologists grappling with the true complexity of our subject. Recently, in the pages of our journals and the corridors of our national meetings, I see and hear discussions of scalar stress, basal unit size (Johnson 1982), and household archaeology (Wilk and Ashmore [eds.] 1988) interdigitated with considerations of regional settlement patterns and the economics of macroregional transport (Drennan 1984). For the most part, these scholars do not view their analyses as mutually exclusive. Rather, they recognize that living systems are hierarchical, and thus they require analysis at several levels and scales simultaneously (see Agnew 1982 for a similar nested or multi-scale approach to political geography, and Brown and Maurer 1989 and Ricklefs 1987 for comparable perspectives for biological ecology). Likewise, these various schools of an ever-more-sophisticated holistic archaeology generally do not neglect the history of human-environment relations, but they also give greater attention and causal significance to the diachronic interplay between human groups and groupings (Trigger 1989a:339). In short, our choices are much broader than classic diffusionism and rigid materialism (cf. Schiffer 1975:842–3).

Admittedly, to date, the interpretive breakthroughs may not be revolutionary. But in areas like Polynesia (Kirch 1984), southern Arizona (Doyel [ed.] 1987;

Gumerman [ed.] 1991), the upper Mantaro of Peru (Costin and Earle 1989; Earle et al. 1987), and Oaxaca, to name just a few regions where sophisticated, multiscale research strategies have been employed, recent findings have become extremely informative. Since it takes decades to build the corpus of archaeological knowledge required to address the questions of greatest comparative breadth, how much should we expect from projects that don't last decades? Clearly, we need many more decades of additional research in many more regions to assess our models and frameworks.

Having recently launched this middle-ground path to significant theoretical insight, we must ask ourselves if this is the time to reverse course and heed the theoretical musings of the Postprocessualists. Clearly, the Postprocessualists are correct in rejecting the mechanical determinism of some of the early New Archaeology (Shanks and Tilley 1987:45). Yet their claims are not new (Gilman 1987), nor do they necessarily engender a blanket rejection of all forms of materialism. A broadly materialist tradition in archaeology can be reconciled with the consideration of ideas and cognition, as well as a more catholic view of causality (Flannery and Marcus 1976; Flannery and Marcus [eds.] 1983; Marcus and Flannery 1990; Renfrew 1989; Spaulding 1988; Trigger 1989a; see also Adams 1978:299–300; Searle 1984; Wolf 1990).

Although the Postprocessualists belittle problem orientation, definition of variables, comparisons, and testing (e.g., Shanks and Tilley 1987, 1989), too much of their own analysis is limited by the structure of their specific research agenda. To seek the meaning behind material culture (such as the meaning of decorated gourds) is little different than seeking an explanation for the earth. In order to pose and answer intelligible questions about material culture or the earth, one would first have to define a set of variables mapped on material culture or the earth (Mayhew 1980; Hull 1988:356–57). "Only after deciding what these variables are is it possible to pose questions about the way they relate to one another, and about how they maintain certain constant relations or change over time" (Mayhew 1980:355). Obviously, such variables need not be measured ordinally nor must statistics be employed for an investigation to have meaning and importance, yet without a more systematic structure for evaluation, how are we to decide between plausible interpretations?

What have we really been offered by the Postprocessual school? Too frequently, some of the more radical proponents seem little concerned with empirical research. As Hodder (1989:16) recently remarked: "in their vision of the 1990s Shanks and Tilley do not mention the collection of new archaeological data, the need for major new excavations, new field surveys, and new prehistories." Yet, even more moderate voices have called on us to abandon the social sciences (Hodder 1988:373) for more interpretive analyses of artifacts (now dressed up under the rubric of "material culture").

Determining the core of the Postprocessual program is not easy, but if we leave aside the political rhetoric and the importance of history, what seems to be left is individualism, the interpretation of contextual meanings, an effort to link meaning with action (or behavior), and a focus on material cultural analysis (Hodder 1985, 1986). Such interpretive analyses may be creative, but they have not proven terribly convincing when applied to prehistoric contexts where the relevant cognitive systems remain largely unknown (Meltzer 1990:187; Smith 1986:221). Often, the links or bridging arguments between the stated theory and the available data have not been explicitly drawn (e.g., Shanks and Tilley 1987:155–71). Yet, even in more contemporary contexts, too many of the Postprocessual interpretations culminate with the conclusion that people do something because they want to (or because their inner selves really want them to). In other words, people do things because they do things. Such conclusions are not explanations nor even analytical interpretations. Rather, they are restatements of data or observations. In short, we are left with a kind of extreme particularism.

I do not offer the above as a critique of cognitive approaches, or contextual studies, or case specific analyses in general. On the contrary, these approaches are essential in a historical science, especially when they are framed in a manner so that comparative and general questions remain possible to address. In another historical science—evolutionary biology—the investigations of specific sequences and general processes, as well as comparative analyses, are all seen as complementary rather than mutually exclusive alternatives. In archaeology, a balance must be found and implemented between general and specific research agendas (e.g., Brumfiel 1983; Kirch and Green 1987; Spencer 1990). Cognitive approaches such as that by Flannery and Marcus on ancient Oaxaca (Flannery and Marcus 1976; Marcus and Flannery 1978, 1990) also have a great deal to offer. Humans are not just automatons carrying cultural baggage (see Kirch 1984:40). People perceive and think, and all societies do not respond in the same manner to comparable stresses (e.g., Giddens 1979; Rappaport 1979; Searle 1984; Speth 1988:203). Yet, whereas Hodder (1985:9) seems to fault the linkage of the ideological with many aspects of the material, I see such efforts at reconciliation and the placement of the entire holistic endeavor on a more empirical basis as a significant strength and a direction well worth pursuing (e.g., Flannery and Marcus 1976; Minc 1986). After all, human action is influenced both by the material conditions of their world and by the manner in which they perceive it (Wetterstrom 1978).

Yet, because the reconstruction of past cognitive systems is admittedly difficult, it becomes even more essential to maintain analytical rigor and to integrate (and cross-check) multiple lines of evidence whenever possible (e.g., Flannery and Marcus [eds.] 1983; Kirch 1984; Trigger 1989b:2–3). We also must be prepared to recognize that cognitive structures, like patterns of human behavior, are not eternal, and, therefore, they too are subject to change.

A Holistic Approach to Ancient Oaxaca

Space does not permit an in-depth discussion of a holistic approach to Oaxaca prehistory. Yet the brief elucidation of such a perspective is important to exemplify and serve as justification for the paradigmatic points raised above. Far too frequently in contemporary archaeology, discussions of regional prehistories and interpretation are divorced entirely from position papers and manifestos that aim to prescribe a paradigmatic course for the field as a whole. However, if the Kuhnian notion of paradigm change is deemed inappropriate for archaeology, then such total segregation (and absence of evaluation that ensues) is not constructive, because it tends to minimize the comparison of analytical frameworks in the face of research questions and data (see Blanton 1990).

Several productive, holistic directions to the study of ancient Oaxaca have been laid out in *The Cloud People* (Flannery and Marcus [eds.] 1983). In discussing and amplifying this prior research, my aim is to provide a framework in which findings from several scales of analysis are linked together as well as insights drawn from both cognitive and material approaches. A further goal is to provoke and illustrate directions for synthetic research; therefore, the findings are not presented as final nor conclusive.

In a series of analyses and simulations, Linda Nicholas and I have investigated settlement and land use in prehispanic Oaxaca (Feinman and Nicholas 1987, 1990; Nicholas 1989). This regional-scale research builds on the landmark study of contemporary agricultural practice in the Valley of Oaxaca by Anne Kirkby (1973), as well as Steve Kowalewski's (1980) pioneering archaeological analyses. As in Kowalewski's earlier analysis, regional population estimates and changing settlement patterns derived from the archaeological survey have a central role in our examination of past human-to-land relations.

Although none of our results leads us to alter a key point made by Kirkby (1973; see also Flannery et al. 1967)—that water is a critical factor in past and present Zapotec agriculture—our studies (Feinman 1991; Feinman and Nicholas 1987, 1990, 1992; Nicholas 1989) do imply that *labor* also was a critical factor in agricultural production. In fact, we have argued that through much of the prehispanic sequence, *labor shortage* tended to be a more serious limit on agricultural production than insufficient land (Feinman and Nicholas 1990, 1992). Both the early center, San José Mogote (the region's largest settlement prior to the founding of Monte Albán in 500 B.C.), and the later site of Monte Albán, were generally surrounded by relatively dense rural populations.

Our land-use studies also point to an important difference between San José Mogote's relationship to its rural environs prior to 500 B.C., and Monte Albán's relationship to its larger hinterland after that date. The population of San José Mogote could have been sustained through its own agricultural production in most years, although the site's emergent leaders were undoubtedly interested in the exaction of surplus and labor from surrounding communities to contribute to mound construction and other activities. In contrast, from the founding of Monte Albán, the population of the city could not sustain itself by using only the land within several kilometers of the site. Consequently, the inhabitants of Monte Albán were dependent on the surrounding rural population for support. Interestingly, while the urban population grew at Monte Albán, the areal extent of the region necessary to sustain the city remained relatively constant in size, remaining approximately a 16 to 20 km radius, or roughly a day's round trip (see Feinman and Nicholas 1987). Nevertheless, the number of rural inhabitants required to feed the center generally increased through time, although the trend was not linear. In other words, rapid demographic increase in the 16–20 km sustaining zone surrounding Monte Albán helped to supply the growing population of the hilltop center.

Marked increases in labor recruitment and surplus mobilization seem likely to have been necessary in Monte Albán I and again in Monte Albán III (see Table 2.1) (periods in which both the population and monumental construction at Monte Albán and other central places increased significantly). Elsewhere, my colleagues and I (Kowalewski et al. 1989:509–12) argue that these transitions (Rosario phase/ Monte Albán I and Monte Albán II/III) were two of the most significant eras of societal change in ancient Oaxaca. Note that the intent here has not been to dissect causality, but rather to establish a changing relationship between the inhabitants of the region's principal center and its environs. The former issue (causality) would require much more extensive discussion and already has been broached elsewhere (e.g., Blanton et al. 1982, 1993; Kowalewski et al. 1989).

When we integrate this material perspective with the consideration of Zapotec cosmology (Flannery and Marcus 1976; Marcus 1978, 1983b, 1989; Marcus and Flannery 1978, 1990, 1994), interesting directions for present and future research emerge. More specifically, we might look for important changes in integrative/ recruitment strategies in Monte Albán I and III. In their path-breaking *American Scientist* article, Flannery and Marcus (1976) discuss the sixteenth-century Zapotec concern with rain, its seasonality (see also Seler 1904), and the distinction between irrigated and nonirrigated fields. Further, they (Flannery and Marcus 1976:380–81; Marcus 1978:174–75, 1983b:344, 348; Marcus and Flannery 1978:75) outline a model in which sacrifices (often of blood) were made to ancestors to intercede for or to induce Lightning to send rain. Ancestors could intercede on one's behalf with the supernatural forces who directly controlled the clouds and rain. For the sixteenth-century Zapotec, the supernatural *Cocijo* (Lightning) had the power to pierce the clouds, releasing rain to earth where man could manipulate it for his purposes. A person sacrificed to encourage Lightning to split the clouds was called *peni guij cocijo* ("man—object of sacrifice—Lightning") (Marcus 1989:152; Marcus and Flannery 1978:75).

Several aspects of this conceptual scheme have been traced back to well before the rise of Monte Albán, through the identification of bloodletting implements and

TABLE 2.1
Valley of Oaxaca Chronology

1500	
1300	
	Monte Albán V
1100	
900	
	Monte Albán IV
700	
	Monte Albán IIIb
500	
	Monte Albán IIIa
300	
A.D. 100	
	Monte Albán II
100 B.C.	
	Monte Albán Late I
300	
	Monte Albán Early I
500	
	Rosario
700	
	Guadalupe
900	
	San José
1100	
1300	Tierras Largas
1500	Espiridión

other archaeological clues (Flannery and Marcus 1976; Marcus 1978, 1989). In the earliest Oaxaca villages, many ritual activities appear to have been conducted at the level of the household. However, by the end of the San José phase centuries later, bloodletting activities also were carried out (using imported stingray and fish spines) in or near public buildings, suggesting that such rituals may have been carried out more publicly, to be viewed by a larger segment of the population, perhaps an entire community or kin group (Flannery and Marcus 1976:380).

During roughly the same period that these ritual sacrifices were conducted at a level above the household, residential communities were organized into two mutually exclusive descent groups, each tracing its descent from a different supernatural (Flannery and Marcus 1976; Marcus 1989:168–75; Pyne 1976). Given the long history of ancestor worship in the Oaxaca highlands, and elsewhere in Mesoamerica, Marcus (1989:190) has postulated that the two sets of symbols found on burial vessels "may have been conceived of as supernatural entities from which two different, broadly based lines of Formative villagers had descended." Thus, a few hundred years after the beginnings of sedentary life in the Valley of Oaxaca, intervillage relationships based on ritual and descent appear to have connected the inhabitants of neighboring communities. At the same time, these bonds may have linked smaller rural communities to San José Mogote, the only settlement where both sets of symbols were represented in separate residential wards and cemeteries.

Above, I postulated that later during Monte Albán I, the nature of labor relations and surplus mobilization may have shifted in Oaxaca (at least in the central part of the Valley of Oaxaca around Monte Albán). Prior to 500 B.C., kinship and community links may have been adequate to support San José Mogote and its emergent leaders. With the foundation of Monte Albán, the Valley of Oaxaca system not only grew markedly in scale, but its primary center was now heavily dependent on surrounding communities for basic subsistence needs. This is not to say that earlier San José Mogote did not exact tribute or labor from surrounding villages, but that with the rise of Monte Albán, the *nature* and *scale* of this exaction changed.

With these points in mind, contemporary shifts in funerary ritual are intriguing. Although the earliest Oaxaca tombs were constructed during the Rosario phase in a few high-status contexts at San José Mogote (Flannery and Marcus 1983), the abundance of these features increased considerably in the subsequent period, Monte Albán I. At that time, tombs frequently included larger quantities of grave goods. Other individuals were interred in less elaborate contexts. One item often buried with the dead was an effigy *olla*. These vessels frequently bore personages costumed to represent *Cocijo,* or Lightning, a common depiction that persisted on later "true" funerary urns (Marcus 1983c). Perhaps, *Cocijo* (an important supernatural symbol in Oaxaca for centuries) and ritual access to this sacred force were in part appropriated by upper-stratum elite families as the nature of Zapotec funerary ritual changed and stratification emerged. The elite controlled access to *Cocijo* by the end of Monte Albán I, and may have used that perceived access through their ancestors (and its long-standing connection to essential precipitation) as a mechanism to attract and recruit the larger labor pools required by the rulers of Monte Albán.

By Monte Albán III, with greater human-labor requirements, funerary ritual was again elaborated. Classic Zapotec urns were mass-produced and were found across the region. Marcus (1983c:144) suggests that many urns depicted venerated remote royal ancestors, sometimes garbed as supernaturals. Other urns are thought to show recently deceased royal ancestors (Marcus 1983c:148). At Monte Albán, the tombs of this period are more variable and more elaborate than during earlier eras (Flannery 1983). Several include numerous secondary burials, while others are topped by commemorative buildings or shrines built (and used) subsequent to burial (Flannery 1983:135). Some of the most elaborate tombs displayed polychrome murals

(Caso 1965; Marcus 1983d; Miller 1988) that depict processions of named ancestors and relatives (Marcus 1983d). Marcus (1983d:143) has suggested that the boustrophedon layout (zigzagging, or "as the ox plows") of contemporaneous carved stones and murals anticipates the layout and content of later Zapotec and Mixtec genealogical records. Miller (1988:256) asserts that Oaxaca tomb murals were all associated with a "cult of the dead." Many Classic tombs were reentered and then resealed, a practice that Lind and Urcid (1983) suggest may have occurred when a living authority required validation by communication with a previous power. In the sixteenth century, Zapotec villagers offered sacrifices to deceased royal ancestors, while the autosacrifices of rulers and elite were used to intercede with the supernatural on behalf of their entire following (Marcus 1983b).

A ritual system linking lightning and rain, ritual sacrifice, supernatural forces, venerated ancestors, and descent has been elaborated by Flannery and Marcus (1976) who have illustrated that this ritual complex long predates the rise of Monte Albán. However, as labor and surplus relations changed through time, the nature of these specific rituals and interpersonal connections appears to have expanded from the household, kin, and community levels to ever larger social networks. Yet, at the same time, there was another change; the Monte Albán urns (and tomb paintings) apparently focused on specific individuals (and their royal ancestors), a specific reference to high-status individuals not found or named on pre-state and pre-Monte Albán funerary ware. Earlier ritual complexes and their associated symbols may have been expanded or co-opted by the elite so that they now bound (through the instrument of fictive kinship) larger labor pools to ruling lords who could mediate with the supernatural. Interestingly, as the material requirements increased during Monte Albán I and Monte Albán III, the preserved remnants of funerary ritual also changed in a manner that extended family allegiances (or fictive kin ties) from ever-larger populations to specific elite families or individuals.

Obviously, many of these arguments are preliminary, and more questions need to be asked. Some of the necessary queries are general in nature, for the recruitment and surplus mobilization problems faced by San José Mogote and Monte Albán certainly were not unique to ancient Oaxaca. For example, Chang (1989) also has argued that the control of labor through kinship principles may have been an extremely important aspect of the early Chinese state. Other questions could be phrased more specifically. For example, we might investigate Marcus's (1983b:351) interesting suggestion that ancestor worship may have been even more important for the prehispanic early Zapotec state than for the ancient Mixtec *cacicazgos*. The latter, for the most part, were organized in smaller polities, so that actual kin-based linkages may have sufficed more effectively. Hopefully, I have illustrated a number of productive paths that could be examined, in which cognitive *and* materialist approaches can be integrated holistically.

Are either of the extreme dichotomous positions in contemporary archaeology more promising or interesting? While the Postprocessualists might call for the disarticulation of these two theoretical frameworks and show limited concern for large-scale processes and relationships, the rigid determinists might ignore the key role of social and ideological factors in the aggregation of population that occurred around important, ancient Oaxaca centers (see Feinman and Nicholas 1987). Alternatively, the arch-empiricists might still be contemplating the intricacies of the plow zone.

Conclusion

Now, I address a final paradox. As is often the case, the extreme approaches have more in common than we might expect. In their call for a discipline focused on artifacts or material culture, many (though not all) Postprocessualists advocate a surprisingly parallel stance to that held by the arch-empiricists, one of the more prominent and extreme processual schools. The Postprocessualists are little concerned with quantitative, relational data and instead suggest the derivation of meaning from artifact analysis. Alternatively, the arch-empiricists view the answers in the application of strict Darwinist principles of natural selection to changes in material culture (e.g., Leonard 1989:496). For example, Dunnell (1984:502) grants utility to only that necessarily small subset of observations and concepts that have "unambiguous representation in the archaeological record."

In a sense, both of these polar positions view archaeology as a discipline narrowly focused on the classification and interpretation of artifacts. Each extreme also calls for a uniquely archaeological theory, which neither has linked convincingly to things larger than what can be held in your hand. Furthermore, both pessimistically challenge archaeology's goal of contributing to the social and historical sciences. Obviously, these polar positions differ markedly in other ways. Yet, they share a narrow revisionist (artifact-centric) bent that would contract the archaeological focus, thereby largely serving to isolate us from the rest of the human sciences.

In sum, I have argued that in this world of too many "sound bites" and not enough substance, we must resist the temptation for only simple answers, especially when those answers are extreme and could serve either to polarize us or to swing us back to positions long ago found inadequate. On the issues of paradigmatic change, the juxtaposition of history and science, the question of scientific method, and the materialist versus idealist debate, I have offered middle-ground positions that place archaeology squarely in the social and historical sciences as a field with unique and important contributions to make about the human past (Trigger 1989a:409). If we are to answer these more general and comparative questions, then we must share, contribute, and interrelate our theories with those in other social and historical disciplines. Finally, I have stressed that archaeology's collective contributions can and must be both general and specific in form. That is, I have called for more long-term archaeological fieldwork and analysis programs that systematically collect information at multiple scales of investigation while keeping a broad overarching research agenda firmly in perspective. Like Trigger (1989a:369), I suspect that growing unity and complementarity of historicism and evolutionism in archaeology should allow our explanations to move beyond the vulgar materialist determinism of the early New Archaeology, the trait-based idealism of historical particularism, and the self-righteous relativism of some of the extreme critical approaches.

Acknowledgments

Many individuals and institutions contributed to the completion of this article, and I am truly grateful to them all. The National Science Foundation generously supported the regional settlement pattern survey of the Valley of Oaxaca. Over the years, necessary permissions and essential assistance were provided by both the Instituto Nacional de Antropología e Historia and the Centro Regional de Oaxaca. Many people were instrumental to the completion of the Oaxaca settlement survey; Richard E. Blanton, Stephen A. Kowalewski (both of whom directed various stages of the research), Laura Finsten, and Linda M. Nicholas were particularly invaluable. I also wish to thank Anna Roosevelt and Samuel M. Wilson, who asked me to prepare an earlier version of this paper for the 55th annual meeting of the Society for American Archaeology. The original work was written while I had the good fortune to be a resident scholar at the School of American Research, an opportunity for which I am grateful to Douglas W. Schwartz, Jonathan Haas, and the entire SAR staff. I am deeply indebted to a number of thoughtful colleagues, including Warren DeBoer, Jeffrey L. Hantman, Susan Kepecs, Jay Knight, Kent G. Lightfoot, Linda M. Nicholas, John Speth, Gil Stein, and Steadman Upham, who all made constructive comments and helpful suggestions on previous versions of this work. Joyce Marcus generously offered detailed and insightful comments on several previous drafts, and her invaluable assistance and advice are greatly appreciated. I also acknowledge the inspiration that I have received since my days as an undergraduate from the words and writings of Kent V. Flannery. Finally, I dedicate this paper to Ron Spores, whose careful, many faceted investigation of the Mixtecs and their history has provided a valued model. None of these colleagues, however, necessarily agrees with this final product for which I take complete responsibility.

References Cited

Adams, Richard Newbold
1978 Man, energy, and anthropology: I can feel the heat, but where's the light? American Anthropologist 80:297–309.

Agnew, John A.
1982 Sociologizing the geographical imagination: Spatial concepts in the world-system perspective. Political Geography Quarterly 1:159–66.

Berger, Bennett
1990 The offenses of sociology. Science 250:1020–21.

Bernal, Ignacio
1965 Archaeological synthesis of Oaxaca. In: Handbook of Middle American Indians, edited by Robert Wauchope. Vol. 3: Archaeology of Southern Mesoamerica, edited by Gordon R. Willey, pt 2, pp. 788–813. Austin: University of Texas Press.
1966 The Mixtecs in the archaeology of the Valley of Oaxaca. In: Ancient Oaxaca: Discoveries in Mexican Archeology and History, edited by John Paddock, pp. 345–66. Stanford, California: Stanford University Press.

Binford, Lewis R.
1962 Archaeology as anthropology. American Antiquity 28:217–25.
1968 Archeological perspectives. In: New Prespectives in Archeology, edited by Sally R. Binford and Lewis R. Binford, pp. 5–32. Chicago: Aldine Press.
1986 In pursuit of the future. In: American Archaeology, Past and Future, edited by David J. Meltzer, Don D. Fowler, and Jeremy A. Sabloff, pp. 459–79. Washington, D.C.: Smithsonian Institution Press.

Blanton, Richard E.
1983 The ecological perspective in Highland Mesoamerican archaeology. In: Archaeological Hammers and Theories, edited by James A. Moore and Arthur S. Keene, pp. 221–31. New York: Academic Press.
1990 Theory and practice in Mesoamerican archaeology: A comparison of two modes of scientific inquiry. In: Debating Oaxaca Archaeology, edited by Joyce Marcus, pp. 1–16. Anthropological Papers of the Museum of Anthropology, University of Michigan, no. 84. Ann Arbor.

Blanton, Richard E., and Stephen A. Kowalewski
1981 Monte Albán and after in the Valley of Oaxaca. In: Supplement to the Handbook of Middle American Indians, edited by Victoria R. Bricker. Vol. 1: Archaeology, edited by Jeremy A. Sabloff, pp. 94–116. Austin: University of Texas Press.

Blanton, Richard E., Stephen A. Kowalewski, Gary Feinman, and Jill Appel
1982 Monte Albán's Hinterland, Part I: The Prehispanic Settlement Patterns of the Central and Southern Parts of the Valley of Oaxaca, Mexico. Memoirs of the Museum of Anthropology, University of Michigan, no. 15. Ann Arbor.

Blanton, Richard E., Stephen A. Kowalewski, Gary Feinman, and Laura Finsten
1993 Ancient Mesoamerica: A Comparison of Change in Three Regions. 2nd ed. Cambridge: Cambridge University Press.

Bloch, Marc
1970 French Rural History: An Essay on its Basic Characteristics. Berkeley: University of California Press.

Braudel, Fernand
1980 On History. Chicago: University of Chicago Press.

Brown, James H., and Brian A. Maurer
1989 Macroecology: The division of food and space on continents. Science 243:1145–50.

Brumfiel, Elizabeth M.
1983 Aztec state making: Ecology, structure, and the origin of the state. American Anthropologist 85:261–84.

Caso, Alfonso
1965 Sculpture and mural painting of Oaxaca. In: Handbook of Middle American Indians, edited by Robert Wauchope. Vol. 3: Archaeology of Southern Mesoamerica, edited by Gordon R. Willey, pt 2, pp. 849–70. Austin: University of Texas Press.

Caso, Alfonso, Ignacio Bernal, and Jorge R. Acosta
1967 La cerámica de Monte Albán. Memorias del Instituto Nacional de Antropología e Historia 13. México.

Chang, Kwang-Chih
1989 Ancient China and its anthropological significance. In: Archaeological Thought in America, edited by Carl C. Lamberg-Karlovsky, pp. 155–66. Cambridge: Cambridge University Press.

Clark, Geoffrey A.
1987 Paradigms and paradoxes in contemporary archaeology. In: Quantitative Research in Archaeology: Progress and Prospects, edited by Mark S. Aldenderfer, pp. 30–60. Newbury Park, Cal.: Sage Publications.

Collins, Randall
1986 Is 1980s sociology in the doldrums? American Journal of Sociology 91:1336–55.

Cordes, Colleen
1990 Doubling of NSF's budget said to bypass individual researchers. The Chronicle of Higher Education 36(27):24–30.

Costin, Cathy Lynne, and Timothy Earle
1989 Status distinction and legitimation of power as reflected in changing patterns of consumption in late prehispanic Peru. American Antiquity 54:691–714.

Cowgill, George L.
1988 Onward and upward with collapse. In: The Collapse of Ancient States and Empires, edited by Norman Yoffee and George L. Cowgill, pp. 244–76. Tucson: University of Arizona Press.

Custer, Jay F.
1981 Comments on David Meltzer's "Paradigms and the nature of change in American archaeology." American Antiquity 46:660–61.

De Garine, I., and W. A. Harrison
1988 Discussions and conclusions. In: Coping with Uncertainty in Food Supply, edited by I. De Garine and G. A. Harrison, pp. 469–75. Oxford: Clarendon Press.

Doyel, David E., ed.
1987 The Hohokam Village: Site Structure and Organization. Southwestern and Rocky Mountain Division of the American Association for the Advancement of Science. Glenwood Spring, Colorado.

Drennan, Robert D.
1984 Long-distance movement of goods in the Mesoamerican Formative and Classic. American Antiquity 49:27–43.

Dunnell, Robert C.
1979 Trends in current American archaeology. American Journal of Archaeology 83:437–49.
1982 Science, social science, and common sense: The agonizing dilemma of modern archaeology. Journal of Anthropological Research 38:1–25.
1984 The Americanist literature for 1983: A year of contrasts and challenges. American Journal of Archaeology 88:489–513.
1985 Americanist archaeology in 1984. American Journal of Archaeology 89:585–611.

Earle, Timothy, Terence D'Altroy, Christine Hastorf, Catherine Scott, Cathy Costin, Glenn Russell, and Elsie Sandefur
1987 Archaeological Field Research in the Upper Mantaro, Peru, 1982–1983: Investigations of Inka Expansion and Exchange. Monograph 28. Institute of Archaeology, University of California, Los Angeles.

Earle, Timothy K., and Robert W. Preucel
1987 Processual archaeology and the radical critique. Current Anthropology 28:501–38.

Eisenstadt, Shmuel N.
1988 Beyond collapse. In: The Collapse of Ancient States and Empires, edited by Norman Yoffee and George L. Cowgill, pp. 236–43. Tucson: University of Arizona Press.

Ellen, Roy
1982 Environment, Subsistence and System: The Ecology of Small-Scale Social Formations. Cambridge: Cambridge University Press.

Fagan, Brian M.
1989 The backward-looking curiosity: A glance at archaeology in the Year of Our Lord 1989. American Journal of Archaeology 93:445–49.

Feinman, Gary M.
1991 Demography, surplus, and inequality: Early political formations in Highland Mesoamerica. In: Chiefdoms: Power, Economy, and Ideology, edited by Timothy Earle, pp. 229–62. Cambridge: Cambridge University Press.

Feinman, Gary M., and Linda M. Nicholas
1987 Labor, surplus, and production: A regional analysis of Formative Oaxacan socio-economic change. In: Coasts, Plains and Deserts: Essays in Honor of Reynold J. Ruppé, edited by Sylvia W. Gaines, pp. 27–50. Anthropological Research Paper, no. 38. Department of Anthropology, Arizona State University. Tempe.
1990 Settlement and land use in ancient Oaxaca. In: Debating Oaxaca Archaeology, edited by Joyce Marcus, pp. 71–113. Anthropological Papers of the Museum of Anthropology, University of Michigan, no. 84. Ann Arbor.
1992 Human-land relations from an archaeological perspective: The case of ancient Oaxaca. In: Understanding Economic Process, edited by Sutti Ortiz and Susan Lees, pp. 155–78. Monographs in Economic Anthropology, no. 10. Lanham: University Press of America.

Flannery, Kent V.
1973 Archeology with a capital S. In: Research and Theory in Current Archeology, edited by Charles L. Redman, pp. 47–58. New York: John Wiley and Sons.
1982 The golden Marshalltown: A parable for the archaeology of the 1980s. American Anthropologist 84:265–78.
1983 The legacy of the Early Urban Period: An ethnohistoric approach to Monte Albán's temples, residences, and royal tombs. In: The Cloud People: Divergent Evolution of the Zapotec and Mixtec Civilizations, edited by Kent V. Flannery and Joyce Marcus, pp. 132–36. New York: Academic Press.

Flannery, Kent V., ed.
1976 The Early Mesoamerican Village. New York: Academic Press.
1986 Guilá Naquitz: Archaic Foraging and Early Agriculture in Oaxaca, Mexico. New York: Academic Press.

Flannery, Kent V., Anne V. T. Kirkby, Michael J. Kirkby, and Aubrey W. Williams, Jr.
1967 Farming systems and political growth in ancient Oaxaca. Science 158:445–54.

Flannery, Kent V., and Joyce Marcus
1976 Formative Oaxaca and the Zapotec cosmos. American Scientist 64:374–83.
1983 The earliest public buildings, tombs, and monuments of Monte Albán, with notes on the internal chronology of Period I. In: The Cloud People: Divergent Evolution of the Zapotec and Mixtec Civilizations, edited by Kent V. Flannery and Joyce Marcus, pp. 87–91. New York: Academic Press.

Flannery, Kent V., and Joyce Marcus, eds.
1983 The Cloud People: Divergent Evolution of the Zapotec and Mixtec Civilizations. New York: Academic Press.

Flannery, Kent V., Joyce Marcus, and Stephen A. Kowalewski
1981 The Preceramic and Formative of the Valley of Oaxaca. In: Supplement to the Handbook of Middle American Indians, edited by Victoria R. Bricker. Vol. 1: Archaeology, edited by Jeremy A. Sabloff, pp. 48–93. Austin: University of Texas Press.

Giddens, Anthony
1979 Central Problems in Social Theory: Action, Structure, and Contradiction in Social Analysis. Berkeley: University of California Press.
1987 Social Theory and Modern Sociology. Stanford, California: Stanford University Press.

Gilman, Antonio
1987 Comment on processual archaeology and the radical critique. Current Anthropology 28:515–16.

Gould, Stephen Jay
1985a Just in the middle. In: The Flamingo's Smile: Reflections in Natural History, pp. 377–91. New York: W. W. Norton.
1985b SETI and the wisdom of Casey Stengel. In: The Flamingo's Smile: Reflections in Natural History, pp. 403–13. New York: W. W. Norton.
1985c Sex, drugs, disasters, and the extinction of dinosaurs. In: The Flamingo's Smile: Reflections in Natural History, pp. 417–26. New York: W. W. Norton.
1986 Evolution and the triumph of homology, or why history matters. American Scientist 74:60–69.
1987a Time's Arrow, Time's Cycle: Myth and Metaphor in the Discovery of Geological Time. Cambridge: Harvard University Press.
1987b An Urchin in the Storm: Essays about Books and Ideas. New York: W. W. Norton.
1988 Pretty pebbles. Natural History 97:14–26.

Gumerman, George J., ed.
1991 Exploring the Hohokam: Prehistoric Desert Peoples of the American Southwest. Albuquerque: University of New Mexico Press.

Hassan, Fekri
1989 Review of "Archaeology as Long-Term History," edited by Ian Hodder. American Anthropologist 91:255–56.

Hodder, Ian
1984 Archaeology in 1984. Antiquity 58:25–32.
1985 Postprocessual archaeology. In: Advances in Archaeological Method and Theory, vol. 8, edited by Michael B. Schiffer, pp. 1–26. New York: Academic Press.
1986 Reading the Past: Current Approaches to Interpretation in Archaeology. Cambridge: Cambridge University Press.
1988 Archaeology and theory. Man 23:373–76.
1989 Comment on archaeology into the 1990s. Norwegian Archaeological Review 22:15–18.

Hodges, Richard
1986 Peer polity interaction and socio-political change in Anglo-Saxon England. In: Peer Polity Interaction and Socio-Political Change, edited by Colin Renfrew and John F. Cherry, pp. 69–78. Cambridge: Cambridge University Press.

Hull, David L.
1988 Science as a Process: An Evolutionary Account of the Social and Conceptual Development of Science. Chicago: The University of Chicago Press.

Johnson, Gregory A.
1982 Organizational structure and scalar stress. In: Theory and Explanation in Archaeology, edited by Colin Renfrew, Michael J. Rowlands, and Barbara A. Segraves, pp. 389–421. New York: Academic Press.

Kaplan, Abraham
1984 Philosophy of science in anthropology. Annual Review of Anthropology 13:25–39.

Kirch, Patrick V.
1984 The Evolution of the Polynesian Chiefdoms. Cambridge: Cambridge University Press.

Kirch, Patrick, and Roger Green
1987 History, phylogeny, and evolution in Polynesia. Current Anthropology 28:431–56.

Kirkby, Anne V. T.
1973 The Use of Land and Water Resources in the Past and Present Valley of Oaxaca, Mexico. Memoirs of the Museum of Anthropology, University of Michigan, no. 5. Ann Arbor.

Kluckhohn, Clyde
1940 The conceptual structure in Middle American studies. In: The Maya and their Neighbors, edited by C. L. Hay et al., pp. 41–51. New York: Appleton-Century.

Knapp, Bernard A.
1987 Comment on processual archaeology and the radical critique. Current Anthropology 28:518–21.

Kowalewski, Stephen A.
1980 Population-resource balances in Period I of Oaxaca, Mexico. American Antiquity 45:151–65.
1990 Merits of full-coverage survey: Examples from the Valley of Oaxaca, Mexico. In: The Archaeology of Regions: A Case for Full-Coverage Survey, edited by Suzanne K. Fish and Stephen A. Kowalewski, pp. 33–85. Washington, D.C.: Smithsonian Institution Press.

Kowalewski, Stephen A., Gary M. Feinman, Laura Finsten, Richard E. Blanton, and Linda M. Nicholas

1989 Monte Albán's Hinterland, Part II: Prehispanic Settlement Patterns in Tlacolula, Etla, and Ocotlán, the Valley of Oaxaca, Mexico. Memoirs of the Museum of Anthropology, University of Michigan, no. 23. Ann Arbor.

Kowalewski, Stephen A., and Suzanne K. Fish

1990 Conclusions. In: The Archaeology of Regions: A Case for Full-Coverage Survey. Washington, D.C.: Smithsonian Institution Press.

Kuhn, Thomas S.

1970 The Structure of Scientific Revolutions. 2nd ed. Chicago: University of Chicago Press.

Leonard, Robert D.

1989 Resource specialization, population growth, and agricultural production in the American Southwest. American Antiquity 54:491–503.

Leone, Mark P.

1986 Symbolic, structural, and critical archaeology. In: American Archaeology, Past and Future, edited by David J. Meltzer, Don D. Fowler, and Jeremy A. Sabloff, pp. 415–38. Washington, D.C.: Smithsonian Institution Press.

Lind, Michael, and Javier Urcid

1983 The lords of Lambityeco and their nearest neighbors. Notas Mesoamericanas 9:78–111.

Marcus, Joyce

1978 Archaeology and religion: A comparison of the Zapotec and Maya. World Archaeology 10:172–91.

1983a Lowland Maya archaeology at the crossroads. American Antiquity 48:454–88.

1983b Zapotec religion. In: The Cloud People: Divergent Evolution of the Zapotec and Mixtec Civilizations, edited by Kent V. Flannery and Joyce Marcus, pp. 345–51. New York: Academic Press.

1983c Rethinking the Zapotec urn. In: The Cloud People: Divergent Evolution of the Zapotec and Mixtec Civilizations, edited by Kent V. Flannery and Joyce Marcus, pp. 144–48. New York: Academic Press.

1983d Stone monuments and tomb murals of Monte Albán IIIa. In: The Cloud People: Divergent Evolution of the Zapotec and Mixtec Civilizations, edited by Kent V. Flannery and Joyce Marcus, pp. 137–43. New York: Academic Press.

1989 Zapotec chiefdoms and the nature of Formative religions. In: Regional Perspectives on the Olmec, edited by Robert J. Sharer and David C. Grove, pp. 148–97. Cambridge: Cambridge University Press.

Marcus, Joyce, and Kent V. Flannery

1978 Ethnoscience of the sixteenth-century Valley Zapotec. In: The Nature and Status of Ethnobotany, edited by Richard I. Ford, pp. 51–79. Anthropological Papers of the Museum of Anthropology, University of Michigan, no. 67. Ann Arbor.

1990 Ideology and archaeology: The case of the ancient Zapotec. Paper presented at Workshop towards an Explicitly Scientific Cognitive Archaeology, co-chaired by Colin Renfrew and Ezra W. Zubrow, Cambridge, April 8–13, 1990.

1994 Zapotec ritual and religion: An application of the direct historical approach. In: The Ancient Mind, edited by Colin Renfrew and Ezra W. Zubrow, pp. 55–74. Cambridge: Cambridge University Press.

Martin, Paul S.

1971 The revolution in archaeology. American Antiquity 36:1–8.

Masterman, Margaret

1970 The nature of the paradigm. In: Criticism and the Growth of Knowledge, edited by I. Lakatos and A. Musgrave, pp. 59–90. London: Cambridge University Press.

Mayhew, Bruce

1980 Structuralism versus individualism: Part 1, shadowboxing in the dark. Social Forces 59:335–75.

Mayr, Ernst

1961 Cause and effect in biology. Science 134:1501–6.

1982 The Growth of Biological Thought. Cambridge: Harvard University Press.

Meltzer, David J.

1979 Paradigms and the nature of change in American archaeology. American Antiquity 44:644–57.

1981 Paradigms lost–paradigms found? American Antiquity 46:662–65.

1990 Review of "Social Theory and Archaeology," by Michael Shanks and Christopher Tilley. American Antiquity 55:186–87.

Meltzer, David J., Don D. Fowler, and Jeremy A. Sabloff, eds.

1986 American Archaeology, Past and Future. Washington, D.C.: Smithsonian Institution Press.

Miller, Arthur

1988 Pre-hispanic mural painting in the Valley of Oaxaca, Mexico. National Geographic Research 4:233–58.

Minc, Leah D.

1986 Scarcity and survival: The role of oral tradition in mediating subsistence crises. Journal of Anthropological Archaeology 5:39–113.

Mithen, Steven

1989 Evolutionary theory and post-processual archaeology. Antiquity 63:483–94.

Nicholas, Linda M.

1989 Land use in prehispanic Oaxaca. In: Monte Albán's Hinterland, Part II: Prehispanic Settlement Patterns in Tlacolula, Etla, and Ocotlán, the Valley of Oaxaca, Mexico, by Stephen A. Kowalewski, Gary M. Feinman, Laura Finsten, Richard E. Blanton, and Linda M. Nicholas, pp. 449–505. Memoirs of the Museum of Anthropology, University of Michigan, no. 23. Ann Arbor.

Orlove, Benjamin S.
1980 Ecological anthropology. Annual Review of Anthropology 9:235–73.

Paddock, John
1966 Oaxaca in ancient Mesoamerica. In: Ancient Oaxaca: Discoveries in Mexican Archeology and History, edited by John Paddock, pp. 83–242. Stanford, Cal.: Stanford University Press.

Patterson, Thomas C.
1989 History and the post-processual archaeologies. Man 24:555–66.

Plog, Stephen, and Jeffrey L. Hantman
1990 Chronology, construction, and the study of prehistoric culture change. Journal of Field Archaeology 17:439–56.

Pyne, Nanette M.
1976 The Fire-Serpent and Were-Jaguar in Formative Oaxaca: A contingency table analysis. In: The Early Mesoamerican Village, edited by Kent V. Flannery, pp. 272–80. New York: Academic Press.

Rappaport, Roy A.
1979 Ecology, Meaning, and Religion. Richmond: North Atlantic Books.

Renfrew, Colin
1980 The great tradition versus the great divide: Archaeology as anthropology. American Journal of Archaeology 84:287–98.
1982 Explanation revisited. In: Theory and Explanation in Archaeology, edited by Colin Renfrew, Michael J. Rowlands, and Barbara A. Segraves, pp. 5–23. New York: Academic Press.
1989 Comment on archaeology into the 1990s. Norwegian Archaeological Review 22:33–41.

Ricklefs, Robert E.
1987 Community diversity: Relative roles of local and regional processes. Science 235:167–71.

Sanders, William T., Jeffrey R. Parsons, and Robert S. Santley
1979 The Basin of Mexico: Ecological Processes in the Evolution of a Civilization. New York: Academic Press.

Schiffer, Michael B.
1975 Archaeology as behavioral science. American Anthropologist 77:836–48.
1988 The structure of archaeological theory. American Antiquity 53:461–85.

Searle, John
1984 Minds, Brains, and Science. Cambridge: Harvard University Press.

Seler, Eduard
1904 The wall paintings of Mitla, a Mexican picture writing in fresco. Bureau of American Ethnology, Bulletin 28:247–324. Washington, D.C.

Shanks, Michael, and Christopher Tilley
1987 Re-constructing Archaeology: Theory and Practice. Cambridge: Cambridge University Press.
1989 Archaeology into the 1990s. Norwegian Archaeological Review 22:1–54.

Sherratt, Andrew
1988 Scouting the objective. The Times Literary Supplement, May 13–19, p. 538.

Smith, Bruce D.
1986 Review of "Ideology, Power, and Prehistory," edited by Daniel Miller and Christopher Tilley. American Anthropologist 88:220–21.

Spaulding, Albert C.
1988 Distinguished lecture: Archeology and anthropology. American Anthropologist 90:263–71.

Spencer, Charles S.
1990 On the tempo and mode of state formation: Neoevolutionism reconsidered. Journal of Anthropological Archaeology 9:1–30.

Speth, John D.
1988 Do we need concepts like "Mogollon," "Anasazi," and "Hohokam" today? A cultural anthropological perspective. The Kiva 53:201–4.

Sterud, Eugene L.
1978 Changing aims of Americanist archaeology: A citations analysis of American Antiquity–1946–1975. American Antiquity 43:294–302.

Taylor, Walter W.
1948 A Study of Archeology. Memoir 69. American Anthropological Association, Menasha.

Trigger, Bruce G.
1982 Archaeological analysis and concepts of causality. Culture 2:31–42.
1984 Archaeology at the crossroads: What's new? Annual Review of Anthropology 13:275–300.
1989a A History of Archaeological Thought. Cambridge: Cambridge University Press.
1989b Archaeology and anthropology: Current and future relations. Canadian Journal of Archaeology 13:1–11.

Upham, Steadman
1990 Analog or digital?: Toward a generic framework for explaining the development of emergent political systems. In: The Evolution of Political Systems: Sociopolitics in Small-Scale Sedentary Societies, edited by Steadman Upham, pp. 87–115. Cambridge: Cambridge University Press.

Watson, Patty Jo
1986 Archaeological interpretation, 1985. In: American Archaeology, Past and Future, edited by David J. Meltzer, Don D. Fowler, and Jeremy A. Sabloff, pp. 439–57. Washington, D.C.: Smithsonian Institution Press.

Wetterstrom, Wilma
1978 Cognitive systems, food patterns, and paleoethnobotany. In: The Nature and Status of Ethnobotany, edited by Richard I. Ford, pp. 81–95. Anthropological Papers of the Museum of Anthropology, University of Michigan, no. 67. Ann Arbor.

Wicker, Tom
1990 Beyond the jackpot. New York Times, January 22, p. 19.

Wilcox, David R.
1988 Rethinking the Mogollon concept. The Kiva 53:205–9.

Wilk, Richard R., and Wendy Ashmore, eds.
1988 Household and Community in the Mesoamerican Past. Albuquerque: University of New Mexico Press.

Willey, Gordon R., ed.
1965 Handbook of Middle American Indians. Vol. 3: Archaeology of Southern Mesoamerica, pt 2. Austin: University of Texas Press.

Wolf, Eric R.
1982 Europe and the People without History. Berkeley: University of California Press.
1990 Distinguished lecture: Facing power–old insights, new questions. American Anthropologist 92:586–96.

Wylie, Alison
1982 Archaeology in a social context: Ethical and epistemological considerations. In: Directions in Archaeology: A Question of Goals, edited by Peter D. Francis and Eric C. Poplin, pp. 369–74. The University of Calgary Archaeological Association, Calgary.

Zeitlin, Robert N.
1987 Comment on processual archaeology and the radical critique. Current Anthropology 28:524–25.

CHAPTER 3

Indian Elites in Late Colonial Mesoamerica[1]

John K. Chance

Arizona State University

The position of village Indian elites in colonial Mesoamerican society has long been a topic of considerable interest to ethnohistorians. *Caciques,* the putative colonial descendants of prehispanic noble families, have attracted much scholarly attention, and with good reason. Their often ambiguous status between Indian commoners (*macehuales*) on the one hand and Spaniards on the other is a fruitful point of entry into the workings of the complex colonial stratification system, a social framework which drew on both indigenous and Spanish cultural models.[2] Traditionally, research on colonial Indian elites has dealt primarily with the sixteenth century, when Indians and Europeans reached their first accommodation (see especially Gibson 1964; López Sarrelangue 1965; Spores 1967, 1983; Carrasco 1975; Carrasco, Broda et al. 1976; Rojas Rabiela 1987).

While the first century of Spanish rule is still the focus of much ethnohistoric work, in recent years an increasing number of scholars have turned their attention to the mature colonial setting of the eighteenth century. These studies are diverse in character, and in this paper I wish to examine just one of their findings: that local elites continued to play important roles in many late colonial Indian communities, and that in some areas elites were significant players in regional political economies as well. It is also becoming increasingly clear that these eighteenth-century elites differed among themselves in various ways, not only in their disparate cultural traditions, but also with respect to their wealth, political power, and prestige.

The purpose of this paper is to take stock of how far we have come in understanding these late colonial elites and to offer suggestions for the direction of future research. Regional differences will be outlined and a typology will be proposed to account for them. Emphasis will be placed on key political and economic forces that shaped the parameters of local elites and conditioned their mode of integration into the wider society.

There are also broader lessons to be learned from a look at this particular social category. The social boundaries and cultural identities of late colonial Indian elites were in most places considerably more fluid and ambiguous than those of their sixteenth-century predecessors. These ambiguities provide a striking example of a basic tension that Fredrick Cooper and Ann Stoler (1989:609) find in many colonial societies: "the otherness of the colonized person was neither inherent nor stable; his or her difference had to be defined and maintained; social boundaries that were at one point clear would not necessarily remain so."

Social Differentiation in the Eighteenth Century

Early writing on colonial Indian elites in Mesoamerica paid scant attention to the years after 1600. If late colonial elites were mentioned at all, their significance was usually minimized and emphasis was placed on the circumstances of their decline (Gibson 1964; López Sarrelangue 1965). Charles Gibson (1964:157–63) stated the case most clearly for the Valley of Mexico:

> The effect of Spanish colonialism on the class stratifications of Indian society was to equalize and compress, to move all classes toward a single level and condition . . . Legitimate cacicazgo had little meaning beyond family pride in the conditions of the late colony.

He went on to note that few *caciques* and *principales*[3] preserved lands and retainers into the seventeenth century, and that *cacique* status became "diluted" in later years as popular criteria for it were broadened.

Gibson's perspective, once widely shared but now undergoing revision, contains a number of inadequacies when viewed from the standpoint of current research. First, it is essentially an outsider's point of view; Gibson had relatively little to say about the meaning of Nahuatl terms like *teuctli* and *pilli,* or Spanish terms such as *cacique* and *principal,* to the inhabitants of late colonial towns and villages. The insider's point of view on such matters is still rather elusive, but ongoing research in Nahuatl sources shows that it is not entirely beyond our grasp (e.g., Lockhart 1982, 1992).

Second, Gibson's view, which I will call the view of the "vanishing nobility," is seemingly predicated on the questionable assumption that the effects of Spanish colonialism on Indian social structure led to uniformity or homogeneity, and that the "destructuring" that occurred in the sixteenth century continued throughout the remainder of the colonial period. Now, however, there is ample evidence that this was not the case, as will be discussed shortly.

Third, the view of the vanishing nobility implicitly treats colonial Indian elites as "vestiges," to use Nancy Farriss's (1983:2–6) term, of the prehispanic past, and underestimates their functional role in late colonial society. It stresses what late colonial nobles had *lost,* particularly land, retainers, and political authority, and gives short shrift to ways in which social differentiation was changing. The problem of how stratification was redefined in the late colonial context received little attention because it was difficult to reconcile with the uniformity or homogeneity thesis.

Research on elites and social inequality during the last two decades has changed this picture substantially. It has become increasingly clear that the period from roughly 1660 to 1810 was more than just an extension of early Indian adaptations to Spanish rule. The depopulation and social destructuring of earlier years gave way to renewed population growth, commercialization, and a vigorous restructuring of indigenous community life in the eighteenth century. Instead of a steady decline and ossification of pre-Conquest and early colonial institutions, there is much evidence that older principles were redefined and reshaped to fit changing circumstances (Carmagnani 1980:1028; Chance 1986:166; Taylor 1979:20).

The persistence during a good portion of the eighteenth century (and in some areas during the entire colonial period) of significant numbers of *caciques, principales,* and the local elites they represent is a case in point. Far from being socially leveled by Spanish institutions, late colonial villages exhibited marked inequalities of various kinds. Eric Van Young (1984:29) has postulated that social differentiation was on the increase in the late colony, and Farriss (1983:29) has suggested that "a colonial native elite with functions similar to those of the pre-Columbian ruling group could perhaps be found all over Mesoamerica." These native elites, I would argue, continued to play important roles in the conduct of both internal and external affairs of late colonial communities. Detailed studies are now available for four Mesoamerican regions, and it is to these that I now turn. The discussion will be brief and synthetic, and the emphasis will be on differences rather than similarities. The interested reader is referred to the original works cited for further details.

Four Regions Compared

Northern Yucatan

In her study of northern Yucatán, Farriss (1984: Ch. 8) makes clear that the cornerstone of elite survival was its retention of political power. To a greater degree than in other parts of colonial Mexico, Maya elites in this region succeeded in rechanneling the new Spanish-imposed municipal offices into the native structure. Colonial *cabildos* (town councils) were monopolized by the *caciques* and *principales* (collectively known as *almehenob* in Maya), who remained the fixed center of each community and the architects of village adaptive strategy. These were individuals of some wealth (the *caciques* at least) and "suitable genealogical credentials," who claimed descent from royal prehispanic ancestors. While Farriss has not been able to confirm or disconfirm such claims,[4] she does show that the source of legitimacy of these groups came more from within than from without. Yucatán's poverty, lack of a developed market system, and absence of local or regional Spanish magistrates (*corregidores* or *alcaldes mayores*) prior to the 1770s led village elites virtually to disappear from Spanish view. In Farriss's (1984:231) words, "They maintained their rank, and more important, many of their traditional privileges, not because the Spanish acknowledged the legitimacy of their claims but because the rest of Indian society did." The persistence of pre-Conquest political structures, if not the ruling families themselves, appears to be at the core of elite adaptation in northern Yucatán.[5]

The Valley of Oaxaca and the Mixteca Alta

In the Valley of Oaxaca and the Mixteca Alta we find a different sort of native elite in the mid-eighteenth century (Taylor 1972:35–66; Spores 1984:99–100, 113–17; Pastor 1987:79–85, 121–27, 165–75, 204–7, 308–27; Carmagnani 1988).[6] Here the *caciques* had lost out in the struggle for political supremacy in local communities 150 years earlier, and had come to share power with Indian *principales* and *macehuales* on the one hand, and with Spanish *alcaldes mayores* on the other. The basis for the *caciques*' existence had become largely economic: they were private owners of titles and lands known as *cacicazgos*. Virtually every major community had a *cacicazgo* attached to it, and in the eighteenth century a few of these in the Valley of Oaxaca were larger than most Spanish haciendas in the region. *Cacicazgos* of different towns were also often fused through marriage alliances.

Unlike the northern Yucatecan *almehenob,* the owners of these Oaxaca estates and their families were very much in Spanish view from the sixteenth century onward. Their landholdings were recognized by colonial law and patterned after the Spanish *mayorazgo,* or entailed estate, with primogeniture as the preferred rule of succession. Furthermore, the *caciques* integrated themselves with the European mercantile economy very early on, and many of them became highly acculturated. Most Valley of Oaxaca *caciques* who could afford it moved to the city of Oaxaca, while in the Mixteca many nobles supplemented their *cacicazgo* income with a wide variety of commercial enterprises. Ronald Spores (1984:100) notes that some Mixtec *caciques* and *principales* "ranked on a par with European bureaucrats or clergy and above certain Spanish civilians, military, and indigents." The persistence of these Oaxaca elites had less to do with the survival of native political organization (though, of course, this factor cannot be entirely discounted) than it did with their ability to acquire an independent economic base and garner a high degree of recognition by Spanish society.

The Sierra Zapoteca of Oaxaca

Yet another type of colonial Indian elite has emerged from my own research in the Sierra Zapoteca of Oaxaca (Chance 1978a, 1986, 1989), where Spanish *alcal-*

des mayores played an active role in maintaining social differentiation in Indian communities. Especially in the Nexitzo-speaking Rincón Zapotec area, a highly exploitive form of political economy was linked to a kind of "status inflation" in the eighteenth century. The remoteness of this region and its mountainous terrain, the absence of haciendas, the weak regional market system, and the small number of Spaniards and other non-Indians all make the Sierra Zapoteca very different from the Valley of Oaxaca and the Mixteca Alta. Sierra Indian communities at the time of Spanish contact were much less populous and less stratified than their Valley Zapotec and Mixteca counterparts. The native nobility was not wealthy and after the Conquest, *cacique* families went into decline, losing much of their political power and prestige. Most landed *cacicazgos* of any consequence were gone by the mid-seventeenth century; the last succumbed shortly after 1730.

Yet status differences in the Sierra were actually on the increase in the eighteenth century. Each town supported a few *cacique* families who were exempt from tribute, but the most noticeable change was the vast proliferation of *principales*. As I have argued elsewhere (Chance 1989: Ch. 5), the growth in this elite group can be attributed primarily to the coercive Spanish trading practice, the *repartimiento de efectos*. Despite its poverty and remoteness, the Sierra's Villa Alta district was a chief source of cochineal dyestuff and cotton cloth in colonial Mexico. The volume of these products increased significantly after 1750, and most of the trade was controlled by the *alcaldes mayores* of Villa Alta through the mechanism of the *repartimiento*. Backed by urban merchants, these officials (through their lieutenants) periodically distributed raw cotton for textiles and cash advances for cochineal production, then returned a few months later to buy back the products at artificially low prices.

This practice was more akin to tribute exaction than to trade, and a key group for its success was the Indian *cabildo* in each town. Zapotec officials, elected yearly, were responsible for the actual collections. They were also in a position to pocket some of the proceeds for themselves, and under these conditions the *cabildo* became the focal point for status achievement and political factionalism. Membership in the *principal* elite could be attained by men through service in high political offices or it could be claimed on the basis of descent. This simultaneous recognition of achieved and ascribed status led to considerable conflict, and many of these disputes ended up on the doorstep of the *alcaldes mayores* in Villa Alta. Never very knowledgeable about (nor probably very interested in) local indigenous culture, and dependent on the cooperation of as many villagers as possible to keep their *repartimientos* running smoothly, the Spanish magistrates more often than not confirmed the hereditary *principal* status sought by the plaintiffs, even when the supporting evidence was weak. As a result, in the latter half of the eighteenth century it was not unusual for over a third of the inhabitants of these small Zapotec villages (most with populations of just a few hundred) to hold *principal* status.

Central Mexico

The Central Mexican plateau, of course, was the core of the colony of New Spain. The Spanish presence here was greater than in Oaxaca or Yucatán, and its impact on Indian society more direct. Nahua communities in this region were highly stratified in prehispanic times, yet we still lack a clear picture of late colonial Indian elites and how much variability they exhibited. Research to date has concentrated on the Valleys of Mexico and Toluca and neighboring Morelos; future work in these and other areas, such as central Puebla, may well reveal important subregional differences.

These problems aside, there is abundant evidence that village Indian elites were present and quite significant in many parts of eighteenth-century central Mexico (Alberro 1981:775; Gruzinski 1989: Ch. 5; Haskett 1987:228; 1988:35–42; Lockhart 1976:21; 1982:368–84; 1992; Martin 1985: Ch. 7; Münch 1976; Taylor 1979:21; Tutino 1976a:270; 1976b:182; 1988:100–102). William Taylor (1979:21) notes that "Almost every rural head town had its small bourgeoisie, composed of notaries, skilled artisans, state officials, tavernkeepers, and traders." James Lockhart provides the best general characterization:

> In central Mexican Indian towns of the middle and later colonial period, there existed an upper group who shared the Nahuatl language and the ethnicity of the rest of the population, but stood out from it in various ways. Heirs of the preconquest nobility, they had more properties and more dependents than the average; they dominated the semiautonomous town governments; they married across town boundaries in quasi-dynastic matches, creating regional familial networks which transcended the individual towns; many of them carried on enterprises not unlike Spanish ones and sold their products in the region's broader Spanish economy; some began to intermarry with the Spaniards, who were growing in number in the main Indian towns. [Lockhart 1982:368–69]

The collaboration of central Mexican *caciques* in the process of colonial domination has been frequently noted by students of this region (Alberro 1981:775; Konrad 1980:293; Martin 1985: Ch. 7; Tutino 1976a:343; 1988:100–102). *Caciques* acted as political and economic intermediaries between Spaniards and Indian commoners, often had good connections with *hacendados* and other non-Indian powerholders, and served as labor brokers for many agricultural and ranching estates. However, while elites were the most land-rich people in their communities, hereditary *cacicazgos* on the scale described for the Valley of Oaxaca and the Mixteca Alta seem to have been rare, at least in the eighteenth century (but see Münch 1976).

The present state of our knowledge of central Mexico does not permit us to go much further than these suggestive generalities. Data from eighteenth-century Morelos, however, reveal an interesting contradiction: at a time when *caciques* and *principales* were becoming increasingly acculturated, their claims to legitimacy emphasized the purity of their Indian ancestry. Cultural differences between Indian elites and commoners had become substantial by 1760, and Serge Gruzinski (1989:172) has gone so far as to say that for elites, the cultural Other by this time was the Indian, not the Spaniard. Yet in Cuernavaca, Robert Haskett (1988:40–42) finds that the earlier elite practice of claiming mixed ancestry from Spanish *and* the indigenous prehispanic nobility had been abandoned in favor of a strategy that invoked only the Indian side, even though some individuals were known to be biological mestizos.

The situation in the central part of the Valley of Puebla may have been similar in some respects. My preliminary research findings on the towns of Tecali and Cuauhtinchan indicate that the title of *cacique* was significant and extensively used in the eighteenth century.[7] In earlier times, both towns were noted for their highly unequal patterns of landholding, a reflection of the strength and exclusivity of their elites (Olivera 1978; Reyes García 1977). Indeed, the *macehuales* of the sixteenth century remained almost entirely landless.[8] By the eighteenth century, both towns experienced periods of heavy Spanish coercive demands for labor and trade, and local elites appear to have been highly acculturated. They were also often intertwined with the Hispanic population, as evidenced by their not infrequent marriages with creoles and mestizos.[9] Some of these *caciques* controlled considerable wealth and power. Don Cayetano de Tovar of Tecali, for example, was reelected *gobernador* for the ninth time (in violation of the law) in 1734 with the backing of the *alcalde mayor*. By all accounts he enjoyed unusual authority. He owned extensive lands worked by several subject hamlets; he collected the customary contributions that paid the local priest's salary and funded the town's lawsuits, fiestas, and annual political ceremonies; he collected tribute and other village fees; he received household servants; and he served as *mayordomo* of the Cofradía de Nuestra Señora de los Dolores for at least four years before his stint as *gobernador* (Taylor 1984:90; Archivo Parroquial de Tecali, Libro de la Cofradía de Nuestra Señora de los Dolores, 1727–37).

Estates called *cacicazgos* existed in central Puebla, but unlike those in Oaxaca they were small, fragmented, and localized, and commonly subdivided among heirs. Consequently, the number of *cacicazgos* and *caciques* multiplied over time, but the amount of land owned by each estate or noble diminished. Olivera (1978:204) counted 55 *cacicazgos* in Tecali at the end of the sixteenth century. By 1755 the town had 123 *caciques,* including 74 men and 49 women (Archivo General de la Nación, Tierras, vol. 1865, exp. 4, folios 6v-7v). These individuals were presumably private owners of lands that they had inherited, and in some cases purchased, from other nobles. *Caciques* in this area were also exempt from tribute, and Spanish magistrates kept records of such privileges. In Cuauhtinchan, all of the town's 110 *caciques* in 1734 were exempt, including 41 married couples, 20 single men, and 8 single women (Archivo Municipal de Cuauhtinchan, Paquete 1, exp. 21).

Certainly, then, the title of *cacique* was significant in late colonial Tecali and Cuauhtinchan. *Caciques* in both communities regularly monopolized the high political offices and top *cofradía* posts. Yet wealth and access to resources was not distributed evenly, and the *caciques* as a whole did not comprise a class. In the first years of the nineteenth century, for example, one illiterate Tecali *cacique* owned little more than three pieces of land and his house. In contrast, a contemporary political official of commoner extraction could boast of a house, 6 pieces of land, 7 teams of oxen, 18 head of cattle, three horses, 120 goats, 22 donkeys, and 25 pigs (Archivo de Notarías del Estado de Puebla, Protocolos de Tecali, Caja 1, Libro 1, exp. 30 and Libro 2, exp. 1).

If the title of *cacique* was no guarantee of wealth and political power, why was it so coveted and so ubiquitous in the documentation? One possibility is that coercive colonial practices in towns like Tecali and Cuauhtinchan promoted the continued existence of formally recognized village elites. Local nobles were well positioned to serve as labor brokers for nearby haciendas and also to help manage the *repartimientos de efectos* of the *alcaldes mayores*. From the point of view of the colonized, *cacique* status was a first line of defense against Spanish exploitation and, for some, a means of upward mobility. Even the poor *caciques* benefited from their exemption from tribute. From the point of view of the colonizers, the title was a reward for services rendered to the Spanish sector.

Recent local and regional studies of eighteenth-century Mexico highlight the increasing inequalities, tensions, and economic exploitation of this period (Chance 1988; Farriss 1984; Hamnett 1986; Menegus Bornemann 1989; Martin 1985; Morin 1979). Some of these social tensions derived from the use of force, which appears to have been prevalent in much of central Puebla. The use of force came from two sources. The first was the region's demographic stagnation and economic depression in the eighteenth and early nineteenth centuries (Thomson 1989; Cuenya 1987; Garavaglia and Grosso 1987). A slender regional market for agricultural products coupled with a falling Indian population after 1735 helped create a labor scarcity on many haciendas (Thomson 1989:25; Vollmer 1973:37). *Hacendados* frequently resorted to labor abuse, particularly from the 1770s on. Nine cases were registered in Tepeaca alone in 1776–78, and in Izúcar, resistance to forced labor nearly led to rebellion in 1781 (Hamnett 1986:85–87).[10]

The second use of force was the heavy *repartimientos de efectos* levied by Spanish magistrates in the region. Puebla *repartimientos* were the forced sale of goods on credit (especially mules, oxen, and horses) or cash advances against the delivery of future goods (primarily wheat, corn, chile, and other agricultural products). The particularly onerous *repartimientos* in Tecali helped ignite a major rebellion in 1735 (Pietschmann 1977, 1988; Taylor 1984).[11] Brian Hamnett sees the survival of *repartimientos* in Puebla villages as a stimulus for the formation of rebel bands in the early nineteenth century. By 1811–1812, the Intendancy of

Puebla had become the "principal theatre of war" in Mexico, with longstanding grievances in several localities, including Tepeaca (Hamnett 1986:150, 152, 160).[12]

Types of Elites: A Model

Having dealt with regional differences among late colonial elites, I wish to propose a matrix of ideal types that will give an explanatory sketch. Of the four regions discussed, central Mexico is clearly the most problematic, and it is impossible to say whether Haskett's (1985, 1987, 1988, 1991) Cuernavaca data and my own preliminary work on Tecali and Cuauhtinchan are indicative of a wider regional pattern in the central highlands. For these reasons the typology presented here is provisional and subject to modification by future research.

"*Elite*" is in the broadest sense "a flexible cover term that refers to the rich, powerful, and privileged in any society, past or present, Western or non-Western" (Marcus 1983:3). The model in Table 3.1 attributes the salient differences in elite structure to regional variations in political and economic integration. The two analytic dimensions are degree of market integration of elites, and degree of direct coercion by non-Indians.

The problem of elite status in late colonial Indian communities is similar in some respects to the problem of ethnic and racial status in the Spanish cities of the time. Just as we have probed the meaning and social significance of terms like *español, mestizo,* and *mulato* (Chance 1978b, 1979), it is time to ask comparable questions about such terms as *cacique* and *principal, pilli* and *macehualli,* in the eighteenth century. In contrast to the declining significance of race in the cities, it appears that the use of noble status terms was on the increase in many Indian communities. Rather than writing off this trend as a "dilution" of a formerly more "authentic" stratification system, it behooves us to come to grips with eighteenth-century community culture on its own terms. I suggest that status terms in use during that period had different connotations in different places, and that their significance had much to do with features of regional political economies.

Northern Yucatán, the Valley of Oaxaca, and the Mixteca Alta were broadly similar in that they all escaped the heavy Spanish pressures of rapid urbanization, mining, and hacienda development that affected much of the central Mexican plateau. Villages retained their land bases, continued to rely on subsistence agriculture, and remained almost entirely Indian in composition. Mining was of little importance and haciendas were either absent or of modest size. These conditions favored the persistence of many aspects of indigenous tradition, including local elites. But as we have seen, there were also important differences among these regions. The typology in Table 3.1 characterizes the northern Yucatecan Maya

TABLE 3.1
Native Mesoamerican Elites in the Mid-Eighteenth Century

	Low Coercion	**High Coercion**
Low Elite Market Integration	*Political Elites* Northern Yucatán	*Dependent Elites* Sierra Zapoteca
High Elite Market Integration	*Economic Elites* Valley of Oaxaca and Mixteca Alta	*Confrontational Elites* Tecali—Cuauhtinchan

elites as political, for their legitimacy was based fundamentally on the continuing integrity of prehispanic political structures. This persistence was made possible by the predominant features of the Yucatecan political economy prior to the 1770s: its relatively weak market integration and low degree of direct coercion by Spaniards. By comparison, class factors and control of Spanish-style wealth loomed much larger among the Zapotec and Mixtec "economic elites" in the Valley of Oaxaca and Mixteca Alta. Not all *caciques* were wealthy, but on the whole, economic factors were here more important than political ones in defining elite status. In these areas of Oaxaca, the prehispanic cultural continuity afforded by the modest amount of Spanish coercion was offset by the elites' high degree of acculturation and integration with the colonial market system.

In the Sierra Zapoteca, the diagnostic features of the political economy were reversed: market integration was weak (this is discussed in detail in Chapter 4 of Chance 1989) and Spanish coercion was strong. Many Zapotecs sought *principal* status in Spanish courts in order to win special privileges and exemption from compulsory community service. At the same time, the Spanish *alcaldes mayores* became more dependent on Indian elites and, through their legal decisions, actively helped to maintain them. The result was a series of community-based "dependent elites" who owed their existence not only to descent and political officeholding, but also to the support of the Spanish political officials.

The Tecali-Cuauhtinchan type of elite, labeled "confrontational" in Figure 3.1, is less well established than the others, but is associated with high elite market integration *and* heavy coercion from non-Indians. The proliferation of *caciques* in Tecali and Cuauhtinchan is similar to the growth in number of *principales* in the Sierra Zapoteca. High levels of coercion in both regions provide the best explanation of this status inflation. The main difference is that in Puebla, by far the wealthier of the two regions, a select few of the titled families also constituted dominant upper classes in their respective communities. This was made possible, I suggest, by their greater involvement in the colonial market economy and their landed wealth, traits that they shared with the elites of the Valley of Oaxaca and the Mixteca Alta. However, the model would predict a greater interest in "passing for Spanish" among Oaxaca's economic elites, while confrontational elites would be more interested in acculturating *without* such emulation, and would place a higher value on the retention of Indian identity. These elites were "confrontational" to the degree that they actively asserted their status as *caciques,* not in the manner of the dependent *principales* of the Sierra Zapoteca, but more from a position of strength based on local tradition, accumulated wealth, and/or participation in the regional market system.[13]

The two axes of the typology represent contradictory forces that were widespread in eighteenth-century Indian society (Stern 1983; Van Young 1984; Gosner 1989). These elements have been most clearly articulated by Steve Stern, who notes that colonialism injected new class forces into Indian villages, furthering differentiation into rich and poor. In many places this led to a high degree of acculturation of Indian elites, in extreme cases transforming elite "insiders" into alien "outsiders" (Stern 1983:35). At the same time, these class tensions also conditioned life within the community, provoking a "struggle for solidarity" which entailed the rise of closed corporate community structures. Stern argues that

> peasants exerted day-to-day pressure on their wealthier and more acculturated counterparts to demonstrate their loyalties to the people to whom they "belonged." By serving the community or ethnic group, "successful" Indians could avoid social ostracism, and even earn prestige and respect. Such services included functioning as protective "brokers" defending community interests against the "outside" world of Hispanic-mestizo exploiters; submitting, at least in part, to rules of "generosity" and community responsibility which redistributed wealth to poorer peasants; and joining in symbolic expressions of solidarity with native society. [Stern 1983:37]

The typology presented here attempts to capture the varying intensity and relations between these two contradictory forces in different regions of late colonial Mesoamerica. Emergent class forces were conditioned most fundamentally by the degree of elite market integration, while the persistence of noble statuses like *cacique* and *principal* was more closely tied to the "struggle for solidarity" against coercive pressures from without.

My analysis also owes much to Eric Wolf's (1955, 1957, 1960) typology of closed corporate and open peasant communities. His model and the one presented here are both based on the same twin pillars of political economy: direct political coercion (a determinant of Wolf's closed corporate type) and market integration (a determinant of the open type). My model differs from Wolf's in that it does not place these variables at either end of a single continuum, but recognizes that they in fact can coexist. And, of course, Wolf's model applies to a whole host of community traits, whereas my model is more limited in scope. But it is the notion of the closed corporate community that is most relevant to this discussion; few colonial Mesoamerican communities produced primarily for external markets (even if some of their elites did), and most were probably closer to the closed, corporate end of the continuum.

Despite its popularity, the closed corporate model has proved difficult to apply ethnohistorically. It has been criticized for being overly egalitarian (Stern 1983; Chance and Taylor 1985); for mistaking some autochthonous institutions as colonial creations (Farriss 1984:382; Hill and Monaghan 1987:xviii); for ignoring important community subunits such as the *calpulli, chinamit,* and *molab* (Hill and Monaghan 1987:xviii-xix); and for its assignment of origins to the seventeenth century (Farriss 1984:382). Wolf has recently addressed these criticisms and now holds that the model as originally formulated is "overly schematic," and that ethnohistoric research over the past 30 years shows "that the overly generalized interpretations of the mid-1950s need to be qualified by much variation both in geographical space and in historical time" (Wolf 1986:326). The typology of elites presented here is offered as one feasible way to address this variation in community structure for the late colonial period.

In sum, it is time to amplify the concept of the closed corporate community and focus on variations in its component parts—such as colonial elites—that are most amenable to ethnohistoric investigation. Such a research strategy will require intensive studies of particular communities, which, oddly enough, are rather rare in Mesoamerican ethnohistory, especially for the eighteenth century.[14] As John Tutino (1988:102) has recently remarked, "The dearth of studies of the internal structure of Mexican peasant communities . . . remains the primary gap in our understanding of Mexican agrarian social history."

The Decline of Colonial Indian Elites

If the Spanish Conquest was not the ultimate source of the more egalitarian sort of Indian peasant community described so frequently by modern ethnographers, then what was? What factors precipitated the decline of native elites and changed the referents of the terms *cacique* and *principal* from noble social strata to latter-day political bosses and village elders? While such questions have received little direct study in the central Mexican highlands, Farriss's (1984) work on northern Yucatán and Rodolfo Pastor's (1987) on the Mixteca Alta of Oaxaca provide valuable insights. Both authors indicate that the disappearance of village elites came late, in some cases after the Mexican wars of Independence that began in 1810.

Yucatán is the best documented example. Farriss (1984:355–79) links the demise of Maya village elites to what she calls the "second conquest" of the late eighteenth century. Beginning with the Bourbon Reforms of the 1770s and extending through the liberal legislation of independent Mexico in the early nineteenth century, a new "neo-colonial era" marked a radical break with the past. State activism and attacks on corporate privilege from various quarters deprived Maya communities of much of their autonomy. The appointment of Spanish *subdelegados* (in an area which never had *corregidores* or *alcaldes mayores*) after 1786, a raid on village *cajas de comunidad* by the provincial treasury in 1777, a takeover of Indian *cofradías* by the Bishop of Yucatán in 1780, the elimination of the *repúblicas de indios* as legal entities in 1812, and growing pressure for land from expanding haciendas in the late eighteenth century all took a tremendous toll on Indian communities. Maya leaders lost control over public revenues and local politics, and "eventually the old boundary between nobles and commoners disappeared. The terms *almehen* and *principal* fell into disuse and *macehual* became synonymous with Indian in general" (Farriss 1984:379).

For the Mixteca Alta, Pastor (1987:165–207) echoes Farriss's emphasis on the Bourbon Reforms, though he posits a more complicated and prolonged period of elite decline. *Caciques*—and their *cacicazgos*—went into eclipse after 1740, victims of their own success. Highly acculturated and frequently living outside their native communities, Mixtec *caciques* became increasingly estranged from their subjects over the years. *Principales* dominated village *cabildos* for a time, but by the end of the eighteenth century they suffered the same fate as the *caciques* before them (ibid.:327). Egalitarian communities began to appear in the Mixteca Alta by the late 1700s, though Pastor places the pivotal turning point in 1832–33, when records indicate a very sudden "pauperization" and economic leveling. Like Farriss, Pastor argues that in the end the old social structure was swiftly destroyed by political command: "The independent government [of Oaxaca] in effect legislated the abolition of the old social regime; it systematically combatted the institutions on which it was founded (particularly the corporations) and promoted privatization" (ibid.:502).

Attempting to generalize for all of Oaxaca, Marcello Carmagnani (1988:230–37) agrees that the turning point came with the enforcement of the Reform laws, but places the period of change between 1847 and 1853. Though his dates differ slightly, his argument is much the same as Pastor's: the old order was destroyed by the political transformation of communal and *cofradía* property into private holdings. Carmagnani bases much of his case on political decrees, military actions, and statistics indicating a sharp decline in village landholdings and in the number of recognized communities in Oaxaca. It remains to be seen just how the stratification systems of particular communities reacted to these events.

While regional differences in timing and state-level politics are to be expected, it appears that the decline of native elites was brought about not by the gradual working of market forces, but by a series of political decisions to destroy corporate forms of property and promote the liberal cause of private ownership. For Indian communities, this amounted to a virtual revolution in the way local power and privilege were distributed. Not only were the old noble status categories dismantled, but if Pastor's findings for the Mixteca Alta can be generalized, there was considerable economic leveling as well.

Conclusion

Clearly, much remains to be done. Our knowledge of late colonial Indian society remains quite fragmentary, and the important central Mexican region in particular needs further study. It appears, however, that village elites and *concepts* of nobility remained a potent—if not unchallenged—force all over Mesoamerica until the early decades of the nineteenth century. Late colonial villages were very different from their sixteenth-century predecessors, and, equally important, their pervasive concern with rank and privilege made them fundamentally unlike the mid-twentieth century communities studied by ethnographers. It is hoped that the typology of elites presented here will serve as a useful point of departure for further research.

The disappearance of elites in the face of the Bourbon and Liberal Reforms also has important implications for other aspects of social structure. As Taylor and I have argued (Chance and Taylor 1985), the very same expropriations and attacks on corporate privilege that destroyed native elites also promoted the rise of that most famous of Mesoamerican institutions, the civil-religious hierarchy, or *cargo* system. It would appear that local hierarchies were essentially *civil* hierarchies, based on political office-holding, as long as village elites remained intact. Religious offices embodied in *cofradías* remained apart for most of the colonial period, but were threatened in the late eighteenth and early nineteenth centuries by expropriation of *cofradía* property by the church and prohibition of communal support of religious fiestas by Spanish political officials. These pressures brought about a shift from collective (i.e., sodality-based) to individual fiesta sponsorship and as a result the civil and religious offices were fused into a unified ladder of prestige. The decline of the Indian nobility was part and parcel of this process and led to a growing concern in the villages that each household should help shoulder the burden of maintaining the cult of the saints. I believe that a better understanding of regional variation among late colonial elites and their various fates in the nineteenth century will also help us to better comprehend the different forms of the prestige-based *cargo* system of twentieth-century communities.

Notes

1. This is a revised and expanded version of a paper presented at the annual meeting of the American Anthropological Association, Phoenix, Arizona, November 16–20, 1988.
2. In colonial parlance, *caciques* were held to be successors of prehispanic rulers or ruling families. *Principales* could be relatives of *caciques,* successors of the prehispanic second-echelon nobility (such as the Nahua *pipiltin*), or those who held or had held political office and their successors (Carrasco 1975:182). In late colonial times there was a

divergence between the legal use of the term *cacique* and its meaning in Indian communities. "Technically, a cacique was the single possessor of the cacicazgo and the heir of the pre-conquest tlatoani" (Gibson 1964:161). But in local usage, sons and daughters (and their descendants) often adopted the title as well.

3. See note 2 above for a definition of this term.
4. A notable exception is the well-documented case of the Xiu family of Mani province (Farriss 1984:230).
5. Kevin Gosner's (1984, 1989, 1992) work on the Maya of highland Chiapas, though not continuing much beyond 1714, is also significant and shows that local elites were a distinct part of community life.
6. Other works by Spores (1967, 1983) on the Mixtec nobility, and Zeitlin (1984, 1989a, 1989b) and Zeitlin and Thomas (1992) on the Isthmus Zapotec, are of central importance, though all confine their attention to the sixteenth century and earlier periods.
7. I visited Cuauhtinchan briefly in the summer of 1988, thanks to a faculty research grant from Arizona State University. Intensive research on the ethnohistory of Tecali was carried out from August, 1991, through May, 1992, in local archives, the Puebla Notarial Archive, the Mexican National Archive, the Archive of the Indies (Seville), and others, with funds from Arizona State University and National Science Foundation Grant BNS-9020551.
8. The same can be said of nearby Tepeaca (Carrasco 1963, 1969, 1973, 1976; Martínez 1983, 1984). However, this community was an important market town and attracted a sizable Spanish population; one early seventeenth-century observer hints that proletarianization among Tepeaca's Indians was already well underway (Mota y Escobar 1939–40:275). Whether a late colonial *cacique* elite was present in Tepeaca remains to be seen.
9. In Tecali there were nine marriages between *caciques* (male or female) and creoles or mestizos between 1735 and 1755 (Archivo Parroquial de Tecali, Libro de Matrimonios, 1735–1755).
10. Puebla's demographic and economic stagnation during this period make it different from other more prosperous regions of New Spain. If population growth was behind the increasing preoccupation with Indian ancestry among eighteenth-century Cuernavaca *caciques* (Haskett 1988:40–42), it does not explain the interest in *cacique* status in Tecali and Cuauhtinchan.
11. Pietschmann (1977: 152–53; 1988:79) argues that Tecali was exceptional and that in most of Puebla, the *repartimiento* system was no longer compulsory by the second half of the eighteenth century. My own view is that such conclusions are premature in light of the mounting evidence on compulsory labor practices in the region.
12. Since this chapter was written, Robert Haskett's dissertation (1985) has been published in book form (Haskett 1991) and James Lockhart's landmark *The Nahuas After the Conquest* (1992) has appeared. Judging from his intensive study of mundane Nahuatl documents from a wide variety of central Mexican communities, Lockhart (1992: Ch. 4) suggests that colonial stratification may have been more pronounced in the eastern Nahua region (which included Tecali and Cuauhtinchan) where the *teccalli,* or noble house, was dominant in prehispanic times, as compared to the western region (which included Cuernavaca), where the *calpolli* was more influential. He also notes that while the whole traditional Nahuatl terminology of nobility fell into disuse in the mid-seventeenth century, differences in social rank continued. By 1700, the term *cacique* had become a loan word in Nahuatl and in the broadest sense meant "any prominent, propertied person of an officeholding family" (p. 133). By this time the term had no Nahuatl counterparts and was used more in dealing with Spaniards than when speaking Nahuatl.

13. The typology presented here has much in common with the one proposed by Margarita Melville (1983:276–80) to distinguish types of ethnicity among Mexican-Americans. Her binary dimensions, use of the same/different environment and symmetrical/asymmetrical power relations, are similar to mine, and her four types of ethnicity—complementary, competitive, colonial, and confrontational—bear a resemblance to my four types of elites. I have followed her lead in using the term "confrontational."
14. Recent notable contributions that focus on particular communities include Cline (1986), González (1974), Haskett (1985), Hill and Monaghan (1987), Kellogg (1979), Martínez (1984), Offner (1983), Olivera (1978), and Thompson (1978). Of these, only Thompson's unpublished dissertation on Tekanto, Yucatan, concentrates on the eighteenth century, and aspects of his analysis of the town's elite have been superseded by Farriss (1984).

References Cited

Alberro, Solange

1981 Inquisition et société: Rivalités de pouvoirs à Tepeaca (1656–1660). Annales, Economies, Sociétés, Civilisations 36(5):758–84.

Carmagnani, Marcello

1980 La ricostituzione delle nazioni indi: Il governo etnico nell'area de Oaxaca nel'700. Quaderni Storici 45:1027–45.

1988 El regreso de los dioses: El proceso de reconstitución de la identidad étnica en Oaxaca, siglos XVII y XVIII. Fondo de Cultura Económica. Mexico City.

Carrasco, Pedro

1963 Las tierras de dos indios nobles de Tepeaca en el siglo XVI. Tlalocan 4(2):97–119.

1969 Más documentos sobre Tepeaca. Tlalocan 6(1):1–37.

1973 Los documentos sobre las tierras de los indios nobles de Tepeaca en el siglo XVI. Comunicaciones 7:89–92.

1975 La transformación de la cultura indígena durante la colonia. Historia Mexicana 25:175–203.

1976 Los linajes nobles del México antiguo. In: Estratificación social en la Mesoamérica prehispánica, edited by Pedro Carrasco, Johanna Broda, et al., pp. 19–36. Instituto Nacional de Antropología e Historia. Mexico City.

Carrasco, Pedro, Johanna Broda, et al., eds.

1976 Estratificación social en la Mesoamérica prehispánica. Instituto Nacional de Antropología e Historia. Mexico City.

Chance, John K.

1978a Indice del Archivo del Juzgado de Villa Alta, Oaxaca: Epoca colonial. Vanderbilt University Publications in Anthropology, no. 21. Nashville.

1978b Race and Class in Colonial Oaxaca. Stanford: Stanford University Press.

1979 On the Mexican Mestizo. Latin American Research Review 14(3):153–68.
1986 Colonial ethnohistory of Oaxaca. In: Supplement to the Handbook of Middle American Indians, edited by Victoria R. Bricker. Vol. 4: Ethnohistory, edited by Ronald Spores, pp. 165–89. Austin: University of Texas Press.
1988 Recent works on Colonial Mexico. Latin American Research Review 23:213–26.
1989 Conquest of the Sierra: Spaniards and Indians in Colonial Oaxaca. Norman: University of Oklahoma Press.

Chance, John K., and William B. Taylor
1985 Cofradías and cargos: An historical perspective on the Mesoamerican civil-religious hierarchy. American Ethnologist 12 (1):1–26.

Cline, S. L.
1986 Colonial Culhuacan, 1580–1600: A Social History of an Aztec Town. Albuquerque: University of New Mexico Press.

Cooper, Fredrick, and Ann L. Stoler
1989 Introduction to tensions of empire: Colonial control and visions of rule. American Ethnologist 16(4):609–21.

Cuenya, Miguel Angel
1987 Puebla en su demografía, 1650–1850: Una aproximación al tema. In: Puebla de la Colonia a la Revolución: Estudios de historia regional, pp. 9–72. Universidad Autónoma de Puebla, Centro de Investigaciones Históricas y Sociales. Puebla.

Farriss, Nancy M.
1983 Indians in Colonial Yucatan: Three perspectives. In: Spaniards and Indians in Southeastern Mesoamerica, edited by Murdo J. MacLeod and Robert Wasserstrom, pp. 1–39. Lincoln: University of Nebraska Press.
1984 Maya Society under Colonial Rule: The Collective Enterprise of Survival. Princeton: Princeton University Press.

Garavaglia, Juan Carlos, and Juan Carlos Grosso
1987 La región Puebla-Tlaxcala y la economía novohispana, 1680–1810. In: Puebla de la Colonia a la Revolución: Estudios de historia regional, pp. 73–124. Universidad Autónoma de Puebla. Centro de Investigaciones Históricas y Sociales. Puebla.

Gibson, Charles
1964 The Aztecs under Spanish Rule. Stanford: Stanford University Press.

González, Luis
1974 San José de Gracia: Mexican Village in Transition. Austin: University of Texas Press.

Gosner, Kevin
1984 Las elites indígenas en los Altos de Chiapas, 1524–1714. Historia Mexicana 33(4):405–23.
1989 Elites, community conflict, and rebellion in Colonial Chiapas. Paper presented at the annual meeting of the American Historical Association, San Francisco, December 27–30.

1992 Soldiers of the Virgin: The Moral Economy of a Colonial Maya Rebellion. Tucson: University of Arizona Press.

Gruzinski, Serge
1989 Man-Gods in the Mexican Highlands: Indian Power and Colonial Society, 1520–1800. Stanford: Stanford University Press.

Hamnett, Brian R.
1986 Roots of Insurgency: Mexican Regions, 1750–1824. Cambridge: Cambridge University Press.

Haskett, Robert S.
1985 A Social History of Indian Town Government in the Colonial Cuernavaca Jurisdiction, Mexico. Ph.D. dissertation, University of California, Los Angeles.
1987 Indian town government in Colonial Cuernavaca: Persistence, adaptation, and change. Hispanic American Historical Review 67:203–31.
1988 Living in two worlds: Cultural continuity and change among Cuernavaca's colonial indigenous ruling elite. Ethnohistory 35(1):34–59.
1991 Indigenous Rulers: An Ethnohistory of Town Government in Colonial Cuernavaca. Albuquerque: University of New Mexico Press.

Hill, Robert M., II, and John Monaghan
1987 Continuities in Highland Maya Social Organization: Ethnohistory in Sacapulas, Guatemala. Philadelphia: University of Pennsylvania Press.

Kellogg, Susan
1979 Social Organization in Early Colonial Tenochtitlan-Tlatelolco. Ph.D. dissertation, University of Rochester, New York.

Konrad, Herman W.
1980 A Jesuit Hacienda in Colonial Mexico: Santa Lucía, 1576–1767. Stanford: Stanford University Press.

Lockhart, James
1976 Introduction. In: Provinces of Early Mexico, edited by Ida Altman and James Lockhart, pp. 3–28. UCLA Latin American Center Publications, Los Angeles.
1982 Views of corporate self and history in some Valley of Mexico towns: Late seventeenth and eighteenth centuries. In: The Inca and Aztec States, 1400–1800, edited by George A. Collier, Renato I. Rosaldo, and John D. Wirth, pp. 367–93. New York: Academic Press.
1992 The Nahuas after the Conquest: A Social and Cultural History of the Indians of Central Mexico, Sixteenth through Eighteenth Centuries. Stanford: Stanford University Press.

López Sarrelangue, Delfina E.
1965 La nobleza indígena de Pátzcuaro en la época virreinal. Universidad Nacional Autónoma de México. Mexico City.

Marcus, George E.
1983 Introduction. In: Elites: Ethnographic Issues, edited by George E. Marcus, pp. 3–27. Albuquerque: School of American Research and University of New Mexico Press.

Martin, Cheryl English
1985 Rural Society in Colonial Morelos. Albuquerque: University of New Mexico Press.

Martínez, Hildeberto
1983 Colección de documentos coloniales de Tepeaca. Instituto Nacional de Antropología e Historia. Colección Científica, no. 134. Mexico City.
1984 Tepeaca en el siglo XVI: Tenencia de la tierra y organización de un señorío. Mexico City: Casa Chata.

Melville, Margarita B.
1983 Ethnicity: An analysis of its dynamism and variability focusing on the Mexican/Anglo/Mexican American interface. American Ethnologist 10(2):272–89.

Menegus Bornemann, Margarita
1989 Economía y comunidades indígenas: El efecto de la supresión del sistema de reparto de mercancías en la intendencia de México, 1786–1810. Mexican Studies/Estudios Mexicanos 5(2):201–19.

Morin, Claude
1979 Michoacán en la Nueva España del siglo XVIII: Crecimiento y desigualdad en una economía colonial. Fondo de Cultura Económica. Mexico City.

Mota y Escobar, Alonso de la
1939–40 Memoriales. Anales del Instituto Nacional de Antropología e Historia, I:191–306.

Münch G., Guido
1976 El cacicazgo de San Juan Teotihuacan durante la colonia (1521–1821). Instituto Nacional de Antropología e Historia. Colección Científica, no. 32. Mexico City.

Offner, Jerome A.
1983 Law and Politics in Aztec Texcoco. Cambridge: Cambridge University Press.

Olivera, Mercedes
1978 Pillis y macehuales: Las formaciones sociales y los modos de producción de Tecali del siglo XII al XVI. Mexico City: Casa Chata.

Pastor, Rodolfo
1987 Campesinos y reformas: La Mixteca, 1700–1856. El Colegio de México. Mexico City.

Pietschmann, Horst
1977 El comercio de repartimientos de los alcaldes mayores y corregidores en la región de Puebla-Tlaxcala en el siglo XVII. In: Jornadas Americanistas, Estudios sobre política indigenista española en América, Vol. 3, pp. 147–53. Universidad de Valladolid, Seminario de Historia de América. Valladolid.

1988 Agricultura e industria rural indígena en el México de la segunda mitad del siglo XVIII. In: Empresarios, indios y estado: Perfil de la economía mexicana (siglo XVIII), edited by Arij Ouweneel and María Cristina Torales Pacheco, pp. 71–85. Centre for Latin American Research and Documentation. Amsterdam.

Reyes García, Luis
1977 Cuauhtinchan del siglo XII al XVI: Formación y desarrollo histórico de un señorío prehispánico. Wiesbaden: Franz Steiner Verlag GMBH.

Rojas Rabiela, Teresa, coord.
1987 Padrones de Tlaxcala del siglo XVI y padrón de nobles de Ocotelolco. Colección Documentos, no. 1. Centro de Investigaciones y Estudios Superiores en Antropología Social, Casa Chata. Mexico City.

Spores, Ronald
1967 The Mixtec Kings and Their People. Norman: University of Oklahoma Press.
1983 The origin and evolution of the Mixtec system of social stratification. In: The Cloud People: Divergent Evolution of the Zapotec and Mixtec Civilizations, edited by Kent V. Flannery and Joyce Marcus, pp. 227–38. New York: Academic Press.
1984 The Mixtecs in Ancient and Colonial Times. Norman: University of Oklahoma Press.

Stern, Steve J.
1983 The struggle for solidarity: Class, culture, and community in highland Indian America. Radical History Review 27:21–45.

Taylor, William B.
1972 Landlord and Peasant in Colonial Oaxaca. Stanford: Stanford University Press.
1979 Drinking, Homicide, and Rebellion in Colonial Mexican Villages. Stanford: Stanford University Press.
1984 Conflict and balance in district politics: Tecali and the Sierra Norte de Puebla in the eighteenth century. In: Five Centuries of Law and Politics in Central Mexico, edited by Ronald Spores and Ross Hassig, pp. 87–106. Vanderbilt University Publications in Anthropology, no. 30. Nashville.

Thomson, Guy P. C.
1989 Puebla de los Angeles: Industry and Society in a Mexican City, 1700–1850. Dellplain Latin American Studies, no. 25. Boulder: Westview Press.

Thompson, Philip C.
1978 Tekanto in the Eighteenth Century. Ph.D. dissertation, Tulane University, New Orleans.

Tutino, John M.
1976a Creole Mexico: Spanish Elites, Haciendas, and Indian Towns, 1750–1810. Ph.D. dissertation, University of Texas, Austin.
1976b Provincial Spaniards, Indian towns, and haciendas: Interrelated agrarian sectors in the valleys of Mexico and Toluca, 1750–1810. In: Provinces of Early Mexico, edited by Ida Altman and James Lockhart, pp. 177–94. UCLA Latin American Center Publications, Los Angeles.

1988 Agrarian social change and peasant rebellion in nineteenth-century Mexico: The example of Chalco. In: Riot, Rebellion, and Revolution: Rural Social Conflict in Mexico, edited by Friedrich Katz, pp. 95–140. Princeton: Princeton University Press.

Van Young, Eric
1984 Conflict and solidarity in Indian village life: The Guadalajara region in the late Colonial Period. Hispanic American Historical Review 64: 55–79.

Völlmer, Gunter
1973 La evolución cuantitativa de la población indígena en la región de Puebla (1570–1810). Comunicaciones 8:37–39.

Wolf, Eric R.
1955 Types of Latin American peasantry: A preliminary discussion. American Anthropologist 57:452–71.
1957 Closed corporate peasant communities in Mesoamerica and central Java. Southwestern Journal of Anthropology 13:1–18.
1960 The Indian in Mexican society. Alpha Kappa Deltan 30(1):3–6.
1986 The vicissitudes of the closed corporate community. American Ethnologist 13: 325–29.

Zeitlin, Judith Francis
1984 Colonialism and the political transformation of isthmus Zapotec society. In: Five Centuries of Law and Politics in Central Mexico, edited by Ronald Spores and Ross Hassig, pp. 65–85. Vanderbilt University Publications in Anthropology, no. 30. Nashville.
1989a Ranchers and Indians on the southern isthmus of Tehuantepec: Economic change and indigenous survival in Colonial Mexico. Hispanic American Historical Review 69:23–60.
1989b Voices against the cacique in sixteenth-century Tehuantepec. Paper presented at the annual meeting of the American Society for Ethnohistory, Chicago, November 2.

Zeitlin, Judith Francis, and Lillian Thomas
1992 Spanish justice and the Indian cacique: Disjunctive political systems in sixteenth-century Tehuantepec. Ethnohistory 39(3):285–315.

CHAPTER 4

Xaltocan under Mexica Domination, 1435–1520

FREDERIC HICKS

UNIVERSITY OF LOUISVILLE

XALTOCAN TODAY IS ONLY a village, but during the thirteenth and fourteenth centuries A.D., it was a city that dominated an extensive area, including all of the northern Valley of Mexico and reaching perhaps as far as the Valley of Toluca to the west, Metztitlan in the north, and Sierra de Puebla to the east (Carrasco 1950:254–55). Archaeological investigations by Elizabeth Brumfiel (n.d.a) indicate that the city reached its maximum size during the Early Aztec period (ca. A.D. 1150–1350). But in 1395, Xaltocan fell to the armies of the expanding Tepanec empire, based at Azcapotzalco. Its king and many of his people fled to Metztitlan; others fled to Tlaxcala; and still others went to Acolhuacan, where they were given lands by the king of Tetzcoco (modern Texcoco). For 35 or 40 years, Xaltocan was depopulated; its lands in surrounding regions were divided up among the kings of Azcapotzalco and Tetzcoco (Anales de Cuauhtitlan 1939: Par. 462–70, 622–28; Alva Ixtlilxóchitl 1975–77, I:323; Carrasco 1950:266–68).

In 1420, however, the empire of Azcapotzalco fell, the result of an uprising by many of its Mexica and Acolhua subjects, and a new power center emerged, dominated by the city of Tenochtitlan (modern Mexico City). Tenochtitlan and its twin city Tlatelolco had been founded by the Mexica who were living on an island in Lake Texcoco; both were subjects of the Tepanec of Azcapotzalco. After 1420, Tenochtitlan, in alliance with Tetzcoco and the small Tepanec city of Tlacopan (modern Tacuba), began the conquests that would result in what is generally called the Aztec Empire. In 1435, Xaltocan was resettled under Mexica leadership. The new settlers were not the descendants of the original settlers, but came from other places. The *tlahtocayotl,* or kingly seat, was not restored, and the newly resettled city remained a direct dependency of Mexico (Anales de Cuauhtitlan 1939: Par. 628, 1017–21).

The above has long been known from published sources. However, there are archival sources, as yet unpublished, that yield additional information. From them, we can learn something of the way Xaltocan was governed under the Mexica, what Xaltocan provided economically to the imperial capital, and the role played by Tlatelolco and Acolhuacan in the area.

These data indicate that the city of Tlatelolco played a prominent role in the Xaltocan area, so a little background on Tlatelolco may be helpful. Although Tenochtitlan and Tlatelolco adjoined each other, each had its own line of kings. Ethnically, both cities were Mexica, and both had been subordinate allies of Azcapotzalco prior to 1420. While it was the king of Tenochtitlan who made the alliance with Tetzcoco and Tlacopan to form what has come to be known as the Aztec Empire, the kings of Tlatelolco were his allies from the beginning. Their forces participated in conquests, and their kings and lords received benefits. They were especially active in the northern Valley of Mexico, and indeed, much of the waters of the northern lakes were assigned to them (Anales de Cuauhtitlan 1939: Par. 1022–23; Barlow 1987:83ff; 1989:109ff). In 1473, however, king Moquihuix of Tlatelolco entered into a conspiracy with several other kings to overthrow the ruler of Tenochtitlan, and a war followed. Tlatelolco was defeated, and its royal line was abolished. From then until 1519, it was governed by a series of noblemen appointed by Tenochtitlan (Anales de Tlatelolco 1948: Par. 16, 276, 280, 285), and according to the historical accounts, many of its lands and the revenue from its market were distributed among Tenochca lords (Tezozómoc 1975: Ch. 46). The Spaniards renamed the city Santiago, but it eventually regained its old name, which it still bears as a section of Mexico City.

The Sources

Pre-Spanish Xaltocan is featured in several of the early chronicles. The *Anales de Cuauhtitlan* (1939, 1975)[1] is a major source, and it gives us the basic chronological framework. A letter written to the king of Spain by Pablo Nazareo and his associates in 1566 (Nazareo 1940) provides royal genealogies and lists of landholdings. Some events involving Xaltocan were recorded by Alva Ixtlilxóchitl (1975–77), and there is occasional mention in other sources. Much of this material has been analyzed by Carrasco (1950).

Of the unpublished sources, the most important are proceedings of early colonial legal disputes. Ron Spores was a pioneer in the use of this kind of source for ethnographic information, and he made extensive use of them in his reconstructions of Mixtec history. (This seems an appropriate, if somewhat tardy, occasion to acknowledge the help and guidance I received, when I was getting ready for my first archival research, from reading the methodological discussions in *The Mixtec Kings and Their People,* Spores 1967). Most useful for this paper are the proceedings of a dispute of Gil González de Benavides (encomendero of Xaltocan) and the Indian governor of Xaltocan against don Juan (Indian governor of Tlatelolco—

presumably don Juan Quauiconoc, who served as colonial "*cacique*" from 1530 to 1537 [Barlow 1989:362]). The document is in the Archivo General de Indias in Seville (AGI Justicia 123/2). The case opened in 1531 and concluded in 1537. Gil González and the governor of Xaltocan complained that don Juan had taken certain lands and "*estancias*" (villages), and forced their inhabitants to serve Tlatelolco, although the *estancias,* he claimed, rightfully belonged to Xaltocan, which could not subsist without them. These *estancias* were Xoloc, Atzompan, Tecalco,[2] Huitznahuatonco, Tonanitlan, and Cuauhtliquizcan (see Fig. 4.1). Also useful is the report of a visit to the Xaltocan area made in 1599 to determine how best to resettle the Indians of the region (AGN Tierras 1584/1); it provides some information about the environment at that time, before the lake drainage projects began. Finally, we get some help from the proceedings of another case against the Indian governor of Tlatelolco, also in the 1530s, this one involving Ecatepec (AGI Justicia 124). We will frequently refer in this paper to these documents, especially the first one.

Because our major source is a case involving Tlatelolco, not Tenochtitlan, we get a clearer picture of the role of Tlatelolco in this area than of Tenochtitlan. Perhaps if the Indian governors of Tenochtitlan had been more aggressive or litigious, our picture would be less skewed, but there was good reason for them not to be. The Spaniards managed to co-opt Tenochca leadership by bringing it into the Spanish administrative system. Cortés granted to the legitimate son and two daughters of Moteuczoma not mere *cacique*ships, but landed estates, that they could bequeath to their heirs. The two daughters received lands that presumably had been part of Moteuczoma's holdings, which they brought as dowries when they married Spaniards. The son, don Pedro Tlacahuepantzin, was given control of Tula and its dependencies. Barlow (1989:189) published a brief chronicle in which he finds that in 1519, the same year the Spaniards arrived, Moteuczoma's nephew, the *tlacateccatl* Cuauhtemoc, established himself as *tlahtoani* in Tlatelolco, thereby reestablishing its *tlahtoani* seat. This interpretation may be correct, since one would expect that in such a case new lands would have been assigned to the *tlahtocayotl,* possibly including some in the northern valley. The war against Spain probably left little time to complete any such assignment, nor to inform all those who would have been affected by it, and the Spanish conquest probably made it all seem irrelevant anyway. But if there were such land assignments, and they were known to the later Indian governors of Tlatelolco, they might have felt justified in pressing claims that to others seemed unjustified.

The Natural Environment

Before the drainage projects begun by the Spaniards in the seventeenth century, the Basin of Mexico contained a series of lakes and marshes. Although among Mesoamericanists there has been a tradition of depicting these lakes as if they were a single expanse of water, they could only rarely have been so, in times of severe

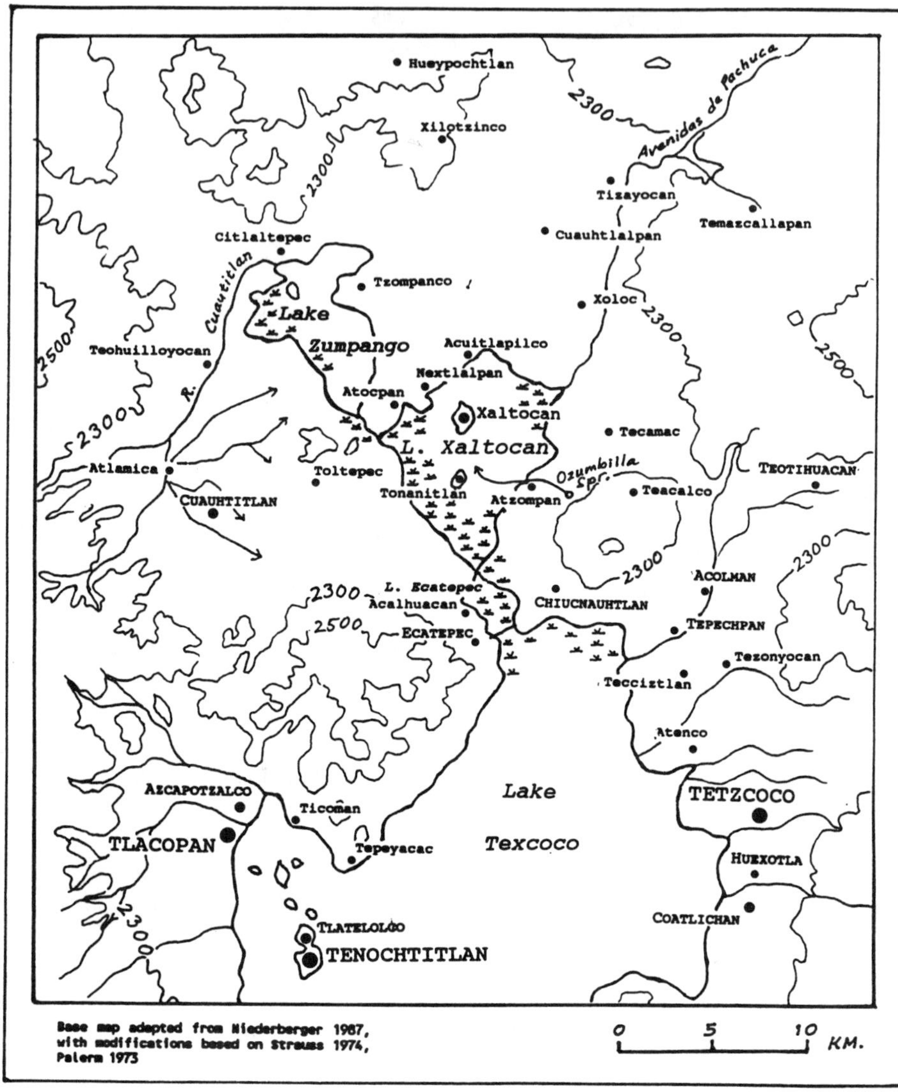

Figure 4.1. Xaltocan and surrounding region in the Basin of Mexico.

flooding. The configuration of the lake system at the time of Spanish contact has been reconstructed by Palerm (1973), Strauss (1974), Rojas (1974), and Niederberger (1987).

Lake Texcoco, in the central valley, was the largest, and also the lowest. It was largely salty, except for the part around Tenochtitlan-Tlatelolco, which was separated from the salt portion to the east by a human-made dike. In the north were Lakes Zumpango and Xaltocan. At times, the water was high enough to produce a third lake, Lake Ecatepec. Although salty or brackish in parts, the northern lakes received enough fresh water to permit its use for irrigation, and in some places, for chinampa farming.

Lake Zumpango received fresh water mainly from the Río Cuauhtitlan, which in 1435 was diverted northward so that it entered the lake near Citlaltepec. Here, there was enough fresh water that chinampa farming may have been possible. The lake also received some rainy season runoff from the Cerro de Xalpa. Lake Xaltocan was fed from the overflow from Lake Zumpango, and also from the important freshwater springs near Ozumbilla, at the base of the Cerro Chiconautla. It also received runoff water during the rainy season, especially from the Avenidas de Pachuca, which before its diversion northward to Lake Zumpango in 1627 probably flowed into Lake Xaltocan.[3] The water in most of this lake was fresh. In 1599, chinampa farming was practiced in parts of the town of Xaltocan, and in its subject communities of Tonanitlan, Nextlalpan, and Atenanco (AGN Tierras 1584/1: f. 9v-13v).

Lake Ecatepec seems to have been really a marsh, which took the form of a small lake only at times of exceptionally high water. Very early colonial accounts indicate there was a dike or causeway between Ecatepec and Venta de Carpio, near Chiconautla. Whether or not this was pre-Spanish is not really certain, but both Strauss and Niederberger believe that successful water control would have virtually required such a dike to prevent excessive water flowing out into Lake Texcoco and endangering the Lake Texcoco cities, as well as causing a water shortage in the north.

The city of Xaltocan was built on an island in the lake; it is depicted that way in a number of early maps (e.g., Linné 1958; Rojas 1974:84). According to Bernal Díaz (1968, I:455–456 [Cáp. 141]), its houses were built in the water of the lake, and there were canals in the city, but it was reachable by a causeway from the mainland (from what part is not clear). The causeway cannot have been very substantial, because the people were able to dismantle it quickly to prevent Spanish horses from entering the city (ibid.; see also Palerm 1973:37–39). Also on an island in the same lake was Tonanitlan, a town long associated with Xaltocan, and claimed by Xaltocan in the 1530s as its subject.

While the freshwater portions of the lake facilitated intensive agriculture, the salt marshes also had resources. The 1599 *visita* mentions that reeds were gathered there for making *petates* (mats); and that the saline soils produced *tequisquitl,* a combination of minerals useful for making soap, and saltpeter for gunpowder. In addition, the diversity of water fowl and aquatic fauna that have been described for the lake system in general (Rojas 1985) was present there. What was lacking was *monte,* wooded land that would have provided firewood, so the principal fuel in the Xaltocan region consisted of corn stalks (AGN Tierras 1584/1, *passim*).

Although the lakes seldom formed one single body of water, canoe travel between them was possible. Both Strauss and Niederberger cite an order from Viceroy Mendoza in 1542, ordering the re-opening of "certain canals and water ways" which, in pre-Spanish times, had connected Lakes Zumpango and Xaltocan with Lake Texcoco and the city of Mexico, and allowed canoe traffic to pass between them.

The Rulership of Mexica Xaltocan

The *Anales de Cuauhtitlan* (1939: Par. 1018) states that although Xaltocan was repopulated under Mexica leadership in 1435, "at no time did they ever establish a tlahtocayotl," until the Spaniards came. In the *Codex Mendoza* (1925: f.17v-18r), Xaltocan is listed (along with Cuauhtochco, Citlaltepec, Tzompanco, Acalhuacan, Coatitlan, and some other places) as administered by governors placed there by the kings of Mexico. In the 1531–1537 dispute as well, at various points in the proceedings, the native lord of Xaltocan is referred to as a *tlacateuctli,* and it is explicitly stated that there was no "señor" in pre-Spanish Xaltocan (AGI Justicia 123/1: 25 ago 1537[4] and *passim*).

In ancient Mexico, the term *tlacateuctli* (sometimes *tlacateccatl*) is one of the most common titles borne by the three or four highest ranking nobles below the *tlahtoani*. Other high dignitaries are designated by titles that vary from polity to polity, but one of them is often *tlacochteuctli* (or *tlacochcalcatl*). Others include Acolnahuacatl, Tlillancalqui, Tecpanecatl, or Huitznahuacatl (Carrasco 1977:230–31; see also Durán 1967, II:103). Collectively, such dignitaries may be termed *teuctlahtoqueh* (singular is *teuctlahto*), a term used frequently in this sense by Chimalpahin (1889, *passim;* cf. Carrasco 1971:352). People bearing one of these titles often appear in the sources as governors of a major section of a kingdom, or of a town which might be regarded as important enough to have a king, but for some reason does not. Generally, nobles appointed as *cuauhtlahtoqueh*—that is, regents or substitutes for a *tlahtoani*—were titled *teuctlahtoqueh*.

These titles are often translated into Spanish or English as either "captains-general," "governors," or "judges," depending on the context, since military achievements were a major path to high political office in ancient Mexico. Probably the *teuctlahtoqueh* would have military attributes, but his duties were not exclusively military.

Van Zantwijk (1967) believes that the Valley of Mexico localities that are listed on folios 17v-18r of the *Codex Mendoza* as ruled by governors represent military garrisons, whose "tribute" obligations consisted of furnishing high functionaries for the garrisons in the eleven more distant localities also listed on those leaves as having governors. That is an intriguing possibility, but there are some problems with it. A gloss at the bottom of folio 18v states that this is the end of the first part of the account—which deals with conquests, not tribute. The tribute lists begin on the next folio, entitled "Second part of the account." Also, there's no proof that titles such as *tlacateuctli* and *tlacochteuctli* necessarily imply "garrisons."

It seems clear that under the Mexica, Xaltocan did not have its own king. The only documentation that might be viewed as dissenting is the well-known letter written by Pablo Nazareo to the king of Spain in 1566 (Nazareo 1940). In it, Nazareo traces his descent from the kings (*dominus naturalis,* "natural lord") of Xaltocan in an apparently unbroken line from pre-Tepanec times to the Spanish conquest. In chronological order these kings are Teuctlacozauhqui, Hopanteuctli, Chalchiuhtlatonac, Xihuitl-Temoc, Hopanteuctli II, Coatzinteuctli, Cuicuitzcatzin, and Coatzinteuctli II. The last three rulers are said by him to have been the daughters of Tenochca princesses, beginning with a daughter of Itzcoatl, and the last was Nazareo's father. However, Alva Ixtlilxóchitl (1975–77, I:322) gives the name of the king of Xaltocan who was defeated in 1395 as Tzompantzin, and his immediate predecessor, according to both Alva Ixtlilxóchitl and the *Anales de Cuauhtitlan* (1939: Par. 624), was named Paintzin or Pantictzin. But the *Anales* (ibid.) also gives the name of Teuctlacozauhqui[5] as, probably, a co-ruler; that is, Xaltocan probably had more than one *tlahtoani* when it was conquered by the Tepanec.

I would infer that these ancestors of don Pablo were descendants of *one* of the kings of Xaltocan—Teuctlacozauhqui—although they did not actually rule, and may not have resided in Xaltocan. Nazareo's account is in a letter to the king of Spain, written in Latin, asking support for his claim to the town of Xaltocan and a number of lands and communities that had served its former kings. Cortés had restored many lands and towns that had been forcibly taken by the Mexica conquerors to those who would otherwise have retained them, and he had restored Xaltocan as well (AGI Justicia 123/1: 13 may 1533), but probably to the descendant of a different king—most likely, Paintzin. Nazareo thought that Cortés should have restored at least part of Xaltocan and its dependencies to him. To make his point, he was concerned to show his descent from people who had been kings in Xaltocan before its fall; it didn't matter what political posts their descendants subsequently held.

We have no good data on lesser nobles in Mexica Xaltocan or its nearby communities, although two prominent nobles of Xoloc, who appeared as witnesses for Xaltocan in 1537, were introduced as the *tlacateuctli* and the *acolnahuacatl* of that town (AGI Justicia 123/1: 3 ene 1537). But a statement by Damián, "*cacique*" of Xaltocan, who appeared as a "confesante" in 1535 after the court had decided in favor of Tlatelolco (the decision was appealed and the case went on for another two years), is of interest. He said that the kings of Tlatelolco

> possessed, after the death of Tlacateotl, some few lands in the said *estancia,* and those of Mexico [i.e., Tenochtitlan] possessed the greater part. In ancient times, the kings, from Tlacateotzin to Moteuczoma, held and planted a certain part of the lands, that they held, in the said *estancias,* and that Mexico had the greater part, and this is true. After the Spaniards came, and this city was conquered, they left the lands, and then this confesante and those of Xaltocan took them; afterwards, those of Mexico and Santiago [Tlatelolco] took them back. [AGI Justicia 123/1: 15 may 1535]

Except perhaps for one or two *teuctlahtoqueh* and their families, there seem to have been no high ranking nobles in Xaltocan itself. In and around the town, and its nearby communities, were lands that provided revenue for the king of Mexico and high nobles of his court, including the governors of Tlatelolco. But these nobles probably did not actually live in Xaltocan. Their lands were most likely administered by stewards—*calpixqueh* or *tequitlahtoqueh*—who saw to it that lands of the kings were cultivated, and their other obligations fulfilled.

This is suggested not only by the ethnohistoric sources, but also by archaeological ones. Brumfiel (n.d.a, 1994), who has carried out an intensive survey and limited excavations in Xaltocan, notes that the town was smaller by about 17% during the period of Mexica domination than it was before its defeat by the Tepanec. She also notes that the larger mounds—those likely to have been temple structures and major administrative structures—date from pre-Mexica times. In addition, decorated serving vessels are less common in the period of Mexica dominance, and those that have been found are less elaborately decorated.

The Settlement of Peasants in the Xaltocan Area

The historical chronicles, such as the *Anales de Cuauhtitlan,* tell us only that Xaltocan was repopulated by the Mexica in 1435. But the 1531–1537 case leads us to believe a more extensive area was involved, and that it included the *estancias* under dispute. In presenting his position, the solicitor for Tlatelolco and Mexico stated that both the *estancias* and Xaltocan itself were "within the boundaries of this city [of Mexico], and as such the lords of Mexico and Tlatelolco, my clients, and Moteuczoma and his predecessors, have had and held them, and they settled and built them, and put in them and in the town of Xaltocan their *maceguales,* some to serve them as fishermen, others as saltmakers, others as farmers and of other *granjerías* and tributes" (AGI Justicia 123/2: 9 may 1533). Later he states that "the said *estancias* and their territories and lands which are under dispute some hundred years ago were depopulated, vacant, and barren, and the first settler of them, who put *maceguales* on them, and settled them and worked them, was a lord of Tlatelolco" (AGI Justicia 123/2: 7 may 1535). Those of Xaltocan replied that whatever dominion Mexico and Tlatelolco had over them was by force and tyranny, and after the Spanish conquest, Cortés undid these tyrannies and restored the legitimate rulers. But they really never explicitly denied the role of Mexico in resettling them.

The *Anales de Cuauhtitlan* states in one place that when Xaltocan was repopulated, it was with people from places called Ixayoctonco, Totollan, Tlapallan, Tlilhuacan, and Ixayoc (*Anales de Cuauhtitlan* 1939: Par. 628). We do not know where these places were (except that at least some of them were within the old kingdom of Xaltocan), but elsewhere, the same source tells us that the new settlers were Acolman people, Colhuas, Tenochcas, and Otomíes (ibid.: Par. 1017). Nothing in the 1531–1537 case gives us any reason to question this, and the report of the 1599 *visita* may even offer support. Although most investigators agree that Otomí was the language of Xaltocan under the old kingdom, before the Tepanec conquest, by the time of the *visita* everyone spoke Náhuatl ("mexicano") (AGN Tierras 1584/I).

We cannot really say that the Xaltocan region was absolutely devoid of human occupation at the time it was resettled by the Mexica. But the native nobility left, and under the unsettled conditions that prevailed in the Valley of Mexico in the late fourteenth century, any small peasant hamlets would probably have been vulnerable to raids, so most of the peasantry most likely left as soon as they could. In any case, the resettlement of Xaltocan may be seen as part of the general population increase in the valley around this time. Archaeological surveys have shown that the population of the Valley of Mexico increased greatly during the century or so just prior to the Spanish conquest (Parsons 1974; Sanders, Parsons, and Santley 1979:209–219 and cf. maps 17 and 18). We have no new data bearing on the cause of this increase, but we may have some on the way space was filled in.

The ancient Mexican economy was such that a shortage of labor was virtually endemic. Land was not a commodity, technology was simple, and productivity depended chiefly on how much human labor could be mobilized (Sanders and Santley 1983). A landed nobleman could almost always use more labor, which, of course, doubled as military power in time of war. A peasant family that for whatever reason (war, natural disaster, flight to avoid punishment) found itself without land, could generally find a lord who would give the family land to work for subsistence, and a measure of protection, in return for service to that lord.

We know from various sources that lords often sought to attract peasants to their lands. A number of published accounts attest to this (e.g., Cortés 1865:542; Anunciación 1940:262; see Hicks 1974 for additional references), and we can also cite testimony in another legal case, this time between Tlatelolco and Ecatepec in 1536, in which a witness for Tlatelolco explained, "it is customary among the natives to move to towns where they are given land to plant, and this witness has seen that many natives have come to live on [the *estancias* under dispute]" (AGI Justicia 124: f. 172r).

But in the early fifteenth century, with the fall of Azcapotzalco and with the Triple Alliance not yet a major power, with so much land available to be settled, and with some competition among lords seeking to extend their domains, it would probably have been too slow and risky to rely on so casual a method. We know that sometimes bands of people, under a leader, came to an established leader and asked to be allowed to settle on his land, as did various groups arriving in Acolhuacan (among them those who fled from Xaltocan after its fall), and as did the Mexica when they first came to the site of Tenochtitlan-Tlatelolco. But there are no indications that this happened in the Xaltocan area.

Rather, there are statements that the rulers of Tenochtitlan and Tlatelolco "put their *maceguales*" on the land, to serve them. This calls to mind the organized operations by which Náhuatl-speaking settlers were recruited to repopulate the devastated lands of Oaxaca and, later, of the Oztoman-Teloloapan region (Durán 1967, II: Ch. 29, 45; cf. Tezozómoc 1975: Ch. 39, 74), and on a smaller scale, the way King Nezahualcoyotl of Tetzcoco settled Calpullalpan (in what is now western Tlaxcala), drawing from each of the six sections of the city a certain number of settlers (Pomar 1941:7; Hicks 1984a:159). These were all major colonizing operations, planned by the state, and apparently intended to colonize an area quickly with large numbers of people. Something like this probably accounts for at least the initial resettlement of the region under the Mexica. Once the communities were established, and the politico-economic structure that tied them to Mexico in place, they probably continued to grow with the occasional arrival of new immigrant families.

The peasants who settled in Xaltocan and nearby communities gave tribute to Tlatelolco and/or Tenochtitlan, and possibly to other lords. We have no information on how this was structured on the local level, but we do know something about who the peasants served and what they gave. Before we can deal with that, however, we have to look at how the relations between Mexico and Acolhuacan developed in this area.

Tribute and the Mexico–Acolhuacan Interface

In the 1531–1537 case, witnesses for Xaltocan acknowledged that in pre-Spanish times the people of the *estancias* gave tribute to Moteuczoma, as did everybody in this land, although they claimed they also gave tribute to Xaltocan. In the words of one witness, a native of Tecamac, "the people of the *estancias* contributed to Xaltocan in some things, and they and the people of Xaltocan contributed some of their fruits to Mexico, until the Spaniards came" (AGI Justicia 123/2: 23 nov

1534). Later, the solicitor for Mexico and Tlatelolco stated that the vassals of his clients included "those of Xoloc and Huitznahuatonco and half of Atzompan and all of the *estancia* of Tonanitlan" (ibid.: 4 dic 1534); the reference to "half of Atzompan" presumably means that half the people there tributed to someone else.

A man named Gerónimo, a witness for Tlatelolco identified as a *principal* of Acolman, said that the *estancias* under dispute "are not in the land or limits of Xaltocan, because Atzompan is in the land of Chiucnauhtlan and Tecalco in the land of Acolman, and all the said lands and *estancias* are in the province of Acolhuacan, which belonged to Tetzcoco in ancient times and not to Xaltocan, and there those of Santiago and Mexico had their lands and *estancias,* and there they planted their crops" (AGI Justicia 123/1: 7 may 1535). Possibly, some of the people of Atzompan continued to give their tribute to Chiucnauhtlan (modern Chiconautla).

The next witness, a man named Matheo who was also a *principal* of Acolman, said he too had heard that in ancient times the lands belonged to Tetzcoco, and that the lord of Tlatelolco mentioned in the question (Tlacateotzin)[6] "had built the said *estancias* and placed *maceguales* in them because the señor who ruled Tetzcoco at that time, who governed all that, gave them to him, and for that reason Tlacateotl populated with *maceguales* the said *estancias* and lands, and so they remained with Tlatelolco and its lords" (AGI Justicia 123/1: 7 may 1535).

This information is consistent with other accounts in which the king of Tetzcoco, or the kings of other allied Valley of Mexico polities, were asked by the emperor of Tenochtitlan to give him lands in their territory. That is, when Tenochtitlan first conquered a city in the Valley of Mexico or near it, some lands were taken and distributed to Mexica nobles (e.g., Tezozómoc 1975: Ch. 15, 17, 20, 26), but afterwards, when the kings of those lands were defined as loyal allies, the kings of Tenochtitlan often asked them for additional lands. Several times the kings of Tenochtitlan asked for and received from the king of Tetzcoco lands in various parts of Acolhuacan (Hicks 1984b). Lands received by the kings of Tenochtitlan in this way were located in many parts of the valley and beyond. They remained under the political control of the king within whose boundaries they lay, but gave tribute to Tenochtitlan—or in this case, to both Tlatelolco and Tenochtitlan. Most likely, it was these lands which were grouped into imperial "tribute provinces," under *calpixqueh* who saw to it that the people attached to them fulfilled their tribute obligations (Hicks 1992).

Xaltocan does not appear in the surviving portions of the pictorial *Matrícula de Tributos* (1980) nor in the tribute-roll portion of the *Codex Mendoza* (1925), and neither do most of the *estancias* under dispute. A place named Tecalco is listed as subject to the Petlacalcatl,[7] meaning that it gave tribute directly to Tenochtitlan, but a Teacalco is listed next to Tonanitlan in the tribute province of Acolhuacan. Xaltocan does appear, however, among places said to have served Tetzcoco in one or another fashion. It was one of the towns which Nezahualcoyotl designated for the service, adornment, and cleaning of the palaces of the king of Tetzcoco (Alva Ixtlilxóchitl 1975–77, I:380; II:114), and Motolinía (1971:394) includes it on a list of twelve towns said to have furnished firewood for the temples of Tetzcoco (which is curious, since the 1599 visitors were struck by the lack of any firewood in the vicinity). Tlatelolco appears in the *Codex Mendoza* (folio 19r), but no subject communities appear with it.

As we have noted, Tlatelolco and Mexico claimed that the peasants settled in their *estancias* served them as fishermen, saltmakers, and farmers. Elsewhere in the proceedings, a questionnaire for Tlatelolco states that "The *maceguales* contributed to the lords of Tlatelolco and served them with much maize and other grains, and maguey fiber (nequén) and maguey fiber blankets, and sandals, and much salt and stone, and other personal and public services in this city" (AGI Justicia 123/2: 23 dic 1536).

The Boundaries of Xaltocan

The *tlacateuctli* of Tlatelolco and his witnesses in the 1531–1537 suit claimed that Xaltocan and its dependent communities were an integral part of the city of Mexico, within its boundaries, and that it was meaningless to speak of the boundaries of Xaltocan, because it didn't have any of its own. This was the only argument they could make in view of the political realities of their day. To the extent that it had merit (the court did find in their favor, after all), it probably means that it was within the *tlahtocayotl* of Mexico (as distinct from Acolhuacan or Tepanohuayan). But what was the extent of the jurisdiction of Xaltocan's *tlacateuctli*?

From the late sixteenth century we have several documents that refer to *sujetos* or outlying communities of Xaltocan at that time, but this is long after the Spanish conquest, time enough for numerous political changes to have occurred; thus, I would be reluctant to assume, without other evidence, that they reflect pre-Spanish conditions. One document is the *Descripción del Arzobispado de México* of 1571, which states that Xaltocan had six barrios or small *estancias,* "some of them to the south, some to the southeast, and some to the northeast" of the *cabecera,* but does not name them (*Descripción del Arzobispado* 1905:35). The 1580 *Relación geográfica* (López de Ribera 1905:169–70) and the 1599 *Visita* (AGN Tierras 1584/1) list the *sujetos* of Xaltocan: nineteen of them according to the *Relaciones geográficas* and eleven according to the *Visita,* but this latter source clarifies that four of them (Tianguistengo, Tequicalco, Huexoyahualco, and Anenesco) were actually barrios of the town, very close to its center. The *Visita* gives the names of the seven *sujetos,* which it says were all within three-quarters of a league of the *cabecera,* as Santa María Tonanitlan, Santa Ana Nextlalpan, San Juan Atenango, San Mateo Acuitlapilco, San Esteban Ecatitlan, Santiago Actoca, and San Pedro Miltengo.

The 1580 *Relación geográfica* adds Ayaca, Tlamelauhcan, Coatlan, Palantan, Toltengo, Caltengo, Tlatelolco, Tlatiltengo, Tlacatecpan, and Jayoque, but omits Tonanitlan and Tequicalco. I have been able to locate only a few of these places on modern maps, so I cannot use them to delineate the extent of Xaltocan's territory.

As for the *estancias* claimed by both Xaltocan and Mexico-Tlatelolco, we have seen that Xoloc probably had its own *teuctlahto,* which would imply that it was not under the authority of Xaltocan. We have no information on how the other *estancias* were governed.

Pablo Nazareo provides a list of "*estancias* or towns adjoining the town of Xaltocan that served personally the aforementioned natural lords of all that had been the province of Xaltocan" (Nazareo 1940:126). The list includes some places that were considered *sujetos* of Xaltocan in the 1580 *Relación geográfica* and the 1599 *visita:* Atocpan, Atenanco, and Tonanitlan, and includes some of the *estancias* that were under dispute in 1531–1537: Xoloc, Tecalco, Atzompan, Tonanitlan again, and Cuauhtliquizcan. But he also lists such places as Tehuiloyuocan, Toltepec, Cuauhtlalpan, and Ticoman, some of which are beyond the region either party claimed in the 1531–1537 dispute. Nazareo also lists towns that were his "patrimony," bequeathed by his predecessors; many of the same places are listed. Almost certainly, these places, which Pablo Nazareo sought to have restored to him, had been within the boundaries of the old kingdom of Xaltocan prior to 1395. They were not necessarily under the administration of Xaltocan under Mexica rule.

Summary

Xaltocan is just one more community in the Valley of Mexico, but since our knowledge of ancient Mexican society is based on data from so few places, any addition to our data base should be helpful. It is somewhat unusual in being a region that was resettled after having been abandoned by its leadership and probably by most of the peasantry, and the resettlement represents an ethnic change, from predominantly Otomí to Náhuatl. The data tell us something about the process of resettlement, and the political and economic administration of the new settlements.

The region was taken to add to the hinterland directly dependent on Mexico (i.e., Tenochtitlan and Tlatelolco), and tribute was given to both cities. The picture we obtain, though certainly incomplete, indicates a population primarily of peasants, under the general command of a *teuctlahto*—or, to judge from the *Codex Mendoza,* of a pair of them. There is no evidence for any other landholding noble establishments in Xaltocan itself, but some of the other communities in the area, such as Xoloc, evidently had their own *teuctlahtoqueh*. This negative evidence is hardly conclusive, however. There is, for example, no mention of *calpixqueh* or *tequitlahtoqueh* (tribute collectors) either, though they must surely have been there.

Tribute and service may have been given directly to the royal palace of Tenochtitlan, but it is not clear who received it in Tlatelolco.

What is curious are the statements, in other sources, that Xaltocan had some tribute obligations to Tetzcoco. It suggests that not only did the king of Tenochtitlan have lands in areas politically subject to Tetzcoco, as we know from other sources, but the reverse may also have been true. Finally, the data show that Tlatelolco, despite its defeat in 1473, remained a significant politico-economic power, at least in the northern Valley of Mexico.

Notes

1. In this paper I cite the 1939 Lehmann edition, by paragraph number, because this edition includes the Náhuatl text, has abundant and helpful notations, and because Lehmann has converted the Aztec years into Christian dates. The 1945 Velázquez edition, which has the advantage of being in Spanish rather than German, contains a concordance, so that a reference to a paragraph in the Lehmann edition can easily be located in the Velázquez edition.
2. The orthography in this and other sixteenth-century documents is a bit irregular, given that most scribes were apparently confused by Mexican names, but this community is pretty consistently given as "Tecalco" (place of someone's house), not "Teacalco" (place of someone's water house [canoe]). There are places with both names in the *Codex Mendoza,* and their glyphs are quite different. It is conceivable that witnesses, questioned orally, misunderstood which town they were being asked about.
3. Strauss (1974) states that before the construction of the Presa del Rey in 1627, the Avenidas de Pachuca emptied into Lake Ecatepec (p. 141) or Lake Texcoco (p. 145), but I am unable to find a route by which its waters could have reached either lake without flowing uphill, unless it reached them via Lake Xaltocan.
4. The folios in this document are not numbered, so citation is by date of the proceedings.
5. The *Anales* actually says it was ruled by "tlaltochtli teuctla coçauhqui çinquani," and Lehmann was not sure if this was one, or more than one, person.
6. Tlacateotl ruled from 1418 to 1428 (Barlow 1989:11), which is too early for him to have administered the resettlement. My impression from reading the testimony of witnesses in many legal cases is that the ancient Mexicans learned their king lists quite well, but were not as good on dates, so they were not always accurate about whose reign a given event occurred in.
7. The chief steward of the empire, who was in charge of the treasury and is mentioned frequently in Tezozómoc (1975) and Durán (1967), as well as in other sources, bore the title of *Petlacalcatl,* literally "man of the mat house [*petlacalli*]." He was apparently within easy call of the Tenochca emperor, and had access to all of the tributes kept in Tenochtitlan (Durán 1967, II: Ch. 40). The gloss in the *Codex Mendoza* refers only to this title (followed by "*gobernador,*" which seems to be the *Codex Mendoza's* standard gloss for someone of *teuctlahto* rank), not to a place, but the glyph is of a place—a house of mats. This led Barlow to postulate the existence of a place called "Petlacalco," but it

could just as well be Petlacalli, which I would infer to be the name of the building that housed the tribute or was otherwise associated with the duties of the Petlacalcatl. I believe that a better interpretation is that these places gave their tribute directly to the Petlacalcatl, in Tenochtitlan, and did not go through a regional *calpixqui*. Barlow (1949) listed Xaltocan in a hypothetical tribute "province" of Citlaltepec and Tlatelolco. However, the towns listed as being in this province (which do not include Tlatelolco) are taken from folio 17v of the *Codex Mendoza* which, as explained in the text, may not be part of the tribute-roll section of this codex and which does not list any tribute.

References

Unpublished Documents

AGI Justicia 123/2
México 1536. Gil González de Benavides y el Gov[or] y Principales de Xaltocan, con los del pueblo de Tlatelolco, sobre ciertas estancias. Archivo General de Indias (Seville), Ramo Justicia, Leg. 123, No. 2.

AGI Justicia 124/1
México 1536. Cristóbal de Valderrama, vecino de la ciudad de México, con Don Juan, indio, principal del barrio de Santiago de México, y los principales de él, sobre el pueblo de Guatepec. Archivo General de Indias (Seville), Ramo Justicia, Leg. 124, No. 1.

AGN Tierras 1584/1
Año de 1711. Testimonio de los autos de reducción que de los naturales de los pueblos sujetos se hizo al de Xaltocan su cabezera, jur[on] de Sumpango de la Laguna, el año de 1599. Archivo General de la Nación (México), Ramo de Tierras, Vol. 1584, No. 1.

Published Works

Alva Ixtlilxóchitl, Fernando de
1975–77 Obras históricas. Edited by Edmundo O'Gorman. Universidad Nacional Autónoma de México, Instituto de Investigaciones Históricas. México.

Anales de Cuauhtitlan
1939 Die Geschichte der Königreiche von Colhuacan und Mexico, edited and translated by Walter Lehmann. Stuttgart: Verlag W. Kohlhammer.
1975 Códice Chimalpopoca: Anales de Cuauhtitlan y Leyenda de los Soles, edited and translated by Primo Feliciano Velázquez. Universidad Nacional Autónoma de México, Instituto de Investigaciones Históricas. México.

Anales de Tlatelolco
1948 Anales de Tlatelolco: Unos annales históricos de la nación mexicana y Códice de Tlatelolco. Fuentes para la Historia de México 2. Antigua Librería Robredo de José Porrúa e Hijos. México.

Anunciación, Fr. Domingo de la
1940 Parecer de Fray Domingo de la Anunciación sobre el modo que tenían de tributar los indios en tiempo de la gentilidad . . . (Chimalhuacan, Chalco, 20 set 1554). Epistolario de Nueva España 1505–1818, edited by Francisco del Paso y Troncoso, Vol. 7:259–66. Porrúa e Hijos. México.

Barlow, Robert H.
1949 The Extent of the Empire of the Culhua Mexica. Ibero-Americana 28. Los Angeles: University of California Press.
1987 Obras de Robert H. Barlow, vol. 1, Tlatelolco, Rival de Tenochtitlan, edited by Jesús Monjarás-Ruiz, Elena Limón, and María de la Cruz Paillés H. Instituto Nacional de Antropología e Historia and Universidad de las Américas. México.
1989 Obras de Robert H. Barlow, vol. 2, Tlatelolco: Fuentes e Historia, edited by Jesús Monjarás-Ruiz, Elena Limón, and María de la Cruz Paillés H. Instituto Nacional de Antropología e Historia and Universidad de las Américas. México.

Brumfiel, Elizabeth
n.d.a The Imperial Subversion of Aztec Xaltocan. Paper presented to the First Joint Archaeological Congress, Baltimore, January, 1989.
1994 Ethnic groups and political development in ancient Mexico. In: Factional Competition and Political Development in the New World, edited by Elizabeth Brumfiel and John W. Fox, pp. 89–102. Cambridge: Cambridge University Press.

Carrasco, Pedro
1950 Los Otomíes: Cultura e historia prehispánicas de los pueblos mesoamericanos de habla otomiana. Universidad Nacional Autónoma de México, Instituto de Historia. México.
1971 Social organization of ancient Mexico. In: Handbook of Middle American Indians, edited by Robert Wauchope. Vol. 10: Archaeology of Northern Mesoamerica, edited by Gordon F. Ekholm and Ignacio Bernal, pt 1, pp 349–75. Austin: University of Texas Press.
1977 Los señores de Xochimilco en 1548. Tlalocan 7:229–65.

Chimapahin Quauhtlehuanitzin, Domingo Francisco
1889 Annales de Domingo Francisco de San Antón Muñón Chimalpahin Quauhtlehuanitzin, Sixième et Septième Rélations (1258–1612), edited and translated by Rémi Siméon. Paris: Maisonneuve et Ch. Leclerc.

Codex Mendoza
1925 Colección de Mendoza o Códice Mendocino: Documento mexicano del siglo XVI que se conserva en la Biblioteca Bodleiana de Oxford, Inglaterra, edited by Francisco del Paso y Troncoso and Jesús Galindo y Villa. Editorial Inovación. México.

Cortés, Hernán
1865 Carta de Hernán Cortés al Consejo de Indias . . . (20 set 1538). In: Colección de documentos inéditos relativos al descubrimiento, conquista y colonización de las antiguas posesiones españolas de América y Oceanía 3:535–43. Madrid.

Descripción del Arzobispado
1905 Descripción del Arzobispado de México (1571). In: Papeles de Nueva España, 2a serie, edited by Francisco del Paso y Troncoso, vol. 3. Madrid: Sucesores de Rivadeneyra.

Díaz del Castillo, Bernal
1968 Historia verdadera de la conquista de la Nueva España, edited by Joaquín Ramírez Cabañas. Editorial Porrúa. México.

Durán, Fr. Diego
1967 Historia de las indias de Nueva España e islas de la tierra firme. Editorial Porrúa. México.

Hicks, Frederic
1974 Dependent labor in prehispanic Mexico. Estudios de Cultura Náhuatl 11:245–66.
1984a Rotational labor and urban development in prehispanic Tetzcoco. In: Explorations in Ethnohistory: Indians of Central Mexico in the Sixteenth Century, edited by Herbert R. Harvey and Hanns J. Prem, pp. 147–74. Albuquerque: University of New Mexico Press.
1984b La posición de Tamazcalapan en la Triple Alianza. Estudios de Cultura Náhuatl 17:235–60.
1992 Subject states and tribute provinces: The Aztec Empire in the northern Valley of Mexico. Ancient Mesoamerica 3:1–10.

Linné, Sigvald
1958 El valle y la ciudad de México en 1550. Statens Etnografiska Museum, New Series, Publ. 9. Stockholm.

López de Ribera, Pedro
1905 Relación de Chiconauhtla y su Partido (1580). In: Papeles de Nueva España, 2a serie, edited by Francisco del Paso y Troncoso, vol. 6:167–77. Madrid: Sucesores de Rivadeneyra.

Matrícula de Tributos
1980 Matrícula de Tributos (Códice de Moctezuma), edited by Frances F. Berdan and Jacqueline de Durand-Forest. Graz: Akademische Druck- und Verlagsanstalt.

Motolinía, Fr. Toribio de Benavente
1971 Memoriales, o Libro de las cosas de la Nueva España y de los naturales de ella, edited by Edmundo O'Gorman. Universidad Nacional Autónoma de México, Instituto de Investigaciones Históricas. México.

Motolinía, Fr. Toribio de Benavente, and Fr. Diego de Olarte
1975 Carta parecer de fray Toribio de Motolinía y de fray Diego de Olarte a don Luís de Velasco el primero, Cholula, 27 agosto 1554. In: Documentos inéditos del siglo XVI para la Historia de México, edited by Mariano Cuevas, S. J., pp. 228–32. Editorial Porrúa. México.

Nazareo, Pablo
1940 Carta al rey don Felipe II, de don Pablo Nazareo de Xaltocan, doña María Axayaca, don Juan Axayaca y doña María Atotoz, México a 17 de marzo de 1566. In: Epistolario de Nueva España 1505–1818, edited by Francisco del Paso y Troncoso, 10, pp. 109–28. Editorial Porrúa. México.

Niederberger, Christine
1987 Paléopaysages et Archéologie Pre-Urbaine du Bassin de Mexico (Mexique). Etudes Mesoaméricaines XI. Centre d'Etudes Mexicaines et Centroaméricaines. México.

Palerm, Angel
1973 Obras hidráulicas prehispánicas en el sistema lacustre del Valle de México. SEP-INAH. México.

Parsons, Jeffrey R.
1974 The development of a prehistoric complex scoiety: A regional perspective from the Valley of Mexico. Journal of Field Archaeology 1:81–108.

Piho, Virve
1972 Tlacatecutli, Tlacochtecutli, Tlacateccatl y Tlacochcalcatl. Estudios de Cultura Náhuatl 10:315–28.

Pomar, Juan de
1941 Relación de Texcoco. In: Nueva colección de documentos para la historia de México, edited by J. García Icazbalceta, pp. 67–205. Salvador Chávez Hayhoe. México.

Rojas R., Teresa
1974 Aspectos tecnológicos de las obras hidráulicas coloniales. In: Nuevas noticias sobre las obras hidráulicas prehispánicas y coloniales en el Valle de México, by Teresa Rojas R., Rafael A. Strauss K., and J. Lameiras, pp. 19–133. SEP-INAH. México.
1985 La cosecha del agua en la cuenca de México. Centro de Investigaciones y Estudios Superiores en Antropología Social, Cuadernos de la Casa Chata 116. México.

Sanders, William T., Jeffrey R. Parsons, and Robert S. Santley
1979 The Basin of Mexico: Ecological Processes in the Evolution of a Civilization. New York: Academic Press.

Sanders, William T., and Robert S. Santley
1983 A tale of three cities: Energetics and urbanization in pre-hispanic Central Mexico. In: Prehistoric Settlement Patterns: Essays in Honor of Gordon R. Willey, edited by Evon Z. Vogt and Richard M. Leventhal, pp. 243–91. Cambridge: University of New Mexico Press and Peabody Museum of Archaeology and Ethnology, Harvard University.

Spores, Ronald
1967 The Mixtec Kings and Their People. Norman: University of Oklahoma Press.

Strauss K., Rafael A.
1974 El área septentrional del Valle de México: Problemas agrohidráulicos prehispánicos y coloniales. In: Nuevas noticias sobre las obras hidráulicas prehispánicas y coloniales en el Valle de México, by Teresa Rojas R., Rafael A. Strauss K., and J. Lameiras, pp. 135–74. SEP-INAH. México.

Tezozómoc, Hernando Alvarado
1975 Crónica Mexicana. Editorial Porrúa. México.

Zantwijk, Rudolf A. M. van
1967 La organización de once guarniciones aztecas: Una nueva interpretación de los folios 17v y 18r del Códice Mendocino. Journal de la Société des Américanistes 56:149–58.

Zorita, Alonso de
1941 Breve y sumaria relación de los señores y maneras y diferencias que había de ellos en la Nueva España . . . In: Nueva colección de documentos para la historia de México, edited by J. García Icazbalceta, pp. 67–205. Salvador Chávez Hayhoe. México.

CHAPTER 5

The Obverse of the Codex of Cholula

Defining the Borders of the Kingdom of Cholula

MICHAEL LIND

SANTA ANA UNIFIED SCHOOL DISTRICT, SANTA ANA, CALIFORNIA

THIRTY YEARS AGO, Mesoamerican ethnohistorians were embroiled in endless arguments about conquests and migrations, or what Flannery (1967) in other contexts has called the "Old Testament effect." Into this fray entered a fresh voice with a new anthropological approach to Mesoamerican ethnohistory. Ron Spores became a pioneer in Mesoamerican ethnohistory and archaeology by advocating the use of ethnohistoric documents to develop models of the cultural systems of ancient Mesoamerican societies and then testing these models against "hard" archaeological data in the field.

In his introductory volume to the Nochixtlán Valley Project, Spores modestly observed:

> The project is somewhat innovative in that it makes direct application of a historically derived model of Mixtec society in an attempt . . . to observe the evolution of those same historic patterns through archaeological survey and excavation. [Spores 1972:ii]

Spores made ethnohistoric data anthropologically and archaeologically relevant in Mesoamerica. My study of the borders of the Kingdom of Cholula attempts to follow in his footsteps.

The Codex of Cholula

The Codex of Cholula is a very large sheet of indigenous *amate* paper which measures 1.12 m × 1.66 m (Glass 1964:106). On both sides are maps or plans with glosses written in Nahuatl. The "front," or obverse, is a map of the Cholula region, while the "back," or reverse, presents plans of the center of the City of Cholula. Unfortunately, no comprehensive study of the original has been published, although Simons (1970) has briefly commented upon it and Luis Reyes (1988:79, 127) cites his own unpublished translation of the glosses.

Apart from the original, which is located in the Museo Nacional de Antropología e Historia in Mexico City, two copies exist. Both are copies of the obverse. Copy 1 is an oil painting on cloth, 1.03 m × 1.72 m, which is on display at the Museo de Cholula (Glass 1964:48). Copy 2, an ink drawing on European paper, measures .92 m × 1.31 m and is in the Museo Nacional (Glass 1964:107). No study of Copy 1 has been published. However, Copy 2 was studied in detail by Bente Simons (1962) in her Master's thesis for the Department of Anthropology of the University of the Americas, and was later published in *Tlalocan* (Simons 1968a, 1968b).

Simons identified, transcribed, translated, and commented individually upon 174 separate glosses in Copy 2 of the Codex and her study, combined with an analysis of the illustrations, provided the data base for my study of the obverse of the Codex of Cholula. The present study analyzes and interprets information in the Codex with regard to the borders of the Kingdom of Cholula around the time of the Conquest. Following a brief overview of the layout of the obverse of the Codex of Cholula, I will discuss the ethnohistoric data and examine their implications for archaeological research.

Plan of the Obverse

The obverse of the Codex of Cholula is a map of the Cholula region, executed between A.D. 1549 and A.D. 1586. The City of Cholula occupies the center of the map with a drawing of the Great Pyramid, or Tlalchihualtepetl, as a focal point. The public barrio buildings form a nearly rectangular frame around the city limits. The "top" portion of the map includes the City of Puebla and the region east of Cholula with the Río Atoyac and the Río Coronango passing through it. The "bottom" portion depicts the region west of Cholula dominated by the two volcanos, Cerro Zapotecas and Cerro Tecajete. The region north of Cholula occupies the left side of the map with the Río Atoyac running along it, and the region south of Cholula is on the right with the Río Nexapa in the lower right hand corner (Fig. 5.1).

The map of the Cholula region is distinctly indigenous in its layout. The peoples of Mesoamerica did not view the four cardinal directions as straight lines as Europeans do. Instead, five areas were conceptualized: center, east, west, north, and south. The center was depicted as a rectangle—just as the City of Cholula is seen in the form of a rectangle at the center of the map. The regions east, west, north, and south of the central rectangle were conceptualized as trapezoidal areas expand-

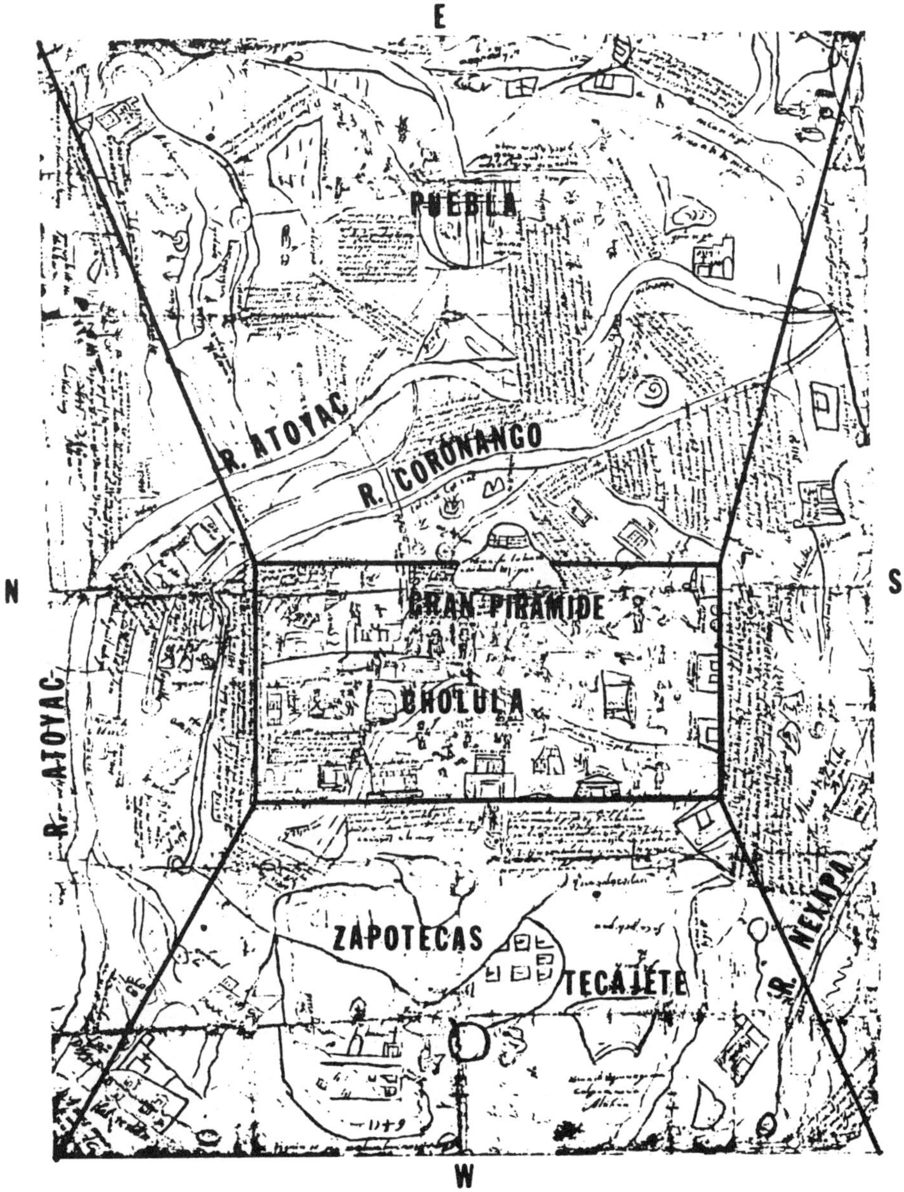

Figure 5.1. Indigenous layout of the Codex of Cholula—Copy 2 (adapted from Glass 1964: Fig. 60).

Figure 5.2. Modern map of the Valley of Puebla.

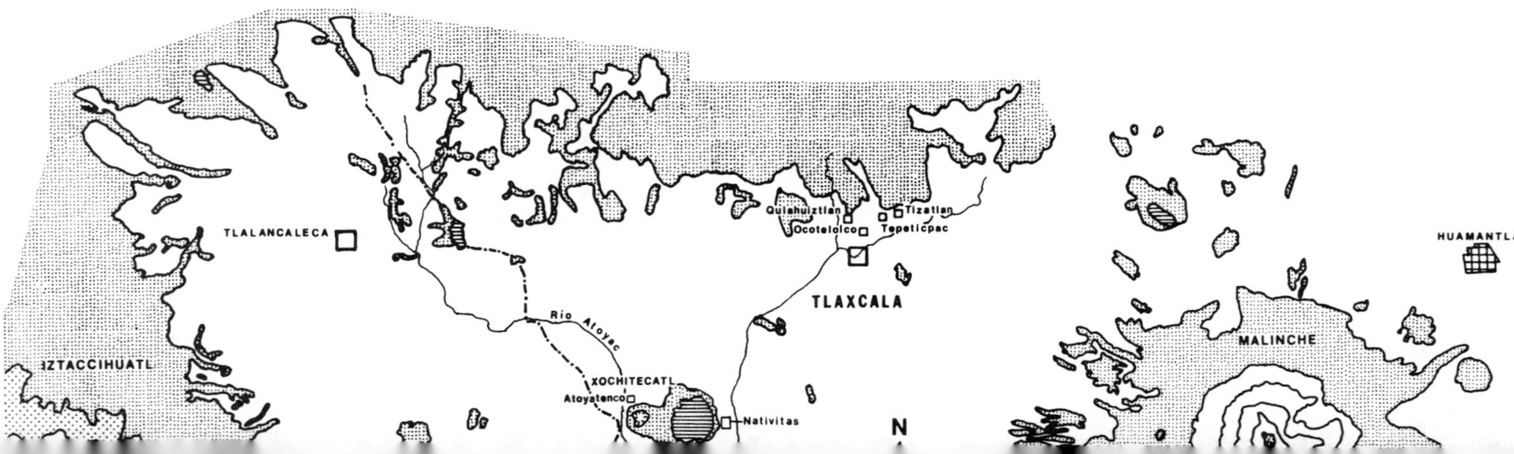

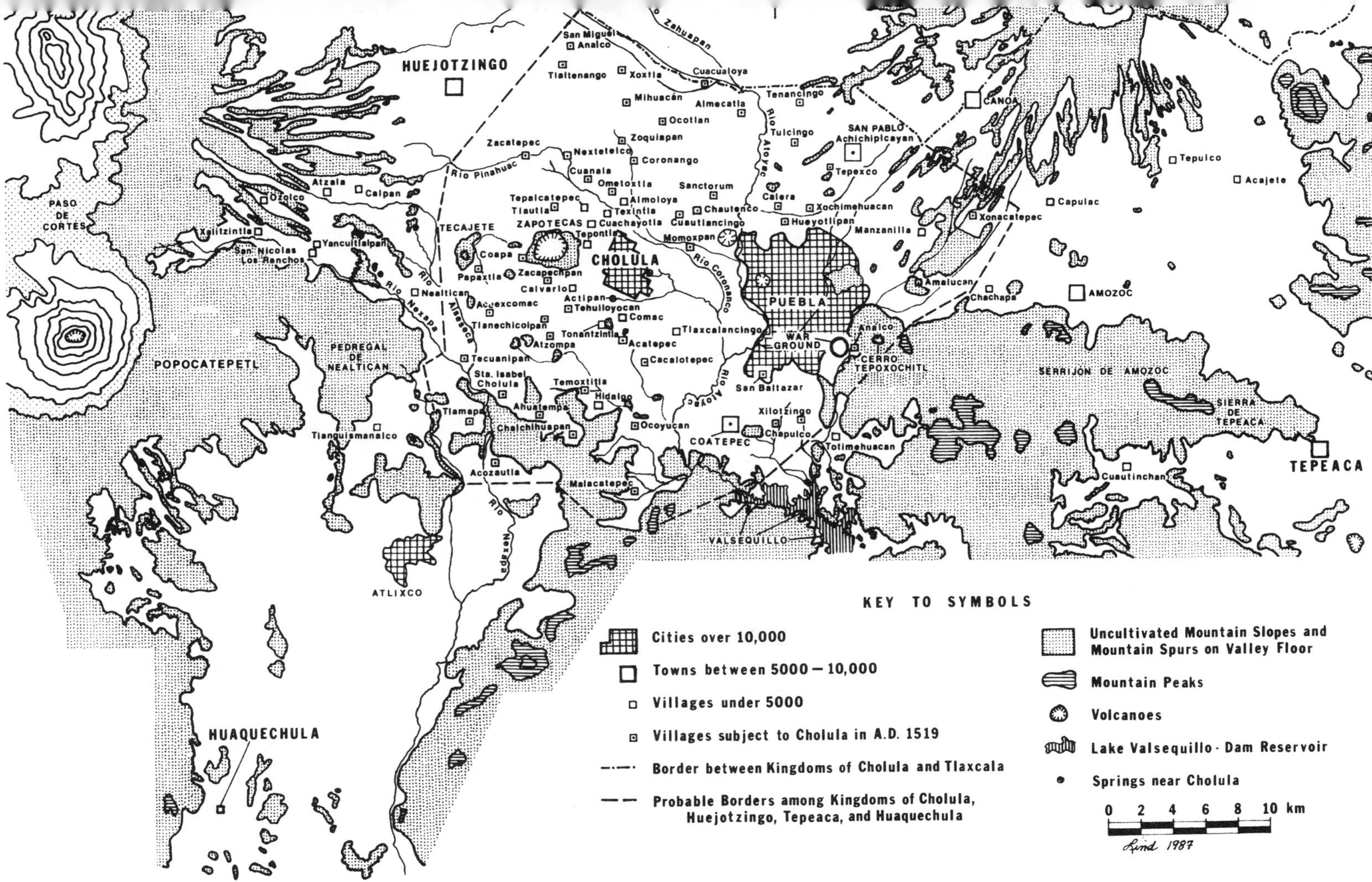
HUEJOTZINGO
PASO DE CORTES
POPOCATEPETL
San Miguel Analco
Tlaltenango
Xoxtla
Zahuapan
Cuacualoya
Mihuacán
Almecatla
Ocotlan
Zoquiapan
Coronango
Zacatepec
Nextetelco
Cuanala
Ometoxtla
Sanctorum
Tenancingo
Tulcingo
Río Atoyac
SAN PABLO Achichipicayan
Tepexco
CANOA
Tepulco
Acajete
Capulac
Xonacatepec
Río Pinahuac
Atzala
Calpan
Ozolco
Xalitzintla
Yancuitlalpan
San Nicolas Los Ranchos
TECAJETE
Tepalcatepec
Tlautla
ZAPOTECAS
Almoloya
Texintla
Cuachayotla
Chautenco
Cuautlancingo
Calera
Xochimehuacan
Hueyotlipan
Manzanilla
Teponti
CHOLULA
Momoxpan
Río Coronanco
Coapa
Papaxtla
Zacapechpan
Calvario
Nealtican
Río Nexapa
Alseseca
Acuexcomac
Actipan
Tehulloyocan
Comac
Tlanechicolpan
Tonantzintla
Acatepec
Tlaxcalancingo
Atzompa
Tecuanipan
Cacalotepec
PUEBLA
WAR GROUND
Analco
CERRO TEPOXOCHITL
Amalucan
Chachapa
AMOZOC
SERRIJÓN DE AMOZOC
SIERRA DE TEPEACA
TEPEACA
PEDREGAL DE NEALTICAN
Sta. Isabel Cholula
Temoxtitla
Hidalgo
San Baltazar
Xilotzingo
Tlamapa
Ahuatempa
Chalchihuapan
Ocoyucan
COATEPEC
Chapulco
Totimehuacan
Cuautinchan
Tianguismanalco
Acozautla
Malacatepec
Río Nexapa
VALSEQUILLO
ATLIXCO
HUAQUECHULA
KEY TO SYMBOLS
Cities over 10,000
Towns between 5000 — 10,000
Villages under 5000
Villages subject to Cholula in A.D. 1519
Border between Kingdoms of Cholula and Tlaxcala
Probable Borders among Kingdoms of Cholula, Huejotzingo, Tepeaca, and Huaquechula
Uncultivated Mountain Slopes and Mountain Spurs on Valley Floor
Mountain Peaks
Volcanoes
Lake Valsequillo - Dam Reservoir
Springs near Cholula
0 2 4 6 8 10 km
Lind 1987

ing out from each side of the central rectangle. The Codex of Cholula, like most Mesoamerican maps, placed the eastern region at the top (Fig. 5.1). To better understand the geographical context of the map, the area covered by the Codex has been outlined on a modern map of the Valley of Puebla (Fig. 5.2).

Borders of the Kingdom

At the time of the Spanish Conquest, Cholula was the capital of an autonomous kingdom, independent from the Aztec state (Durán 1951:I, 239). The Kingdom of Cholula was bordered by the Kingdoms of Tlaxcala, in the north; Huejotzingo, in the west; Huaquechula (Atlixco), in the south; and Tepeaca, in the east (Fig. 2). Because Puebla was founded within a decade of the Conquest on lands belonging to Cholula, the eastern border of the Kingdom of Cholula has been difficult to define from Colonial documents (Nolasco 1967:70). Fortunately, since the obverse of the Codex of Cholula specifies the lands ceded to Puebla and since the land boundaries of the Kingdom of Cholula are related to specific topographical features illustrated in the Codex, the frontiers of the Kingdom of Cholula can be determined with a degree of accuracy heretofore unprecedented.

Being a map of the land boundaries of the Kingdom of Cholula, the obverse of the Codex represents a relatively accurate plan of mountains, rivers, barrancas, and springs—those topographic features which serve as reasonably permanent landmarks for territorial borders. These topographic features can be seen more clearly when separated from the plethora of glosses and illustrations which fill the obverse of the Codex. A tracing illustrating these features has been prepared for Copy 2 of the Codex (Fig. 5.3). That the Codex illustrates the topographic features of the Cholula region with reasonable accuracy can be seen by comparing it with a modern topographic map of the region (Fig. 5.4). Most of the topographic features in the Codex can be identified easily on the modern map (Table 5.1).

A series of glosses in Nahuatl around the edges of the Codex name the kingdoms and towns which bordered the Kingdom of Cholula. These glosses are located near specific topographic features which marked the boundary between Cholula and its neighbors. Each of these glosses, as translated by Simons (1962, 1968a, 1968b), is placed in its proper location on the tracing of the Codex (Fig. 5.3).

With regard to the lands ceded to Puebla, the Codex states:

> Here they shall see what we gave the Spaniards. They shall settle down at Cuitlaxcohuapan-Tenexatzinco. We give them our land of the plain; they, the lords, also receive it. They shall be near us there at the river. Toward the east . . . At a league's distance there is a mountain called Tepoxuchitl, it is our property, our land of Cholula. [Simons 1962; 1968a, 1968b: Gloss II-B5]

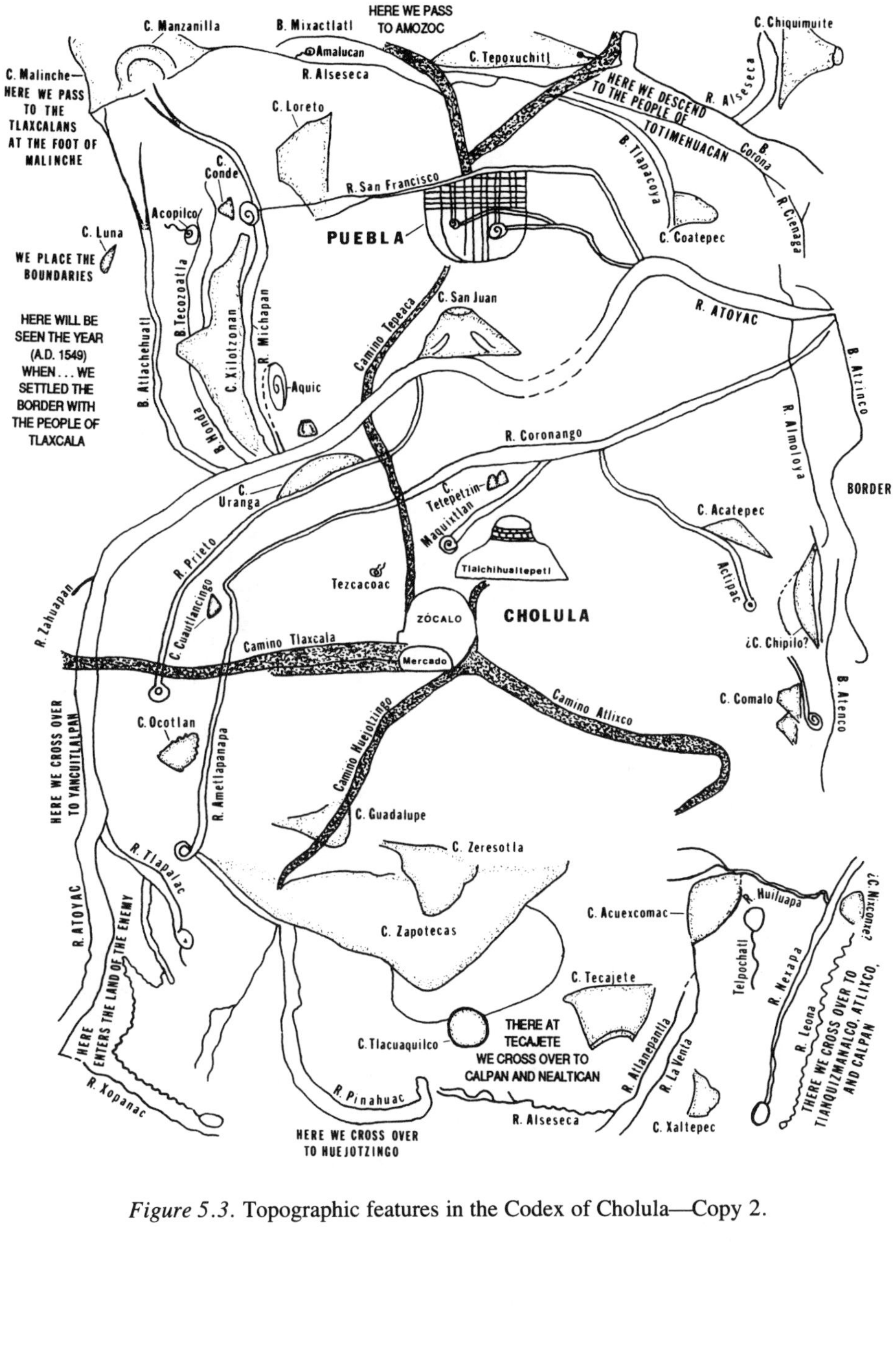

Figure 5.3. Topographic features in the Codex of Cholula—Copy 2.

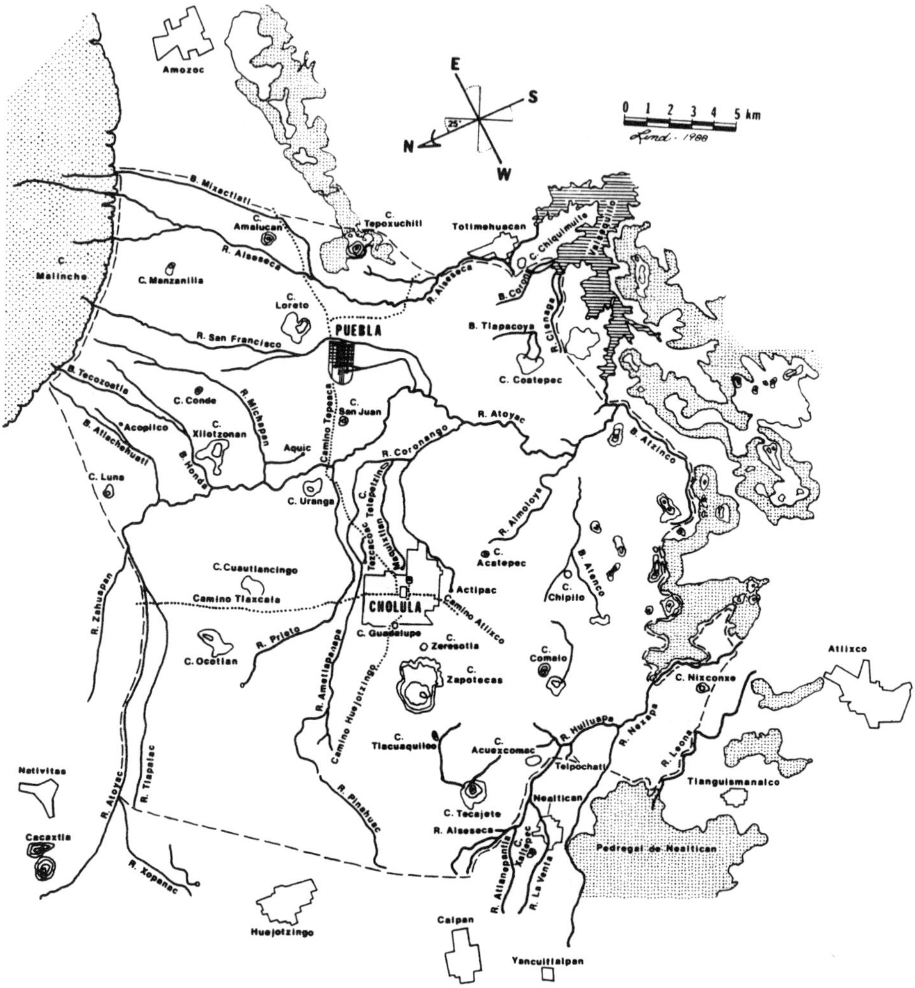

Figure 5.4. Topographic features in the modern Valley of Puebla.

Near the center of the upper edge (east) of the Codex, Cerro Tepoxuchitl is illustrated and appropriately labeled (Fig. 5.3). The eastern boundary of the Kingdom of Cholula, then, clearly included Cerro Tepoxuchitl.

However, the Codex is even more specific regarding the eastern border of the Kingdom. A road leaving Puebla and heading east first crosses the Río Alseseca East[1] and, then, farther east it crosses the Barranca Mixactlatl. At the point where

[1]Two rivers in the Valley of Puebla are called Alseseca. They will be referred to as the Alseseca East and Alseseca West to distinguish them.

the road crosses the Barranca Mixactlatl is a gloss (Fig. 5.3) which reads: "Here we pass to Amozoc" (Simons 1962; 1968a, 1968b, Gloss I-B1). The Barranca Mixactlatl, then, formed the eastern border of the Kingdom of Cholula from the foot of Cerro Malinche to Cerro Tepoxuchitl. From Cerro Tepoxuchitl to the base of Cerro Chiquimuite, the eastern boundary followed the Río Alseseca East (Fig. 5.4). Directly north of Cerro Chiquimuite along the west bank of the Río Alseseca East is a gloss (Fig. 5.3) which reads: "Here we descend to the people of Totimehuacan" (Simons 1962; 1968a, 1968b: Gloss I-C2).

The eastern border of the Kingdom joined the southern border at Cerro Chiquimuite. A small tributary of the Río Alseseca East (illustrated, but unnamed, on both the Codex and the modern map, Figs. 5.3–4) and the Cañada La Corona marked the juncture of the eastern and southern borders. From La Corona the southern border followed the Río Ciénaga to its headwaters south of Cerro Coatepec. In the absence of any notable topographic feature, the southern border followed an imaginary line from the headwaters of the Río Ciénaga to a small tributary of the Río Atoyac (Fig. 5.4). The tributary (shown, but unnamed, on both the Codex and the modern map, Figs. 5.3–4) enters the Río Atoyac from the north, and directly opposite it, the Barranca Atzinco joins the Río Atoyac from the south. The Barranca Atzinco has a gloss (Fig. 5.3) along its southern bank which reads simply, "Border" (Simons 1962; 1968a, 1968b: Gloss III-C4).

From the headwaters of the Barranca Atzinco to the Río Nexapa, a range of rugged mountains separates the Valleys of Puebla and Atlixco, and this mountain range served as a natural continuation of the southern border (Fig. 5.4). The Río Nexapa and the Río La Leona flank a natural pass between the Valleys of Puebla and Atlixco. At the head of this pass, north of Atlixco and east of the Río Nexapa, the small Acozautla sub-valley formed the southernmost border of the Kingdom of Cholula. Cerro Nixconxe, directly opposite the Acozautla sub-valley, served as a boundary marker for the southern border between the Río Nexapa and the Río La Leona (Fig. 5.4).

The southern border joined the western border of the Kingdom at the Río La Leona. A gloss (Fig. 3) along the southwest bank of the Río La Leona reads: "There we cross over to Tianquizmanalco, Atlixco, and Calpan" (Simons 1962; 1968a, 1968b: Gloss V-C1). From the headwaters of the Río La Leona, the western border of the Kingdom followed the edge of the Pedregal de Nealtican to the Río Nexapa. From this point, the western border was formed by an imaginary line which crossed the Río Nexapa and extended to a spring which fed a small tributary of the Río Huiluapa. The spring is shown, but not named, on the modern map (Fig. 5.4); it is named the "Telpochatl" on the Codex (Fig. 5.3).

From the point where the Telpochatl enters the Río Huiluapa, the western border followed the Río Huiluapa upstream to the Río Atlanepantla. The western border continued along the Río Atlanepantla to a point where the Río Alseseca West joined it behind (west of) Cerro Tecajete (Fig. 5.4). A gloss (Fig. 5.3) on the east bank

TABLE 5.1
Topographic Features of the Cholula Region

Features[a]	Gloss in Copy 2 of Codex	Gloss No.[b]
MOUNTAINS		
Acatepec	Acatepec	III-C6
Acuexcomac	Aculcomon tepetl	IV-C4
Chipilo	Nepalualtopel	III-C8
Chiquimuite	—	—
Coatepec	Quahtepe	I-C4
Comalo	—	—
Conde	Tepopolo	II-A8
Cuautlancingo	Tçcauhyocan	III-A17
Guadalupe	Yztzocan	IV-A14
Loreto	—	—
Luna	—	—
Malinche	Matlalcueye	I-A9
Manzanilla	—	—
Nixconxe	Tepanchi tepec	IV-C16
Ocotlan	Teyocan	IV-A11
San Juan	Çentepec	II-B6
Tecajete	Tecaxic	V-C5
Tepoxuchitl	Tepch xochio	I-B10
[Tetepetzin]	Tetepetzin	III-B17
Tlacuaquilco	Tlacoa quita	V-B4
Uranga	—	—
Xaltepec	—	—
Xilotzonan	—	—
Zapotecas	Tzapoteca	V-B5
Zeresotla	—	—
RIVERS		
Almoloya	—	—
Alseseca East	Chiyecan?	I-B2
Alseseca West	—	—
Ametlapanapa	Metlapanapan	III-A12
Atoyac	Atoyac	III-A7
Atlanepantla	—	—
Cienaga	—	—
Coronango	—	—
Huiluapa	—	—
La Venta	—	—
Leona	—	—
[Michapan]	Michapan	II-B8
Nexapa	Nexac	V-C3
Pinahuac	Pinahuiçac	V-A6
Prieto	—	—
San Francisco	—	—
Tlapalac	—	—
Xopanac	—	—
Zahuapan	—	—
BARRANCAS		
Atenco	—	—
Atlachehuatl	Atlacahtli	II-A4
Atzinco	—	—
Corona	—	—

Table 5.1 (cont.)

Features[a]	Gloss in Copy 2 of Codex	Gloss No.[b]
Honda	Atlauhtli?	II-A5
Mixactlatl	Tepoxxchatla?	I-B2
Tecozoatla	ocao tlaza can	I-A8
Tlapacoya	—	—
SPRINGS		
Acopilco	—	—
Actipac	Yaticpac	III-C11
Amalucan	Amalihcan	I-B3
[Aquic][a]	Aquinexac	II-A3
[Maquixtlan][a]	Maquiçtlan	III-B13
[Telpochatl][a]	Telpochatl	IV-C15
[Texcocoac][a]	Tezca coac	III-B18

[a]Features in brackets glossed in Codex but not labeled on modern topographic maps of region.
[b]Gloss number in Simons (1962, 1968a, b).

of the Río Alseseca West reads: "There at Tecajete we cross over to Calpan and Nealtican" (Simons 1962; 1968a, 1968b: Gloss V-B1).

Instead of following the Río Alseseca West to its headwaters, the western border followed two tributaries of the Alseseca West to their headwaters. These tributaries are illustrated, but not named, on the Codex and the modern map (Figs. 5.3–4). From the headwaters of these two tributaries, the western border followed an imaginary line to a large bend in the Río Pinahuac. On the western bank of this large bend in the Río Pinahuac is a gloss (Fig. 5.3) which reads: "Here we cross over to Huejotzingo" (Simons 1962; 1968a, 1968b: Gloss V-A3). An imaginary line from the bend in the Río Pinahuac to the headwaters of the Río Tlapalac completed the western border and linked it to the northern border of the Kingdom. At the headwaters of the Río Tlapalac is another gloss (Fig. 5.3) which reads: "Here one enters the land of the enemy" (Simons 1962; 1968a, 1968b: Gloss V-A2).

The headwaters of the Río Tlapalac, which begin near where the Río Xopanac joins the Río Atoyac, mark the point on the Río Atoyac where the northern border of the Kingdom began (Figs. 5.3–4). A gloss (Fig. 5.3) along the northern bank of the Río Atoyac reads: "Here we cross over to Yancuitlalpan" (Simons 1962; 1968a, 1968b: Gloss IV-A1). This gloss would appear to be incorrect since today there is a Yancuitlalpan to the west, not north, of Cholula (Fig. 5.4). However, Simons (1968a:303) states that the area glossed in the Codex was, in fact, called Yancuitlalpan in the sixteenth century. Today it includes modern Santa María Natívitas. Therefore, the gloss is correct.

The northern border followed the Río Atoyac to the Río Zahuapan. From the point where the Río Zahuapan enters the Río Atoyac to Cerro de la Luna, the northern border followed an imaginary line. Two glosses occur next to Cerro de la Luna (Fig. 5.3). One reads: "Here will be seen the year [A.D. 1549] when . . . we settled the border with the people of Tlaxcala" (Simons 1962; 1968a, 1968b: Gloss II-A1). The other, placed directly beneath a box which encloses Cerro de la Luna, reads: "We place the boundaries" (Simons 1962; 1968a, 1968b: Gloss I-A2). Cerro de la Luna, then, was clearly established as a boundary marker between Cholula and Tlaxcala.

From Cerro de la Luna, the northern border extended to the headwaters of the Barranca Atlachehuatl on the slopes of Cerro Malinche, around the 2400 m elevation. A gloss (Fig. 5.3) at the headwaters of the Barranca Atlachehuatl reads: "Here we pass to the Tlaxcalans at the foot of Malinche" (Simons 1962; 1968a, 1968b: Gloss I-A1). The northern border continued along the 2400 m level to cross the Barranca Tecozoatl, Río Michapan, Río San Francisco, Río Alseseca East, and finally joined the eastern border at the Barranca Mixactlatl (Fig. 5.4).

Conclusions

Since the Codex specifies the lands ceded by Cholula to establish the Spanish settlement of Puebla, or Cuetlaxcohuapan, in A.D. 1531, Simons (1968a:271) has noted that the land boundaries in the obverse of the Codex represent the frontiers of the Kingdom of Cholula as they existed in A.D. 1519 on the eve of the Spanish Conquest. With the exception of the contested border with Tlaxcala in the vicinity of Cerro de la Luna, which was settled in A.D. 1549, Simons' observations are valid. Within these ancient borders, the Kingdom of Cholula extended about 30 km from east to west and about 33 km from north to south. It covered about 800 km^2. Few, if any, Prehispanic kingdoms, known to be autonomous polities, have had their borders defined as precisely as the Kingdom of Cholula where specific topographic features have been identified as boundary markers. The implications of this for the direct historical approach in archaeology are of great significance.

In archaeology, as in all science, it is necessary to move from the known to the unknown in solving problems. One problem that has long concerned archaeologists is how to define the boundaries of autonomous political units, or polities, from archaeological remains. Two hypotheses have commonly been proposed to solve this problem: (1) the borders of polities can be defined on the basis of the distribution of characteristic ceramic types; or (2) the borders of polities can be defined on the basis of "breaks" in site distribution which represent "no man's lands" between neighboring polities.

Knowing the borders of the Kingdom of Cholula, these hypotheses can be tested and verified or rejected. Sites on either side of the borders can be sampled to see if they show characteristic differences in ceramic types. Site surveys can be conducted along the borders to see if breaks occur in site distributions representing no man's lands. If archaeological evidence of boundaries can be identified along the known borders of Cholula, then the path is open to recognize this evidence as indicative of the borders of kingdoms that can only be known archaeologically.

Recently, an archaeological survey of the Atlixco Valley has been completed by Patricia Plunket and Gabriela Uruñuela of the Universidad de las Américas in Cholula. The survey showed that Cholulteca ceramic types—including Nila and Catalina polychromes—diagnostic of the Martir phase (ca. A.D. 1350–1550) were distributed in the northern part of the Valley of Atlixco (north of the city of Atlixco) in the region of the Acozautla sub-valley where the Codex marks the southern boundary of the Kingdom of Cholula. However, in the southern part of the Valley of Atlixco in the region around Huaquechula, late Aztec, and not Cholulteca, ceramic types predominate. In fact, a break in settlement distribution representing a no man's land existed in the central part of the Valley of Atlixco between the City of Atlixco and Huaquechula (Plunket 1990). This survey along the southern border of the Kingdom of Cholula, then, supports both hypotheses. However, additional surveys need to be conducted along the eastern, western, and northern borders of the Kingdom of Cholula to determine if the same situation prevails.

Ron Spores pioneered the use of ethnohistoric documents to create anthropological models of ancient Mesoamerican societies which could be tested against archeological data. In this study, an ethnohistoric model derived through an analysis of the obverse of the Codex of Cholula has explored the nature of border definition in an ancient polity, the Kingdom of Cholula. Guidelines have been presented for future archaeological research into the general problem of defining borders of ancient polities from archaeological remains, using the Kingdom of Cholula as a test case.

References Cited

Durán, Fray Diego
1951 Historia de las indias de Nueva España y islas de tierra firme. 2 tomos. Editora Nacional. México.

Flannery, Kent V.
1967 Culture history vs. culture process: A debate in American archaeology. Scientific American 217(2):119–22.

Glass, John B.
1964 Catálogo de la colección de códices. Museo Nacional de Antropología e Historia. México.

Nolasco, Margarita

1967 La región de Cholula. In: Cholula: Informe preliminar, edited by Miguel Messmacher, pp. 65–76. Editoral Nueva Arqueología. México.

Plunket, Patricia

1990 Arqueología y etnohistoria en el Valle de Atlixco. Notas Mesoamericanas, 12:3–18. Universidad de las Américas. Cholula.

Reyes, Luis

1988 Cuauhtinchán del siglo XII al XVI: Formación y desarrollo histórico de un señorío prehispánico. Puebla: Estado de Puebla, CIESA, Fondo de Cultura Económica.

Simons, Bente

1962 The Codex of Cholula: A Preliminary Study. M.A. Thesis, University of the Americas, Cholula, Puebla.

1968a The Codex of Cholula: A Preliminary Study–Part I. Tlalocan V (3):267–88.

1968b The Codex of Cholula: A Preliminary Study–Part II. Tlalocan V (4):289–339.

1970 The City of Cholula and its Ancient Barrios. 38th International Congress of Americanists, 2:139–50.

Spores, Ronald

1972 An Archaeological Settlement Survey of the Noxchixtlan Valley, Oaxaca. Vanderbilt University Publications in Anthropology, no. 1. Nashville.

CHAPTER 6

A Codex-Style Vessel from Nochixtlan, Oaxaca

JOHN PADDOCK

INSTITUTO DE ESTUDIOS OAXAQUEÑOS, OAXACA, MEXICO

THE THEME OF THIS TRIBUTE to Ronald Spores is a striking piece of Mixtec pottery—a globular tripod olla colorfully decorated in codex style—that has been attributed to the Pueblo Viejo of Nochixtlan, a site on which Spores has reported.

Beginning with Eduard Seler's publication (1904 [1888]:257), this vessel was reproduced in many works on prehispanic art.[1] In fact, many books and articles published between fifty and one hundred years ago featured this vessel, but recently it has been almost excluded from use as an illustration.

When Alfonso Caso and Ignacio Bernal decided to display it in its own small glass case in the Period V area of the Sala Oaxaca in the National Museum of Anthropology, I agreed completely, without having examined in detail the scenes on the piece. Its impact on one accustomed to handling damaged sherds was such that I remained almost blind to the iconographic content of the olla.

Seler's first article says almost nothing about the piece except that it was one of three vessels in the Musco Nacional that reminded him strongly of Cholula polychrome, and that other examples had been noted in Ejutla and Zoquitlan as well as around Zimatlan in the Valley of Oaxaca.

In a later article, however, Seler gave special attention to the olla (1908 [1906]:522–32). Seler's second article reveals that the olla had been in the collection of Dr. Fernando Sologuren, a Oaxacan who sponsored pre-archaeological (but not exactly looting) excavations. Sologuren apparently attributed the three poly-

[1]A few examples of illustrations showing the Nochixtlan olla are the following: Seler 1904 [1888]: *Gesammelte Abhandlungen* II: 357 (Quetzalcoatl). Poor photograph, showing also the olla and the cajete; Seler 1908 [1906]: *Gesammelte Abhandlungen* III: 523 (neck and feet only); 524 (rollout drawing, the entire central body); Marquina 1928: (second leaf after page 78; color painting, Quetzalcoatl); Caso 1938b: (color photograph, Quetzalcoatl); Toscano 1952 [1944]: page 438, black-and-white photo, Tezcatlipoca-Tonacatecuhtli; Bernal 1967: color slide no. 47 (Tex.-Tonaca.; no. 46 is of the Nochixtlan pitcher); Moser 1973: 62 (black-and-white photo, Quetzalcoatl).

chrome vessels to the Pueblo Viejo of Nochixtlan; Seler probably saw a note to that effect included with the pieces, and Alfonso Caso confirmed that when he examined the collection.

Including the olla among his thirteen masterpieces of prehispanic Mexican art (Caso 1938b:45–50, 109–12), Caso accepted most of what Seler said about the iconography, even though Caso was already developing his own ideas about the Mixtec codices. Seler had almost exclusively interpreted the vessel in terms of Aztec religion and the Borgia Group of codices.

There is probably a connection between Caso's visit to the Nochixtlan site in 1933, "taking photographs and making drawings of carved stones" at a number of sites in the region (1938a:41), and his interest in the vessel, although he adds no details regarding the Pueblo Viejo of Nochixtlan.

On March 1, 1934, Eulalia Guzmán (1934:31–32), in another rapid visit, noted "sótanos," or late Mixtec-style tombs, at the Pueblo Viejo of Nochixtlan, but said she found not a single sherd of polychrome ware.

During the 1930s, Caso and Eduardo Noguera had agreed that the region merited special attention. Caso planned to enter it from the Valley of Oaxaca, and Noguera from the Valley of Puebla. Both were soon involved in high administrative responsibilities that prevented such fieldwork, however.

Beginning in 1966, Ron Spores directed the first detailed study of the Nochixtlan Valley. The valley, while not extremely large, turned out to have so many sites that the first report by Spores on the Pueblo Viejo was brief (25 lines), though eloquent. As he says, it was "one of the largest, most complex, most heavily utilized, and most disturbed" late sites. Much remained visible, even though "the site has been devastated by looters, stone robbers, and adobe collectors" (1972:130–31). He added a photograph (1972: 134, Fig. 38).

Though he cites "disturbed burials," Spores does not mention finding polychrome sherds. Special attention was given to late highland polychromes in a Master's thesis prepared by Michael D. Lind in 1967, under the supervision of Eduardo Noguera. Still unpublished, the thesis includes photographs of all four scenes portrayed on the vessel. These excellent photographs were taken in the Museo Nacional by Chris Moser. (There is also a photograph of the olla that was the second piece in the lot; the photograph by Moser shows the side that is invisible the way the piece is displayed in the Museo Nacional. The third piece, a tripod cajete lacking two of its supports, was not located by Lind and Moser.)

Having excavated near Nochixtlan, Lind has special knowledge of the area and of its polychrome pottery. In his Master's thesis, Lind (1967) clearly established that several types of late polychrome are easily distinguished. That of the Mixteca Alta is similar to that of Cholula in some ways, but sharply distinguished not only in details of decoration, but also by differences in shape. In 1967, he clarified the existence of a third type, found in the Chinantec region; later examinations of regional variants have established several other easily distinguishable types.

Lind (pers. comm.) places this Nochixtlan tripod olla in the Las Pilitas polychrome type of the Mixteca Alta, which is abundantly illustrated by Caso, Bernal, and Acosta (1967: Láminas XIII-XXVIII, following page 464). Las Pilitas is site N-237 in the Spores survey (Spores 1972:78, 126). Lind's excavations nearby have clarified many details about the polychrome pottery that occurs there (Lind 1978, 1987).

Why did this gorgeous polychrome olla lose its popularity as an illustration? In part, no doubt, this was precisely because it had become too popular and, therefore, was avoided by authors seeking to find fresher materials. In addition, recent times have also brought forth a strong preference for pieces found in scientific excavations and, therefore, with secure proveniences.

The three pieces attributed to the lot from Pueblo Viejo of Nochixtlan are of extraordinary technical quality and, at least the two I have seen, of equal aesthetic quality. There would be nothing strange in their having come from some other production center, if they were offered in the burial of a wealthy ruler. Such a person might well have been proud to own ceramic pieces finer than those produced by nearby potters. It is even conceivable that some extraordinarily fine ceramicist in Nochixtlan or the surrounding area had risen significantly above the level of his colleagues in both technique and art.

A more difficult point is raised by Alfonso Caso. Clearly enough, in 1938, his thinking about iconography had not reached its full development; some twenty years later, after having analyzed various codices with the aid of the Mapa de Teozacoalco, he might have expressed differently what he perceived in the Nochixtlan olla.

There are two figures represented, each of them facing a large, elaborate place sign. Caso proposed that one was Quetzalcoatl, the other Tezcatlipoca. (The Nahua names of the gods were not imposed simply in obedience to Aztec imperialism; not knowing the Mixtec names for them, we use the Nahua names even in contexts as purely Mixtec as this one.)

Quetzalcoatl (Fig. 6.1) has both usual and unusual traits. He is shown bearded, indicating advanced age. Here he is a wind god, with the bird-beak mouth mask that occurs in later contexts, but not in Teotihuacan. His snail-shell necklace, with a centerpiece cut from a section of a large shell, is also familiar.

But here he is not standing; he sits on a prehispanic "throne" like that of a ruler. His distinctive conical headdress has been replaced by a jaguar head. In one hand he holds, apparently as an offering, a human head. Since Quetzalcoatl is the most pro-human of all the gods, a decapitated head may be the most disturbing of all the unexpected traits that appear here.

The other figure, identified by Seler as Tonacatecuhtli and by Caso as Tezcatlipoca, likewise has unusual traits. He too is seated, not on a throne but on a jaguar-skin cushion, like a human ruler in the codices. He too wears a jaguar helmet. His feet are normal, but at the back of his head is a smoking mirror that

Figure 6.1. Nochixtlan vessel (photo courtesy of Chris Moser).

led Caso to identify him as Tezcatlipoca (whose smoking mirror is not always a substitute for one foot). His face is that of an old man, bearded and toothless. In his hand is a smoking offering, probably copal.

Each of the two figures clearly has two right arms and no left arm; this is a common device in codex painting, where human figures are, in the words of Donald Robertson (1967), assembled from standard parts. In fact, the painter of this vessel reveals a complete mastery of codex style suggesting experience in painting codices, in spite of the unusual iconographic details.

Having checked the Seler drawing against the vessel itself in November, 1990, I am confident of its accuracy. (The artist's nearly illegible signature may say Koch, but might be read as Wood.) Even more unusual are the place signs before which the two figures make their offerings. The throne of Quetzalcoatl rests upon a serpent head that may show feathers, symbolizing the god himself. A huge feathered serpent is seen behind the elaborate codex-style temple (Fig. 6.2) he faces, and a section of snail shell tops its roof. Its base may be another serpent head.

Tezcatlipoca (mirror-its-smoke) or Tonacatecuhtli (our-flesh-god), also known as Ometecuhtli (duality-lord), sits before a place sign (Fig. 6.3) without a temple. It is a huge earth-monster symbol, made by combining two alligator heads. Inside its mouth is a body of water containing a fish. The overall form suggests the mountain sign of the codices, and, in fact, it may symbolize a combination of two mountains, for the two halves are differently decorated.

Specialists in iconography may be able to explain much more of the richness this piece presents. Whereas the Quetzalcoatl figure seems to sit before a temple of Quetzalcoatl, as a human priest of the cult might do, the figure Caso called Tezcatlipoca appears to be celebrating an earth symbol. If he were a creator-god, like Ometeotl, or a priest of that cult, Seler would have been more correct than Caso in his identification.

Like many other questions this piece provokes, this question can be settled only by thorough analysis and comparison. Meanwhile, I can suggest only some possible lines of investigation based on impressions.

1. Its relations with the codices may be with the beginnings, the mythical sections. That is, it might be portraying the divine origins of some ruling dynasty.
2. The "place signs" might then refer to mythical rather than real places.
3. Sitting on symbols of rulership, the two figures seem more like men than like gods.
4. The head that is offered by Quetzalcoatl might not be a decapitated human one from a sacrifice, but rather a jewel representing a head.
5. In any case, the reference might be to some remote single event rather than to a practice; we should remember that the abundant crucifixes in Christian usage do not show crucifixion as a current practice.

Figure 6.2. Nochixtlan vessel (photo courtesy of Chris Moser).

References Cited

Bernal, Ignacio
1967 Museo Nacional de Antropología de México (con 100 diapositivas y 314 ilustraciones en blanco y negro). México: M. Aguilar Editor, S.A.

Figure 6.3. Nochixtlan vessel (photo courtesy of Chris Moser).

Caso, Alfonso

1938a Exploraciones en Oaxaca, quinta y sexta temporadas 1936–1937. Instituto Panamericano de Geografía e Historia. México.

1938b Thirteen Masterpieces of Mexican Archaeology (Trece obras maestras de arqueología mexicana). México: Editoriales Cultura y Polis.

Caso, Alfonso, Ignacio Bernal, and Jorge R. Acosta

1967 La cerámica de Monte Albán. Instituto Nacional de Antropología e Historia. México.

Guzmán, Eulalia

1934 Exploración arqueológica en la Mixteca Alta. In: Anales del Museo Nacional de Arqueología, Historia y Etnografía, V época, I:17–42.

Lind, Michael D.

1967 Mixtec Polychrome Pottery: A Comparison of the Late Preconquest Polychrome Pottery from Cholula, Oaxaca, and the Chinantla. Master's thesis, University of the Americas.

1977 Mixtec Kingdoms in the Nochixtlan Valley: A Preconquest to Postconquest Archaeological Perspective. Ph.D. dissertation, University of Arizona.

1979 Postclassic and Early Colonial Mixtec Houses in the Nochixtlan Valley, Oaxaca. Vanderbilt University Publications in Anthropology, no. 23. Nashville.

1987 The Sociocultural Dimensions of Mixtec Ceramics. Vanderbilt University Publications in Anthropology, no. 33. Nashville.

Marquina, Ignacio

1928 Estudio arquitectónico de los monumentos arqueológicos de México (contribución al XXIII Congreso de Americanistas). México: Secretaría de Educación Pública.

Moser, Christopher L.

1973 Human Decapitation in Ancient Mesoamerica. Dumbarton Oaks, Washington, D.C.

Robertson, Donald

1970 The Tulum murals: The international style of the late Post-Classic. In: Verhandlungen des XXXVIII Internationalen Amerikanistenkongresses, Stuttgart-München, 1968, 2:77–78. München: Klaus Renner.

Seler, Eduard

1904 Die archäologischen Ergebnisse meiner ersten mexikanischen reise. In: Gesammelte Abhandlungen 2:289–367. (Presented to VII International Congress of Americanists, Berlin, 1888.)

1908 Einige fein bemalte alte Thongefässe . . . In: Gesammelte Abhandlungen 3:522–32. (Presented to XV International Congress of Americanists, Quebec, 1906.)

Spores, Ronald M.

1972 An Archaeological Settlement Survey of the Nochixtlan Valley, Oaxaca. Vanderbilt University Publications in Anthropology, no. 1. Nashville.

Toscano, Salvador
1952 Arte precolombino de México y de la América Central. 2nd ed. Universidad Nacional Autónoma de México. México.

CHAPTER 7

Why the Second Codex Selden was Painted[1]

Mary Elizabeth Smith, Professor Emerita

Tulane University

The Codex Selden is one of a group of screenfold manuscripts from the Mixtec-speaking region of southern Mexico.[2] The contents of these manuscripts are genealogical and historical in that they present a chronological account of the native rulers of some of the communities in this region.

The Codex Selden, as we know it today, consists of twenty screenfold pages and sets forth the ruling line of a single Mixtec town. The manuscript focuses on Jaltepec, located in the southwestern section of the Valley of Nochixtlán, the first major valley northwest of the Valley of Oaxaca. The Nochixtlán Valley is located in the mountainous subregion known as the *Mixteca Alta* (Figs. 7.1, 7.2); the second subregion in northern Oaxaca and southern Puebla is known as the *Mixteca Baja* because its average altitude is somewhat lower than that of the Alta; the third subregion, the *Costa,* is the hot lowland area bordered by the Alta on the north and the Pacific Ocean on the south.

The Codex Selden presents over five and one-half centuries of Jaltepec's native nobility in the period prior to the Spanish Conquest and continuing into early Colonial times. The earliest historical date in the manuscript is probably A.D. 988, and the latest date is unquestionably 1556—over three decades after the arrival of the conquistadors in the Mixtec-speaking region.[3]

The codex is today in the Bodleian Library in Oxford, a bequest of the noted English lawyer, John Selden, who died in 1654. We do not know from whom Selden acquired the manuscript nor anything of its history in the century between its completion around 1560 and the death of Selden. The best reproduction of the codex is a color photographic facsimile published in 1964, with a detailed commentary by Alfonso Caso.[4]

Almost three-quarters of the Codex Selden as we know it today is a palimpsest—that is, a "recycling" or reutilization of an earlier manuscript (Burland 1958:361–62; Dark and Plesters 1959; Caso 1964:14–18, 62–66). The original manuscript

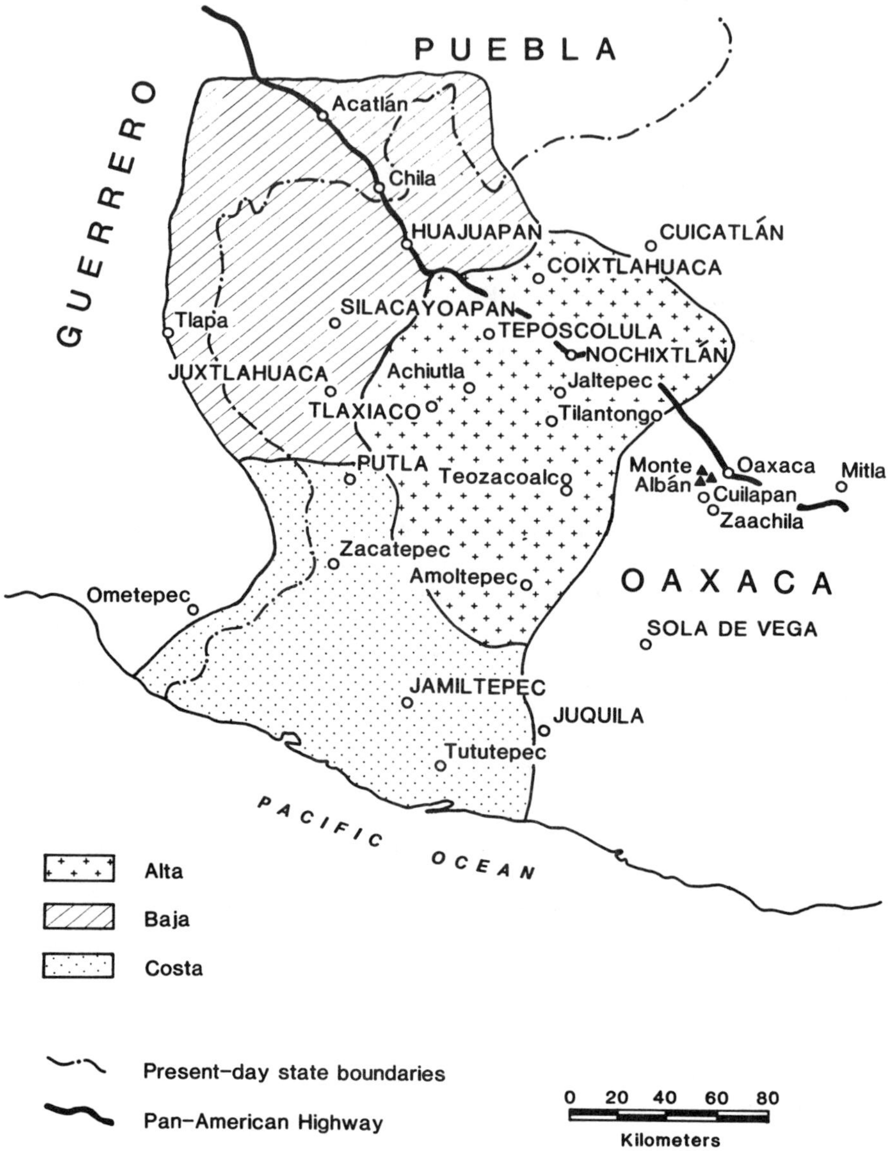

Figure 7.1. Map showing approximate locations of the Alta, Baja, and Costa subregions of the Mixteca.

Figure 7.2. The eastern Mixteca Alta.

was composed of four glued hides, measuring slightly over four meters in total length, and equivalent to screenfold page 1 through almost the end of page 15 of the codex as it is paginated today. At an unknown time, the earlier manuscript was intentionally obliterated: it was partially erased and then covered with an exceptionally thick, gritty coating of the white gesso typically used as the background in prehispanic manuscripts. The painted narrative that we can now see was then added to only one side of the screenfold.

On what is today the reverse of the Codex Selden, barely visible but still illegible traces of the first painting can be glimpsed. All that can be determined of the earlier manuscript's format is that (1) the original codex was painted on both sides of the screenfold (as illustrated in Dark and Plesters 1959:535), (2) the screenfold pages were divided into five registers by red guidelines, and (3) the overall reading order was horizontal.

Presumably at the same time that the earlier codex was covered with white gesso, two hides were added at the end of what is now page 15, making the total length of the codex about five and one-half meters. In the present codex, the upper portion of line IV of page 15, as well as the final pages 16 through 20, were painted on one side of these added hides, with no evidence of an earlier painting on the other side. In addition, the two appended hides are pliable and not as stiff as those of the original codex, perhaps implying that they were not given as careful treatment as the hides on which the earlier manuscript was painted.

The format of the second, visible codex is also different from the now-covered codex. The screenfold pages of the visible Codex Selden are divided into four rather than five registers by red guidelines, and its overall reading order is vertical, from bottom to top, rather than horizontal.

The Codex Selden as we know it today was drawn and painted by the same artist or group of artists (Caso 1964:47, 94). The painted narrative is all "of a piece," notwithstanding the addition of the two hides at the top or end of the manuscript which might imply that later material was added by different hand(s) following the Spanish Conquest. Moreover, even though it was painted over a generation after the Conquest, it does not exhibit obviously intrusive European motifs such as Christian churches, figures with Spanish costumes and metal swords, sun disks with human faces, crescent moons, and the like. It does, however, seem to have been painted very rapidly (Burland 1958:362). Some of the flat areas of paint extend beyond the black frame lines that were added after the paint was applied to the figures. Areas of paint outside the contour lines are especially evident in the forms whose interior is a golden yellow, the color used for human flesh, feline hides, borders of place signs, and the lower borders of women's skirts.

In summary, the Codex Selden, as we know it today, presents the genealogy of the native rulers of the Mixtec community of Jaltepec, and this manuscript was painted with dispatch after 1556, in a traditional native style. Three-quarters of the visible codex was placed on top of one side of an earlier codex that was first completely covered with white gesso, and the remainder of the visible codex is on two added hides that were not made stiff as were the hides of the original manuscript. The arrangement of guidelines and overall reading order of the second codex were completely different from those of the illegible first codex. Is the codex that we know today a revised version of the material presented in the original manuscript, or does it represent different, unrelated material? We cannot answer this question until it is possible to recover at least part of the text of the first codex. In the meantime, I would like to offer a suggestion as to why the second Codex Selden was painted.

The Dispute Between Jaltepec and Yanhuitlán Over Zahuatlán

Beginning at least as early as 1539, Jaltepec—the town whose native rulers are the principal subject of the visible Codex Selden—was engaged in a major dispute with its neighbor, Yanhuitlán, the most important town in the northern section of the Valley of Nochixtlán. Both Jaltepec and Yanhuitlán claimed the community of Zahuatlán as a subject town. (As can be seen in Fig. 7.2, Zahuatlán is located in the southwestern section of the Nochixtlán Valley, about 8 km north of Jaltepec and 18 km southeast of Yanhuitlán.) I believe that the second Codex Selden was painted *specifically* to be presented in court to support Jaltepec's side in the litigation over Zahuatlán.

Regrettably, the documents engendered by the Jaltepec-Yanhuitlán dispute have not yet been located, if they still exist. But the case was of sufficient importance and duration that it was described in early Colonial documents that were concerned with other matters.

AGN-Inquisición 37, expedientes 7–10

This document in Mexico's national archive, the Archivo General de la Nación (AGN), deals with a famous idolatry case of the mid-1540s, in which the native nobility of Yanhuitlán were accused of performing prehispanic ceremonies, including human and animal sacrifice. Portions of this important case have been quoted in a commentary on the Colonial Codex of Yanhuitlán by Wigberto Jiménez Moreno and Salvador Mateos Higuera (1940), and the litigation has also been discussed by Ronald Spores (1967:25–27, 96–98, 134–35, 228–31) and Richard E. Greenleaf (1969:75–80; 1985:172). The entire document has recently been published with introductory essays by Richard E. Greenleaf and Maarten E.R.G.N. Jansen (1991).

In this trial, one of the arguments in defense of the accused, Domingo de Guzmán, the native ruler of Yanhuitlán from the time of the Spanish Conquest until 1558, was that neighboring towns, including Jaltepec, were maliciously presenting false information about him and his co-defendants. In 1545, witnesses were asked whether the native ruler and secondary nobility of Jaltepec were, and continued to be, mortal enemies of Domingo de Guzmán because Jaltepec and Yanhuitlán had, roughly six years earlier (ca. 1539), engaged in serious lawsuits and disputes over the subject town of Zahuatlán and other lands and boundaries (exp. 9, fol. 281, question viii).

We do not know the results of the litigation over Zahuatlán mentioned in the Inquisition document. But, even if a ruling on the case had been made prior to 1545, the decision apparently did not satisfy both claimants. Both Jaltepec and Yanhuitlán listed Zahuatlán as a subject town in the *Suma de visitas,* a survey of Mexican towns compiled between 1547 and 1550 that provides information on the tribute-paying population (Paso y Troncoso 1905–1906, I:131, 309–10).

AGI-Escribanía de Cámara 162-C, legajo 5

This important document in the Archivo General de Indias (AGI) in Seville deals with the claim of the town of Tecomatlán that it had never been a subject of Yanhuitlán but was an independent town in its own right. Tecomatlán is in the southwestern section of the Valley of Nochixtlán, only 5 km west of Zahuatlán (Fig. 7.2). The document is over five hundred folios and details litigation that took place in the early 1580s.[5] It has been utilized extensively in the book-length studies on prehispanic and posthispanic Mixtec culture by Ronald Spores (1967, 1984), who has published excerpts of the original document (1967:194–219).

In this litigation, as in the earlier Inquisition proceedings, a definite anti-Yanhuitlán faction is identified, and this faction again includes the town of Jaltepec.[6] When a group of witnesses is asked why Jaltepec opposes the claims of Yanhuitlán, they state that Jaltepec is against Yanhuitlán because of an earlier dispute between the two communities over a subject town that one witness names as Zahuatlán. They further state that there is animosity between Jaltepec and Yanhuitlán because Gabriel de Guzmán, the native ruler of Yanhuitlán from 1558 to 1591, refused to marry a noblewoman from Jaltepec nor would he allow his son to marry a noblewoman from that town.[7]

Thus, the Jaltepec-Yanhuitlán legal battle over the two towns' rival claims to control Zahuatlán is referred to in documents of the mid-1540s and early 1580s, in two different legal cases involving two generations of native rulers of this region. By the time of the 1580s *Escribanía de Cámara* document, the dispute would seem to have been settled in favor of Yanhuitlán because in this document, witnesses from Zahuatlán testify on behalf of Yanhuitlán.[8] Moreover, a 1565 listing of Yanhuitlán's subject towns that is included in the *Escribanía de Cámara* document (published in Spores 1967:194–96) contains the Mixtec name of Zahuatlán: *yucu nicata,* or "the hill that danced." Nonetheless, one of the witnesses who testifies as to why Jaltepec is anti-Yanhuitlán is from Zahuatlán, and in this instance the town is described as a "subject of Jaltepec" (fol. 230v). Again, in the 1580s, as in the mid-1540s, even though an official ruling may have been reached in the Zahuatlán case, there still seems to have been dissenting opinions on the decision.

Without question, Jaltepec and Yanhuitlán were involved in a mid-sixteenth-century dispute over the town of Zahuatlán, even if we do not know the location of the documents that described this litigation. If, as postulated, the Codex Selden was painted to support Jaltepec's claim that Zahuatlán was its subject, how is Zahuatlán presented in the pictorial text of the codex?

The Sign of Zahuatlán in the Codex Selden

The pictorial sign of the town of Zahuatlán was first identified in the Colonial screenfold known as the Codex Muro (Smith 1973b, 1983a), a manuscript that lists the rulers of San Pedro Cántaros and San Miguel Adeques, located east of the Nochixtlán Valley. In this codex, the sign appears accompanied by the inscription *yucu nicata* ("the hill that danced"), the Mixtec name of Zahuatlán given in the *Escribanía de Cámara* document's 1565 list of Yanhuitlán subjects (Spores 1967:195). The pictorial sign in the Codex Muro (Fig. 7.3d) consists of the standardized bell-shaped hill form (*yucu*) with a male figure holding a flower in one hand and a rattle or weapon in the other, depicting the verb "to dance" (*cata,* prefaced by the past-tense prefix *ni-*).

The Zahuatlán sign occurs three times in the Codex Selden. In its earliest appearance (Fig. 7.3a), it is the third of fourteen signs of places listed between pages 3-IV and 4-III of the codex acknowledging the authority of the first ruler of Jaltepec in the late tenth century.[9]

The second appearance of the sign is on page 11-II (Fig. 7.3b), where it is shown as the hometown of the parents of a woman who marries a ruler of Jaltepec. This marriage is not accompanied by a date but probably took place in the first half of the fourteenth century, over three centuries after the first appearance of Zahuatlán in the codex. The ruler of Jaltepec who intermarries with Zahuatlán has a calendrical name of 13 Wind and a personal name of "Enemy-Ballcourt," and he seems to re-establish the Jaltepec ruling line after over a century of confusion that occurs in the pictorial narrative on the previous two pages of the manuscript. That is, the succession of rulers on pages 9 and 10 is unclear, because the section between pages 9-II and 11-III contains no dates, and the Jaltepec sign does not appear between 9-II and 10-IV.

The third and final appearance of the sign Zahuatlán is on page 13-II (Fig. 7.3c), where it is shown as being conquered by Jaltepec—specifically, by 13 Wind's son 9 Lizard "Flames-Face with Diagonal Black Lines," who is attacking the town of his mother. This conquest may have occurred in the year 1383.[10]

On the line immediately following the conquest of Zahuatlán is the marriage of 9 Lizard's son to a woman descended from rulers of the important Mixteca Alta town of Tilantongo and Teozacoalco. Beginning with this marriage, and continuing throughout the remaining seven and one-half pages of the Codex Selden, the pictorial narrative settles into a very standardized and explicit genealogical document in its presentation of the final nine generations of Jaltepec's rulers (Table 7.1, a-b). These rulers and their siblings are born, and they marry. The fourth, fifth, and sixth of the final nine rulers are each shown as making a single conquest (Selden 15-IV, 16-III, 17-II). But no one ruler's biography is treated in any detail, and no one from Jaltepec is shown as being conquered or sacrificed.[11] The only major break in the Jaltepec ruling line depicted in the final pages of the codex occurs between generations 7 and 8 in Table 7.1b, when the Jaltepec ruler apparently dies without heirs, and the rulership of that town is assumed by a nobleman from Tilantongo whose mother was from Jaltepec (Caso 1964:45, 92; Aróstegui 1977).[12]

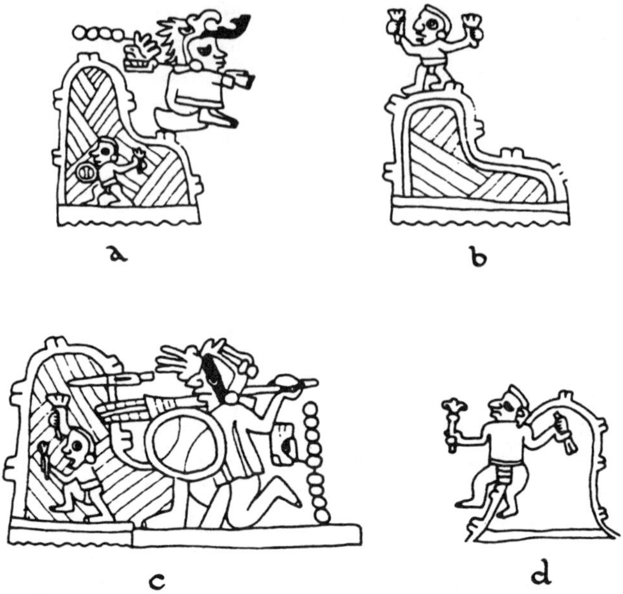

Figure 7.3. The place sign of Zahuatlán: (*a*) Codex Selden 3-IV; (*b*) Codex Selden 11-II; (*c*) Codex Selden 13-II; (*d*) Codex Muro 7.

What the pictorial text of the Codex Selden seems to be saying about Zahuatlán and its relationship to Jaltepec is as follows: Zahuatlán has acknowledged the sovereignty of the Jaltepec nobility since the time of Jaltepec's first ruler (Selden 3–4). After a century of confusion (Selden 9–10), a woman of Zahuatlán married a ruler of Jaltepec (Selden 11-II), and since that time the Jaltepec line has continued in a line of direct descent (*por línea recta*) into the Colonial period. The control of Zahuatlán by Jaltepec was definitely settled in 1383 (Selden 13-II) by the conquest of Zahuatlán by a ruler of Jaltepec who was the legitimate son of his father, who also ruled Jaltepec, and his mother, a noblewoman of Zahuatlán. Since 1383, Zahuatlán has been a subject of Jaltepec, not of Yanhuitlán.

Atypical Features of the Codex Selden

In many respects, the Codex Selden is similar to Mixtec manuscripts that are considered to have been painted before the Conquest, such as the codices Nuttall, Bodley, and Vindobonensis. All were painted on screenfolds of animal hide, with each screenfold page divided into registers by red guidelines. The arrangement of the guidelines may vary from one codex to another, but in all instances they

TABLE 7.1a
The Final Nine Generations of Jaltepec's Rulers in the Codex Selden

Part A: Generations 1-5

Generation	Male	Female	Place
1	♂ 2-Tiger "Tiger-Smoking Earth Monster"	♀ 1-Serpent "Sun"	TILANTONGO - TEOZACOALCO
2	♂ 5-Water "Tiger-Visible Eye"	♀ 7-Rain "Feather Fan-Visible Eye"	TLAXIACO
3	♂ 10-Monkey "Rain Deity-Sky-Wavy Lines"	♀ 5-Water "Earth Figure Emerging from Jewel"	PLAIN WITH CROSSED STONE LEGS
4	*♂ 3-Death "Eagle-Quetzal" (died 1444)	♀ 3-Serpent "Garland of Cocoa Flowers"	HILL WITH BLACKENED TOP, SWIRL OF WATER
5	*♂ 1-Monkey "Rain Deity-Sun (died 1480)"	*♀ 7-Water "Sun-Quetzal Feathers" (died 1477)	TILANTONGO

Continued on Part B with son ♂ 4-Serpent

* Death Indicated by a mummy bundle

delineate a reading order that is a meander or boustrophedonic pattern. In addition, as noted above, the Codex Selden has no obvious European motifs.

Nonetheless, at least four features of the codex suggest that it was painted for an audience other than the native nobility of Jaltepec whose genealogy is set forth in the manuscript. More specifically, these features seem to corroborate the hypothesis that the codex was painted to be used in a Colonial court of law.

TABLE 7.1b
The Final Nine Generations of Jaltepec's Rulers in the Codex Selden

Part B: Generations 6-9

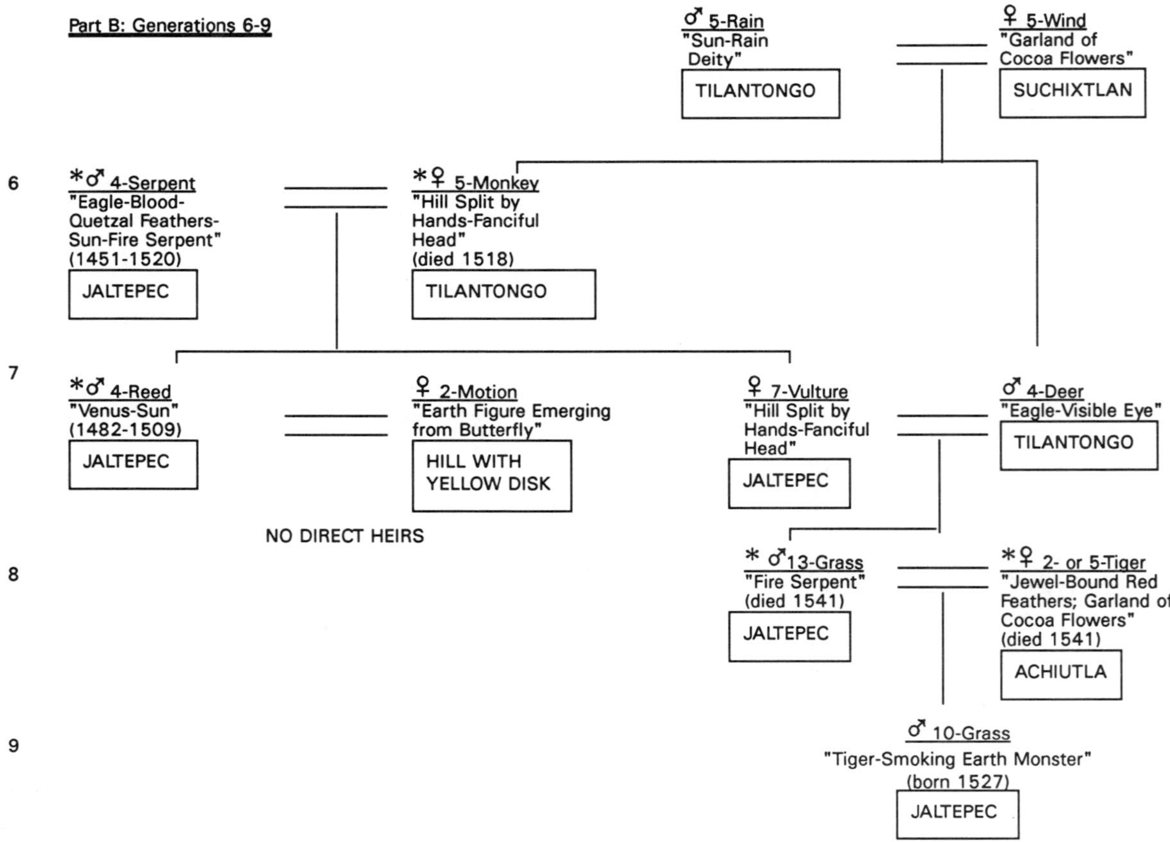

* Death indicated by a mummy bundle

Presentation of the Genealogy of a Single Community

Mixtec manuscripts that are considered to be prehispanic, such as the Codex Bodley and the genealogical side of the Codex Nuttall (pages 1–41 of the 1902 edition), present partial genealogies of the native nobility of more than one community.[13] By way of contrast, Mixtec manuscripts painted after the Conquest characteristically present the hereditary rulers of only one community and usually include only those rulers who inherit, while omitting subsidiary offspring or any mention of actual or potential conflict over succession. The simple one-community king list is a standard feature of Colonial Mixtec genealogical manuscripts whether they are painted on traditional hide screenfolds, such as the codices Egerton 2895 (Burland 1965; König 1979) and Muro (Smith 1973b); on *tiras* or long strips of hide not scored in a screenfold fashion, such as the Codex Tulane (Smith and Parmenter 1991); on *lienzos,* or large cloth documents, such as the second Lienzo of Tequixtepec (Caso 1979:239; Parmenter 1982:56–58); or on European paper, such as the two genealogies on the map painted to accompany the 1580 *Relación geográfica* of Teozacoalco (Caso 1949; Acuña 1984, II:129–47).

The simplified king lists of the Colonial period were made to demonstrate to the Spanish administrators that the native nobility of a single town descended in a direct line. In these lists, the possible competitors for the community's rulership—brothers, sisters, cousins, nephews and nieces—are not mentioned. Rather, the genealogy is presented as a *fait accompli* of uncontested legitimate succession.

Thus, because it deals with the rulers of only one town, the Codex Selden was intended for a Colonial rather than a native audience. But the codex names many of the subsidiary offspring of the principal town, as well as showing the sacrifice of offspring who did not inherit and some of the diplomatic problems of those who did. For this reason, the Codex Selden seems to be transitional between such prehispanic manuscripts as the codices Bodley and Nuttall with their genealogical complexities and the typical Colonial king lists that depict only the inheriting rulers and their spouses.

Format

The Codex Selden is the only extant screenfold manuscript from the Mixtec-speaking or any other region of Mesoamerica whose overall reading order is vertical (from bottom to top) rather than horizontal (Paso y Troncoso 1898:204–5, note l; Burland 1958:362; Nicholson 1967:257). Even those Colonial Mixtec screenfolds that present a simple king list of one community have an overall horizontal reading order, as exemplified by the codices Egerton 2895, Muro, and the Vienna portion of Becker II.

The principal source of information on the prehispanic use and display of the painted screenfolds is the seventeenth-century Dominican friar Francisco de Burgoa, who wrote prolix accounts of some of the towns in Oaxaca in the 1660s—well over a century after the Spanish conquest of this region (Burgoa 1934a, 1934b).

Concerning the screenfolds, Burgoa stated that they were customarily unfolded to their full length and affixed to rooms belonging to the nobility. Then those who were knowledgeable of their contents would explain the stories depicted in them.[14]

This type of display of an unfolded screenfold is eminently possible with manuscripts whose overall reading order is horizontal. But it would be difficult to impossible with the Codex Selden because of its unique vertical reading order. When unfolded, this codex is about five-and-one-half meters in height, and thus it would have been impractical to display it in a typical domestic space. I believe that the manuscript's format indicates that it was not painted to be used by the native nobility of Jaltepec in a traditional manner, but to be presented to outsiders—in this case, the judge who presided over the Jaltepec-Yanhuitlán dispute over Zahuatlán.

The Date on the Outside Front Cover

A prehispanic style of date is the only visible pictorial motif on the outside front cover of the Codex Selden. (I am using the term "outside front cover" to refer to the screenfold section that is on the back of the first page of the codex as we know it today.) This date is definitely associated with the second or visible codex because at the corners of the cover where the white ground has worn away, vestiges of the palimpsest or earlier codex can be seen.[15]

The date is appended to a prehispanic style of "A-O year sign," used in central Puebla and southward into the Mixtec region to signal a year-date. The date on the cover is the year 2 Flint and the day 5 Reed.

To my knowledge, the painting of a prehispanic style date on the outside of a screenfold manuscript is unique to the Codex Selden, as is this codex's overall vertical reading order. What year does the date represent, and why was it painted on the codex?

Alfonso Caso (1950; 1964:11–14, 49, 61–62, 95) believed that the date was prefatory, referring to a year that was earlier than the first date on page 1 of the manuscript. Philip Dark (1958b:1–2; 1959:524) suggested that the date was an ending date that represents the year 1560. He postulated that the codex might have been painted in that year because the latest date on the final page of the manuscript is 1556. Dark's suggestion seems to me to be the more plausible, although we may never be able to correlate this date with certainty because of its unique placement on the outside cover and because any Mixtec year-date can occur once every fifty-two years. Moreover, the date on the outside of the codex does not seem to relate to any of the dated events in the narrative presented in the twenty painted pages of the manuscript.[16]

If the date on the cover of the Codex Selden corresponds to 1560, this may have been the year the codex was presented in court. In many respects, this date seems to be equivalent to that given in the opening sentence of Colonial legal documents. But, instead of giving a date in the European manner, such as "on the twenty-sixth day of the month of March of 1569," the date on the outside of the codex gives a date in the prehispanic manner: "on the day 5 Reed in the year 2 Flint." By the time this codex was painted, the native nobility of the Mixtec region were well aware of the requirements of the Spanish Colonial legal system. Thus, the date on the outside of the manuscript, although very much prehispanic in style and content, may have functioned in the same manner as the dates in alphabetic script in Colonial documents.

Mummy Bundles

Another unusual feature of the Codex Selden is the large number of mummy bundles that appear in the concluding pages of the manuscript (Smith 1973a:34, note 54). The mummy bundle is a typical prehispanic convention used to indicate that a person is dead. In the Mixtec manuscripts, it generally consists of a vertical oval of cloth bound with diagonal patterns of ropes and with the head of the deceased person shown on top of the bundle.

The quantity of mummy bundles in the final four pages of the Codex Selden is atypical because the deaths of most individuals in the Mixtec manuscripts are not shown at all. They are born, they marry, their children are born, and then they do not appear again. The exceptions to this generalization are usually persons who meet a dramatic end by sacrifice or those whose deaths are shown to clarify problems of succession. In the Codex Selden, prior to page 16-II, only two mummy bundles occur.[17]

Beginning on page 16-II, five of the final six male rulers of Jaltepec are shown as mummy bundles with the dates of their deaths given. (The last ruler of Jaltepec in the codex, born in 1527, was still alive when the manuscript was painted.) Even more unusual is the depiction of the deaths of three of the wives of the five rulers shown as mummy bundles. Like their husbands, the deaths of the women are indicated by mummy bundles accompanied by dates. Only one woman in the Mixtec codices is shown as a mummy bundle, and female deaths are rarely recorded at all.[18] The names of Jaltepec nobility who appear as mummy bundles in the concluding pages of the codex are indicated by an asterisk in Table 7.1. In addition, on Selden 20-I is an enthroned mummy bundle of a man whose personal name is "Eagle-Quetzal Feathers" but whose identity is uncertain.[19] Thus, the final three-plus pages of the codex contain nine mummy bundles: five of Jaltepec's male rulers, three of their wives, and one of a male ruler who may have had a potential claim to inherit Jaltepec. Why does this plethora of mummy bundles occur on the concluding pages of the manuscript, with the death-dates explicitly given?

I believe that the mummy bundles, although unquestionably a prehispanic convention, are being used in the Codex Selden to convey information to a Colonial court of law. Specifically, the bundles express the Spanish phrase *ya difunto* ("now deceased"). This phrase occurs frequently in Colonial documents, especially in those in which legitimate succession is being established. A native ruler will state that he is legitimately descended in a direct line from his ancestors, whom he will name; and, if they are dead, he will describe them as *ya difunto*.

The type of information that the final four pages of the Codex Selden conveys is similar to that presented in a late Colonial and completely European style of genealogical tree (Fig. 7.4). This drawing was made in 1783 to support the claim of Manuel de los Reyes to the native rulership of Juxtlahuaca in the western Mixteca Baja (AGN-Ramo de Tierras 1097, exp. 8). Manuel maintained that he was the only possible male heir to the rulership, formerly held by his father's cousin Rafael (whose name appears within the circle with an elaborate flower on the left side of the drawing). To demonstrate that he is the logical heir, the names of all family members who might also be possible inheritors and who are now dead are followed by the Spanish word *muerto* ("deceased"). This word accompanies the names of all the relatives of Manuel's father's generation and his grandfather's generation, as well as the names of two of Manuel's three brothers. (A third brother, Antonio, is considered mentally incompetent [*mantecoto*]).

The mummy bundles on the last three-plus pages of the Codex Selden are comparable to the word *muerto* in the late eighteenth-century drawing. The bundles indicate which ancestors and relatives of the Jaltepec ruling line were deceased and demonstrate to Colonial administrators that this rulership descended in a straight line (illustrated by the central trunk of the genealogical tree in Fig. 7.4).

The specific indication of which members of a family were deceased was not necessary in codices that were painted for local use in the community. Within any given community, everyone would know who was dead and who was not. But an official in a law court outside of the community would not have this knowledge; and thus, indicating those who were deceased—as the presentation of the genealogy of a single community—would eliminate the number of potential claimants to the native rulership.

Thus the mummy bundles in the final pages of the Codex Selden are not obviously Colonial motifs, but the information they convey was necessary for Colonial litigation. In essence, they represent an adaptation of the prehispanic writing system to produce a text that would satisfy Colonial officials.

Conclusions

Three features of the Codex Selden are unique to this manuscript and do not occur in the other extant Mixtec screenfolds: the overall vertical reading order, the prehispanic style date on the outside cover, and the carefully recorded and dated deaths of the rulers on the final pages of the codex.

These features seem to indicate that the manuscript was painted for an audience outside the community of Jaltepec, whose native rulers were the primary concern

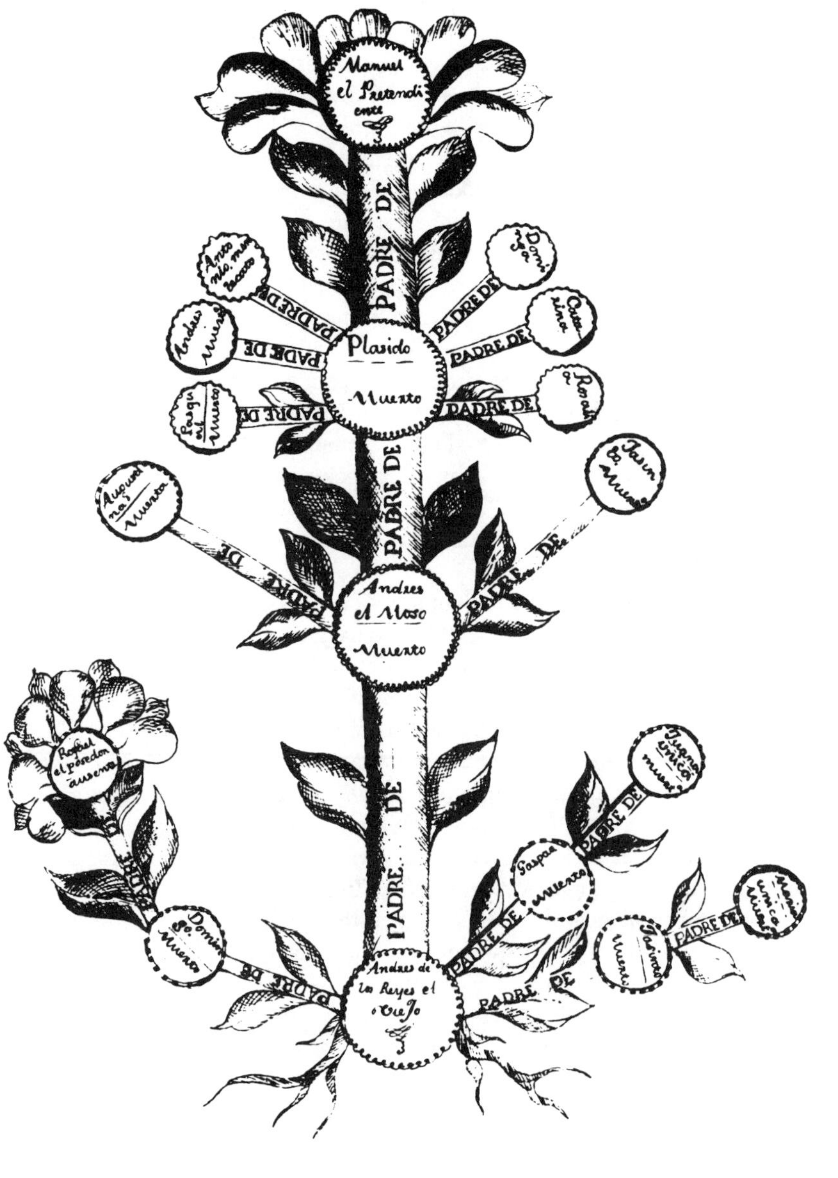

Figure 7.4. Genealogical tree of Manuel de los Reyes of Juxtlahuaca, 1783. Archivo General de la Nación, Ramo de Tierras 1097, expediente 8, folio 19.

of the codex. The vertical reading order of the Selden would make it difficult to display around the walls of a room, as was reported to have been done when a manuscript remained in the community. It could, however, have been unfolded on a table in a courtroom, much as the facsimile can be unfolded on a library table today. The date on the cover can be correlated with the year 1560, four years after the latest date at the end of the codex. Possibly 1560 was when the codex was presented in court, and the prehispanic style date may have functioned in the same manner as dates written in European script that prefaced Colonial legal documents. The explicitly dated deaths of five of the six final rulers of Jaltepec and three of their wives, all of whom are shown as mummy bundles, informed the Colonial administrators that these persons were deceased (*ya difunto* or *muerto*). This type of information was not necessary in codices painted for the native nobility, and thus the deaths of very few persons were recorded in prehispanic manuscripts.

In presenting the genealogy of a single community, the Codex Selden is transitional between prehispanic manuscripts that include partial genealogies of several towns and the standard Colonial "king lists" that set forth only the inheriting rulers of one town. The codex depicts subsidiary non-inheriting offspring, but focuses on the Jaltepec ruling line.

The Codex Selden, although undoubtedly commissioned by the native nobility of Jaltepec, was painted to be presented to outsiders. It seems to me probable that the manuscript, which seems to have been completed very rapidly, was prepared as evidence in the major litigation in which Jaltepec was engaged in the early Colonial period: the town's dispute with Yanhuitlán over the town of Zahuatlán, claimed by both Jaltepec and Yanhuitlán to have been its subject. This hypothesis is substantiated by the contexts in which Zahuatlán appears in the pictorial text of the Codex Selden. According to this text, Zahuatlán acknowledged the authority of Jaltepec's first ruler and later sent a daughter to marry a Jaltepec ruler, with the son of this marriage shown as conquering Zahuatlán. As far as the nobility of Jaltepec was concerned, this conquest settled the question of Zahuatlán more than a century before the Colonial dispute with Yanhuitlán.

The Codex Selden illustrates the adaptation made by the native nobility in the Colonial period in its attempt to cope with an imported legal process. The writing system and pictorial style of the codex are essentially pre-Conquest, as is the screenfold format with the division of each page into registers separated by red guidelines. But prehispanic forms such as mummy bundles were used to convey explicit information to outsiders—in the case of this motif, to tell a court of law that individuals who were potential heirs were deceased. The narrow focus on a single community seen in the Codex Selden is also characteristic of early Colonial Mixtec pictorial documents. This focus is even more restricted in contemporaneous manuscripts, which show only the couples who actually inherit one town. In the Mixtec-speaking region, the adaptation and reduction of the rich pictorial narratives of the prehispanic period continued until almost the end of the sixteenth century, when the more economical form of writing in European script supplanted the pre-Conquest writing system.

Notes

1. In 1978, a fellowship from the John Simon Guggenheim Memorial Foundation made it possible for me to conduct research in the Archivo General de Indias in Seville and to study the Codex Selden in the Bodleian Library in Oxford. Helpful comments and suggestions on this paper were offered by Nicholas Johnson, Ross Parmenter, Emily Rabin, and Nancy P. Troike. Figures 7.1 and 7.2 were drawn by Shelley Choy, and Figure 7.3 by Caren Walt. Table 7.1 was prepared by Kathleen Burke.
2. As defined by James Cooper Clark (1912:7, 33), this group includes—in addition to the Codex Selden—the codices Nuttall (Troike and Anders 1987), Bodley (Caso 1960), Colombino (Caso and Smith 1966), Becker I (Nowotny 1961a), and Vindobonensis (Adelhofer 1974). (The references given above are for the best reproductions of these manuscripts.) Prior to the establishment of a Mixtec origin for these manuscripts by Alfonso Caso (1949), this corpus was also called the "Nuttall Group" (Glass and Robertson 1975:171) after one of the best-known manuscripts in the group, the Codex Nuttall. Except for the Codex Selden, all the screenfolds listed above are considered to have been painted before the Conquest. In addition to these screenfolds, there has survived from the Mixtec-speaking region a substantial number of Colonial pictorial manuscripts that still exhibit elements of native style (Glass 1975:67–73; Welte 1981).
3. Alfonso Caso (1950, 1964) proposed correlations for the year-dates in the Codex Selden, but these correlations are in the process of being revised by Emily Rabin (1981). She believes, however, that beginning with the 3 Flint year-date on page 16-II of the codex (correlated by Caso as 1444) and continuing through the end of the manuscript, the Caso correlation is correct (Emily Rabin, pers. comm.). Table 7.1 of this paper, which sets forth the final nine generations of Jaltepec's rulers in the Codex Selden, includes only those dates on which Caso and Rabin are in agreement.

   I am proposing that the earliest historical date in the manuscript is the 2 Flint date on page 3-I, associated with the beginning of the ceremonies participated in by the first Jaltepec ruler. Rabin considers this date to be 988 in the Christian calendar. The dates on the opening two pages are probably metaphorical or mythological rather than historical (Furst 1978b; Jansen 1988).
4. The Codex Selden was first published in a color lithographic edition of a copy drawn by A. Aglio in Lord Kingsborough's monumental *Antiquities of Mexico* (1831, volume 1). José Corona Núñez (1964–1967) published some of the pictorial manuscripts included in Kingsborough, illustrating them in color photographs rather than reproducing the earlier lithographs from Kingsborough. In the Corona Núñez edition, the Codex Selden appears on pp. 77–99 of the second volume, with the screenfold pages of the codex on the recto pages and a short description of their contents on the facing verso pages. The quality of this color reproduction is not as good as that of the facsimile accompanying the Caso 1964 commentary. The Bodleian Library, Oxford (1972), has published a pamphlet on its collection of Mexican codices, with a brief introduction by

A.R. Pagden and black-and-white photographs of the entirety of pages 1, 5, 6, 8, 10, 11, and 13 of the Codex Selden, as well as a detail of page 6. The pioneering study by Alfonso Caso (1949) on the map that accompanied the 1580 *Relación geográfica* of Teozacoalco was the impetus for later studies that dealt exclusively or primarily with the Codex Selden. In a paper on the reverse or historical section of the Codex Vindobonensis, Caso (1950) included a list of his proposed correlation of dates in the codex, and this was reprinted, with slight revisions, in his 1964 commentary on the manuscript. As mentioned in note 3, this correlation is currently being revised by Emily Rabin. Cottie A. Burland (1958) characterized some of the ethnographic features of the codex, such as costume, weapons, architecture, and ceremonial objects.

Philip Dark (1958a) used the Codex Selden, as well as the obverse of the Codex Bodley, to analyze the genealogical relationships in the Mixtec codices. Caso (1959) wrote a detailed review of this book-length study. Dark (1958b) also related the pictorial narratives of the codices Selden and Bodley with the archaeological sequences of southern Mexico. He further suggested that the Codex Selden might be from, or at least related to, the town of Amoltepec in the southern Mixteca Alta because of a gloss in European script on the cover containing the phrase "*yuchaña* . . .", which he felt was *yucu nama,* the Mixtec name of Amoltepec (Dark 1959). Dark and Joyce Plesters (1959) published one of the first detailed discussions of the palimpsest problems of the codex, although the palimpsest had been discovered in 1950 by Caso (1964:14–18, 62–66) and described in the same year by Burland (1950 report summarized in Burland 1958:361–62, and quoted in Caso 1964:14–15, 62–63). H. B. Nicholson (1967), in a review of Caso's 1964 publication of the Codex Selden, summarized the status of Mixtec studies in the mid-1960s and was the first to suggest that Caso's correlations of Mixtec dates with the Christian calendar might need revision.

The Codex Selden was also given major consideration in Caso's two-volume work, *Reyes y reinos de la mixteca,* published almost a decade after his death on November 30, 1970. In the first volume, the genealogical material from the codex is considered in a chronological context and related to contemporaneous data in other manuscripts (Caso 1977:60–67, 72–76, 90–98, 154–55). The second volume (Caso 1979) is a biographical dictionary of the persons in the Mixtec and Mixtec-related pictorial documents and includes the *dramatis personae* of Selden.

In a paper delivered at the 1974 International Congress of Americanists in Mexico City, I suggested that the town with which the Codex Selden is most concerned is Jaltepec in the Nochixtlán Valley (Smith 1983a). The sign representing this town's name had previously been described in English as "Cloud-Belching Mountain" by Spinden (1935) and in Spanish as "Montaña que Escupe" by Caso (e.g., 1951, 1964, 1977, 1979). I further postulated that the phrase "*yuchaña* . . ." written on the cover of the codex was not, as thought by Dark (1959), the Mixtec name of Amoltepec, but the name of Chachoapan (*yuta ñani*) in the Nochixtlán Valley.

Carlos Aróstegui (1977) discussed the Codex Selden's depiction of frequent intermarriage between Jaltepec and Tilantongo in the century and a half prior to the Spanish Conquest. In the summer of 1978, at a conference held in Oaxaca (summarized in Jansen and Gaxiola 1978), several scholars made important observations about the codex. Maarten Jansen and Wigberto Jiménez Moreno independently discovered that the calendrical names of the ancient ancestors on the opening two pages of the manuscript (the male 2 Grass and female 8 Rabbit), who are the parents of the first historical ruler, occur as a metaphorical date in Codex Vindobonensis 42d and 1a. John Pohl pointed out that the two bundles being tied by priests on Selden 3-I are associated with this pair of ancient ancestors. Jiménez Moreno also identified a place sign that consists of a platform and flames as Achiutla in the Mixteca Alta. Not only do the rulers of Jaltepec in the Codex Selden intermarry with nobility from this town (pages 17-IV and 19-II), but the male ancient ancestor 2 Grass is shown as being born from a tree at Achiutla (page 2-I).

In a paper on the nonhistorical dates in Mixtec codices, Jansen (1988:170) noted that the first date in the codex—the year 3 Reed and the day 2 House—is used commemoratively in Bodley 32–31, II, by the important early twelfth-century Mixtec ruler 4 Wind, whose mother 6 Monkey was from Jaltepec. On pages 8-IV of the Selden Codex, the biography of 4 Wind is not related in the detail that it is on pages 34–28 of the Bodley reverse, where the 3 Reed, 2 House date was apparently deliberately chosen for 4 Wind's enthronement. The 3 Reed date in the lower right corner of the first page of the Codex Selden is partially damaged and had been interpreted earlier by Caso (1964:23, 71) as being 4 or possibly 5 Reed.

Several segments of the Codex Selden have received more detailed study. The most frequently analyzed portion is the biography of the female ruler 6 Monkey on pages 6 through 8 of the manuscript. The story of this woman, who lived in the late eleventh century, was first told by Herbert J. Spinden (1935) in an important early study of Mixtec manuscript painting. Since then, the life and times of 6 Monkey have been discussed by Caso (1964:32–37, 79–84; 1979:259–62), Jansen and Pérez (1986), Anders and Jansen (1988:173–83), and Byland and Pohl (n.d.). Joseph Whitecotton (1990:78–106) has suggested that 6 Monkey and her husband 11 Wind were named as the first rulers of the town of Iztepec (present-day Santa Cruz Mixtepec in the southwestern section of the Valley of Oaxaca) in a Colonial Zapotec painting on hide known as the "Yale Genealogy." In addition, three generations of this couple's descendants depicted on Selden 8-IV through 9-IV also appear in the same genealogical relationship in the Yale manuscript.

Pages 11–13 have also been the subject of more detailed consideration. I focus on these pages in a paper on the regional viewpoint of the codex (Smith 1983b). Maarten Jansen (1983, 1989:73–74) discusses the excursion by the principal male ruler depicted in these pages—9 Lizard "Face with Diagonal Black Lines"—to the region of central Puebla north of the Mixteca, including his marriage to a woman of Cuauhtinchan, Puebla.

The Codex Selden has also been discussed in general studies of the Mixtec-speaking region and its manuscripts (e.g., Dahlgren 1954; Caso 1960b, 1966; Nowotny 1961b; Smith 1973a, 1988; Furst 1977; Anawalt 1981; Robertson 1982; Jansen 1989) and in works devoted to other Mixtec manuscripts such as the codices Bodley (Caso 1960a), Colombino-Becker I (Caso in Caso and Smith 1966; Troike 1974), and Vindobonensis (Furst 1978a; Jansen 1982a). Brief descriptions of the codex have been included in the listings of Mexican manuscripts compiled by Lehmann (1905:271, no. 4), Alcina Franch (1955:480, no. 7), and Glass and Robertson (1975:195–96, no. 283).

5. The dispute between Tecomatlán and Yanhuitlán is also described in documents in Mexico's AGN: Ramo de Tierras 985 and 986, exp. 1. The genealogy of rulers claimed by Tecomatlán in volume 986 has been published by Berlin (1947).
6. In addition to Jaltepec, the towns whose citizens consistently testified against Yanhuitlán were: Etlatongo (on the western edge of the Nochixtlán Valley), Mitlatongo and Malinaltepec or present-day Yucuañe (in the Mixteca Alta outside the Valley of Nochixtlán), Ixcuintepec or present-day Peñoles (west of the Valley of Oaxaca), Tenango (in the District of Etla), and Tutla (presumably Santa María Tutla on the northern edge of the Mixteca Alta bordering the Mixteca Baja).
7. As far as can be determined from the Codex Selden, no intermarriage occurred between

Jaltepec and Yanhuitlán prior to the Conquest, as well. More specifically, no one from Jaltepec married anyone from a town represented by the known or conjectured signs of Yanhuitlán (Caso 1966 and 1977:110–14; Smith 1973a:62–65). Nonetheless, the native rulers of Jaltepec did intermarry with the secondary nobility who controlled at least one of Yanhuitlán's subject towns. In the Inquisition document discussed above, one witness (a priest named Juan Ruanes) testified in 1545 that he always thought that Jaltepec and Yanhuitlán were friendly because a daughter of the native nobility of Jaltepec had married a *principal* (secondary noble) of Yanhuitlán (AGN-Inquisición 37, exp. 9, fol. 283). This marriage is probably depicted on page 19-III of the Codex Selden where a woman from Jaltepec is shown as marrying a man from Suchixtlán (whose sign is a platform with white four-petaled flowers), a town considered to have been a subject of Yanhuitlán in the sixteenth century. (For example, in 1591 Suchixtlán, called "Ixquixochitlan," is considered a subject of Yanhuitlán in AGN-Ramo de Tierras 985, cuaderno 2, fol. 42v, 49v.) The Jaltepec woman in Selden 19-III was born in 1528, so her marriage could have taken place prior to the Inquisition testimony of 1545.

8. Other towns that were described as Yanhuitlán's subjects and whose citizens give pro-Yanhuitlán testimony are: Yxitlán (present-day Sachio), Guautla (Huauclilla), and San Francisco Jaltepetongo. In addition, witnesses from a formidable number of communities in the Mixteca Alta testify on behalf of Yanhuitlán, including: Patlaystlahuaca (present-day Yodocono), Nochixtlán, Soyaltepec, Tiltepec, Chachoapan, Tilantongo, Tonaltepec, Teposcolula, Tamazola, Tataltepec, Achiutla, Teozacoalco, Sosola, Apoala, Texupa, and Tamazulapan.

   During the litigation recorded in the *Escribanía de Cámara* document, Yanhuitlán presented a pictorial manuscript which, as was usual in Colonial documents, is generically described as a *pintura*. The Yanhuitlán *pintura* is said to have shown twenty-four generations of the town's native rulers, covering a period of five hundred years (Spores 1967:94, 96). Witnesses are called to testify to the veracity of the *pintura* (and, undoubtedly, the Codex Selden was the subject of the same type of interrogation when Jaltepec presented it in court). In the testimony on the Yanhuitlán pictorial document, one witness from Yxitlan (Sachio) stated that the *pinturas* are as accurate as documents written in European script (fol. 133v: "son tan ciertas y verdaderas como escrituras entre españoles"). A witness from Jaltepetongo claimed that every major town (*cabecera*) in the Mixteca had similar *pinturas* (fol. 123v), and another from Chachoapan said that his town and many others also had *pinturas* (fol. 155v). Still another witness from Tilantongo testified that Yanhuitlán's pictorial document was very similar to one in his town (fol. 166v). Where are the manuscripts described by these witnesses? We do not know.

9. The sequence between Selden 3-IV and 4-III has sixteen named men as well as fourteen place signs. (Four of the place signs have two men, with none associated with the final two place signs.) This sequence seems, in some ways, to be analogous to the confirmation of the first ruler of Zacatepec in the Lienzo of Zacatepec 1 from the Costa (Smith 1973a:110–15; Caso 1977:137–139; Jansen 1982a:253–54). Persons who congregate at the rulership ceremonies of Zacatepec's first ruler are not accompanied by place signs as are the individuals on Selden 3-IV through 4-III, but ten of the fourteen participants in the rulership ceremonies at the top of the Zacatepec lienzo appear with place signs within the cartographic rectangle of this manuscript (Smith 1973a:114). I believe that this implies that some of the men who confirm the first ruler of Zacatepec are the secondary nobility (*principales*) who control the subject towns within Zacatepec. (On the relationship of the secondary nobility to the primary rulers, see Spores 1967:9–11, 93–96, 164, 176.) The same may also be true of the fourteen towns named in this section of the Codex Selden, which seem to be subjects of Jaltepec, as well as several of the

subjects of Yanhuitlán that bound Jaltepec on the east and north, such as Sachio and Andúa (Smith 1983a:251–252).

10. In his commentary on the Codex Selden, Alfonso Caso (1964:41, 50, 88, 96) correlated the 7 Reed date on which Zahuatlán was conquered as 1331. Emily Rabin (pers. comm.) suggested that the date may be 1383, or one 52-year cycle later.

    Eleven years earlier than the conquest of Zahuatlán by 9 Lizard, his two oldest sons are shown as dead (Selden 12-IV). Both of these sons appear as mummy bundles, along with a configuration with a bow and arrow, on a long slope containing metal axes. Considering the very local character of the Codex Selden, this place with axes may be a mound between Jaltepec and Tamazola (Jaltepec's neighbor to the south) named *yucuñucaa* or "hill where there are metal axes" (*yucu* = "hill"; *ñu* = "place where something exists"; *caa* = "metal axes"). In the eighteenth century, this site was described as the "pueblo despoblado" of Santiago Yucuñucaa, and it functioned as a boundary between Jaltepec and Tamazola (AGN-Ramo de Tierras 990, exp. 1, cuaderno 2, fols. 23, 45, and Tierras 2257, exp. 1, fols. 158, 205). Facing the two dead sons (Selden 13-I) is a male ruler whose calendrical name is 6 Water and whose personal name is "Colored Strips." This man holds a club, and Caso (1964:39–40, 87) suggested that he probably killed the two older sons of 9 Lizard. The armed 6 Water is seated at a place sign that consists of a feather-mat field or plain and a *cacaxtli,* a device of bound slats used to carry heavy loads. Caso (1966; 1977:92, 111–13) postulated that Cacaxtli Plain is one of the signs of Yanhuitlán or the sign of Cuilapan in the Valley of Oaxaca. Jansen (1989:78–79) thought that the Cacaxtli Plain sign was most likely Cuilapan due to the appearance of the *cacaxtli* motif in a drawing in the Manuel Martínez Gracida papers in the Casa de Cultura in Oaxaca (volume V, plate 46 of the papers; published in Martínez Gracida 1986:8). The drawing is entitled "Coat of Arms of Ancient Coyolapan [Cuilapan]," and on its right side a prominent *cacaxtli* appears on a hillock within a declivity between a hill with a tree containing a crowned eagle and a hill with a nopal cactus.

11. Contrasting with the capsule biographies of rulers on the final seven and one-half pages of the codex are the more detailed stories presented in earlier sections of the manuscript: the establishment of Jaltepec's ancient ancestors on pages l-2, the installment of the town's first ruler on pages 3–4, the biography of the noblewoman 6 Monkey on pages 6–8, and the biography of 9 Lizard on pages 11-II through 13-II.

    On Selden 5-IV and 6-I, the older brothers of noblewoman 6 Monkey hold the long rectangular flags traditionally carried by prisoners, implying that they were sacrificed; and the demise of the two eldest sons of 9 Lizard appears on Selden 12-IV. These deaths were probably included to show why subsidiary offspring inherited: the woman 6 Monkey because her brothers had been killed, and the third son of 9 Lizard because his two older brothers were dead. The codex seems to be telling us that the ruling line of Jaltepec had no serious succession problems following the conquest of Zahuatlán.

12. The passage of the Jaltepec line to an offspring of Tilantongo follows the guidelines for succession provided in early Colonial documents quoted by Caso (1964:45, 92) and Spores (1967:131–38, 150–51). Nonetheless, a hint that the inheritance of Jaltepec by 13 Grass—the son of a Tilantongo father and a Jaltepec mother—may not have been all that peaceful is given in a motif attached to the figure of 13 Grass on Selden 19-II. Extending from the right side of the seated 13 Grass are curved parallel lines that terminate in a circle, a motif identified by Spinden (1935:432–34) as an umbilical cord. In the codices Selden and Bodley, this motif is usually attached to a ruler in his or her first appearance following the parents' marriage, to indicate specifically the parent-child relationship; it can also connect the figure of an offspring to a year-date giving the

person's birthdate. The use of the umbilical cord on Selden 19-II is highly unusual because this is the second appearance of 13 Grass in this manuscript, and he is shown as being married in this scene. Nor is the umbilical cord part of his personal name, which is given on Selden 19-I as "Fire Serpent." Another atypical feature of the cord on 19-II is that it contains the chevron pattern that represents the Mixtec word for "enemy" (Smith 1973a:33). Could the implication have been that 13 Grass was "born an enemy" (*nicacu yecu* in Mixtec)? If so, then perhaps the ascension of 13 Grass to the Jaltepec throne was not quite as uneventful as it appears.

13. The Codex Bodley is an encyclopedic manuscript painted on both sides of the screen-fold. Philip Dark (1959:525) postulated that this manuscript may be from Tilantongo because an entire genealogy of twenty-four generations of the rulers of this important Mixteca Alta town appears on the front of the manuscript. A different origin was suggested by Wigberto Jiménez Moreno (implied in a paper summarized in Jansen and Gaxiola 1978:11–13; stated more explicitly in unpublished discussion at a 1979 conference at Dumbarton Oaks on *The Art and Iconography of Post-Classic Central Mexico*). He felt that this codex may have come from the region of Tlaxiaco and Achiutla in the Mixteca Alta because the genealogies of these two towns are emphasized at the end of the reverse.

    The Codex Nuttall was also painted on both sides, but each of the two sides set forth a different type of story. One side, illustrated as pages 42–84 of the Nuttall 1902 edition of the manuscript, presents a detailed biography of the important Mixtec nobleman 8 Deer "Tiger Claw," who lived from 1063 to 1115. This side was formerly thought to be the reverse of the codex, but Nancy P. Troike (1969) has convincingly demonstrated that it was painted first and that the opposite side was added at an unknown date afterward. The second side (pages 1–41 of the Nuttall 1902 edition) contains partial genealogies of Tilantongo (pages 22–27) and Teozacoalco (pages 27-IV through 33-II), culminating on pages 33–35 with a short genealogy of a place whose sign consists of a river with a quetzal bird and a bent hill with a plant. Whereas the genealogical material in the Codex Bodley continues up to the time of the Conquest, that of the Codex Nuttall ends in the late fourteenth century. The manuscript may have been painted for the town of the latest genealogy on pages 33–35 (Paddock 1983:61). Caso (1966) suggested that the town in question was Cuilapan in the Valley of Oaxaca, and Jansen (1982b, 1989:75–81), that it was nearby Zaachila in the same valley because the persons in this genealogy also appear in the Colonial Zapotec Lienzo of Guevea that names rulers of Zaachila. Paddock (1983:87) believed that the native nobility on Nuttall 33–35 ruled both Cuilapan and Zaachila. As mentioned in note 10, Jansen (1989:78–79) thought that the town of Cuilapan was represented by the Cacaxtli Plain sign. Furst (1987) postulated that the naming practices on the genealogical side of the Codex Nuttall seemed more Zapotec than Mixtec and noted that the painter of this side of the codex often rendered incorrectly the traditional Mixtec poses of the human figures.

14. According to Burgoa (1934a:210), "solía poner estos papeles o como tablas de cosmografía pegados a larga en las salas de los señores." To commemorate their ancestors, the native rulers owned "algunas historias pintadas, en papel de cortezas de árboles, y pieles curtidas, de que hacían unas tiras muy largas de un tercio de ancho, y en ellas pinturas de sus caracteres, con que los indios doctos en estas leyendas les explicaban sus linajes, y descendencias, con los trofeos de sus hazañas, y victorias" (Burgoa 1934b, I:288).

15. In addition to the prehispanic style of the date, the outside front cover also has a three-line gloss in Mixtec and Spanish that has been discussed by Dark (1959:526–28),

Caso (1964:18–20, 66–67), and Smith (1983a:249–50). Also on the cover is the numeral "87," the manuscript's number in the catalog of former owner John Selden (Caso 1964:18, 66; see also Barratt 1951), as well as the circular stamp of the Bodleian Library.

16. The year-date 2 Flint only occurs twice within the pictorial narrative of the codex: on page 3-I, as the earliest historical date associated with the biography of Jaltepec's first ruler (A.D. 988), and on page 8-IV, as the birthdate of the nobleman 4 Wind (A.D. 1092). It does not seem likely that the date on Selden 3-I is related to the 2 Flint date on the cover because the line 3-I date—the year 2 Flint, day 3 Rain—is 54 days earlier than the year 2 Flint, day 5 Reed on the cover.

    Other problems in relating the date on the cover to the visible narrative concern the date's orientation and style. The date's placement on the cover gives it a diametrically opposite reading order from that of the visible codex (Caso 1964:20, 67), as well as to that of the short text in European script. In addition, as Nancy Troike has astutely observed (pers. comm.), the year-sign on the cover is drawn in a style different from the year-signs in the remainder of the codex. One possible explanation for the differences between the orientation and style of the cover date and the remainder of the codex is that, following the erasure and resizing of the first Codex Selden, the date was placed on the cover in 1560 by one artist, with the expectation that the second codex would be painted on what today is the reverse of the manuscript. For unknown reasons, this did not occur, and thus the orientation of the date is 180 degrees different from that of the visible narrative. Alfonso Caso (1964:20, 67) suggested that the person who painted the date on the cover did not know how to read the codex and that perhaps he was Spanish rather than a native artist. It seems implausible that a European would have been responsible for adding a prehispanic style of sign to the codex. Caso (1964:13–14, 62) also postulated that the date on the cover might have referred to the original codex that is now covered by the visible manuscript. I also find this unlikely, for the earlier codex was so determinedly obliterated (first by being scraped and then covered with a very thick mixture of white clay) that it does not seem plausible that a motif from this erased manuscript would be preserved.

    Nor does the date on the cover seem to be a "metaphorical" or nonhistorical date, such as the "in the beginning" date of the year 1 Reed, day 1 Alligator (Furst 1978b; Jansen 1988). The year 2 Flint, day 5 Reed date on the Selden cover does not appear on the obverse of the Codex Vindobonensis, whose dates are all nonhistorical, or in other contexts that have dates that cannot be correlated with specific days and years in the calendar.

17. The two bundles in question are on Selden 12-IV and depict the deaths of the first two sons of Jaltepec ruler 9 Lizard "Flames-Face with Diagonal Black Lines." Concerning the deaths of these two heirs, see note 10. Two sacred bundles that are not mummy bundles are on Selden 3-I, and these are associated with the ancient ancestors of Jaltepec whose mythological origin is given in the first two pages of the codex (John Pohl, summarized in Jansen and Gaxiola 1978:8).

    As for mummy bundles in other Mixtec manuscripts, the Codex Bodley is the most extensive of the genealogical-historical codices and also has the most mummy bundles. On pages 3-III through 4-III are mummy bundles of men who died in the "War of Heaven" (Rabin 1979), with two of the individuals on 4-III also appearing as mummy bundles on page 35-I of the Bodley reverse. This early eleventh-century war was characterized by Caso (1960:74–76) as one of the "crises in Mixtec history." Other mummy bundles in the Codex Bodley, all but one of male rulers, are:

8-V: 5 Alligator "Sun-Rain Deity" (father of 8 Deer "Tiger Claw")
14-IV: 8 Deer "Tiger Claw" (following his sacrifice by 4 Wind [Troike 1980])
15-IV: 4 Water "Blood-Eagle" of Teozacoalco and his son 9 Alligator "Flints-Eagle"
31-V: 11 Wind "Blood-Tiger" (father of 4 Wind "Fire Serpent")
29-I: 1 Eagle "Rain Deity" and his mother or wife 1 Grass "Feather Headdress"
28-II: 4 Wind "Fire Serpent"
26-II: 12 Rain "Fire Serpent-Blood-Tiger" of Tlaxiaco
23-II: 5 Reed

In the case of four of the Bodley mummy bundles, these conclude biographies that are told in detail in this manuscript: those of 8 Deer's father, 5 Alligator (Bodley 6-I through 8-V); 8 Deer himself (Bodley 7-V through 14-IV), and 4 Wind and his father 11 Wind; the story of 4 Wind is given more space than that of any other individual in this codex (Bodley 34-III through 28-II), with his ancestral background detailed on pages 40 through 34-II. The remaining four mummy bundles (the two on 15-IV and 29-I and those on 26-II and 23-II) clarify matters of succession to some of the major ruling lines depicted in the Codex Bodley.

In the Codex Nuttall, six men who lost their lives in the "War of Heaven" are shown as mummy bundles on pages 4-II and 20, II and III. In addition, in the 8 Deer biography in this codex, 8 Deer's half-brother 12 Motion is shown as a mummy bundle following his dramatic sacrifice in a steambath (Nuttall 81-I).

In addition to his being shown as a mummy bundle, a person's death can also be indicated by his appearing in a seated position with his eyes closed. This is the case for a male ruler named 3 Lizard on Nuttall 44-I, and for this individual and two other men in a cognate scene on Colombino 4-II. This convention for death is also used to record the deaths of three important male rulers on the reverse or historical side of the Codex Vindobonensis: 2 Rain "Twenty Tigers" on V-1, 5 Alligator "Sun-Rain Deity" on VII-1, and 8 Deer "Tiger Claw" on IX-2. One of these three, 2 Rain "Twenty Tigers," who died mysteriously at the age of 21, is shown twice on Bodley 5-I, once with a blackened eye lacking a pupil and once with his eyes closed. On page 20 of the Codex Nuttall, within one of this manuscript's accounts of the "War of Heaven," two seated men with closed eyes are roped to plants (20-II), and the head of another man with closed eyes is placed on its side and appended to the base of another plant (20-I). At times, a ruler's death is implied rather than explicitly shown in the Mixtec codices. This is the case for the three male offspring of Jaltepec who were the brothers of the woman 6 Monkey. In the Codex Selden (5-IV and 6-I), these three sons hold the long rectangular banners associated with prisoners, and they do not appear again in this codex, nor do they appear at all in any other manuscript. The implication is that they were sacrificed, even though their actual deaths are not depicted.

The biography of the male ruler 11 Wind "Blood-Tiger" in three different codices exemplifies three different versions of showing or not showing a nobleman's death. In the Codex Selden (8-III), 11 Wind's last appearance is as a husband and a father, and his death is not presented. In the Codex Bodley (34-IV), he appears as a mummy bundle, and his death is recorded by a date. On pages 10–11 of the Codex Becker I, the cause of his death is given explicitly: he is a prisoner and sacrificed.

18. The one mummy bundle of a female ruler occurs on Bodley 29-I, where a woman named 1 Grass "Feather Headdress" appears on a burning scaffold along with the mummy bundle of a man named 1 Eagle "Rain Deity," who may be her son or second husband (Caso 1960:65). This woman's first husband was a descendant of the important ruler 4

Wind "Fire Serpent" whose biography is told in detail in this section of the Codex Bodley, and the enigmatic scene in which she is shown as a mummy bundle seems to occur shortly before or after 4 Wind's death. The implication of the scene may be that she and 1 Eagle were eliminated as possible successors to 4 Wind. One notable female death occurs on page 11 of the Codex Becker I, where the woman named 6 Monkey is sacrificed along with her husband 11 Wind. Another female who seems to be dead is 4 Flint in her appearance in the Codex Bodley (5-III) as one of two sisters who marry the ruler of Tilantongo. In the Bodley, this woman is shown with the blackened eye lacking a pupil that is also seen to record the death of 2 Rain "Twenty Tigers" on the same page (5-I) of this manuscript. The woman 4 Flint is shown with an eye with a pupil (i.e., as alive) in both the codices Nuttall (23-III) and the Vindobonensis reverse (V-3), so that the implication of her being depicted as dead in the Bodley may be that her sister, not she, was the mother of the Tilantongo ruler's children.

Thus, the representation in the Codex Selden of three wives of Jaltepec rulers as mummy bundles (Table 7.1) is very different from the norm for the genealogical codices. In the case of one Jaltepec wife whose death is not shown—the woman named 2 Motion "Earth Figure Emerging from a Butterfly," who marries Jaltepec ruler 4 Wind "Venus-Sun," a marriage that has no heirs—her fate following her husband's death is made explicit in the Selden (18-IV). She returns to her hometown, Hill of the Yellow Disk, and, with her second husband, witnesses the transfer of the rulership of Jaltepec to a son of the rulers of Tilantongo. Apparently it was not necessary for this woman's death to be shown because she had eliminated herself from inheriting Jaltepec by returning to Hill of the Yellow Disk.

On Selden 20, I-II, the Tilantongo inheritor of Jaltepec, 13 Grass "Fire Serpent," and his wife from Achiutla are both shown as dying in the same year, 1541 (Table 7.1b). Perhaps both died from smallpox or measles, diseases that greatly diminished the native population of the New World in the early Colonial period.

19. This mummy bundle is accompanied by a date of the year 3 Reed (1535) and the day-date 12 Death. In his commentary on the Codex Selden, Caso (1964:46, 93) suggested that the 12 Death day-date probably gives the day on which the ruler died rather than his calendrical name, because the other deaths in the concluding section of the codex are accompanied by a year-date and day-date. He also noted that a Jaltepec ruler named 4 Serpent has "Eagle-Quetzal Feathers" as part of his personal name, but that the death of this man was recorded three lines earlier in the Codex Selden (19-II). In his biographical dictionary of the persons in the Mixtec manuscripts, Caso (1979:157, 164) postulated that the mummy bundle on Selden 20-I may be that of the Tilantongo ruler, 4 Deer, whose son 13 Grass assumed the rulership of Jaltepec. By Caso's calculations, 4 Deer would have been almost 70 years old in 1535, the death-date of the ruler on 20-I. One problem with this interpretation is that 4 Deer's personal name is not the "Eagle-Quetzal Feathers" of the Selden mummy bundle, but "Eagle-Visible Eye." Nonetheless, Caso's suggestion makes genealogical sense, because 4 Deer's son had become ruler of Jaltepec, and, thus, it was important to record the deaths of Tilantongo nobility who were now potential heirs to Jaltepec.

References Cited

Acuña, René, ed.
1984 Relaciones geográficas del siglo XVI: Antequera. 2 vols. Universidad Nacional Autónoma de Mexico, Serie Antropológica, nos. 54 and 58. Mexico.

Adelhofer, Otto
1974 Codex Vindbonensis Mexicanus I. Graz: Akademische Druck- und Verlagsanstalt.

Alcina Franch, José
1955 Fuentes indígenas de Méjico: Ensayo de sistematización bibliográfica. Revista de Indias, año XV, nos. 61–62:421–521. Madrid.

Anawalt, Patricia Reiff
1981 Indian Clothing Before Cortés: Mesoamerican Costumes from the Codices. Norman: University of Oklahoma Press.

Anders, Ferdinand, and Maarten Jansen
1988 Schrift und Buch im alten Mexiko. Graz: Akademische Druck- und Verlagsanstalt.

Aróstegui, Carlos B.
1977 Marriage, alliance, and succession in Precolumbian Mixtec society. Paper presented at the annual meeting of the Society for American Archaeology, New Orleans.

Barratt, D. M.
1951 The library of John Selden and its later history. The Bodleian Library Record 3–31:128–42. Oxford.

Berlin, Heinrich
1947 Review of Howard F. Cline, "The Terrasgueros of Guelatao Oaxaca, Mexico." Boletín Bibliográfico de Antropología Americana, 9:200–1. Mexico.

Bodleian Library, Oxford
1972 Mexican Pictorial Manuscripts, with an introduction by A. R. Pagden. Oxford University Press, Bodleian Picture Books, Special Series, no. 4. Oxford.

Burgoa, Francisco de
1934a Palestra historial. Publicaciones del Archivo General de la Nación, XXIV. Mexico: Talleres Gráficos de la Nación.
1934b Geográfica descripción. 2 vols. Publicaciones del Archivo General de la Nación, vols. XXV–XXVI. Mexico: Talleres Gráficos de la Nación.

Burland, Cottie A.
1958 Ethnographic notes on Codex Selden in the Bodleian Library of the University of Oxford. Miscelánea Paul Rivet Octogenario Dicata, 1, pp. 361–72. Mexico: Universidad Nacional Autónoma de México.
1965 Codex Egerton 2895. Graz: Akademische Druck- und Verlagsanstalt.

Byland, Bruce E., and John M. D. Pohl
n.d. In the Realm of 8-Deer: The Archaeology of the Mixtec Codices. Norman: University of Oklahoma Press.

Caso, Alfonso
1949 El Mapa de Teozacoalco. Cuadernos Americanos, año VIII, 47(5):145–81. Mexico.
1950 Explicación del reverso del Codex Vindobonensis. Memoria de El Colegio Nacional V-5:9–46. Mexico.
1959 Review of Philip Dark, Mixtec ethnohistory: A method of analysis of the codical art. American Anthropologist 61(1):147–51.
1960a Interpretation of the Codex Bodley 2858. Mexico: Sociedad Mexicana de Antropología.
1960b The Historical Value of the Mixtec Codices. Boletín de Estudios Oaxaqueños, no. 16. Museo Frissell, Mitla.
1964 Interpretación del Códice Selden 3135 (A.2) / Interpretation of the Codex Selden 3135 (A.2). Mexico: Sociedad Mexicana de Antropología.
1966 The Lords of Yanhuitlan. In: Ancient Oaxaca, edited by John Paddock, pp. 318–35. Stanford: Stanford University Press.
1977 Reyes y reinos de la Mixteca, vol. 1. Mexico: Fondo de Cultura Económica.
1979 Reyes y reinos de la Mixteca, vol. 2: Diccionario biográfico de los señores Mixtecos. Mexico: Fondo de Cultura Económica.

Caso, Alfonso, and Mary Elizabeth Smith
1966 Interpretación del Códice Colombino / Interpretation of the Codex Colombino (by Caso); Las glosas del Códice Colombino / The Glosses of Codex Colombino (by Smith). Mexico: Sociedad Mexicana de Antropología.

Clark, James Cooper
1912 The Story of "Eight Deer" in Codex Colombino. London: Taylor and Francis.

Corona Núñez, José
1964–1967 Antigüedades de México basadas en la recopilación de Lord Kingsborough. 4 vols. Mexico: Secretaría de Hacienda y Crédito Público.

Dahlgren de Jordan, Barbro
1954 La Mixteca: Su cultura e historia prehispánicas. Mexico: Imprenta Universitaria.

Dark, Philip
1958a Mixtec Ethnohistory: A Method of Analysis of the Codical Art. Oxford: Oxford University Press.
1958b Speculations on the Course of Mixtec History prior to the Conquest. Boletín de Estudios Oaxaqueños, no. 10. Museo Frissell, Mitla.
1959 Evidence for the date of painting and provenience of Codex Selden and Codex Bodley. 33rd International Congress of Americanists 2:523–29. San José de Costa Rica.

Dark, Philip, and Joyce Plesters

1959 The palimpsests of Codex Selden: Recent attempts to reveal the covered pictographs. 33rd International Congress of Americanists 2:530–39. San José de Costa Rica.

Furst, Jill Leslie

1977 The tree birth tradition in the Mixteca, Mexico. Journal of Latin American Lore 3(2):183–226.

1978a Codex Vindobonensis I: A Commentary. State University of New York, Institute for Mesoamerican Studies, Publication 4. Albany.

1978b The year 1 Reed, day 1 Alligator: A Mixtec metaphor. Journal of Latin American Lore 4(1):93–128.

1987 Mixtec narrative conventions and variations: Problems in defining Codex Nuttall as Mixtec. Latin American Indian Literatures Journal 3(1):9–26.

Glass, John B.

1975 A survey of Native Middle American pictorial manuscripts. In: Handbook of Middle American Indians, vol. 14, edited by Howard F. Cline, pp. 3–80. Austin: University of Texas Press.

Glass, John B., in collaboration with Donald Robertson

1975 A census of Native Middle American pictorial manuscripts. In: Handbook of Middle American Indians, vol. 14, edited by Howard F. Cline, pp. 81–252. Austin: University of Texas Press.

Greenleaf, Richard E.

1969 The Mexican Inquisition of the Sixteenth Century. Albuquerque: University of New Mexico Press.

1975 Inquisición y sociedad en el México colonial. Madrid: Ediciones José Porrúa Turanzas.

Greenleaf, Richard E., and Maarten E. R. G. N. Jansen

1991 Mixtec Religion and Spanish Conquest: The Oaxaca Inquisition Trials, 1544–1547. Madrid: José Porrúa Turanzas.

Jansen, Maarten E. R. G. N.

1982a Huisi Tacu: Estudio interpretativo de un libro mixteco antiguo: Codex Vindobonensis Mexicanus I. 2 vols. Centrum voor Studie en Documentarie van Latijns Amerika, Incidentele Publicaties 24. Amsterdam.

1982b Viaje al otro mundo: La Tumba 1 de Zaachila. In: Coloquio Internacional: Los indígenas de México en la época prehispánica y en la actualidad, edited by M.E.R.G.N. Jansen and Th. J.J. Leyenaar, pp. 87–118. Leiden: Rijksmuseum voor Volkerkunde.

1983 La expedición hacia Cuautinchan: Contactos entre mixtecos, chocho-popolocas y nahuas en la epoca postclásica. Paper presented at the annual meeting of the Grupo de Trabajo Latinoamericano de la Universidad de Leiden.

1988 Dates, deities and dynasties: Non-durational time in Mixtec historiography. In: Continuity and Identity in Native America: Essays in Honor of Benedikt Hartmann, edited by Maarten Jansen, Peter van der Loo, and Roswintha Manning, pp. 156–92. Leiden: E. J. Brill.

1989 Nombres históricos e identidad étnica en los códices mixtecos. Revista Europa de Estudios Latinoamericanos y del Caribe 47, pp. 65–87.

Jansen, Maarten E. R. G. N., and Margarita Gaxiola
1978 Primera Mesa Redonda de estudios Mixtecos: Síntesis de las ponencias. Centro Regional de Oaxaca, Instituto Nacional de Antropología e Historia, Estudios de Antropología e Historia, no. 15. Oaxaca.

Jansen, Maarten E. R. G. N., and Gabina Aurora Pérez
1986 Iyadzehe Anute: Valor literario de los códices Mixtecos. In: Etnicidad y pluralismo cultural: La dinámica étnica en Oaxaca, edited by Alicia M. Barabas and Miguel A. Bartolomé, pp. 173–211. Instituto Nacional de Antropología e Historia, Colección Regiones de Mexico. Mexico.

Jiménez Moreno, Wigberto, and Salvador Mateos Higuera
1940 Códice de Yanhuitlan. Museo Nacional. Mexico.

Kingsborough, Lord [Edward King]
1831 Antiquities of Mexico. 7 vols. London.

König, Viola
1979 Inhaltliche Analyse und Interpretation von Codex Egerton. Hamburgischen Museum fur Völkerkunde, Beitrage zur mittelamerkanischen Völkerkunde, XV. Hamburg.

Lehmann, Walter
1905 Les peintures Mixteco-Zapotèques et quelques documents apparentes. Journal de la Société des Américanistes de Paris, n.s. 2(2):241–80. Paris.

Martínez Gracida, Manuel
1986 Los indios oaxaqueños y sus monumentos arqueológicos. Oaxaca: Gobierno del Estado de Oaxaca.

Nicholson, H. B.
1967 Review of Alfonso Caso, Interpretación del Códice Selden 3135 (A.2). American Antiquity 32(2):257–58.

Nowotny, Karl Anton
1961a Codices Becker I/II. Graz: Akademische Druck- und Verlagsanstalt.
1961b Tlacuilolli: Die mexikanischen Bilderhandschriften, Stil und Inhalt. Berlin: Verlag Gebr. Mann.

Nuttall, Zelia
1902 Codex Nuttall, Facsimile of an ancient Mexican codex belonging to Lord Zouche of Harynworth, England. Peabody Museum of American Archaeology and Ethnology, Cambridge.

Paddock, John
1983 Lord 5 Flower's Family: Rulers of Zaachila and Cuilapan. Vanderbilt University Publications in Anthropology, no. 29. Nashville.

Parmenter, Ross

1982 Four Lienzos of the Coixtlahuaca Valley. Studies in Pre-Columbian Art & Archaeology, no. 26. Dumbarton Oaks, Washington, D.C.

Paso y Troncoso, Francisco del

1898 Descripción, historia y exposición del códice pictórico de los antiguos Nauas que conserva en la Biblioteca de la Cámara de Diputados de Paris. Florence: Tipografía de Salvador Landi.

1905–1906 Papeles de Nueva España, segunda serie, geografía y estadística. 7 vols. Madrid: Est. Tipográfico "Sucesores de Rivadeneyra."

Rabin, Emily

1979 The War of Heaven in codices Zouche-Nuttall and Bodley: A preliminary study. 42nd International Congress of Americanists 7:173–82. Paris.

1981 Chronology of the Mixtec historical codices: An overview. Paper presented at the American Society for Ethnohistory annual meeting, Colorado Springs.

Robertson, Donald

1982 Some comments on Mixtec historical manuscripts. In: Aspects of the Mixteca-Puebla Style and Mixtec and Central Mexican Culture in Southern Mesoamerica, edited by Doris Stone, pp. 15–26. Tulane University, Middle American Research Institute Occasional Paper 4. New Orleans.

Smith, Mary Elizabeth

1973a Picture Writing from Ancient Southern Mexico: Mixtec Place Signs and Maps. Norman: University of Oklahoma Press.

1973b The relationship between Mixtec manuscript painting and the Mixtec language: A study of some personal names in codices Muro and Sánchez Solís. In: Mesoamerican Writing Systems, edited by Elizabeth P. Benson, pp. 47–98. Dumbarton Oaks, Washington, D.C.

1983a Codex Selden: A manuscript from the Valley of Nochixtlán? In: The Cloud People: Divergent Evolution of the Zapotec and Mixtec Civilizations, edited by Kent V. Flannery and Joyce Marcus, pp. 248–55. New York: Academic Press.

1983b Regional points of view in the Mixtec codices. In: The Cloud People: Divergent Evolution of the Zapotec and Mixtec Civilizations, edited by Kent V. Flannery and Joyce Marcus, pp. 260–66. New York: Academic Press.

1988 It doesn't amount to a hill of beans: The frijol motif in Mixtec place signs. In: Smoke and Mist: Mesoamerican Studies in Memory of Thelma D. Sullivan, part ii, edited by J. Kathryn Josserand and Karen Dakin, pp. 696–710. BAR International Series 402(ii). Oxford.

Smith, Mary Elizabeth, and Ross Parmenter

1991 The Codex Tulane. Tulane University, Middle American Research Institute, Publication 61. New Orleans.

Spinden, Herbert J.

1935 The Indian Manuscripts of Southern Mexico. Annual Report of the Smithsonian Institution, 1933:429–51.

Spores, Ronald
1967 The Mixtec Kings and Their People. Norman: University of Oklahoma Press.
1984 The Mixtecs in Ancient and Colonial Times. Norman: University of Oklahoma Press.

Troike, Nancy P.
1969 The provenience of the Mixtec codices Nuttall and Colombino-Becker. Paper presented at the 68th Annual Meeting of the American Anthropological Association, New Orleans.
1974 The Codex Colombino-Becker. Ph.D. dissertation, University of London.
1980 The identification of individuals on the Codex Colombino-Becker. Tlalocan 8:397–418. Mexico.

Troike, Nancy P., and Ferdinand Anders
1987 Codex Zouche-Nuttall. Graz: Akademische Druck- und Verlagsanstalt.

Welte, Cecil R.
1981 Pre-Conquest and Early Colonial Pictorial Manuscripts of the "Oaxaca Area." Oficina de Estudios de Humanidad del Valle de Oaxaca, Welte's Ready Reference Release no. 5. Oaxaca.

Whitecotton, Joseph W.
1990 Zapotec Elite Ethnohistory: Pictorial Genealogies from Eastern Oaxaca. Vanderbilt University Publications in Anthropology, no. 39. Nashville.

CHAPTER 8

Irrigation and Ecological Complementarity in Mixtec Cacicazgos

JOHN MONAGHAN

VANDERBILT UNIVERSITY

IN ONE OF Ronald Spores' early publications on Oaxaca, he pointed out that the geographical diversity between highland and lowland areas was important in stimulating trade in the ancient Mixtec economy. Coastal areas, for example, specialized in products such as cotton and cacao, while highland regions specialized in products such as pulque, which were exchanged in periodic markets held throughout the Mixteca (Spores 1967:5–7). Later, Rodolfo Pastor (1987:43–44) went on to suggest that large, prehispanic *cacicazgos,* or "kingdoms," such as Coixtlahuaca, spanned these zones, controlling several smaller "political units" through conquest, marriage, and other means (Spores 1974, 1983a). This control gave these *cacicazgos* a "vertical integration," of the sort that Andean societies are often said to have had—that is, they were located in an area where several diverse ecozones exist by virtue of a steep gradient, and the *cacicazgos* integrated the zones into a single productive system.

What I suggest here is that vertical integration was not solely a characteristic of large, expansionist kingdoms, but was important to the structure of even small Mixtec *cacicazgos*. By discussing the transitional zone between the Mixteca Alta and the Mixteca de la Costa, I will show that a number of *cacicazgos* controlled lands situated on different ecological floors, an indication that the strategy of vertical integration was practiced widely in the region. I will then go on to suggest that settlement patterns, ritual exchanges, and local political dynamics characteristic of this zone of the Mixteca should be placed within the context of this strategy, and that vertical integration may be a local response to pressures operating more generally in Oaxaca, pressures that led to the development of many different forms of agricultural intensification in the region.

The Transitional Zone

There are three large geographic subdivisions within the Mixteca: the *Mixteca Alta,* a cold, mountainous region; the *Mixteca Baja,* a high, dry region to the northeast of the Alta; and the *Mixteca de la Costa,* a lowland strip lying between the Alta and the Pacific Ocean. The area of particular interest to me is one I call the "transitional zone" between the Alta and the Costa (see Fig. 8.1). This region is marked by a series of sharp ridges, called "El Nudo Mixteco," running roughly north to south, which divides the Alta from the Costa. To the east of the ridges is the *tierra fría* of the Alta. To the southwest of the ridges is the *tierra caliente* of the Costa.

An important feature of the transitional zone is a series of small rivers, flowing roughly from the northeast to the southwest, which begin in the Alta, run off the high ridges, and empty into the Costa. Along their paths they form a number of narrow canyons, which, as the rivers grow, become small valleys, called *cañadas* in the area. Four of the rivers flow down from the mountainous lands of the Trique communities of Copala and Chicahuaxtla, where they water the level fertile lands called the Llano de Putla. These rivers join one another, and form the large Río de Putla, which eventually flows into the Río Verde, and then into the Pacific Ocean. To the south, another *cañada,* the Cañada of Yosotichi, is cut by streams that flow out of Chicahuaxtla, Ocotepec, and Yucuhiti. This is followed by the narrow Cañada of Jicaltepec, the tiny Cañada of Nopalera, and finally the Cañada of Nuyoo.[1] The last is longest at 26 km, and is exceedingly narrow at places, but opens up to form a wide valley at Asunción Atoyaquillo. All of the *cañadas* drain into the Río de Putla, which runs parallel to the ridges. Each *cañada* lies about 4 km from those to the north or south of it, separated from the others by hilly zones that climb as much as 2000 m from the *cañada* floors.

Although each of the rivers begins in the mountains of the Mixteca Alta, they quickly plunge off the ridges, forming what are usually spectacular waterfalls. The river in the Cañada of Nuyoo, for example, begins in streams and mountain springs at 3000 m; it then cascades into a narrow canyon alongside present-day centers of Santiago Nuyoo and Santa María Yucuhiti, at 1000 m. As this "river" continues its journey to the Río de Putla, other streams feed into it, and it eventually drops to below 500 m at Atoyaquillo.

The *cañadas* combine two features that make them particularly valuable to the people of the region: (1) they offer a sharp contrast with the nearby highlands of the Mixteca Alta, and (2) they contain some lands that can be irrigated. I will discuss each of these in turn.

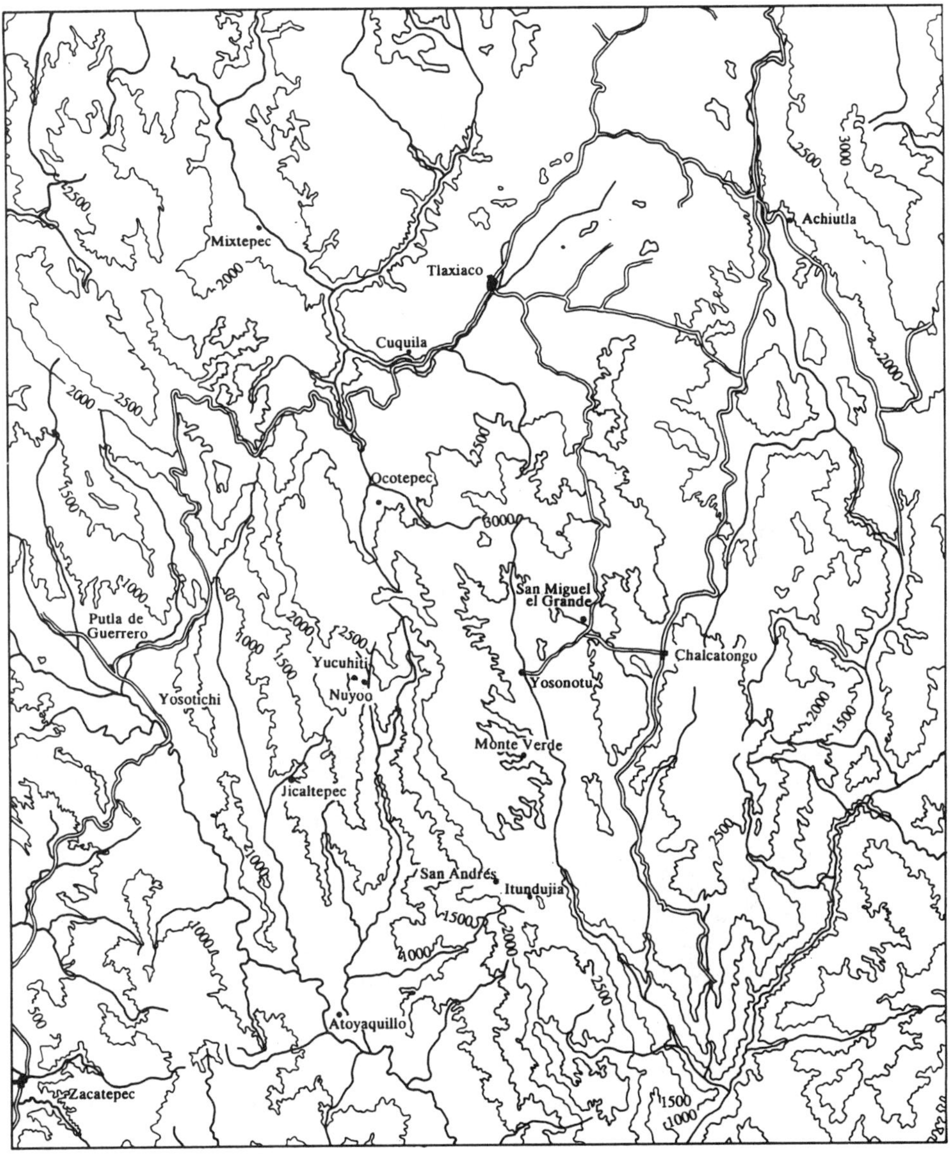

Figure 8.1. The Mixtec area, showing the "transitional zone" between the Mixteca Alta and the Mixteca de la Costa.

Ecological Floors

The highland areas to the east of the ridges that separate the Mixteca Alta from the Costa are *tierra fría,* where annual mean temperatures range from 14–18° C, and it is not uncommon in January and February to wake to see ice on the ground (cf. Secretaría de Programación y Presupuesto 1981). This is a mountainous area, with peaks that reach as high as 3200 m. Except for some level areas around Tlaxiaco, Ocotepec, and Chalcatongo, the terrain is steep, rocky, and cut by canyons and stream beds.

The present-day inhabitants of the highlands cultivate corn, beans, squash, potatoes, and maguey, from which they produce pulque. Pulque has high nutritional value, and is an important ritual drink. Women cultivate a variety of greens and condiments in household gardens, or gather them wild (such as manzanilla, garlic, camomile and *epazote;* cf. Katz 1990). Although cherry, plum, apple and peach trees grow in the area, few other fruits can be produced. Game, particularly deer, is available in the mountain forests, and *chilacayote,* a cold weather squash identified as *Cucurbita ficifolia* (Katz 1990:247) is grown on lands above 1500 m.

Cañada lands are quite distinct from the highland regions. *Cañada* lands lie below 1000 m, with annual mean temperatures from 22–24° C (Secretaría de Programación y Presupuesto 1981). The average mean rainfall also increases in the *cañadas*. While the Tlaxiaco area in the highlands receives 800–900 mm of rainfall during the May to October rainy season, the *cañada* areas receive from 1200–1400 mm around Nuyoo and Yucuhiti, and from 1700–2000 mm around Putla (Secretaría de Programación y Presupuesto 1984). These differences allow for the cultivation of a variety of tropical plants that will not produce fruit in the highlands, or will simply die from the cold and lack of moisture. Such plants include bananas, mamey, mangos, pineapples, oranges, guayabas, *anonas, cidras, zapote, zapote negro,* limes, lemons, avocados, tomatoes, and *cuajinicuil,* many of which were important in the diets of prehispanic people. Moreover, several varieties of chile, warm weather squash (*calabaza,* or *Cucurbita mixta* [Katz 1990:248]), *camotes,* and *nopales,* which will not survive highland conditions, can be grown.

Besides the chile and fruits given above, cacao and perhaps cotton were cultivated in the *cañadas* in the sixteenth century.[2] These crops were extremely important in the prehispanic economy. They were the raw ingredients of several forms of native wealth, and people used them in rituals, bridewealth payments, gift exchange, tribute payments, and sumptuary trade. The *cañadas* are also the home of several highly valued game animals that cannot be found in the highlands. These include the iguana (from which the Cañada of Yosotichi derives its name), and freshwater trout, which abound in the rivers at the lower ends of the *cañadas*. Finally, plants that are not food sources, but have important ritual uses, were produced in *cañada* lands. Chief among these were tobacco, and brightly colored flowers. Tobacco and flowers were important sacrificial offerings in prehispanic times (e.g., Acuña 1984:294, 314), and in the Cañada of Nuyoo today, *mayordomos* come from as far away as Chila in the Mixteca Baja for the sole purpose of picking flowers to bring home to use in church rituals.

Although the variety of plant and animal species available in the *cañadas* would have attracted the inhabitants of the region to these areas, it is in the production of one crop, corn, that these lands take on critical importance. Corn, for people in this region, as is true throughout Mesoamerica, is the main subsistence crop, considered to be the basis of good nutrition, and consumed at every meal. While farmers today sow corn in both highland areas and in the *cañada* lands, its cycle of growth is highly sensitive to altitude. In the highland areas, from 2000 to 2400 m, *temporal* corn (corn that depends on seasonal rains) must be planted in April or May, to be harvested in November or December. In areas above 2400 m, where the clouds trapped by the mountains moisten the ground, farmers plant corn as early as February, but do not harvest it until the following December or even January, which makes the cycle of growth almost a year long. At an elevation of 1500 m, however, along the sides of the *cañadas,* the growing cycle of corn is considerably shortened. Planting is in May, and harvest is late October to early December. But it is the lands at the base of the *cañadas* where the *temporal* cycle is shortest. Here, on lands under 1000 m, corn is sown in late May to late June, and harvested as early as late August (see also Katz 1990).[3]

The *cañada* lands present advantages for the growing of corn, not only because it is in those lands where the *temporal* cycle is shortest, but because the lower the elevation, the more productive the cornfields tend to be. One reason for this is that corn does better in frost-free environments that have relatively high mean temperatures. In a survey of six municipalities with lands located, for the most part, above 1800 m, corn production averaged .448 tons per hectare; in contrast, the average produced in five municipalities with lands located primarily below 1200 m, was .591 per hectare, 32% more than that in the highlands.[4]

Another reason corn productivity is so high in the *cañadas* is that the less time corn spends in the ground, the less that can happen to it. This became particularly clear to me when highland areas adjacent to the Cañada of Yosotichi and Cañada of Nuyoo lost their entire harvests in both 1984 and 1985, due to freezes and strong winds. But the fields in the *cañadas* produced a bumper crop, since they did not suffer the freeze, and the winds struck only after the harvest period ended. It is also true that the *cañadas* occasionally suffer bad years, with little harvest, while the crops sown in the mountains are unaffected. In the early 1920s for example, swarms of locusts descended on the Mixteca, consuming everything in the Costa. In contrast, crops in the Alta survived, because, as the locusts advanced into the highlands, they were killed by the cold, often in mid-flight (people promptly scooped them into sacks, to be roasted and eaten). It is, however, much more common for corn harvests to be lost in the highlands than in the lowlands, and highland peoples regard the coast as a "place of abundance," and regard the sowing of corn there as less risky than in highland zones.

The different growing environments created by abrupt changes in altitude from highlands to lowlands suggests that one way to protect against sudden swings in corn yields might be to plant corn in the different ecozones created by the steep gradient. This multiple field strategy is something the modern inhabitants of the region readily recognize. Most of those who lost milpas in the highland areas in Yucuhiti and Nuyoo in 1984 and 1985 also had corn planted in the 1000–1500 m zone, where harvests were reduced by only about one third, since only the winds affected them, and not the freeze.

Thus far, I have been speaking primarily about rainfall agriculture. Yet the *cañada* lands are also set off from highland areas by the amount of irrigated lands they contain. It is true there are some irrigated plots in the highlands near the old *cacicazgo* seats of Chalcatongo, Tlaxiaco, and Ocotepec, and these lands may have been an important factor in their location. However, the irrigated plots are small, and sometimes people simply plant rainy season corn in them, supplementing the natural rainfall with water from nearby rivers, to ensure that the crop receives adequate moisture. In contrast, the long, meandering rivers in the *cañadas* create many alluvial fans, upon which inhabitants have built extensive systems of dikes and canals.[5] The largest irrigated areas are around Putla, followed by a long stretch in the Cañada of Yosotichi, and then the area around Atoyaquillo. The Cañada of Jicaltepec, and the top of the Cañada of Nuyoo, in the lands of Santa María Yucuhiti, also contain smaller patches of irrigated lands. Corn is sown in the irrigated lands from January to March, depending on the elevation and on how quickly the farmers work. It is then harvested in mid-June to early August, depending on when it was planted. Because farmers are assured of an adequate supply of moisture, and because the corn is growing in a warm zone, the irrigated lands of the *cañadas* are extremely productive. Today, people in the Cañada of Yosotichi produce more corn than they consume, and sell the surplus in the market. While the amount of rainy season corn produced ranges between .75 to 1 ton per hectare in the region, the amount of corn produced on irrigated lands ranges from 3 to 16 tons per hectare (Anuario Estadístico 1988:1167–68).

The productivity of the *cañadas* is important because the highland areas in the transitional zone run a deficit in corn. Today in the highlands, there is a period called *yoo yuu* or "months of starvation," from August to September, when corn from the previous year has run short and people anxiously await the harvest. Until roads were built into the area in the 1970s, and a supply of corn from other areas became readily available, people had to subsist on famine foods, and make long journeys out of the highlands to the coast to buy corn.[7]

This pattern of *cañada* surplus and highland deficits characterized the region in the early sixteenth century as well. Evidence for *cañada* surpluses comes from the

1580 *Relaciones geográficas,* which note that people from settlements in *cañada* lands, such as Putla, paid tribute in corn and traded corn in surrounding markets for other products (Acuña 1984:290–1, 317). If the inhabitants of *cañada* lands were able to use corn for tribute and trade, this suggests that they produced more corn than necessary to meet local subsistence needs. Evidence for highland deficits comes from Burgoa, writing in the mid 1600s, who tells us that in the "*montes de* Chicahuaxtla" adjacent to Putla and Juxtlahuaca, people did not produce enough corn to meet their needs, and had to trade for corn in nearby markets to make up for the shortfall (Burgoa [1674] 1989:359). Highland corn deficits became a critical problem in the Colonial period, when Spanish planters recognized the value of *cañada* lands, and began to enter the area. They planted sugar cane on the irrigated plots, sharply reducing the amount of corn produced in the *cañadas*. Once the native populations began to recover after the plagues of the sixteenth century, a severe subsistence crisis developed, because the population of the highlands lost the supply of *cañada* corn that traditionally saw them through the "months of starvation" (Monaghan 1990).

The takeover of *cañada* lands by the Spaniards, and the subsistence crisis it created, is crucial to understanding the political and economic dynamics of this region of the Mixteca during the last 400 years (Monaghan 1990). However, my purpose here is only to suggest that the different productive zones created by altitude differences in this part of the Mixteca made the highlands and *cañadas* a single subsistence system. By exploiting different zones, human populations in the region were not only able to obtain access to a wide range of animal and plant species, but more importantly, were able to obtain the corn required to meet basic dietary needs. This made the highlands dependent upon *cañadas,* because the *cañadas* produced a surplus of corn, and because the corn crop produced in the *cañadas* would be harvested precisely when it was needed most in the highlands, in July and August, at the outset of the months of starvation. *Cañada* settlements also experience a period of shortage in mid-March to mid-May. Although these shortages occur with less frequency than in the highlands, supplies of corn from the highlands have been used to alleviate the stress on subsistence in the *cañadas,* since March marks the end of the harvest in the highlands, and corn is most plentiful there at this time.

The Articulation of Ecological Floors

There are many ways that different ecological zones can be productively articulated. In Oaxaca, we have the example of the Tomellín Cañada, where different ethnic groups occupied different zones, and exchanged products and labor (Hopkins 1983:266–67). We also have the example of a long-distance ecological complementarity, where, during the Late Formative, the Valley of Oaxaca Zapotec conquered the Cuicatlán Cañada and forcibly exacted from the local population fruits and other goods that could not be grown in the Valley of Oaxaca (Marcus 1983:107–8; Redmond 1983; Spencer and Redmond 1983:117–20). However, in the transitional zone between the Mixteca Alta and Costa it was usually the individual *cacicazgo* that integrated different ecozones into a productive system. Spores described these *cacicazgos* or "community-kingdoms" as:

> small, socially stratified states, each controlled by a privileged ruling aristocracy and consisting of a territory normally traversable by foot in a day, one or more agricultural settlements with adjacent farm plots and resource areas, and a resident population differentiated into a ruling lineage, a nobility, a class of commoners, and in some cases, a group of tenant farmers subject to direct control of the ruler. [Spores 1983a:255]

In the sixteenth century, each *cacicazgo* in the transitional zone laid claim to *cañada* lands. Most had their seats in the Mixteca Alta, in the highlands immediately to the east of the ridges that separate the Alta from the Costa. These sites range from 1800 to 2300 m in altitude. Tlaxiaco, for example, at 2000 m, had lands in the Cañada of Yosotichi (below 800 m).[8] Burgoa described the kingdom as having "tanta variedad de templos, que saliendo de la región de la nieve, se baja a la del fuego" (Burgoa [1674] 1989:306). Similarly, Chicahuaxtla lies at 2300 m and controlled extensive lands on the Llano de Putla, and in the northern part of the Cañada de Yosotichi (García Alcarez 1973:279–96, see especially "mapa político del área Triqui" p. 296; Huerta Ríos 1982:20). Ocotepec, at 1800 m, also controlled lands in the Cañada de Yosotichi, and, according to oral history, had plots that bordered the Capilla de Putla on the Llano de Putla (Monaghan 1989). Finally, Chalcatongo, at 2250 m, controlled most of the Cañada of Nuyoo, perhaps the small Cañada of Nopalera and the Cañada of Cortez.

Putla, at 740 m, and Zacatepec, at 350 m, were two coastal *cacicazgos* that had lands in the *cañadas*. Putla sits in the wide, fertile *llano* watered by the rivers flowing out of Chicahuaxtla (the territory it controlled in the sixteenth century appears to have been much smaller than today). Zacatepec, a *cacicazgo* lying to the west, appears to have controlled the Cañada of Jicaltepec,[9] and at least some lands in the Cañada of Yosotichi (Smith 1973:91). It is difficult to determine if the domains of these coastal *cacicazgos* extended into the highlands, but we do know that their territories bordered on the high ridges separating the Alta from the Costa, something that indicates that they controlled at least some areas where highland products could be grown. It is also possible that control over highland areas was not as critical to coastal *cacicazgos* as control over lowland areas was to highland *cacicazgos*. There appear to be few highland agricultural products that coastal people needed, and historically the area appears to have produced a surplus of corn (for a comparable situation, see Marcus and Silva 1988, which discusses the possibility that verticality was more significant to highlanders than to lowlanders in the Andes).

The establishment of vertical ecological integration can enable a polity to be self-sufficient (Murra 1972; Pastor 1987:44), and this was also the goal of Mixtec polities. Self-sufficiency would have been an important strategic goal of Mixtec *cacicazgos*: they were often in conflict with one another, and having to depend on neighbors for subsistence crops while at war would have been a distinct disadvantage. Desiring to be self-sufficient may also be a reason for the many conflicts that developed between *cacicazgos* in the region during the sixteenth century. As might be expected, most conflicts were over *cañada* lands. An epic dispute took place between Ocotepec and Tlaxiaco over the Cañada of Yosotichi, beginning at least as early as 1554,[10] and is not yet fully resolved (Monaghan 1990). Another dispute occurred between Ocotepec and Chalcatongo over lands in the Cañada of Nuyoo. Lands in the Cañada of Nuyoo appear to have changed hands several times. Nuyoo was originally a settlement established in *cañada* lands by people sent out from Chalcatongo. Later, Nuyoo was listed as a cattle *estancia* for Ocotepec in the sixteenth century; and, according to oral history we know that Nuyoo again became part of Chalcatongo some time in the seventeenth century.[11] Putla, Chicahuaxtla, and Tlaxiaco appear to have been in constant disagreement over boundaries in the *cañada* lands that form the Llano de Putla, and the three were entangled in disputes over lands in the northern part of the Cañada of Yosotichi.[12] Chicahuaxtla once held lands right up "to the door of the Chapel of Putla," which later became part of Putla. Place signs in the Lienzo of Ocotepec, as well as archival sources, indicate that Chicahuaxtla did have lands in the Cañada of Yosotichi, which later became part of Tlaxiaco, again after considerable litigation (García Alcarez 1973:279–96; Smith 1973:150–51). Today, the same aim of controlling lands in different ecozones is behind many ongoing land disputes in the region, as highland groups attempt to push their way down onto *cañada* lands.

To protect their rights to *cañada* lands, it appears that the ancient kingdoms in the area established subordinate settlements that could both exploit the surrounding resources and guard against encroachments. We can see this reflected in the origin myths of the people of several settlements in the region, where the ancestors of today's inhabitants traveled from an ancient *cacicazgo* seat through a tunnel to their present location, remaining connected—as if by an umbilical cord—to the center of *cacicazgo* power. One settlement's name, Yosotato, can be translated as "plain of the guardian," and people today say Yosotato was founded by a group sent out from Tlaxiaco to protect against incursions onto Tlaxiaco's lands in the Cañada of Yosotichi. These settlements may have been especially important in defense because they lie at what, according to Spores (1983a:255), was the geographical limit of the *cacicazgo*—about one day's walk from the *cacicazgo* center.

Labor Allocation

In controlling lands located on different ecological floors, the *cacicazgos* of the transitional zone not only faced the problem of how to defend against incursions by rival *cacicazgos,* but also how to organize labor supplies so that each zone could be productively exploited. In this the *cacicazgos* appeared to have had several options. One, as I noted, was to control permanent settlements in the *cañadas,* whose population would then labor on the surrounding agricultural lands. However, the settlements of most *cacicazgos* with lands in the *cañadas* do not appear to have had sufficient population to provide the labor needed to maintain irrigation canals, and to sow, weed, and harvest large plantings of corn, chile, cacao, and other crops. For these polities, a series of settlements on the ridges overlooking the *cañadas* (e.g., the *estancias* of Itundujia, San Andrés, and Santa Lucía of Chalcatongo, the *estancias* of San Pedro and Santa María of Ocotepec) appear to have been of key importance in their exploitation of *cañada* lands.

There are two reasons why ridge settlements played such an important role in *cañada* agriculture. First, one can reach the *cañada* floors from these places in no more than two or three hours. The climb back up is much longer, especially if one is carrying a heavy load, but a round trip can easily be made in one day. Second, the agricultural cycles of the two zones mesh in such a way that peak times in one area coincide with lulls in the other. As I noted, the time for planting irrigated corn in the *cañada* is from January to March. At the 1500–2000 m level this is a slack period, since by this time the rainy season corn is harvested, and farmers do not begin to clear their fields for planting until late March or April. Also, the time for harvesting the irrigated corn in the *cañada* would fall between the first and second weedings of the rainy season corn at the 1500–2000 m level, another slack period. The co-occurrence of lulls in one area with peaks in the other suggests that labor could be supplied from ridge settlements to work in the *cañada* lands without interfering with productive activities in the highlands. A pattern of seasonal labor migration between highland settlements and *cañada* lands is something that existed throughout the Colonial period, and goes on even today, as people descend from the mountains to harvest corn and sugar cane during the *yoo yuu,* "months of starvation," in June, July, and August. The native elite could have organized such migration in prehispanic times. Commoners owed the elite personal service, which often meant they would have to change residence (Dahlgren 1966:194). It would have been a simple matter for the elite to require populations of ridge settlements to travel down into the *cañadas* to work on *cacicazgo* lands. An even bigger pool of labor may have been available in the *cacicazgo* seats themselves, since they are also within a long day's walk to the *cañadas.*

Exchange Mechanisms

Beyond mobilizing labor to exploit *cañada* lands, *cacicazgos* faced the problem of how to distribute the different products produced on the various ecological floors. One way this distribution could be accomplished would have been for people to simply sow plots at different elevations and micro-environments, and supply themselves with what they needed, like the inhabitants of many towns in the region today. Another way would be to circulate the products of different zones through marketplaces. Early Colonial sources report the presence of some markets in the Mixteca, and it appears that much of the daily trade involved products from different ecological zones (Spores 1963).[13]

There is also evidence for the circulation of products between different ecozones through non-market exchanges. In the early part of this century, Mixtecs from the highlands descended into the Cañada of Yosotichi to claim lands that belonged to their sixteenth-century ancestors. Soon after, they initiated reciprocal trading partnerships between themselves and people who remained in the highlands. Households in the *cañada* would bring loads of corn into the highlands during the "months of starvation" in late July, August, and September, to leave with selected partners. These partners would then return an equal amount of highland rainy season corn in mid-March to mid-May, during the months when corn supplies are low in the *cañada*. These exchanges took place during major fiestas held in the two zones. Thus, people from Teponaxtla and Siniyubi would bring a load of corn to their partners in Yucuhiti during its patronal fiesta in August, and those of Yucuhiti would travel to Teponaxtla and Siniyubi to leave off their load of corn during Lent, when these towns held fiestas. Note that this kind of exchange is based upon a set of moral ties between transactors that are much stronger than those that unite people bartering in the market. Indeed, the people from Teponaxtla, Siniyuvi, and Yucuhiti who formed trading partnerships were bound by ritual kinship, affinal and consanguineal ties (for an Andean case, see Marcus and Silva 1988).

Although market exchange, reciprocal trading partnerships, and the exploitation of different ecozones by single domestic units may each have been important in distributing goods produced on different ecological floors throughout the *cacicazgo,* the extensive circulation of products via these mechanisms is predicated, in part, on individual household rights to agricultural lands, and individual household rights to the products of its labor. The problem is that these rights only slowly developed during the Colonial period. In the sixteenth century, land ownership appears to have been vested in corporations, and production appears to have been collectively organized. Moreover, the most productive lands were in the hands of the elite (Spores 1983b:229–30). If exchange was important in circulating goods from different ecozones within the *cacicazgo,* then this suggests the presence of redistributing mechanisms where a central authority would play a mediating role. The most important mechanism of this type, if one can judge by how often early

Spanish observers of the Mixteca mention it, is the *viko* or "fiesta," as the Spaniards translated it.

Sixteenth-century *viko* can be classified into two kinds: those commemorating some religious event, and those commemorating some life-crisis transition of the elite, such as marriage. In each *viko,* non-elite were required to furnish the materials needed to feed participants in the celebrations and provide the sumptuary goods needed for elite exchanges. We know that in Tilantongo, commoners brought these goods to the elite during the fiesta as tribute payments, and that the collection of tribute was an important function of the fiesta (Paso y Troncoso 1982:72–73). In the Colonial period, settlements in the transitional zone also paid tribute to their *cacicazgo* seats during important fiestas. Thus, Yosotichi paid its tribute to Tlaxiaco during the latter's patronal fiesta, as did Nuyoo with Chalcatongo.[14]

Tribute in the Mixteca is a complex topic, and it is not clear what proportion of the payments made by commoners to the elite in the fiesta were "taxes" and how many were sacrifices made to an elite who were seen as manifestations of the sacred (Monaghan n.d.). In any event, what is important here is the way the celebration of the *viko* required the consumption of products from different ecological zones. From the highlands, for example, the important drink pulque was needed. Also, game animals from the forests of the highlands were needed for the banquets that were part of every fiesta. From the *cañada* lands, cacao was needed for ritual drinks, to make bridewealth payments, to make distributions to allied groups, and to make gifts to the elite of other centers. Indeed, dependent settlements located in the transitional zone paid tribute in products produced in the zone. Nuyoo, for example, paid tribute in bananas to the *cacica* of Chalcatongo,[15] Yosotichi paid Tlaxiaco a tribute in palm, flowers, and freshwater trout[16] and Mixtepec, a low-lying settlement, paid Tlaxiaco, at 2000 m, tribute in corn and beans (Acuña 1984:293). This made the *viko* into a kind of magnet, pulling in goods from throughout the different ecozones of the kingdom through tribute payments, sacrifice, and perhaps other transactions as well.

Yet it was not simply the case that goods were flowing into the hands of a group of elite, who then expended them for their own purposes. Several sources suggest that a wide range of people took part in the feasting and other distributions that occurred during the *viko*. As one early observer noted: "comían todos y bebían hasta embrigarse: esta, un día o dos [que era lo que] duraba la fiesta, y luego cada uno se iba a su casa" (Acuña 1984:307; see also Acuña 1984:285–6, 294, 307; Alvarado 1962:182; Pastor 1987:53). If people from throughout the *cacicazgo* participated, and if fiestas were times when goods from throughout the *cacicazgo* would be amassed, then this would have allowed people from the highlands to receive *cañada* products, and people from the *cañadas* to receive highland products. It is also quite probable that the location of at least some of these fiestas were periodically shifted from settlement to settlement. We know from the Mixtec codices that the elite would make the rounds of their domains, staying at various places during their circuits (Smith 1973; Marcus 1992:320). Fiestas held in different ecozones would have given participants the chance to sample products from a variety of places during the year. Moreover, by holding fiestas in areas where production was at its peak, the pressure of supporting the elite and their retainers could be shifted from settlements where food stocks might be scarce, to ones where food was more abundant.

In summary then, the fiesta could have played an important role in regulating the exchange of products between different ecozones in the *cacicazgo*. On the one hand, goods from both the highlands and the *cañadas* were collected to celebrate the fiestas, and these goods were distributed among fiesta participants. On the other hand, fiestas may have been held in different zones, drawing on the resources of areas where food was most plentiful. It should be kept in mind that while the elite may have played a crucial mediating role in the fiesta, this does not mean that the only exchanges that took place were between elite and commoners. If some form of trading partnership existed in the past, then the exchange of products between commoners living in different zones may also have occurred at this time. Also, markets may have been held concurrently with the fiesta. If this were the case, the products received in one exchange, say by bartering in the market, may have also circulated in another, perhaps as tribute to the elite. This would have made the fiesta a nexus of different transactions, which, in their totality, had the consequence of distributing goods produced in different ecozones to persons from throughout the *cacicazgo*.

Conclusion

In this paper, I have suggested that the different *cacicazgos* of the transitional zone between the Alta and the Costa each attempted to control swaths of territory that encompassed lands in the highlands, on the shelves of land alongside the *cañadas,* and in the *cañadas* themselves. In this way, they were able to ensure themselves access to a broad range of products, and, more importantly, sufficient supplies of corn.

As I noted in the Introduction, Ronald Spores was the first to point out the importance of ecological complementarity in Mixtec economies, and Rodolfo Pastor went on to relate ecological complementarity to large *cacicazgos* like Coixtlahuaca, which controlled vast extensions of territory by incorporating smaller polities through conquest, marriage alliance, guarantees of protection, and other means. As the discussion of ecological complementarity in the transitional zone makes clear, however, is that even small *cacicazgos* like Ocotepec and Chicahuaxtla articulated different productive zones into a single subsistence system.

This suggests that vertical integration is more important for understanding Mixtec polities than previously thought, since it was a characteristic of a range of different kinds of *cacicazgos,* not just of large expansionist kingdoms.

The notion that the vertical integration of different ecozones was a widespread feature of Mixtec *cacicazgos* does not mean that this articulation could not have different expressions. "Small" *cacicazgos* like Ocotepec or Chicahuaxtla demonstrate a kind of "compressed" type of ecological complementarity, where different ecozones lie in close proximity to one another (Brush 1976:161). This proximity allowed them to establish key settlements along the ridges that straddled the *cañadas* and highlands, which were no more than three or four hours from the *cañada* floors. In this location, inhabitants could both exploit the highland zones around the settlements (which at 1500–2000 m may have been particularly productive for rainfall farming [Flannery 1983:330]), and travel down into the *cañadas* to work during peak times in the agricultural cycle. The "large" kingdom of Tlaxiaco, on the other hand, demonstrates an "archipelago" type of ecological complementarity (Brush 1976; Murra 1972). Instead of achieving vertical integration by controlling adjoining environmental zones, Tlaxiaco secured access to *cañada* products by controlling islands of land that did not share borders with the main body of its territory. The most important of these archipelagos was in the Cañada of Yosotichi—separated from Tlaxiaco in the sixteenth century by Ocotepec, Cuquila, and Chicahuaxtla—which was about a two-day journey (some merchants say they can make the journey from Tlaxiaco to the Cañada of Yosotichi in twenty hours). Tlaxiaco's archipelago pattern may have been the result of a strategy that targeted specific resource areas for inclusion within the *cacicazgo,* leapfrogging over less desirable lands, or it may have been the result of the division of *cacicazgo* plots among royal heirs. In any event, Tlaxiaco appears to have been a patchwork of territories on its outer fringes, and it was unable to establish settlements on the ridges straddling the two zones, which remained in the hands of other kingdoms. As a consequence, it maintained a large satellite settlement, Teponaxtla, right in the Cañada of Yosotichi. In 1548 Teponaxtla contained 105 households, over 11% of the *cabecera* of Tlaxiaco's total population, which made it far larger than any other settlement in the *cañada,* and about a third the size of Chicahuaxtla, and over half the size of Putla (Paso y Troncoso 1905:101, 177, 282–83). There is no information on why Tlaxiaco maintained such a large settlement in the *cañada,* but one can speculate that because Tlaxiaco was physically separated from its archipelagos, it faced the problem of how to maintain a presence in an area where rapid transfers of defensive forces and labor were not possible. By establishing such a large settlement, Tlaxiaco was able to discourage encroachments from neighboring *cacicazgos* (such as Teponaxtla, or "war drum"), and avoid having to organize large labor parties to travel to *cañada* lands, since its main supply of labor was already resident in the zone.

These two patterns of vertical integration may also be associated with a different emphasis on exchange for the circulation of products among the various zones of the *cacicazgo*. While the populations of the small *cacicazgos* in the settlements along the ridges had access to the different ecozones created by the sharp gradient, most of Tlaxiaco's population did not, and would be faced with the problem of moving goods from Teponaxtla to Tlaxiaco. Tribute payments and other forms of exchange mediated by an elite may have been much more important in circulating goods from *cañadas* to highlands in Tlaxiaco's case than for other *cacicazgos* in the region.

From a broader perspective, we can view both patterns of ecological complementarity as a regional response to demographic and political forces operating more generally in Oaxaca. We know that the prehispanic history of Oaxaca was characterized by increasingly heavy demands placed on agricultural systems by a combination of growing population, increased demands by elites, and, in the fifteenth century, tribute payments imposed by the Mexica empire. These developments are associated with a number of innovations designed to increase agricultural output in the region (Flannery 1983:339; see also Spores 1969; Hopkins 1983:269). The "compressed" and "archipelago" types of ecological complementarity found in the Mixteca can perhaps be added to this catalog. As we have seen, the migration of workers between highlands and *cañadas* would have increased labor productivity, and the development of an extensive system of irrigation in the *cañadas* would have increased agricultural output. Unfortunately, the zone of the Mixteca that I have focused on here has not been studied archaeologically, and our knowledge of the antiquity of this system is limited to what the early Colonial documents tell us. One of the challenges for future archaeologists will be to determine its time depth.

Notes

1. The Cañada de Cortez, running southeast from San Miguel el Grande and draining into the Río de Cuanana probably should be included among these other *cañadas*.
2. Archivo Municipal de Santa María Yucuhiti, Memoria de las huertas de tierras y huertas de cacao que tienen los indios de las estancias de San Pedro y Santa María sujetos al pueblo de Ocotepec en las partes donde los indios de Tlaxiaco hicieron sus linderos, 1591.
3. Farmers in the region have at their disposal several different varieties of corn seed, each adapted to specific altitudes and environmental conditions, which Katz discusses at some length (Katz 1990:246–248).
4. Anuario Estadístico del Estado de Oaxaca, Tomo II (1988:1027, 1030–1035, 1161, 1164, 1167–1169). The highland municipalities surveyed were Tlaxiaco, Yosonatu,

Ocotepec, San Miguel, Itunyoso, and Chalcatongo. The lowland towns surveyed were Ixtayutla, Mixtepec, Zacatepec, Tijaltepec, and Yucuxaco.

5. Irrigation is also mentioned in the Spanish sources from the sixteenth century (e.g., Archivo Municipal de Santa María Yucuhiti, Memoria de las huertas de tierras y huertas de cacao que tienen los indios de las estancias de San Pedro y Santa María sujetos al pueblo de Ocotepec en las partes donde los indios de Tlaxiaco hicieron sus linderos, 1591).
6. Famine foods consumed in the area include acorns and the roots of bananas, both of which are ground and mixed with corn dough to make tortillas.
7. *Suma de Visitas* 1548, in Paso y Troncoso (1905, Tomo I, p. 283).
8. Archivo Municipal de Santa María Yucuhiti, Títulos de ejecutoria, posesión y confirmación de ella de las tierras pertenecientes a el pueblo de Santa María Ocotepeque, 1588.
9. Archivo General de la Nación, Mercedes 4, fa. 39, 1554.
10. Map in the possession of the Comisariado de Santiago Nuyoo.
11. See especially Archivo General de la Nación, Tierras 1331, exp. 1.
12. Markets are mentioned in 1542 at Cuquila ("Para que Rodrigo de Xerez, corregidor de Teposcolula, sobre lo que se queja, Bartolomé Baldez," transcribed in Spores 1992:1) and in 1555 at Yanhuitlán and Soyaltepec, where markets were held every five days, as was the custom in prehispanic times ("Yanguitlan," transcribed in Spores 1992:17). Of course, participation in particular markets may not have been restricted to the inhabitants of single *cacicazgos,* but may have operated expressly to exchange products between *cacicazgos*. It is for this reason I qualified the statement that different ecozones in the area were articulated into a single system by the *cacicazgo,* because the market may also have done this in prehispanic times.
13. Archivo General de la Nación, Indios 36, exp. 102; map in the possession of the Comisariado de Santiago Nuyoo. People in Nuyoo continued to bring bananas to Chalcatongo's fiesta through at least the 1940s.
14. Map in the possession of the Comisariado de Santiago Nuyoo.
15. Archivo General de la Nación, Indios 36, exp. 102. The people of Yosotichi paid 225 fish each year, and beginning in 1588 were required to pay 100 cargas of bananas.

References Cited

Acuña, René, ed.
1984 Relaciones geográficas del siglo XVI: Antequera. Mexico: Universidad Nacional Autónoma de México.

Alvarado, Francisco de
1962 Vocabulario en lengua Mixteca. Facsimile of 1593 edition. México: Instituto Nacional Indigenista y Instituto Nacional de Antropología e Historia.

Anuario Estadístico
1988 Anuario estadístico del estado de Oaxaca 1987, tomo II. Aguascalientes: Instituto Nacional de Estadística, Geografía e Informática.

Brush, Steven
1976 Man's use of an Andean ecosystem. Human Ecology 4 (2):147–66.

Burgoa, Fray Francisco de
1989 Geográfica descripción. vol. 1. México: Editorial Porrúa.
[1674]

Dahlgren de Jordán, Barbro
1966 La Mixteca: Su cultura e historia prehispánicas. México: Universidad Nacional Autónoma de México.

Flannery, Kent V.
1983 Precolumbian farming in the valleys of Oaxaca, Nochixtlán, Tehuacán and Cuicatlán: A comparative study. In: The Cloud People: Divergent Evolution of the Zapotec and Mixtec Civilizations, edited by Kent V. Flannery and Joyce Marcus, pp. 323–39. New York: Academic Press.

García Alcarez, Agustín
1973 Tinujei. México: Comisión del Río Balsas.

Huerta Ríos, César
1981 Organización socio-política de una minoría nacional. México: Instituto Nacional Indigenista.

Hopkins, Joseph W.
1983 The Tomellín Cañada and the Postclassic Cuicatec. In: The Cloud People: Divergent Evolution of the Zapotec and Mixtec Civilizations, edited by Kent V. Flannery and Joyce Marcus, pp. 266–70. New York: Academic Press.

Katz, Esther
1990 Prácticas agrícolas en la Mixteca Alta. In: Agricultura indígena: Pasado y presente, edited by Teresa Rojas Rabiela, pp. 239–76. México: Ediciones de la Casa Chata.

Marcus, Joyce
1983 The conquest slabs of Building J, Monte Albán. In: The Cloud People: Divergent Evolution of the Zapotec and Mixtec Civilizations, edited by Kent Flannery and Joyce Marcus, pp. 144–48. New York: Academic Press.
1992 Mesoamerican Writing Systems: Propaganda, Myth, and History in Four Ancient Civilizations. Princeton, New Jersey: Princeton University Press.

Marcus, Joyce, and Jorge E. Silva
1988 The Chillón Valley "Coca Lands": Archaeological background and ecological context. In: Conflicts Over Coca Fields in XVIth-Century Perú, by María Rostworowski de Diez Canseco, pp. 1–32. Studies in Latin American Ethnohistory & Archaeology, vol. 4. Memoirs of the Museum of Anthropology, University of Michigan, no. 21. Ann Arbor.

Monaghan, John
1989 Geography and history in the Lienzo of Ocotepec. Paper read at the Annual Meetings of the American Society for Ethnohistory, Chicago, Illinois.

1990 La desamortización de la propiedad comunal en la Mixteca: Resistencia popular y raíces de la conciencia nacional. In: Lecturas históricas del estado de Oaxaca: El siglo XIX, edited by Angeles Romero Frizzi, pp. 343–85. Instituto Nacional de Antropología e Historia y el Gobierno del Estado de Oaxaca. Mexico.
n.d. Sacrifice and the Symbolics of Power in Ancient Mesoamerica.

Murra, John
1972 El "control vertical" de un máximo de pisos ecológicos en la economía de las sociedades andinas. In: Visita de la provincia de León de Huánuco (1562), Iñigo Ortíz de Zuñiga, Visitador, vol. 2, pp. 429–76. Huánuco, Perú: Universidad Hermillo Valdizán.

Paso y Troncoso, Francisco del
1905 Papeles de Nueva España, 2a serie, geografía y estadística, tomo I. Madrid: Est. Tipográfico "Sucesores de Rivadeneyra."
1982 Papeles de Nueva España, 2a serie, geografía y estadística, tomo IV. Facsimile of 1905 edition. México: Banca Confía.

Pastor, Rodolfo
1987 Campesinos y reformas: La Mixteca, 1700–1856. El Colegio de México. México.

Redmond, Elsa M.
1983 A Fuego y Sangre: Early Zapotec Imperialism in the Cuicatlán Cañada, Oaxaca. Studies in Latin American Ethnohistory & Archaeology, vol. 1. Memoirs of the Museum of Anthropology. Ann Arbor.

Redmond, Elsa M., and Charles S. Spencer
1983 The Cuicatlán Cañada and the Period II Frontier of the Zapotec State. In: The Cloud People: Divergent Evolution of the Zapotec and Mixtec Civilizations, edited by Kent V. Flannery and Joyce Marcus, pp. 117–20. New York: Academic Press.

Secretaría de Programación y Presupuesto
1981 Carta de temperaturas medias anuales, México. México: Secretaría de Programación y Presupuesto.
1984 Carta de efectos climáticos regionales, Mayo–Octubre, Oaxaca. México: Secretaría de Programación y Presupuesto.

Smith, Mary Elizabeth
1973 Picture Writing from Ancient Southern Mexico. Norman: University of Oklahoma Press.

Spores, Ronald
1967 The Mixtec Kings and Their People. Norman: University of Oklahoma Press.
1969 Settlement, farming technology and environment in the Nochixtlan Valley. Science 166:557–69.
1974 Marital alliances in the political integration of Mixtec kingdoms. American Anthropologist 76:297–311.
1983a The origin and evolution of the Mixtec system of social stratification. In: The Cloud People: Divergent Evolution of the Zapotec and Mixtec Civilizations, edited by Kent V. Flannery and Joyce Marcus, pp. 227–38. New York: Academic Press.

1983b Postclassic Mixtec Kingdoms: Ethnohistoric and archaeological evidence. In: The Cloud People: Divergent Evolution of the Zapotec and Mixtec Civilizations, edited by Kent V. Flannery and Joyce Marcus, pp. 255–60. New York: Academic Press.

1992 Colección de documentos del Archivo General de la Nación para la etnohistoria de la Mixteca de Oaxaca en el siglo XVI. Vanderbilt University Publications in Anthropology, no. 41. Nashville.

CHAPTER 9

Irrigation in Cuicatlán

The Question of Río Grande Waters[1]

ROBERT C. HUNT

BRANDEIS UNIVERSITY

IN 1972, EVA HUNT REVIEWED the ethnohistoric evidence for irrigation among the Cuicatec. While there was massive evidence for irrigation from small streams, she found no evidence for the use of water from the Río Grande in Cuicatlán before the twentieth century. Puzzled, she examined population, technology, and the water demand of crops as explanations, and concluded that there was no visible reason why the Río Grande was *not* used during the Postclassic (E. Hunt 1972).

Since that time, much additional research relevant to this problem has been published. There has been a survey of archaeological settlements in the Cañada by Redmond (1983), an excavation of a Postclassic canal by Hopkins (1984), and an excavation at Dominguillo by Spencer (1982). Kirkby's magnificent study of agriculture in the Valley of Oaxaca appeared in 1973. SARH published the Papaloapan Commission data on climate and river regimes, which include the 1969 floods (Atlas Climatológico 1975). Doolittle's book on irrigation technology in Mesoamerica appeared in 1990. Due to the additional studies of irrigation systems worldwide, we now understand far more about the technology, organization, and social effects of irrigation than we did in 1972.

Given the accumulation of new data, it is appropriate now to take another look at the question of when the Río Grande waters were used for irrigation. This paper will review the archaeological and ethnohistoric evidence for the use of Río Grande water, and consider plausible economic and technological reasons for its use and non-use through time.

Setting: North Oaxaca Valley

The Puebla/Basin of Mexico area, and the Valley of Oaxaca, are two major population and cultural centers of highland Mesoamerica. One of the two main travel routes between them runs through the Tehuacán Valley and the Cañada de Cuicatlán. This is a low altitude path with reliable year-round supplies of water for human consumption.

The Cañada de Cuicatlán and the southern Tehuacán Valley are usually treated as separate regions. E. and R. Hunt, Hopkins, Redmond, and Spencer have all written on the Cañada, while MacNeish, Woodbury, and Neely have written on the Tehuacán Valley, as if they were separate places. The Cañada has been treated as a political and/or cultural subject of the Valley of Oaxaca, while the Tehuacán Valley has, at least at times, been treated as linked to Puebla, that is, facing northwards. But these two hydrological basins (1) form a continuous valley floor through high mountains, (2) have been a major transport route between Guatemala and the Basin of Mexico for millennia, and (3) have had a homogeneous agricultural tradition since early Classic times. The boundary of political dominance (between the Valley of Oaxaca and the Puebla area) has wandered up and down the valley for 2000 years. I suggest that there was one cultural zone and often two or more political zones. Only rarely were the borders of the political zones coincident with the place where the Río Salado and the Río Grande join (just north of Quiotepec). In consequence, the common tendency among all of us to separate the Tehuacán Valley from the Cañada as some sort of natural and sociopolitical provinces is misleading. Instead, I propose that we identify the entire North Oaxaca Valley as a single general zone, subdivided *hydrologically* into the Tehuacán Valley and the Cañada.[2]

The Environment

The North Oaxaca Valley has a single environment. The valley floor (below 1000 m asl) is low, hot, and relatively dry (precipitation less than 550 mm, all in summer), while the mountain ranges on either side (up to 3000 m) are cooler and receive considerably more rain (greater than 1000 mm) for more months in the year (Atlas Climatológico 1975). As a consequence, the valley floors have high rates of evapotranspiration and a year-round growing season. The North Oaxaca Valley contains two major rivers, the Río Salado in the Tehuacán Valley, and the Río Grande in the Cañada. These are the two main tributaries in the upper basin of the Río Papaloapan. The minor tributaries of these two rivers, usually called *ríos chiquitos,* can be ephemeral, and always end on fertile alluvial fans where they join the main rivers.

The settlements on and adjacent to these alluvial fans are said to have two kinds of agricultural land—low alluvium and high alluvium (Redmond 1983; Spencer 1982; following Kirkby 1973). The low alluvium is, for the most part, a product of the main rivers. It is relatively flat and level, occurs next to the bed of the river, and is subject to inundation in the worst floods. The high alluvium is on the alluvial fan, and, for the most part, is not easily reached with water from the main rivers. Instead, it is easily reached by water from the *ríos chiquitos*.

In the North Oaxaca Valley the permanent settlements have always (from the Formative to the present) been on, or next to, the alluvial fans. And for the entirety of this time period, the cropping patterns have been a combination of the subsistence crops (maize, beans, chile, squashes) and tropical fruits for export (coyol palm, chicozapote, ciruela, and the recently introduced orange and mango). Given the climate, then, water control has been a major factor for agriculturalists living on the valley floors. Those of us who have worked in the North Oaxaca Valley have all been interested in irrigation, and with good reason. The environment stimulates an enduring interest in water management.

There is apparently little or no irrigation possible from the Río Salado (because of high salt content), whereas the Río Grande has water that is chemically fit for irrigation. Our task in this paper is to understand the use of the Río Grande for irrigation in Cuicatlán. A significant part of our problem is to understand the differences between the *ríos chiquitos* and the Río Grande.

Hydrology

There are a number of streams tributary to the Grande and Salado.[3] Some are perennial, due to the high rainfall in the surrounding mountains. Their flow rates can vary considerably. All are relatively small streams, and therefore generate relatively small forces for the irrigator to manage. At the headworks[4] of the irrigation system, the Río Chiquito of Cuicatlán is 2 m wide, and 30 cm deep. The flow in the streams is highest in the rainy season (May to October), generally lowest in the hot dry season (March to May), and can be suddenly augmented by a large storm in its basin.[5] These streams are short and have steep gradients. The Río Chiquito de Cuicatlán falls 2400 m in 23 km (104 m/km). Like other *ríos chiquitos*, its flow is augmented by springs. Rarely does a situation occur in which a mountain community, located at the headwaters of one of these streams, can affect the water supply of the community down at the mouth, where the stream joins the Río Grande.[6]

Water control in the North Oaxaca Valley started in a truly massive way in the Formative period with the Purrón Dam, a storage facility on an ephemeral *río chiquito* (Woodbury and Neely 1972; Spencer 1979). The Purrón Dam is the first evidence of water storage technology in the New World, and was a monumental achievement. At its peak it was 18 m high, with a storage capacity greater than 3×10^6 m^3, and it stayed in use for about 800 years.[7] Irrigation with the use of the *ríos chiquitos* is as old as irrigation in this valley, and therefore goes back to at least the Late Formative (Redmond 1983).

Compared to the *ríos chiquitos*, the Río Grande is a large and turbulent river. The dry season river at Cuicatlán is 10 m wide, and up to 1 m deep in places, although fords exist where one can easily walk or drive across. In the rainy season, the river can be 30 m wide or more, and 2 m or more deep. The bed of the river has less gradient than the *ríos chiquitos*. For its course in the settled part of the

Cañada it drops 90 m in the 30 km from Dominguillo to Quiotepec (3 m/km). The river carries a very substantial load of silt. The amount is highly variable as to month of the year, with 98% coming during the rainy season, from May to October (Comisión del Papaloapan 1975: Lámina XXIV).

For the Papaloapan Basin as a whole, the upper basin provides 66% of the solid matter, and only 11% of the water. The Río Grande produces 81% of the water of the upper basin, and 59% of the solid matter (see Table 9.1).

The speed of the water flow in the natural source affects the durability of irrigation facilities. The headworks can be flimsily built if the water is flowing very slowly in the stream. But the water supply in nature can be highly variable, and it is highly variable in the North Oaxaca area. Hurricanes and other storms occasionally soak the area with large amounts of rain, which results in sudden increases in water velocity in the streams. The Río Grande mean water flow per month at Matamba and Quiotepec are presented in Table 9.2. A number of storm surges at Quiotepec can then be understood against this background flow (Table 9.3). The visible pattern indicates rapid changes in volume (and velocity and height of water). Increases of three to five times may occur in one day.

The year 1969 was a major wet one in the Valley of Oaxaca (Kirkby 1973), and was the year of the most devastating floods remembered in Cuicatlán. Several hurricanes struck Mexico that year. Table 9.4 records the storm surges (in m^3/s) produced by five hurricanes (Debbie, Emily, Eve, V-6, and Francella) at Matamba and Quiotepec in August and September, 1969.

The data show eleven storm surges on the Río Grande between 1950 and 1969, or an average of one surge every 1.8 years.[8] These surges occurred during the summer growing season. Their impact on irrigation works was enormous. For the major floods of 1969, even the Matamba Dam was threatened, although in the end it held. The ordinary headworks of brush, mud, and stones would have been obliterated in 1950, 1958, 1960, and 1969 (conservatively setting the threshold for destruction at a very high 500 cubic meters per second).

The implication of this for canal irrigation using the Río Grande is clear. Any irrigation facility using Río Grande water will be difficult to construct and very expensive to maintain. Impermanent facilities will be threatened or destroyed several times each summer growing season.

Agricultural Soils

The agricultural soils in the Cañada have been divided by Spencer and Redmond (following Kirkby 1973) into two types: low alluvium and high alluvium. Redmond (1983) presents a map of the distribution of these two land forms, from Tecomavaca to Dominguillo, but the scale of the maps is such that they are difficult to read, and are very difficult to transfer to the larger-scale topographic maps of the Papaloapan Commission.[9]

The Río Grande runs in a bed that is fairly wide, and at low water the stream is

TABLE 9.1
Physical Attributes of Upper Basin

	Area Drained (km^2)	Annual Water Flow (million m^3)	Annual Solids (thous. m^3)
Río Salado	7370	247	2672
Río Grande	4832	1172	3193

SOURCE: Com. Papaloapan 1975, Láminas XXII, XXIII.

TABLE 9.2
Mean Water Flow per Month, Matamba and Quiotepec

	J	F	M	A	M	J	J	A	S	O	N	D
Matamba	40	30	20	20	30	120	150	200	140	100	80	80
Quiotepec	50	40	30	25	30	50	180	175	250	210	80	80

SOURCE: Com. Papaloapan 1975: Lámina XXIV.
Flow in cubic meters per second.

TABLE 9.3
Storm Surges in the Cañada

October 1950: 6th 150, 11th 200, 12th 500, 16th 200
Source: Com. Papaloapan 1975, Lámina XXXII
June-July 1954: 28th 60, 30th 200, 2nd 300, 3rd 400, 6th 200
Source: op. cit.: Lámina XXXVI
October 1958: 5th 90, 13th 100, 15th 550, 23rd 150
Source: op. cit: Lámina XLIV
August-September 1960: 29th 125, 30th 450, 31st 675, 1st 450, 11th 200
Source: op. cit.: Lámina XLVI

Flow in cubic meters per second.

braided. At Cuicatlán on the eastern side of the river there is a bench some three to five meters higher than the floodplain. This low alluvium bench is fairly flat, slopes gently downhill with the river, and is now a very productive, major agricultural zone.

The *ríos chiquitos* have deposited alluvium where they enter the Cañada. As many have remarked, all settlements in the Cañada proper are found on these alluvial fans. I assume that these are the "high alluvium" of Redmond and Spencer. These fans have more relief than the low alluvium.

In terms of irrigation potential, both the high and low alluvium can be reached with water from a *río chiquito*. The *ríos chiquitos* pose few technical problems. They flow across fertile alluvial fans. They do not contain a great deal of water, the water quality is quite high, and they are easy to divert onto the various slopes

TABLE 9.4
Río Grande Flood Surges, Hurricanes of 1969

Date	Matamba Dam	Quiotepec
August 19	100	150
August 21	300	500
August 24	500	700
August 25		500
August 27	200	
September 3		500
September 5	350	500
September 6	650	650
September 9	300	500
September 11	600	708
September 15	200	300
September 19	150	200

SOURCE: Com. Papaloapan 1975: Lámina L
Flow in cubic meters per second

of the fan. From the very beginning of permanent settlement they were used for human consumption and for crops. There is little mystery about these features.

The mystery concerns the use of the waters of the Río Grande in the Cañada. The water from the Río Grande can reach only the low alluvium.[10] As we have seen, the Río Grande is a very large river generating huge forces and containing large quantities of solid matter. During the major floods, the low alluvium is inundated and the irrigation headworks and main canals erased. Construction is, therefore, necessary after every substantial flood. The engineering and resource problems of harnessing the Río Grande are very much greater than those posed by the *ríos chiquitos*.

When Eva Hunt and I were doing field work in Cuicatlán in the early 1960s, there were three or four short canals (less than 1 km in length) from the Río Grande, mostly used for watering cane. But there were very few of them, and most of the interest in town seemed to focus on the waters of the *ríos chiquitos*. In her ethnohistoric survey, one of the questions Hunt (1972) addressed was the history of the use of the Río Grande water, particularly in the major settlement in the Cañada Cuicatlán.

Eva Hunt's Argument

In her article in the Tehuacán Project series, Hunt (1972:195) noted that the ethnohistoric sources described irrigation from the *ríos chiquitos,* but did not mention using Río Grande water in Cuicatlán (1972:195). She considered two possible reasons for this non-use: technology, and the water demand of crops. The problems with the Río Grande itself were seen as the silt-load, and the lack of lift technology. After a discussion of statements that in 1580 there was sufficient water for irrigation from the Río Chiquito in Cuicatlán, she pointed out that during the Postclassic, Cuicatlán had extensive fruit orchards with an attendant high water demand.

Hunt (1972:195) rejected the technology argument because another *cacicazgo* on the river, Atlatlauca, did use Río Grande water (1972:195), and because the Río Salado was used for irrigation (1972:196). These two cases, for her, implied that lack of technological knowledge could not be a reason for not using the Río Grande at Cuicatlán. The high population and high water demand of Postclassic Cuicatlán, combined with the presence of the necessary technology, should have resulted in use of the Río Grande waters in Cuicatlán, and she suggested that evidence for such use might be found archaeologically (1972:195).

She concluded that:

> At present, we do not know why control and utilization of only streams was their only culturally viable solution, common also in other areas of Mesoamerica. It is possible, however, that before Spanish entry, when population pressures must have been greater, the Rio Grande waters were used for local canal feeders. If this was the case, it may be possible to retrieve some archaeological evidence. [E. Hunt 1972:195]

With new environmental, archaeological, and ethnographic data, and new understandings of irrigation, it seems appropriate to re-open the question. Is there any new evidence regarding the use of Río Grande water in Cuicatlán? If there is still no evidence for its use, do we have a better understanding of why?

The Second Look

New Data

Climate and hydrological data for the Papaloapan Basin were published in 1975, covering the period from the early 1940s to 1969 (Comisión del Papaloapan 1975).

Some of the new data derive from archaeological work. Hopkins wrote his thesis on Cañada material, based on survey and some excavation (Hopkins 1977, 1984). Redmond did a survey of the Cañada from Tecomavaca to Dominguillo (Redmond 1983), looking particularly at settlement distribution and population levels. Spencer surveyed the Purrón Dam area in the Tehuacán Valley (1979); he also excavated at Dominguillo, paying particular attention to irrigation (1982). In addition, there are other publications from the Redmond-Spencer team (Redmond and Spencer 1983; Spencer and Redmond 1979).[11] Doolittle's survey of irrigation features in the archaeological literature of northern Mesoamerica (including North Oaxaca) was published in 1990.

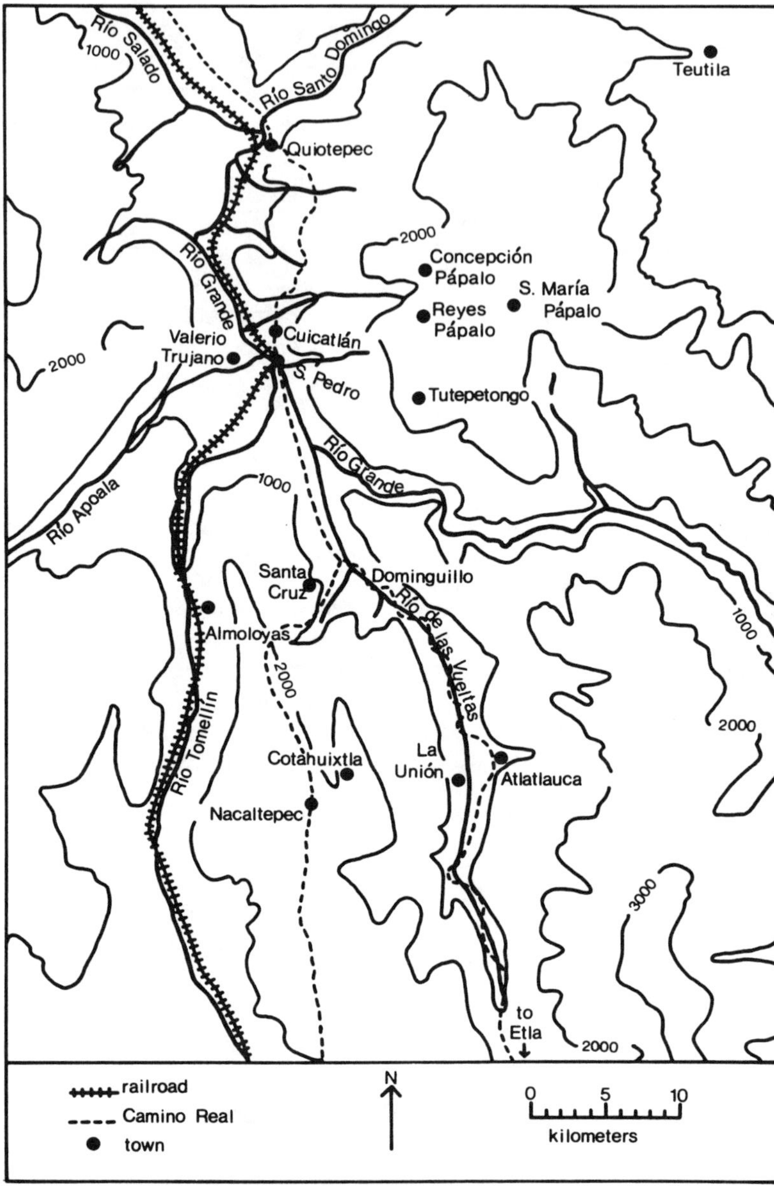

Figure 9.1. The Cuicatec Cañada: Atlatlauca to Quiotepec (redrawn from Hopkins 1984: Fig. 1).

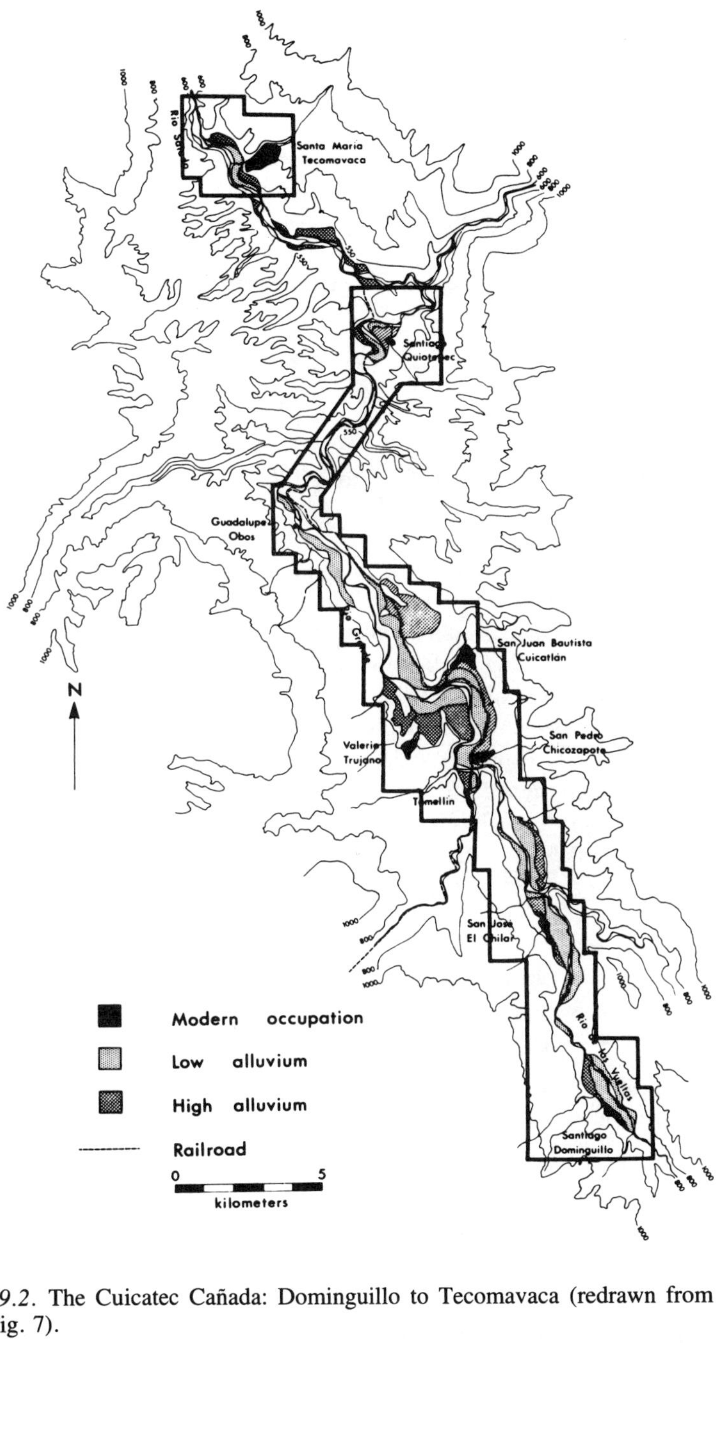

Figure 9.2. The Cuicatec Cañada: Dominguillo to Tecomavaca (redrawn from Redmond 1983: Fig. 7).

Two ethnographic publications appeared after the 1972 monograph, both on the social organization of irrigation in Cuicatlán (E. and R. Hunt 1974, 1978; R. and E. Hunt 1976). Kirkby published her important monograph on Valley of Oaxaca agricultural systems, which contains considerable information on irrigation (1973); Susan Lees' monograph on the organization of irrigation in the Valley of Oaxaca was also published in 1973. In addition, in the time period after 1972, a vast amount of literature on the social organization of irrigation from many other parts of the world has been produced.[12]

Everybody seems to have accepted Eva Hunt's original ethnohistoric work on this question (cf. Hopkins 1984). The archaeological surveys and excavations have turned up no evidence for use of the Río Grande waters for irrigation before the modern period. Hunt's conclusion that the Río Grande was not used for canal irrigation has not been challenged.

In the remainder of this paper, I take a second look at plausible reasons for the lack of use of the Río Grande water in Cuicatlán from A.D. 1100 to 1965.

Evidence for Irrigation

Finding and dating direct archaeological evidence for canal irrigation is notoriously difficult (cf. discussion in Sanders 1976). Even quite large canal irrigation systems can be constructed of ephemeral materials. If the dam is made of brush and sticks, and the canals dug in dirt, one massive flood can wipe out all surface indications of the system. Direct archaeological evidence of irrigation exists when the system has left evidence of headworks (usually massive) and/or canals whose temporal dimensions are firmly established. It is usually fairly easy to determine some time period when these facilities were in use. The dating of construction, on the other hand, is usually very difficult.

Historical documentation is another source of direct evidence. In the *Relaciones geográficas* of the *Papeles de la Nueva España,* for example, there are direct statements that local crops were irrigated, often including the name of the water source.

> Baxa d vna sierra comarcana a este pueblo vn arroyo de mucha y buen agua, con las qual se rriega toda la arboleda, y avn las simenteras y legunbres qaue sienbran los naturales de este pueblo, y ansi mismo por la parte de medio dia le desciende otro arroyo de buen agua y mucha, con aue se rriega otra parte de frutales y simenteras que los naturales tienen en laderas y mesas quo a fecho el Rio grande. [Paso y Troncoso 1905, IV:187][13]

These statements must be used with caution, of course. But where a sixteenth-century description presents details of the crops grown with irrigation, and of the water source, there seems to be no reason to deny the existence of irrigation agriculture.

Direct evidence for past canal irrigation can be very difficult to obtain. It is probably the case that most sites that had canal irrigation have left no direct evidence.

There are two primary forms of indirect evidence for irrigation—plant remains and settlement patterns. If the environment is too arid to support certain plants without human-provided moisture, then evidence of the growing of those plants in that environment creates a high probability of some form of irrigation. This evidence is almost entirely derived from archaeological excavation, rather than by survey.

If excavations turn up substantial plant remains that could be grown in that area only with irrigation, and, in addition, these remains include growing plant parts (rather than simply the fruits, which could be imported), then we have the strongest indirect evidence of irrigation. It must be remembered that only two excavations of any substantial size have been conducted in the whole of the region—one at Purrón Cave, and the other at Dominguillo. Our evidence of plant remains for the last 2500 years is entirely from these two sites.

The other form of indirect evidence is settlement pattern. Some settlement patterns strongly imply the presence of irrigation. If any of these alluvial fans had a permanent settlement of at least 2.5 ha, it follows that they were probably irrigating their basic crops. Furthermore, as population grew, and settled on or on the edge of irrigable land, the probability that irrigation was taking place increases.

In the Postclassic, the Cañada population (see Table 9.5) was greater than at any time before about A.D. 1980, and we find vastly greater numbers of small sites, all of them located on the edge of alluvium, with most of them located very close to present-day canals.

My conclusion is that the land had to have been irrigated during the Postclassic in order to provision the substantial local population.

The Question of Río Grande Water

The claim for earliest use of Río Grande water comes from Spencer (1982) and Redmond (1983) who state that simple flood-water irrigation was used on the low alluvium in early times, with canal irrigation being used later on the high alluvium. There are three varieties of flood-water farming: arroyo, flood-recession, and hillside harvesting. None of them, in my judgment, were viable on the low alluvium.

In general, the Cuicatec area has high relief, and a multitude of permanent streams. The Cañada settlements were all located on or next to alluvial fans associated with permanent *ríos chiquitos*. For these settlements, there was no reason to resort to flood irrigation, for canal irrigation would be far more effective. There are other reasons why "simple flood-water irrigation" was unlikely to have been used in the Cañada.

Arroyo harvesting was an unlikely option. Most of the major tributaries of the

TABLE 9.5
Estimates of Population in Cuicatlán

Author	Time Period	Population
E. Hunt	Post Classic	5,000[a]
E. Redmond	Post Classic	3,650-4,000[b]
J. Hopkins	Colonial—1548	1,063[c]
J. Hopkins	Colonial—1560	1,403[c]
J. Hopkins	Colonial—1569	840[c]
Mexican Census	1930	1,818[c]
Mexican Census	1960	2,456[c]
Mexican Census	1990	3,469

[a]E. Hunt estimated 5,000 (1972).
[b]Redmond's Tables 41 and 42 permit an estimate of 3,650-4,000 (1983:160, 161).
[c]J. Hopkins 1984:47.

Río Grande in the Cuicatec Cañada are perennial, at least on the east side of the river. There would be no reason to get involved in arroyo harvesting when the arroyos contained perennial streams. Hill harvesting was also an unlikely option. There is very little rain in the Cañada, and there would have been very few occasions where substantial amounts of rain fell. Furthermore, no archaeological or other kind of survey has as yet revealed the construction features of hill-side harvesting.

Flood-recession farming was also unlikely to have been practiced. As seen in the section on the rivers, the Río Grande is subject to frequent storm surges between June and October. Such surges are incompatible with flood-recession agriculture—such a surge would wipe out a crop nearly ready for harvesting. The river regime is simply too unpredictable. Furthermore, the alluvial terrace that was cultivated is several meters above the low-water level of the river. It is only the occasional flood that comes up onto that terrace. Agriculture that depended upon a flood on average once every two years, and that might see a sequence of several years without a flood, would be very chancy indeed. Flood recession agriculture on the low alluvium seems to be, at best, a very distant possibility.

My conclusion, then, is that flood-water farming on the low alluvium in the Cañada area, and particularly around Cuicatlán, was extremely unlikely.[14] Canal irrigation from the Río Chiquito seems highly probable. I disagree with the conclusions of Redmond and Spencer on this matter.

In terms of canal irrigation, short (less than 1 km) main canals with brush weirs were in use on the Río Grande in Cuicatlán in the 1960s, and the first evidence of their use is in the twentieth century. At that time, they were used on the low alluvium. It is possible that these short and ephemeral weirs and canals could have been used at any time, including the Formative period. It is difficult to imagine any kind of surface archaeological evidence for (or against) such features. The headgates were ephemeral. The canals were short, and subject to destruction by the frequent floods. There was no settlement, and no housing, along or near these short canals. Therefore, surface archaeological evidence for canals is unlikely to be found. There is no ethnohistoric mention of their existence.

Longer canals (greater than 5 km) could have delivered Río Grande water to several large areas of low alluvium (Grassland, on Map I from Hunt and Hunt 1978). Located higher up the slopes than the short ones, they would likely have left some archaeological trace, although the frequent large floods would have washed their headworks away. No sign of such canals has been reported. There are Postclassic settlement traces in the Grassland area (low alluvium), following a contour that would have been natural for a canal. However, this string of sites could also have been reached by the right bank canal from the Río Chiquito de Cuicatlán. In my opinion, these sites are evidence for irrigation, but are not evidence of irrigation from the Río Grande.[15]

There is no evidence for long canals from the Río Grande before A.D. 1965, and there is no evidence for any kind of canal irrigation with Río Grande water in the early Colonial and Postclassic periods. I will assume, for the purposes of this paper, that the lack of evidence represents non-use. I will now consider the technological sophistication, the political situation, and the changing water demands of the Postclassic and later periods to see if these provide any explanation for the lack of Río Grande canals.

The Río Salado and Atlatlauca Evidence

Eva Hunt cited use of the Río Salado in the Tehuacán Valley as evidence that the technology was in place. Her primary reference was to the *Suma de Visitas* for Teotitlán del Camino (Paso y Troncoso 1905, IV:213–33). A close look at the entries shows clearly that Teotitlán and the subject towns were using water from the *ríos chiquitos,* not from the Río Salado, for irrigation.

Hunt noted that Atlatlauca was recorded as using Río Grande water, the only site in the Cañada to do so. This fact was a major piece of evidence for her conclusion that the technology for using the Río Grande had existed in Postclassic times. Of the modern investigators who have worked in the Cañada, only Hopkins reports actually having visited the site. In fact, the major river at Atlatlauca is not the Grande, but the much smaller Jayacatlán, a tributary of the Grande. Atlatlauca is on the Río Jayacatlán, upstream from Dominguillo. The Jayacatlán is joined by a *río chiquito* at Atlatlauca, and both are used for irrigation, according to the *Relación* of 1580. The Río Jayacatlán at Atlatlauca is much smaller than the Río Grande at Cuicatlán. Table 9.6 presents the basic facts about the basins, water flow, and solids in the water for the four subsystems. Table 9.7 compares four gauging stations: the Grande at Matamba (upstream from the following three rivers), the Jayacatlán at Dominguillo, the Tomellín at Tomellín, and the Apoala at Apoala.

If none of the upstream flow is removed before the Grande reaches Cuicatlán, then the Grande at Cuicatlán would be a drainage area greater than 3959 km^2, water volume greater than 1044×106 m^3, and a total volume of solids greater than 2408×10^3 m^3.[16] In other words, the volume of water and solids at Cuicatlán itself is many times higher than that of the tributary streams. The area drained by the Jayacatlán is 18% of the Grande at Cuicatlán; the water in the Jayacatlán is 7% of the Grande at Cuicatlán; and the solid matter is also 7% of the Grande at Cuicatlán, measured at the mouth of the Jayacatlán, not upstream at Atlatlauca. The Río Jayacatlán is thus vastly smaller than the Grande at Cuicatlán. If I am correct about the size of the Jayacatlán River at Atlatlauca, Hunt's argument that technology for handling the Río Grande was in existence and used during the Postclassic, based on the ethnohistoric record of Atlatlauca, is seriously weakened. I conclude that the use of the Río Jayacatlán for irrigation at Atlatlauca is not proof that the technology for managing irrigation from the Grande was in existence in the Postclassic.

Construction Problems

There are a number of tasks that are universally found in canal irrigation systems: construction, allocation of the water, maintenance, accounting, and conflict resolution (R. Hunt 1988). There is no reason to think that allocation, accounting, and conflict resolution were any more (or less) problematic in the past, or that they would affect the use of Río Grande water in Cuicatlán.

Physically, the most challenging of these tasks are construction and maintenance. Construction requires the existence of an engineering technology, and it includes the design of the facility, the marshalling of construction resources (labor, materials, food, tools, etc.), and application of effective incentives to the work force.

A major water storage facility, the Purrón Dam, was built in the Early Formative in the North Oaxaca Valley, and, therefore, an advanced water-containing technology was already available (Woodbury and Neely 1972; Spencer 1979). According to Doolittle (1990), canals, sometimes built of masonry, were used to irrigate from *ríos chiquitos* early in the Formative, but he presents no evidence that headgates on major rivers existed until the late fifteenth century. It is, of course, possible that such engineering technology existed and was absorbed by the Spaniards. If this were true in Cuicatlán, it has left no trace whatsoever, and I am confident that long Río Grande canals would have left some historical trace. It is doubtful, but possible, that major headworks in rivers would have been within prehispanic capacity.

TABLE 9.6
Area Drained, Total Water Flow, and Total Volume Solids

River	Site	Area Drained[a]	Water Volume[b]	Solids Volume[c]
Grande	Matamba	2,143	887	1,624
Jayacatlán	Dominguillo	695	77	173
Tomellín	Tomellín	780	51	467
Apoala	Apoala	341	29	144

[a]Square kilometers, from Com. Papaloapan 1975: Lámina XXII.
[b]Millions of cubic meters, op. cit., Lámina XXIII.
[c]Thousands of cubic meters, op. cit., Lámina XXIII.

TABLE 9.7
Volume of Water (Millions of Cubic Meters) per Month, Upper Basin

Month	Matamba	Dominguillo	Tomellín	Apoala
January	20	2	0	0.7
February	25	2	0	0.5
March	20	1	0	0.3
April	20	1	0	0.5
May	20	1	0	0.4
June	30	2	9	2.3
July	120	7	10	3.3
August	160	17	18	6.3
September	200	21	17	7.9
October	150	17	6	3.5
November	100	6	2	1.7
December	80	4	0	1.1

SOURCE: Com. Papaloapan 1975: Lámina XXIV
Note: The data for Apoala are from a chart, and are copied exactly. The data for the rest are interpolated from graphs and have unknown errors.

On the other hand, it is perfectly clear that the technology to build and operate short canals from a river existed. If such canals, in fact, existed in Cuicatlán during the Postclassic, they too have left no historical or archaeological trace. I agree with Hunt's conclusion that the construction technology for short canals existed and, therefore, construction technology can not be a plausible reason for not using the Río Grande waters.

There is also no doubt in my mind about resources and their organization. Postclassic population was high enough, and was highly organized. The existence of pyramids and ballcourts is evidence that the Postclassic political leadership had the capacity to organize material, food, and labor. The ability to mobilize incentives for this work also seems clear. Those incentives probably did not include wage labor, but rather were of the corvée type.

Maintenance Problems

Maintenance, when compared with construction, is very differently organized. While construction tends to take a short time, and a large effort from large numbers of people, maintenance is tedious and small scale, requiring frequent small efforts from a large number of people. It is easier to mobilize people to construct a facility than to maintain it. The intensity of the job, and the visibility of the results, may well be important aspects of the difference.

Maintenance of a canal irrigation system demands both sufficient labor and adequate organization of that labor. The solid matter in the Río Grande is high, much higher than in the *ríos chiquitos*. The consequence of this fact for operating canals from the Río Grande can not be overemphasized. Currently (1990) there is a 24 km main canal drawing water from the Río Grande at the Matamba Dam, about 10 km upstream from Cuicatlán. Water from this canal can reach the entirety of the low alluvium, and small amounts of the high alluvium as well. The canal has a cross section of 1 square meter, and a capacity of 2 cumecs (cubic meters/second). Portions of the main canal fill with silt in less than a year. From my brief observations in 1990, more than 10,000 cubic meters of soil needs to be removed every year. This means that the whole of the canal has to be cleaned, when needed, in order for any water at all to get to the end. Currently, the Unidad de Riego is responsible for this cleaning, which is done in November. Every member has to supply a number of days of labor, proportional to the land owned in the system, to the cleaning effort. Hundreds of men turn out to do the digging.[17] The routine maintenance of canals from the Río Grande is, therefore, not a trivial task.

But not only is the physical system subject to constant silting—there is also danger from floods. In central Mexico, the hurricane season coincides with the wet season. In September of 1969, six hurricanes occurred within a few days of each other, precipitating massive floods. Such floods wipe out most or all human-made features on the low alluvium. Headgates are destroyed, canals are obliterated, and the annual crops and other field features are a total loss. The Matamba Dam survived the 1969 floods, but even it was damaged (SAHR engineer 1990: pers. comm.).

The population to provide labor for construction and maintenance was clearly in existence in the Postclassic. The amount of labor available should have been high during the Postclassic; it fell to a very low figure by 1600, and has very slowly climbed back, reaching Postclassic levels only in the late twentieth century. The population to support the maintenance of long canals from the Río Grande probably existed in the Postclassic, and was probably absent in the Colonial period.

Also, the social organization to maintain long canals was very likely in existence in the Postclassic, and during Colonial times as well. Since at least the 1910 Revolution, local social organization would have found it much more difficult to organize the construction and maintenance. Wage labor might have been available, but it is unlikely that command labor (including corvée) would have been feasible for large-scale projects. It would have to have been done by a highly capitalized entity. Eventually the State organized, and largely paid for, the construction of the Matamba Dam and its 24 km long main canal in the 1960s.

The incentives for individuals to work on maintenance during the Postclassic certainly included the corvée. It is unclear whether there was wage labor as well. During the Colonial period, both corvée and wage labor existed. In the modern period (after 1910), wage labor and corvée co-exist (there is some common-property labor which belongs to the Irrigation Community; see R. Hunt 1991).

It is my conclusion that the labor supply for headworks and main canal maintenance would have been adequate during the Postclassic and inadequate during most of the Colonial period, becoming available again only during the late twentieth century. The social organization to mobilize it was certainly present up to the Revolution of 1910.

Eva Hunt suspected that maintenance would be a problem, given the solid matter in the Río Grande during the wet season. My conclusion is that the executive organization and labor demands for maintenance would be very high. But there seems to be no reason why the Postclassic phase of occupation in Cuicatlán could not have met these demands. During the Colonial period, the executive capacity was surely present, but with the low population, the labor supply looks to be problematic.

Water Demand by Crops

Eva Hunt asserted that there were prehispanic crops which demanded a good deal of water, including chicozapote. We will probably never obtain even approximate figures on water demand of prehispanic cultivars (generalizing from contemporary varieties to 1490 is almost certainly a mistake). However some crops introduced by the Spaniards (mango, orange, various vegetables) had seasonal patterns of water need that were very close to the crops already present.

Two new crops that did have different water demands were rice and sugar. Rice is an annual, and while it needs a great deal of water at some stages of growth, it would be grown during the rainy season when water is relatively plentiful.

Cane sugar, in contrast, has a very different pattern of needs. Sugar grows for twelve to eighteen months, and must be watered intensively over much of that cycle. It is not a perennial tree, with varying water needs over the year. It is more like an annual, with high water demands during both the wet and dry seasons.

Sugar was introduced in the Colonial period when population was much lower than during the Postclassic. Thus, the increased demand for water by sugar was almost certainly counterbalanced by the decreasing demand for water for subsistence crops, due to falling population. There may have been a net decrease in water demand.

There is a widespread tendency to regard the demand for water as somehow fixed in nature, whereas the supply is variable. In actuality, the demand for water is under far more human control than is the supply. The demand is a product of the water demand of each plant multiplied by the number of those plants, summed over the whole of the irrigated area. Many irrigated plants are annuals, and so each year the variety and numbers of plants are the product of human decisions, and so, therefore, is water demand. In modern times, with markets and rising populations, there is a tendency for irrigators to push the limits of the water system.[18] The point here is that these decisions are made every year, and so the water demand is a function of the crops, and not set by nature. The crop varieties alone of the Postclassic would not have automatically generated a water scarcity (or surplus) situation. It would have been a question of the relationship of the total demand to the total supply for any given year.

Hunt asserted that Postclassic agriculture in Cuicatlán presented as much demand for water as any subsequent period. I see it very differently. No known Postclassic crop had high water water needs at critical time periods that the Colonial sugar cane did.

Discussion

The first evidence of short canals from the Río Grande dates from the twentieth century. These short canals, ephemeral because of the floods, could well have been built and destroyed many times during the past three millennia. By their very nature they would not leave archaeological traces on the land surface. However, there is no reason why they would not have left historical traces.

There is no evidence that Cuicatlán had long (greater than 5 km) canals using water from the Río Grande prior to A.D. 1965. There should be archaeological and ethnohistoric traces if the longer canals existed, and so far no traces have been found. It is reasonable to conclude, based on the evidence available so far, that such canals did not in fact exist. The question then is why there were no long canals using Río Grande waters?

Several factors which would have made such canals possible have been considered. The technology for construction of both the canals and the headgates was in existence, and had been for centuries. The labor force, and the social organization to mobilize it, certainly existed in the Postclassic. There is no reason to think that maintenance would have been impossible in the Postclassic. The labor force, and the social organization, to maintain the canals would surely have been in place. The Postclassic population of Cuicatlán was large enough. All of these social conditions would seem to support, or at least not constrain, the installation of the long Río Grande canals. These factors can not, therefore, be used to explain the lack of the feature.

Hunt asserted that the Postclassic crops had high water demand. I claim that this assertion is not bolstered by evidence. It is not how often a crop must be watered that counts, but how much water it must receive at the critical times, and how much water supply there is during that time period. Sugar needs water during the dry seasons, when water is least plentiful. If any crop would have stimulated additional water supplies, surely it would have been sugar cane.

But sugar was introduced after the Conquest, and by the time it was well established, the native population had already decreased substantially. The falling population would have meant a reduction in the amount of land being cultivated, and, therefore, a reduction in the demand for water. Furthermore, the reduction in population meant a reduction in the size of the work force.

Events in the Colonial period would have both worked for, and against, the use of Río Grande waters. If sugar was an incentive to acquire more water, the low population (with lower amounts of labor, and lower demand for water) would have worked against it. It seems plausible to conclude that the sum of these vectors would have worked against the use of Río Grande waters. The population climbed back to early Colonial levels in the twentieth century, which is also when we have our first evidence for the use of (short) Río Grande canals. This is probably not a coincidence.

Conclusion

There is still no evidence that Río Grande water was used for irrigation in Cuicatlán at any time prior to the twentieth century. The argument that Colonial period large-river irrigation existed in Atlatlauca and Teotitlán has been rejected.

The technology for building short canals from the Río Grande surely existed in the Postclassic, for it would have been identical to the technology used to irrigate the *ríos chiquitos* in the same area, which had been irrigated since the Formative. We do not know whether there were short canals abstracting water from the Río Grande prior to the twentieth century, but no evidence for them has been presented. Most of the conditions were favorable. The social organization and the labor were presumably available during the Postclassic. There was a demand for water year-round for tropical fruits, and presumably also for a dry-season crop of corn and beans. So the demand would have been there. Short canals would have been relatively impermanent, due to floods. Their existence would not have required any greater amount of organization than already existed to build and operate the canals from the Río Chiquito.

Several factors are plausibly involved in operating long canals from the Río Grande. The technology for building permanent headgates probably did not exist (the forces generated by the Río Grande in flood are massive). Impermanent headgates were available, if expensive of labor. The labor force and social organization necessary to manage the maintenance demands probably existed during the Postclassic. The population to supply labor was probably too low during much of the Colonial period.

The demand for water is another key element in the puzzle. It is not at all clear that the demand for Río Grande water existed during the Postclassic. Sugar, in sufficient amounts, would have required more water during the dry season, and would have been an incentive to harness the Río Grande. But when sugar was introduced during the Colonial period, the population was also very low.

Long canals with impermanent headgates were never installed on the Río Grande at Cuicatlán. A long canal (24 km) with a permanent headgate was not built until 1965, when the technology existed; the social organization to fund and build it was interested (the State); the water demand was present (sugar, fruit trees); the population was high enough to support the demands of maintenance; and the social organization to manage it was in place. The co-occurrence of all these conditions did not take place until the middle of the twentieth century A.D.

Notes

1. I am grateful to Judy Zeitlin and Joyce Marcus for involving me in this project. Fieldwork in Cuicatlán has been supported by NSF GS82 (1962–64), and by the University of Illinois (1967, 1968). Comparative work on irrigation has been supported by ACLS (1975–76), and by NSF 1990–1992. I am appreciative for all their support. I am grateful to the editors for their intelligent and firm advice, and to Scotty MacNeish and Elsa Redmond for checking the manuscript. Irene Winter and William E. Doolittle have responded at length with very helpful suggestions.
2. When Judy Zeitlin and Joyce Marcus first approached me about my interest in writing a paper for this volume, my response was that I would have another look at the irrigation literature. That survey covered the territory from the Purrón Dam in the Tehuacán Valley to Atlatlauca in the southern Cañada. (That paper is now at 107 pages and climbing. I have extracted one of the arguments from it for this paper.)
3. There are at least three such *ríos chiquitos* in use in the Cañada today, one descending from Yepaltepec to Quiotepec, the Río Chiquito de Cuicatlán, and the Río Chiquito de San Pedro Chicozapotes. There are others at Dominguillo, Guendulain, and almost

certainly at Atlatlauca. For the rest of this paper, the analysis will concentrate on Cuicatlán, and on the Río Chiquito de Cuicatlán.

4. Headworks are the human-made facilities where the irrigation system transfers the water from a natural source to the system. They can include wells, qanats, weirs, barrages, and storage dams.
5. Although the Papaloapan Commission took many measurements of the natural environment in the 1940s and 1950s, they apparently never put a gauge on any of the *ríos chiquitos*. What I have reported here is the result of talking with informants, and observing the behavior of the stream.
6. The major exception is, of course, Yepaltepec and Quiotepec (E. Hunt 1972).
7. The Purrón Dam has not received the attention it deserves, either from social scientists, or from engineers.
8. 1950 October
   1952 June
   1954 June-July
   1955 July
   1955 September
   1956 July
   1958 October
   1960 August-September
   1961 July-August
   1969 August
   1969 September
9. In what follows, I will be applying the Kirkby division of low and high alluvium to the only area of the Cañada I know well from walking, riding, and driving—that on the eastern side of the river including Cuicatlán. I have visited the Purrón Dam, Tecomavaca, Teotitlán, Valerio Trujano, and Quiotepec and so I know something of their environment. I have made a low-altitude flight over Atlatlauca, El Chilar, and Dominguillo, but I have not walked those areas. I obviously know less about some areas than about others, and do not know the extent to which the analysis can be generalized to them. My study of the 1:50,000 topographic maps drawn by the Papaloapan Commission leads me to suspect that they will conform to the ones I have visited. In this study, as in all others of the region, there are important data that simply are not currently available. Redmond (1983) and Spencer (1982) also use the Kirkby division. My use of the division may vary from theirs.
10. Río Grande water could reach the high alluvium, but it would require a main canal of great length and technical complexity. Even with the modern Matamba Dam, only incidental amounts of the high alluvium is watered from the Río Grande.
11. Most authors have written about more than one site in the region. The overlap among them, however, is different. Johnson and Neely surveyed from Purrón to Tecomavaca. Redmond surveyed from Tecomavaca to Dominguillo, and Hopkins worked from Cuicatlán to Atlatlauca with a probe further south. E. Hunt was concerned with Quiotepec and Cuicatlán. Woodbury and Neely wrote of irrigation features in the Tehuacán Valley, including the Purrón Dam, and Spencer did a detailed survey of the Purrón Dam. Doolittle was not concerned with regional cultural complexes.

    The time period of these studies also varies. The Purrón Dam occurs in the Formative. Spencer and Redmond's work concentrates on the Formative and Classic, but extends to the end of the Postclassic, and the Tehuacán Valley Project covered all time periods to the end of the Postclassic, concentrating on the earlier ones. Hopkins concentrates on the Postclassic but extends to modern times, E. Hunt combines the sixteenth century A.D. with some twentieth-century material, and E. and R. Hunt have written about irrigation around Cuicatlán in the 1960s.

A major issue in studies of the region, therefore, has to be variation in how the spatial and temporal boundaries of the study area are set. This paper concentrates on Cuicatlán between A.D. 1100 and 1990.

12. There is no convenient way to get access to the bibliography of the world irrigation literature. It is scattered across several disciplines (anthropology, sociology, rural sociology, development engineering). Some of it is gray literature (reports receiving limited circulation), available to those few of us who specialize in the topic, but not widely available. The libraries of IIMI, ICID, USAID, and the World Bank do not have complete collections.
13. This is part of section 19 for Cuicatlán. These two arroyos are certainly the Río Chiquito de Cuicatlán, and probably the Río Chiquito de San Pedro Chicozapotes. The Río Grande is mentioned in this passage, but only as a source of fish. All references to irrigation are to *ríos chiquitos*.
14. Professor William E. Doolittle has written me to say that he disagrees with my position here. I quote (with permission) from his letter dated 13 August 1992:

> (1) The low alluvium could have been cultivated, and via flood-recession. As the name implies, this form of agriculture takes place after the flood water recede. If this is in October and there is a year-round growing season then planting could have taken place in Oct.-Nov. with harvests a few months later. (2) "Arroyo harvesting" *is* likely; and early on when the population was small and demands were low would have been preferred over floodplains of perennial streams. The latter would have been heavily vegetated, probably with mesquite bosques, prior to cultivation, and would have to be cleared. . . . (3) Just because surveys didn't reveal hillside harvesting features doesn't mean they are not there. . . . Even trained observers can fail.

All these positions are possible, but none are based on field data. In my opinion the resolution of this issue requires several of us to visit the sites in northern Oaxaca in an attempt to investigate, in the field, the relevant dimensions.

15. The first successful permanent head gate using Río Grande water is the Matamba Dam. It commenced operation in 1965 A.D., survived the massive floods of 1969, and it has led to a massive change in the organization of irrigation in Cuicatlán. It demanded labor, capital, skilled engineers, and management. It was designed, built, and paid for by outside interests, in this case the State. Operation has been turned over to the local farmers, who now run everything but the maintenance of the dam. There is no longer any water shortage in the town. Rather, now there is a shortage of irrigable land. The stratification within the land-owning category is now far less than it was in 1963. The difference between the land-owner and the landless is if anything greater than it was, and the landless have increased in number (the population of the town is now [1990] 9,000—it was 2,500 in 1963.)
16. The numbers would be even larger on account of the unmeasured tributaries to the Grande. The Río Chiquito de San Pedro Chicozapotes, and the Río Chiquito de Cuicatlán both join the Grande, and are not measured. On the other hand, most of the water from these small tributaries is taken for irrigation, and so does not join the Grande, at least on the surface. The differences should be small.
17. I had a chance to observe the process in November of 1990 when I was in Cuicatlán for a few days. I was unable to obtain a measure of the total number of person-days it took to clean the main canal. I hope to return soon and obtain the correct figures.
18. That this is not solely a modern phenomenon is proved by Valencia, where there has been pressure on the size of the system since the fourteenth century. The newly created

areas of the system have junior rights, and must cut back under water scarcity conditions before the senior rights holders have to do so (Glick 1970; Maass and Anderson 1978).

References Cited

Comisión del Papaloapan
1975 Atlas climatológico e hidrológico de la Cuenca del Papaloapan. Mexico, D.F.: Secretaría de Recursos Hidráulicos.

Doolittle, William E.
1990 Canal Irrigation in Prehistoric Mexico. Austin: University of Texas Press.

Glick, Thomas
1970 Irrigation and Society in Medieval Valencia. Cambridge, MA: Harvard University Press.

Hopkins, Joseph W., III
1977 Irrigation and the Cuicatecs: Environmental manipulation and ecosystems. The Western Canadian Journal of Anthropology 7:129–50.
1984 Irrigation and the Cuicatec ecosystem: A study of agriculture and civilization in North Central Oaxaca. Studies in Latin American Ethnohistory & Archaeology, vol. 2, edited by Joyce Marcus. Memoirs of the Museum of Anthropology, University of Michigan, no. 17. Ann Arbor.

Hunt, Eva
1972 Irrigation and the socio-political organization of the Cuicatec Cacicazgos. In:The Prehistory of the Tehuacán Valley. Vol 4: Chronology and Irrigation, edited by Frederick Johnson, pp. 162–248. Austin: University of Texas Press.

Hunt, Eva V., and Robert C. Hunt
1974 Irrigation, conflict and politics: A Mexican case. In: Irrigation's Impact on Society, edited by Ted Downing and McGuire Gibson, pp. 129–57. Tucson: University of Arizona Press.
1978 Irrigation, conflict and politics: A Mexican case. (Revised version of 1974 paper.) In: Origins of the State: A Symposium, edited by Ronald Cohen and Elman R. Service, pp. 69–123. Philadelphia: ISHI Press.

Hunt, Robert C.
1988 Size and the structure of authority in canal irrigation systems. Journal of Anthropological Research 44:335–55.
1991 Property in common property: Irrigation in Mexico. Paper presented at the 1991 Annual Meeting, International Association for the Study of Common Property, Winnipeg.
n.d. North Oaxaca Irrigation. In preparation.

Hunt, Robert C., and Eva V. Hunt
1976 Canal irrigation and local social organization. Current Anthropology 17:389–411.

Kirkby, Anne V. T.
1973 The use of land and water resources in the past and present Valley of Oaxaca, Mexico. In: Prehistory and Human Ecology of the Valley of Oaxaca, vol. 1, edited by Kent V. Flannery. Memoirs of the Museum of Anthropology, University of Michigan, no. 5. Ann Arbor.

Lees, Susan
1973 Sociopolitical aspects of canal irrigation in the Valley of Oaxaca. In: Prehistory and Human Ecology of the Valley of Oaxaca, vol. 2, edited by Kent V. Flannery. Memoirs of the Museum of Anthropology, University of Michigan, no. 6. Ann Arbor.

Maass, Arthur, and Raymond Anderson
1978 . . . and the Desert Shall Rejoice. Cambridge, MA: MIT Press.

Paso y Troncoso, Francisco del
1905 Papeles de la Nueva España, segunda serie, geografía y estadística, tomo IV, Relaciones Geográficas de la Diócesis de Oaxaca. Madrid: Sucesores de Rivadeneyra.

Redmond, Elsa M.
1983 A Fuego y Sangre: Early Zapotec Imperialism in the Cuicatlán Cañada, Oaxaca. Studies in Latin American Ethnohistory & Archaeology, vol. 1, edited by Joyce Marcus. Memoirs of the Museum of Anthropology, University of Michigan, no. 16. Ann Arbor.

Redmond, Elsa, and Charles Spencer
1983 The Cuicatlán Cañada and the Period II Frontier Zapotec state. In: The Cloud People: Divergent Evolution of the Zapotec and Mixtec Civilizations, edited by Kent V. Flannery and Joyce Marcus, pp. 117–20. New York: Academic Press.

Sanders, William T.
1976 The agricultural history of the Basin of Mexico. In: The Valley of Mexico: Studies in Pre-Hispanic Ecology and Society, edited by Eric R. Wolf, pp. 101–59. A School of American Research Book. Albuquerque: University of New Mexico Press.

Spencer, Charles S.
1979 Irrigation, administration and society in Formative Tehuacán. In: Prehistoric Social, Political and Economic Development in the Area of the Tehuacan Valley, edited by Robert D. Drennan, pp. 13–109. Technical Report of the Museum of Anthropology, University of Michigan, no. 11. Ann Arbor.
1982 The Cuicatlán Cañada and Monte Albán: A Study of Primary State Formation. New York: Academic Press.

Spencer, Charles S., and Elsa Redmond
1979 Formative and Classic developments in the Cuicatlán Cañada. A preliminary report. In: Prehistoric Social, Political and Economic Development in the Area of the Tehuacan Valley, edited by Robert D. Drennan, pp. 201–12. Technical Report of the Museum of Anthropology, University of Michigan, no. 11. Ann Arbor.

Woodbury, Richard, and James A. Neely
1972 Water control systems of the Tehuacán Valley. In: The Prehistory of the Tehuacán Valley. Vol. 4: Chronology and Irrigation, edited by Frederick Johnson, pp. 81–153. Austin: University of Texas Press.

CHAPTER 10

The Cacicazgo

An Indigenous Design

ELSA M. REDMOND AND CHARLES S. SPENCER

AMERICAN MUSEUM OF NATURAL HISTORY, NEW YORK

ON DECEMBER 16, 1492, ten days after making his first landfall on the northwest coast of Hispaniola, Christopher Columbus encountered his first native ruler. From his ship, Columbus noticed the respect accorded this young man by his party of more than 500 men on the shore. A handful of elders served as the ruler's spokesmen and as his intermediaries with Columbus's messengers, whom the ruler received with dignity. He agreed to come aboard the ship, where Columbus treated him to a Castilian meal. The ruler brought the food to his mouth in a formal show of appearances and then silently passed it to his accompanying retainers. Two days later, the Taíno ruler returned by litter with more than 200 men for another feast on board ship. As he joined Columbus in the aft cabin he directed, merely with hand signals, the members of his party to remain on deck, save two elders who sat down at his feet; the latter were his spokesmen and the recipients of his meal. The meeting concluded with an exchange of gifts: the young sovereign presented Columbus with a girdle and two pieces of worked gold, and Columbus gave him the tapestry over his bed, his necklace of amber beads, red shoes, and a vial of orange-blossom water. After being ferried ashore, the ruler mounted his litter and departed, followed by his son who was borne on the shoulders of one of his men. Farther behind walked the ruler's brother, escorted arm-in-arm by two nobles. From this brother of the Taíno ruler, Columbus learned that in the language of that island their sovereign was called *cacique* (Colón 1945:230–35; Las Casas 1951, I:262–67).

Thus recorded in Columbus' journal, the Arawakan Taíno term *cacique* entered the ethnohistoric literature. When subsequent conquistadores and chroniclers encountered other New World cultures that were politically centralized but not true urban civilizations, they often called their native leaders *caciques* and the societies they ruled *cacicazgos*. Notwithstanding the zeal with which Europeans adopted and applied these terms, it is clear that their linguistic roots are strictly indigenous. Using the dictionaries and grammars compiled by Moravian missionaries who lived among Arawak-speaking Indians in British and Dutch Guiana in the eighteenth century, Brinton proposed that the Taíno term *cacique* might have been derived from the mainland Arawak term *kassiquan,* "owner of a house (*ussequa*) or houses" (Brinton 1871:438). According to Brinton, the same term (such as *ussequa*) served to designate both the singular and plural forms (house, houses). The prefix *ka* is also found in the Arawak term *kannikún,* "many, a large number," and *kassaku,* "the firmament, big with all things which are" (Brinton 1871:434,440). Thus *cacique* might have alluded to being "big" by virtue of having or owning many houses. Lovén suggested that *cacique* originally referred to the rulers of towns, which in the case of fifteenth-century Hispaniola could consist of 1,000 houses and more than 3,000 men (Lovén 1935:336, 504; Colón 1945:227). Goeje defined the Taíno term *kasike* as superior chief, and compared it to the Arawak prefix *ka* and *isiri,* "first born" (Goeje 1939:9). Regardless of the precise native meaning of the term, it is evident from the ethnohistoric record of the Americas that the rule and domain of *caciques*—the *cacicazgo*—was an indigenous, pre-Columbian phenomenon.

More recently, when Oberg (1955) referred to the Circum-Caribbean *cacicazgos* as "chiefdoms" and outlined their centralized political organization, he used the fifteenth-century Taíno of Hispaniola to exemplify these "multi-village territorial chiefdoms governed by a paramount chief under whose control are districts and villages governed by a hierarchy of subordinate chiefs" (Oberg 1955:484). Carneiro (1981:38) has also equated *cacicazgo* with the concept of chiefdom, which he defines as "an autonomous political unit comprising a number of villages or communities under the permanent control of a paramount chief" (1981:45). Chiefdoms, of course, have been widely discussed in the anthropological literature. They are characterized by the permanently centralized but nonbureaucratic decision-making authority of chiefs, generalized leaders who assume the administrative duties and functions of leadership, and who have the capacity to summon laborers and warriors and to collect other forms of tribute from local communities. The leadership of a chiefdom is a hereditary institution that focuses on the chiefly office and title, which is usually passed on to designated heirs within an elite lineage. Underscoring their special status, members of the chiefly elite are set off from the remainder of society, usually enjoying an array of sumptuary privileges befitting their high social rank (Sahlins 1968:24–27; Carneiro 1981:45; Wright 1977:381; Flannery 1972:402–3; Peebles and Kus 1977:422; Johnson 1978:101–3).

Although *cacicazgos* were "particularly well represented in the Circum-Caribbean area" (Carneiro 1981:38) in the sixteenth century, archaeological research has demonstrated both the widespread distribution and antiquity of this political institution. Chiefdoms appear to have emerged by 1500 B.C. on the north-central Peruvian coast of South America, by 1000 B.C. in Mesoamerica, by A.D. 500 in the

Intermediate and Circum-Caribbean areas, and by A.D. 1000 in the Greater Antilles (Pozorski 1980:108–9; Wright 1986:343; Lange and Stone 1984; Spencer and Redmond 1992; Rouse 1982:52; Rouse 1991:125, 135; Wilson 1990a:20).

The emergence of prehistoric chiefdoms in these areas tends to be associated with two- or three-level settlement hierarchies and the construction of monumental architecture at large regional centers (Carneiro 1981:53). Other evidence of organized productive activities on the community and regional levels reflect the production, collection, and storage of surplus under the chief's direction (Peebles and Kus 1977:430–33; Spencer 1982:160–67). In addition, the pervasive social inequality that exists in chiefdoms is manifested in their residence patterns, burial treatment, and by the chiefly elite's differential participation in ritual and preferential access to exotic prestige goods (Spencer 1982:131–43; Spencer 1987).

This centralized but nonbureaucratic political institution appears to have flourished under diverse environmental and sociopolitical conditions. The multi-village chiefdoms and supra-regional chiefly confederations of the Circum-Caribbean existed in an area where prehistoric state societies never arose. In the nuclear areas of Mesoamerica and the South American Andes, by contrast, *cacicazgos* existed alongside and in interaction with a series of very large state societies that had emerged there in pre-Columbian times. Still widespread at the time of the Spanish conquest, the Spaniards referred to these non-state centralized societies as *cacicazgos,* as they did in the case of those of the Circum-Caribbean, or the Mixteca Alta and Cuicatlán Cañada regions of southern Mexico (Steward and Faron 1959:174–75; Spores 1967; Hunt 1972). In parts of South America they were designated *curacazgos* (Salomon 1986:10). There were also the *cuchcabalob* in the Yucatán peninsula (Roys 1943, 1957), and the *señoríos* of Central Mexico (Gibson 1964; C. Davies 1968).

Many of these autonomous *cacicazgos* had been incorporated for a time into prehispanic states to varying degrees, but they often appear to have survived more or less intact long after the collapse of these more powerful, expansionist neighbors. Still other such autonomous "city-states" or "kingdoms," as they have also been referred to, arose following the demise of large, imperial states (Marcus 1989a; Bray 1972; Hodge 1984). In some areas, native *cacicazgos* persisted for nearly a century after the first Spanish incursions and the imposition of Spanish rule. Indeed, when Spores outlined the principal features of the *cacicazgos* of the Mixteca Alta on the eve of the Spanish conquest, he remarked that "one of the most durable facets of Mixtec experience that was to survive the Conquest and persist through the sixteenth century was hereditary native rule and the community kingdom" (Spores 1967:29).

Was the widespread use of *cacicazgo* only the result of expedient labeling by Spanish *conquistadores* concerned with dominating native New World societies, or could it be that underlying the many *cacicazgos* was a common, pan-American design, so that the term can be usefully applied to Taíno chiefdoms and Mixtec kingdoms alike? Also, how could some *cacicazgos* have emerged relatively intact from their previous interaction with, and sometimes their incorporation into, the tributary domains of expansionist states? We wish to take some steps toward answering these questions by investigating the regional organization and rulership of *cacicazgos* in two areas where they existed under quite different sociopolitical conditions. In the first case, we will examine the Taíno *cacicazgos* of Hispaniola, which existed without close contact with more complex pre-Columbian state societies. Secondly, we will review the prehistoric sequence of *cacicazgo* development in the Cuicatlán Cañada, an area taken over to varying degrees by two Mesoamerican states. By examining and comparing the nature and extent of their regional organization and their control by autonomous *caciques,* we will explore whether these examples can be considered manifestations of the same underlying sociopolitical design. Such an undertaking might also help us to understand why the *cacicazgo* was apparently so pervasive in the Americas and why it persisted well into the Colonial period in some areas.

The Taíno Cacicazgos of Hispaniola

In 1492, the mountainous island of Aiti, as Hispaniola was called by its native inhabitants, was populated by a mosaic of large *cacicazgos*. The island's total population has been variously estimated as ranging between 100,000–600,000 persons to over 1,200,000 and as many as 8,000,000 inhabitants (Rouse 1948:522; Cook and Borah 1971; Mártir de Anglería 1964, I:363; Dreyfus 1981:229). The Taíno of Hispaniola were organized into multi-village *cacicazgos* under the centralized authority of *caciques*. Rouse presents the most succinct description of their regional political organization:

> each province had its own chief, called a "cacique." In addition, there are said to have been some 30 subchiefs in control of local districts within each province and 70 to 80 headmen in charge of the villages of the province. . . . The authority of the headman apparently extended no farther than his own village, but the subchief also had a certain control over the other villages in his district, while the chief's authority extended over the entire province. [1948:528–29]

Similarly, Fewkes (1907:33) suggested that each *cacicazgo* (he used the term "caciquedom") or province was subdivided into smaller divisions, comprising the inhabitants of valleys and isolated villages, governed by subordinates.

We are fortunate that Las Casas recorded the native Taíno designations for this two- or three-level control hierarchy made up of regional, district (or valley), and village leaders (Table 10.1). They were distinguished by their positions of authority over others, and hence, they constituted the chiefly elite or nobility and called themselves *nitaínos* (Las Casas 1967, II:309). Derived from the word *taíno,* "good" or "noble," Taylor has suggested that the term *nitaíno* meant "his nobles," in reference to the *cacique* (Taylor 1960:348). This translation is supported by the note Las Casas made in his transcription of Columbus' journal, that "cacique era nombre de rey, y nitayno era nombre de caballero y señor principal" or "principal y señor después del Rey" (Colón 1945:245; Las Casas 1951, I:275). Brinton did not consider the first syllable a pronominal prefix, and he thought the term derived from the Arawak *nüddan* "to look well, to stand firm, to do anything well or skillfully" (Brinton 1871:439).

As listed in Table 10.1, *guaoxerí* was the lowest grade of chief or of nobility, whose administrative status, if any, is not indicated by any of the chroniclers. *Baharí* was the title assigned to village chiefs, or to the sub-chiefs or "house-rulers" who ruled villages (Brinton 1871:437). The third and highest grade of chief was *matunherí,* the title reserved by the Taíno for their supreme "kings" or paramount chiefs (Las Casas 1967, II:309). The commoners or laborers who made up the remainder of Taíno society were the *naborías* ("the remainder, the rest of them"), who served the chiefly elite (Taylor 1960:348; Lovén 1935:499–501).

The Taíno's regional settlement patterns consisted of numerous villages, located near cultivated fields "in every situation," since "there appears to have been no rule as to where a settlement should be made" (Roth 1887:280–81). Fifteenth-century Taíno villages could consist of a single, multi-family dwelling, or as few as seven or eight houses, to as many as 30, 100, 200, and 500 multi-family houses. Las Casas described their communal houses as round structures with conical-shaped, thatched roofs, 30–40 feet in diameter, with no interior partitions. Each house could accommodate ten to fifteen household heads or *vecinos,* their wives, and children. The houses of a village were closely spaced and they were clustered around a flat, rectangular plaza (*batey*) on which the village chief's house faced (Las Casas 1967, I:244; Roth 1887:281; Rouse 1948:524–25; Sauer 1966:63).

The seats of paramount chiefs were larger settlements, like the first one visited by Columbus's crew on the north coast of Hispaniola, which consisted of 1,000 houses and an estimated population of more than 3,000 household heads (*hombres*) (Colón 1945:227). Great chief Guacanagarí's center featured a plan of streets and houses and a central plaza where its inhabitants—2,000 men, their wives, and their children—assembled (Colón 1945:244–45). Las Casas described a center in the eastern region of Higüey that had a cruciform plan of streets, 50 paces wide and the length of a crossbowman's shot, where warriors gathered in the event of an attack (Las Casas 1967, I:23). Las Casas might also have been referring to the military jousts that warriors conducted in such public spaces, an activity that Columbus' brother, Bartolomé, witnessed in chief Behechio's center in the province of Xaraguá in 1497. Considered by the Europeans to be the royal court of all of Hispaniola, Behechio's center featured a plaza large enough for Behechio's entire chiefly elite, including his allies (numbering 32 nobles in one account and

TABLE 10.1
Taíno Terms and the Meanings Assigned to Them

Term	Las Casas	Brinton	Coll y Toste
Nitaínos (Nitayno)	"principal y señor despues del Rey" (Colón 1945:245) "nombre de caballero y señor principal" (1951:275)	title applied to petty chiefs, from Ar. *nüddan*, "to look well, to stand firm, to do anything well or skillfully" (1871:439)	"jefe subalterno, o lugar-teniente a las órdenes del cacique" (1907:93, 177)
Guaoxerí (Guaojerí)	lowest grade of chief, "vuestra merced" (1967, II:309)	lowest class of inhabitants, from Ar. *wakaijaru*, "worthless, dirty" (1871:438)	lowest order of chief "alférez," second lieutenant, "señor" (1907:94, 183)
Baharí (Bajarí)	second grade of chief, "señoría" (1967, II:309)	title of subchiefs ruling villages, from Ar. *bajü*, "house," "house-ruler" (1871:439)	second order of chief, "teniente," lieutenant, "señor" (1907:94, 183)
Matunherí (Matunjerí)	"a los reyes supremos," "Vuestra Alteza" (1967, II:309)	title applied to the highest chiefs (1871:439)	highest order of chief, "capitán" (1907:94)
Naborías (Naborí)	"indios de quien se servían, que no les faltaba sino sólo el nombre de esclavos" (1951, III:23), "sirviente o criado" (1967, II:178)	servants (1871:439)	"miembro de la tribu," "hombre más inferior" (1907:93, 95)
Guamiquina (Guamechyna, Guamí kení, Guamoquina)	"el señor grande" (1951, I:372)	lord, supreme ruler of all things, and chiefest of all divinities" (1871:440, 443-44)	"señor de tierra y agua," "jefe superior" (1907:177, 244)

	Zayas y Alfonso	Goeje	Taylor
	"denominación comparable a la nobleza, como caballeros, hidalgos, que figuraban en la compañia y séquito de los caciques," "por grande" (1931, II:220)	important man (1939:9)	"his nobles" (referring to the cacique) (1960:348)
	"el tratamiento de menor categoría que se daban a los nitaynos, o nobles" (1931, II:58)	title of address to head, chief (1939:17)	
	"el segundo grado de dignidad o estado, equivalente a 'señoría'" (1931, I:73)	lord, nobleman Ar. *basari*, old headman (1939:9)	
	"el tratamiento más alto de los tres que recibían los nitaynos o nobles" (1931, II:197-98)		
		client, servant (1939:9)	"the rest of them," L. *budia*, "remainder, rest" (1960:348)
	"señor principal," "señor grande" (1931, II:34)	Ar. *Kulimina*, god or demi-god (1928:28)	

more than 80 in another), and subjects from a province that extended over more than 40 leagues (220 km) to assemble:

> infinitas gentes y muchos señores y nobleza, que se ayuntaron de toda la provincia con el rey Behechio y la reina Anacaona, cantando sus cantares y haciendo sus bailes, que llamaban areytos, cosa mucho alegre y agradable para ver cuando se ayuntaban muchos en número, especialmente; salieron delante 30 mujeres, las que tenía por mujeres el rey Behechio . . . toda la gente demás, que era innumerable, hacen todos grandes bailes y alegrías, y con toda esta fiesta y solemnidad, . . . llevaron a D. Bartolomé Colón a la casa real o palacio del rey Behechio. [Las Casas 1951, I:441]

When Nicolás de Ovando visited Xaraguá in 1501, he was treated to similar *areítos* and ball games here. Bordering the plaza was Behechio's residence (*caney*), which was larger and more elaborate in its wood and thatched-roof construction than other houses. Behechio's *caney* was large enough to accommodate well over 80 and 100 people, according to the accounts of activities that took place on two occasions inside. We know that the *cacique's* residence was the site of chiefly rituals (*cohobas*) and feasts; foreign guests were housed here, and tribute goods were brought and stored here as well (Las Casas 1951, I:441–43; 1951, II:236; 1967, I:32, 680; 1967, II:173; Wilson 1990a:122–24).

The precise number and size of Taíno *cacicazgos* in fifteenth-century Hispaniola is still being debated by scholars, and several versions of their political geography exist in the literature (Wilson 1990a:110). Since we are concerned with assessing the nature of regional organization and political rule by *caciques,* we should examine the two earliest and most complete descriptions of the island's political geography. In 1508, Andrés de Morales was commissioned to survey the coast and interior of Hispaniola. The resulting map and report were subsequently lost, but a copy of the map appeared in a 1516 edition of Pietro Martire d'Anghiera's *Décadas,* along with what is generally agreed to have been Martire d'Anghiera's transcription of Morales' report (Sauer 1966:41; Mártir de Anglería 1964, I:349–72). Martire d'Anghiera's "island cosmography" as he referred to it, consisted of five provinces, which he did not characterize politically—other than to consider them "kingdoms." Nor did he name their rulers; he said only that this territorial division of provinces made up of smaller regions with their ancient names had served the natives of Hispaniola since time immemorial (Table 10.2). Although Morales' map did not indicate the boundaries of the named provinces, Martire's account showed how their limits coincided with the island's major geographic units composed of river valleys and mountain ranges (Fig. 10.1) (Mártir de Anglería 1964, I:354–55; Sauer 1966:44–46). Using Morales' map and Martire d'Anghiera's account, Bernardo Vega has been successful in reconstructing and locating the majority of the Taíno *cacicazgos* (Vega 1980:46, Mapa 4).

Las Casas arrived on Hispaniola in 1502 and began writing his *Historia de Las Indias* and *Apologética Historia Sumaria* in 1527, the stated goals of which in-

TABLE 10.2
Andrés Morales' Political Geography of Hispaniola

Province	Member Regions	Additional Information
Caizcimú (Caicimy)	Higuei, Guanamá, Reyré, Xaguá, Aramaná, Arabo, Hazoa, Macorix, Gayacoa, Guayagua, Baguanimaho, Haití.	"en su lengua 'cimú' quiere decir 'frente' o 'principio'" (Mártir 1964, I:354).
Huhabo (Hyabo, Huhabum)	Xamaná, Canabacoa, Cuhabo, "y otras muchas cuyos nombres ignoro" (Mártir 1964, I:356).	
Cayabo (Caihabo, Cayabum)	Maguá, Cocacubana*, Cubana*, Baioháigua*, Dahaboon, Cybaho, Manabaho, Cotoy.	*"hablan una lengua muy distinta de los otros de la Española, y les dicen 'macoryxes.'" Chief Guarionex of Maguá was its paramount ruler (Mártir 1964, I:362; Vega 1980:25).
Bainoa	Maguana, Jagohaiucho, Bauruco, Dabiagua, Attibuní, Caunoa, Buiací, Dahabonici, Mayaguarití, Atici, Maccazina, Guahabba, Anniuici, Marien, Guaricco, Aruaguei, Xaragua, Jaguana, Azzuei, Jacchi, Honorucco, Diaguo, Camaie, Neibaimao	three times larger than preceding provinces (Mártir 1964, I:359). Chief Beuchio of Xaragua was its paramount ruler (Mártir 1964, I:371-2).
Guaccayarima	Mauicarao, Guahagua, Manabaxao, Zauana, Habacoa, Ayqueroa	"a la que llaman así por ser la parte extrema de la isla,...pues 'marima' significa ano en su lengua"(Mártir 1964, I:355).

cluded recounting the history of the discovery and conquest of Hispaniola and of its neighboring islands, and describing its native inhabitants, their nations, and customs. Although Las Casas' description of Hispaniola and its native political divisions was written at a later date than Morales' report, when in his own words its provinces were utterly depopulated, it is useful because it includes information on the territorial extent of many provinces, as he referred to them (Las Casas 1967, I:9–53; Table 10.3). His data also suggest that in pre-Columbian times five supreme *caciques* of *matunherí* title (Lovén 1935:518) ruled over supra-valley polities or "provinces" that embraced many smaller subject regional chiefdoms, also designated "provinces" (Fig. 10.2). Elsewhere, Las Casas (1967, II:308–9) listed the names of these paramount rulers and of their provinces (see Table 10.4). Figure 10.3 plots the territorial extent of the Taíno chiefdoms for which Las Casas provided estimates.

The effectiveness of chiefly rule over these heavily populated, multi-tiered political units was actually witnessed and extolled by Columbus and fellow chroniclers like Las Casas. Shortly after being received by Guacanagarí on the eve of his

TABLE 10.3
Las Casas' Political Geography of Hispaniola

Province	Size Information	Additional Information
1. Bainoa	25-30 leagues* long 12-15 leagues wide	
2. Guahaba	the same as above	
3. Marién	extends >15 leagues and possibly up to 30 leagues	ruled by Guacanagarí
4. Macorix de Abajo		chief Guanacouel (Lovén 1935:74)
5. unnamed province east of R. Yaque, where Isabela located, traversed by R. Bahabonico	20-25 leagues	
6. Cubao (Macorix de Arriba)	15-20 leagues long 8-10 leagues wide	
7. Ciguayos	extends >30 leagues	ruled by Mayobanex
8. Higüey	45-50 leagues of coast, extends 30 leagues inland	ruled by Higuanamá, includes Adamaney and Mona islands, and provinces of Cotubanamá and Macao
9. Cayacoa	30 leagues of coast	
10. Azúa	30 leagues of coast 10-15 leagues inland	
11. Baoruco	25-30 leagues of coast >20 leagues inland	
12. Yaquimo	30-40 leagues long 12-15 leagues wide between sea and Gulf of Xaraguá	
13. Haniguayagua (Haniguayaba)	>25 leagues long 12-15 leagues wide	autonomous chief with many subjects (Las Casas 1967: II:309) Guacayarima at western tip
14. Iguamuco		
15. Banique		
16. Hatiey	>20-25 leagues long >15 leagues wide	
17. Zahay		
18. Bainoa	>25 leagues of R. Hatibonico valley	"a otras excede,...otra [provincia] sin la que primero que todas descrebimos" (Las Casas 1967, I:32)
19. Xaraguá	>40 leagues in diameter	"donde fue la corte de toda la isla" (Las Casas 1967: I:32)
20. Caiguaní	>30 leagues round	Careibana center
21. Cibao	30-40 leagues long >20-25 leagues wide	ruled by Uxmatex who could mobilize16,000 warriors when Guarionex demanded (Las Casas 1967, II:308). This province's gold mines controlled by Caonabó of Maguana (Las Casas 1951, I:357)
22. Maguana	>30 leagues long >20-25 leagues wide	ruled by Caonabó (Las Casas 1951, I:357)

TABLE 10.3 (cont.)

Province	Size Information	Additional Information
23. Bonao	15-20 leagues long "y otras tantas de ancho" (Las Casas1967, I:43)	
24. Maniey		
25. Cotuy		
26. Maguá (La Vega Real)	80 leagues long from sea to sea, 12-15 leagues maximum width	ruled by Guarionex from center where Concepción de la Vega established. Other member "naciones" or "provincias" included Marién, Macorix de Abajo, Macao, Samaná, and Canabocoa (Las Casas 1967, I:52-53)
27. Macao	10-12 league-long savannas at eastern end of La Vega Real	possibly part of province of Higüey (Las Casas 1967, I: 22)
28. Samaná	>20 leagues round	center of Icaguá, one league from the sea
29. Canabocoa	>20 leagues round at eastern end of La Vega Real	

*The Spanish land league is equivalent to 5.5 kilometers

fateful landfall at Navidad, Columbus wrote down his favorable, first impressions about the *cacicazgos* of Hispaniola and about the nature of chiefly authority:

> es maravilla las cosas de acá y los pueblos grandes de esta Isla Española, . . . y las casas y lugares tan hermosos, y con señorío en todos como juez o señor dellos, y todos le obedecen que es maravilla, y todos estos señores son de pocas palabras y muy lindas costumbres, y su mando es lo mas con hacer señas con la mano, y luego es entendido que es maravilla. [Colón 1945:246]

It seemed to Las Casas (1967, II:316–17) that the Taíno *caciques* ruled *manu regia* over so many villages and innumerable people by their good judgment and free will. He likened their authority to that of a *paterfamilias:*

> La gobernación que estos reyes y todos los señores sus inferiores por toda esta isla puesta tenían, era naturalísima, porque en ninguna cosa de la paterna que los padres usan con sus hijos, teniendo fin principalmente al bien dellos, como libres difiría. Tratábanlos como si todos los súbditos fueran sus propios hijos, y ellos como a propios padres, por amor y no por temor los reverenciaban y obedecían. [1967, II:312]

> Y siendo, como eran, estas gentes tan sin número en esta isla, y que un rey y señor tenía en su reino y señorío infinitos, no pasaba más trabajo en los gobernar que un padre de familia tiene con su casa sola, mujer e hijos. [1967, II:313]

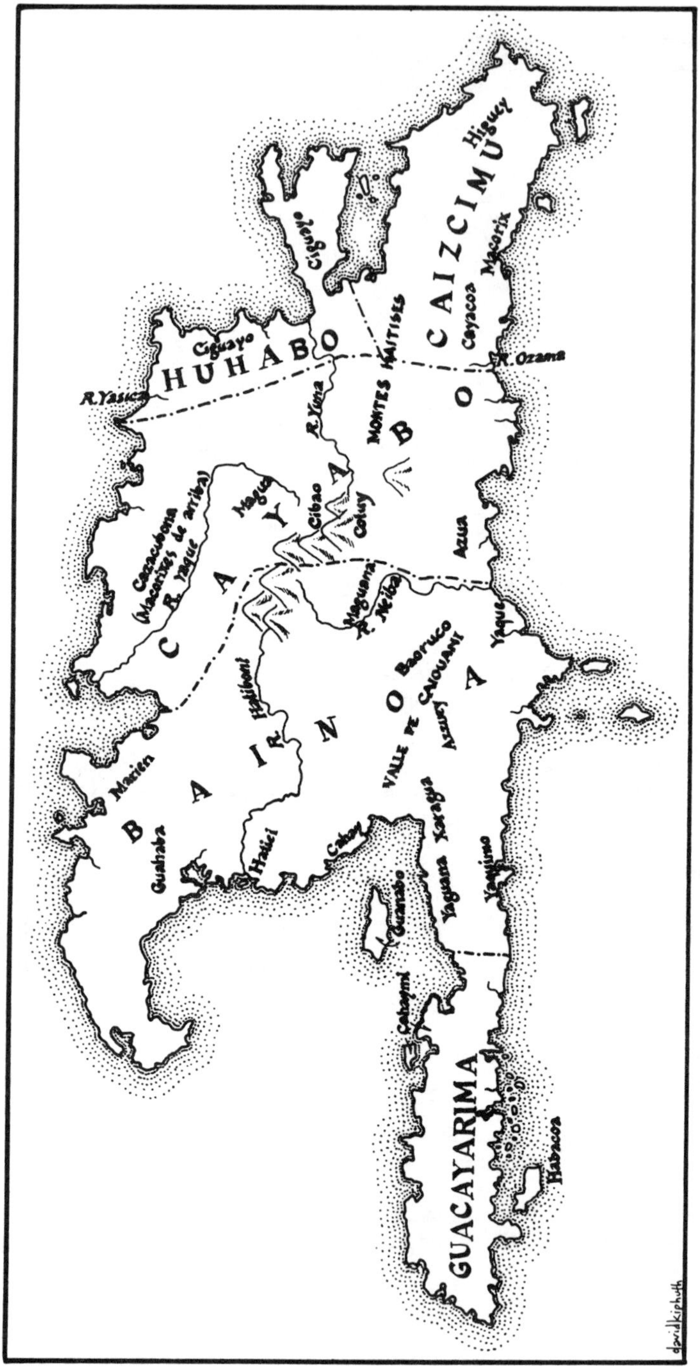

Figure 10.1. Native *cacicazgos* of Hispaniola according to Andrés de Morales and Pietro Martire d'Anghiera (redrawn from Sauer 1966).

Figure 10.2. Map of Taíno provinces based on Bartolomé de Las Casas' description of Hispaniola's native provinces (redrawn from Vega 1980).

TABLE 10.4
Rulers of Principal Provinces in Fifteenth-Century Hispaniola

Ruler	Province
Guarionex	Maguá
Guacanagarí	Marién
Behechio	Xaraguá
Caonabó	Maguana
Higuanamá	Higüey

Centralized regional authority focused on the hereditary chief, whose power was absolute, unquestioned, and legitimized in several ways. One of the most complete discussions of chiefly rule is by Lovén (1935:503–19). Although none of the Taíno *cacique*-kings was referred to as a *guamiquina,* or "lord of land and water" (see Table 10.1), this supreme or divine ruler of all things stood over them, and clearly sanctified their authority.

They invoked his divinatory powers through chiefly rituals that they performed in the privacy of their sanctuaries, where they fasted, took narcotic snuff (*cohoba*), sounded drums, danced and sang their *areítos* that commemorated the supernatural and human aspects of their authority before their personal effigy figures (*cemís*) (Pané 1974:21, 34, 42, 47; Las Casas 1967, II:173–79; Roth 1887:260–63; Mártir de Anglería 1964, I:191, 195–98; Arrom 1975:19–43). Wilson (1990a:88) has suggested that the *cemís* were the *caciques*' supernatural allies, whom they venerated and courted. Not only did *caciques* boast of possessing the best *cemís,* but "it was only caziques that after death were worshipped as zemis" (Lovén 1935:586). By revering their *cemís,* therefore, Taíno chiefs invoked the help of their ancestors, who resided in the supernatural world of the *cemís,* to benefit their living descendants (Lovén 1935:583–84; Pané 1974:35, 37, 42). Taíno chiefs also enjoyed privileged access to esoteric knowledge relating to their myths, their rituals, and the history of their lineage (Lovén 1935:506; Roth 1887:260, 273).

Caciques were entitled to wear special gold-studded insignia, to be borne in litters, to take as many wives as they pleased, and to possess finely carved wooden stools (*duhos*), large canoes, and many other prestige goods (Mártir de Anglería 1964:I:158, 371). They were also accorded lengthy titles at birth. Paramount chief Behechio of Xaraguá, for example, possessed the following epithets: *Turéiga Hobin* ("resplendent as brass"), *Starei* ("shining"), *Huiho* ("sublimity"), *Duiheyniquen* ("rich river"), and more than 40 other chiefly titles, which often referred to the brilliant ornaments that *caciques* like Behechio were entitled to wear (Mártir de Anglería 1964, I:371; Lovén 1935:517). Indeed, so revered were Taíno chiefs that they frequently spoke through intermediaries, and used mere gestures to direct their followers, as Columbus witnessed.

The centralized regional authority enjoyed by the great Taíno chiefs was fueled by their alliances with as many as 70 or 80, 100, and in the case of Behechio, perhaps more than 200 village chiefs (Roth 1887:265; Las Casas 1967, II:309–10). Roth noted that village chiefs were not obliged to render tribute to the *cacique*-kings, but that at harvest time they brought their first fruits to the paramount chief's *caney* and offered them to his *cemí* (Las Casas 1967, II:173). Benzoni described one of these chiefly rituals, at which the paramount chief received all his subjects and presided over the ritual observances to him and his *cemí,* after which "every man, highly elated and content, returned to his own home" (Benzoni cited in Roth 1887:263).

The ties between a paramount chief and local village chiefs were strengthened by elite intermarriage and exchange, whereby the movement of prestige goods was linked to the movement of high-ranking spouses (Wilson 1990a:130–31). Wilson goes on to outline how the practice of exogamous marriage by the Taíno elites and the *cacique's* practice of polygamy served to consolidate the multi-village alliances between a paramount chief and village chiefs (Wilson 1990a:139–40). For example, most of chief Guarionex's many wives came from the highest-ranking families of the 70 or more villages in the central Vega Real that he controlled; "his marriages helped forge the social and political bonds that held the chiefdom together" (Wilson 1990b:46). In return, paramount chiefs could call upon village chiefs "to assist them in their wars and till the ground" (Roth 1887:265).

It was the *cacique*'s duty, according to Lovén (1935:505), to represent his people in their relations with the outer world, which in turn solidified his authority at home. Relationships between the Taíno chiefdoms were shaped largely by alliances, exchange, and warfare. As Columbus observed, the *caciques* hosted elaborate feasts for foreign visitors, complete with welcoming ceremonies at which gestures of friendship and reverence of the foreign dignitaries were enacted, as well as musical *areítos,* ball games, and military jousts (Las Casas 1951, I:259, 264, 441; Las Casas 1951, II:236–37).

Such encounters between high-ranking delegations of separate polities usually concluded with the exchange of gifts, often personal ornaments and clothes. At the conclusion of Bartolomé Colón's visit to Xaraguá in 1497, chief Behechio's sister, Anacaona, presented him with an array of prestige goods, including finely polished wooden stools and cotton textiles (Las Casas 1951, I:266, 286–88, 447). In addition to exchanging material items, Taíno chiefs exchanged esoteric knowledge with one another. Chief Guarionex of Maguá had taught neighboring chief Mayobanex of the Ciguayos an *areíto* of his region, a gift which Mayobanex valued highly (Las Casas 1951, I:462). *Caciques* also exchanged their titles with one another, by means of which they became formal allies or blood kin (*nataios, guatiaos*) (Fewkes 1907:34). On the occasion of the birth of a chief's son, neighboring chiefs came to visit and bestow the infant with some of his many titles or epithets, a practice which probably stemmed from their relationship as allies (Mártir de Anglería 1964, I:371). The Spaniards soon adopted this form of exchange in their dealings with Taíno chiefs. In the process of subduing the province of Higüey in 1503, Captain Juan de Esquivel exchanged names with chief Cotubanamá:

> A éste, como a señor principal y señalado, el capitán general dió su nombre, trocándolo por el suyo, diciendo que se llamase desde adelante Juan de Esquivel, y que él se llamaría Cotubano, como él. Este trueque de nombres en la lengua común desta isla se llamaba ser yo y fulano, que trocamos los nombres, guatiaos, y así se llamaba el uno al otro guatiao; teníase por gran parentesco y como liga de perpetua amistad y confederación y así el capitán general y aquel señor quedaron guatiaos, como perpetuos amigos y hermanos en armas. [Las Casas 1951, II:234]

Finally, Taíno chiefs exchanged their daughters and sisters in marriage. Fray Ramón Pané, who was sent by Columbus in 1495 to live among the Taíno and record their customs—and can justifiably be considered the first ethnographer of New World Indians—reported that commoners had two or three wives, while chiefs had 10, 15, and 20 wives (Pané 1974:56). Behechio of Xaraguá was held up as a chiefly standard by the chroniclers for having 30 wives (Las Casas 1967, II:317–18; Mártir de Anglería 1964, I:176). The resulting marriage alliances forged closed kinship relationships among the chiefly elite of Hispaniola. Moreover, the political alliances stemming from these royal marriages constituted a significant mechanism in the consolidation of smaller polities into larger *cacicazgos,* like Guarionex's Maguá, Caonabó's Maguana, and Behechio's Xaraguá (Dreyfus 1981:243; Wilson 1990a:139–40).

In the case of Xaraguá, chief Behechio's sister, Anacaona, was the wife of neighboring Caonabó, a powerful *cacique* in his own right, and probably a close ally of Behechio's (Las Casas 1951, I:357). At the time of Bartolomé Colón's visit to Xaraguá in 1497, Anacaona was the apparent successor to Caonabó, who had been seized by the Spaniards and had died two years earlier. Referred to by the Spaniards as "queen," Anacaona was an equal partner to her brother, Behechio, in the festivities and transactions with Bartolomé Colón (Las Casas 1951, I:406–8, 440–43, 447–48; Mártir de Anglería 1964, I:157; Wilson 1990a:130). It seemed to the Spaniards that the provinces of Xaraguá and Caonabó were ruled jointly by Behechio and his sister; we have seen how Morales and Martire d'Anghiera listed Caonabó's territory (Maguana) as one of the member regions of Behechio's province (Table 10.2; Mártir de Anglería 1964, I:356; Dreyfus 1981:241). The next recorded Spanish encounter with the native rulers of Xaraguá came in 1503, when Nicolás de Ovando visited the province. He was received by Anacaona, who, following Behechio's death, had ordered the most beautiful of Behechio's wives to be buried alive with him, and who now ruled Xaraguá and presumably the adjacent territory of Caonabó as well (Mártir de Anglería 1964, I:371; Las Casas 1951, II:235). When she learned about Ovando's visit, Anacaona "mandó convocar todos los señores de aquel reino y gentes de los pueblos, que viniesen a su ciudad de Xaraguá a rescibir y hacer reverencia y festejar" (Las Casas 1951, II:236). The apparent consolidation of Caonabó's *cacicazgo* into the *cacicazgo* centered at Xaraguá proved to be short-lived. It ended when Ovando trapped 80 or so members of the gathered chiefly elite in a *caney,* burned them alive, and hanged Anacaona, an act which effectively destroyed the last remaining native *cacicazgo* of Hispaniola (Wilson 1990a:134).

Interpolity marriage alliances were so important in the external relations of the Taíno that a failure to honor an agreed-upon marriage contract was cause for war, as were revenge motives and boundary trespasses (Las Casas 1967, II:317; Lovén 1935:515). According to Martire (Mártir de Anglería 1964, I:153), chief Behechio was pursuing expansionist warfare outside his territory along the Río Neiba—30 leagues (165 km) from his chiefly center—when Bartolomé Colón first encountered him. As supreme military commanders, Taíno *caciques* presided over allied military councils and *cohobas,* and led large allied fighting forces, as large as 100,000 warriors in one encounter against the Spaniards (Wilson 1990a:89–90). Their fighting forces were made up of able-bodied men, and women too when needed, who were called upon to defend their territory in times of war (Las Casas 1967, II:344–45).

Yet the military confederacies mounted by Guarionex against the Spanish forces in the Vega Real illustrate the ephemeral nature of these military alliances as well as the oscillating powers of their commanding chiefs. When the Spaniards set out from Isabela to make war on the inhabitants of the Vega Real in 1495, they were confronted by an allied force of over 100,000 men, organized by a number of the eastern Hispaniola's chiefs, including Guatiguaná, the brothers of Caonabó, and Guarionex, who was the Vega Real's preeminent *cacique* (Las Casas 1951, I:414, 416; Wilson 1990a:89–90, 101; Wilson 1990b:45). The next major military confrontation occurred in 1497, when the region's chiefdoms were close to an internal revolt over how to rid themselves of their Spanish overlords. At a military council hosted by Guarionex and attended by at least fourteen allied chiefs, he agreed to lead an allied attack against the Spaniards with 15,000 men (Mártir de Anglería 1964:I:155–56; Las Casas 1951, I:445–46). This military alliance was shattered by a successful Spanish counter-raid on the eve of the planned attack, and just a year later Guarionex abandoned the Vega Real and sought refuge in the mountainous territory of neighboring chief Mayobanex, who honored his long-standing alliance with Guarionex by defending him until both *caciques* were pursued over the next three months by Bartolomé Colón's men and captured (Mártir de Anglería 1964, I:159–61, 172–77; Las Casas 1951, I:458–65; Wilson 1990a:107–8).

Thus, not only did Guarionex's military alliance prove to be short-lived, but it became the agent of his own political downfall in a mere two years at the hands of the Spaniards. Although Guarionex was the Vega Real's most powerful chief, his failed military alliance suggests that he might have overstretched his regional chiefly authority. Moreover, it is possible that supra-regional chiefly confederations like the one Guarionex presided over might well have been ephemeral in nature. As Fewkes pointed out, "leagues of more or less strength were undoubtedly formed . . . for special purposes, such as resistance to a common foe, but such a union was loose and its organization feeble" (Fewkes 1907:34).

The available information on the territorial extent of Taíno *cacicazgos* underscores the dramatic difference in scale between the regional chiefdoms and the supra-regional polities. Table 10.5 lists the thirteen provinces for which territories can be estimated in square kilometers, using Las Casas' figures (Table 10.3). Four of these are the supra-regional polities or "kingdoms" of Higüey, Xaraguá, Maguá, and Maguana, the mean territory size of which is 33,552 km^2. The other nine are regional *cacicazgos,* which have a mean territory size of 12,639 km^2. This bipartite distinction is supported by the histogram in Figure 10.3, which reveals a bimodal distribution of estimated territories. Moreover, a two-sample T-test on the difference of mean territory sizes between regional and supra-regional polities produced the following results: $T = 5.121$; $df = 11$; $p < .001$. Homogeneity of the group variances (an assumption required by the T-test) was indicated by a Bartlett test result of 1.862 ($p = .20$). In addition, the two groups yielded a Mann-Whitney U of 1.0 ($p = .009$). All these procedures suggest that the supra-regional polities called "kingdoms" by the chroniclers had territories that were significantly larger than those of the regional *cacicazgos*.

If Las Casas' figures accurately portray the territories administered by Taíno *caciques* at the time of Spanish contact, then these are substantial territories indeed, considerably larger than has been reported for chiefdoms in some other areas (Spencer 1990:7). The available data on distances between the paramount centers of the Taíno are consistent with territories of impressive size. Columbus was told that it was a four-day journey overland from Guacanagarí's paramount center, located 4–5 leagues (22–27.5 km) inland from the port of Santo Tomás (Las Casas 1951, I:275) to Guarionex's center at La Concepción in the Vega Real (Fig. 10.2; Las Casas 1951, I:287; Las Casas 1967, I:53; Sauer 1966:89). The gold-rich province of Cibao—controlled by Caonabó, according to one account (Las Casas 1951, I:357)—lay some 30 leagues (165 km) from Guacanagarí's center (Las Casas 1951, I:275). Guarionex's center at La Concepción was located more or less 30 leagues (165 km) from the neighboring provinces of Samaná and Canabocoa (Las Casas 1967, I:53). Behechio's center, located 8 leagues (44 km) east of the Gulf of Xaraguá, was more than 50 leagues (275 km) distant from the neighboring province of Haniguayaba to the west (Las Casas 1967, I:33–34; Las Casas 1967, II:309).

As the first example makes clear, the distances between the centers of some of the major Taíno *cacicazgos* would have represented several days of travel. Close to five days of overland travel would have separated Behechio's center from neighboring Haniguayaba, using one estimate (56 km) of a day's walking distance (Spencer 1982:23). By contrast, in the case of the chiefdoms of ancient Panama,

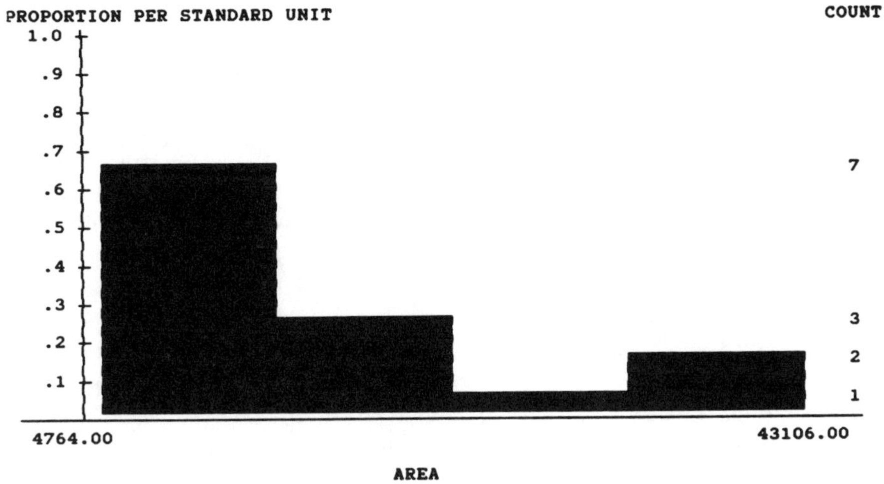

Figure 10.3. Histogram of Taíno territories.

neighboring regional paramount centers were located between 26 to 35 km apart, a distance that could have been easily traversed in one day's travel (Helms 1979:51–53). Similar travel times would have been obtained by canoe, since it was estimated that the Taíno could travel approximately 10 leagues (55 km) over sea in one day in their canoes (Las Casas 1951, I:225).

Although we have noted above how impressed the Spaniards were by the authority with which the Taíno *caciques* ruled over their large domains and many subjects, we might question how provinces of this size could have been administered effectively by a single paramount chief, whose centralized rule was nonbureaucratic and generalized (Spencer 1982:8–9, 1990:7; Wright 1977:381). We suggest that the considerable travel time between regional *cacicazgos* would have made supra-regional confederacies under the centralized authority of even a powerful *cacique* like Guarionex difficult to maintain on a long-term basis. We also agree with Wilson (1990a:109) that the boundaries drawn by Morales and Las Casas for the major Taíno *cacicazgos,* including these large provinces, usually referred not to integrated polities of considerable longevity, but instead to the temporary alliances that bound neighboring chiefdoms for the purpose of exchange and warfare. This would help to account for the discrepancies that exist among the Taíno political geographies as they were recorded by the chroniclers and as they continue to be interpreted today. From this viewpoint, the supra-regional polities the Spaniards called kingdoms represent short-term departures from the more usual and persistent situation of regional *cacicazgos*. We would, therefore, propose that the Taíno *cacicazgos* were fundamentally regional polities that centered upon the hereditary *cacique*, whose authority was strongest over the many villages of his domain, with whom he celebrated rituals and feasts, exchanged wives, and fought wars when necessary. We also suggest that the island's five major *cacicazgos*—or kingdoms, as the Spaniards perceived them in 1492—were entities created by strategies of external alliance actively pursued by some of the island's *caciques* at that time. They represented the marriage alliances, exchange relationships, and military alliances that were maintained by powerful *caciques* such as Guarionex, whose power "most likely derived from his ability to convince other leaders through persuasive rhetoric, through appeal to kinship relationships which seem to exist among most of the Taíno elite, through gifts or displays of generosity in competitive feasts, or through more Machiavellian political maneuvering" (Wilson 1990a:102). Helms reports similar supra-regional confederacies in sixteenth-century Panama, where "each centrally located—and possibly more powerful—ruler, together with his perhaps less significant elite neighbors, is seen as composing what I am terming a regional 'field of influence'" (Helms 1979:39–40). Dependent upon the vagaries of individual chiefs, their personalities, and their ambitions, the supra-regional spheres of influence of powerful *caciques* can be seen as the product of their political fortunes. Consequently, they were especially prone to cycles of political growth and decline that often characterize the political dynamics of chiefdoms (Wright 1977:381–82; Spencer 1990:11).

The Cacicazgos in the Cuicatlán Cañada

The Cuicatlán Cañada is a narrow 30-km-long canyon in the southern highlands of Mexico where we have documented archaeologically the development of prehispanic *cacicazgos* (Redmond 1983; Spencer 1982). We can trace their origins back to the Middle Formative period (650–300 B.C.), when a two-level hierarchy of settlement sizes appeared in the region for the first time. Two of the region's twelve settlements were significantly larger in size, and they were located on high alluvial terraces overlooking the largest expanses of prime farmland in the Cañada (sites Cs 10 and Cs 19 in Fig. 10.4). Moreover, they were the only two Middle Formative sites with three 2–4 m tall pyramidal mounds arranged around an open plaza. Our excavations at one of the smaller settlements in the region (Cs 25) revealed some low platforms arranged around the interior courtyards of a residential compound, which we have reason to think were the loci of public ceremonies (Spencer 1982:137–43).

On the basis of the region's two-level settlement size hierarchy and the corresponding two orders of public architecture, we have proposed that two chiefdoms

Figure 10.4 (opposite). Middle Formative sites in the Cuicatlán Cañada.

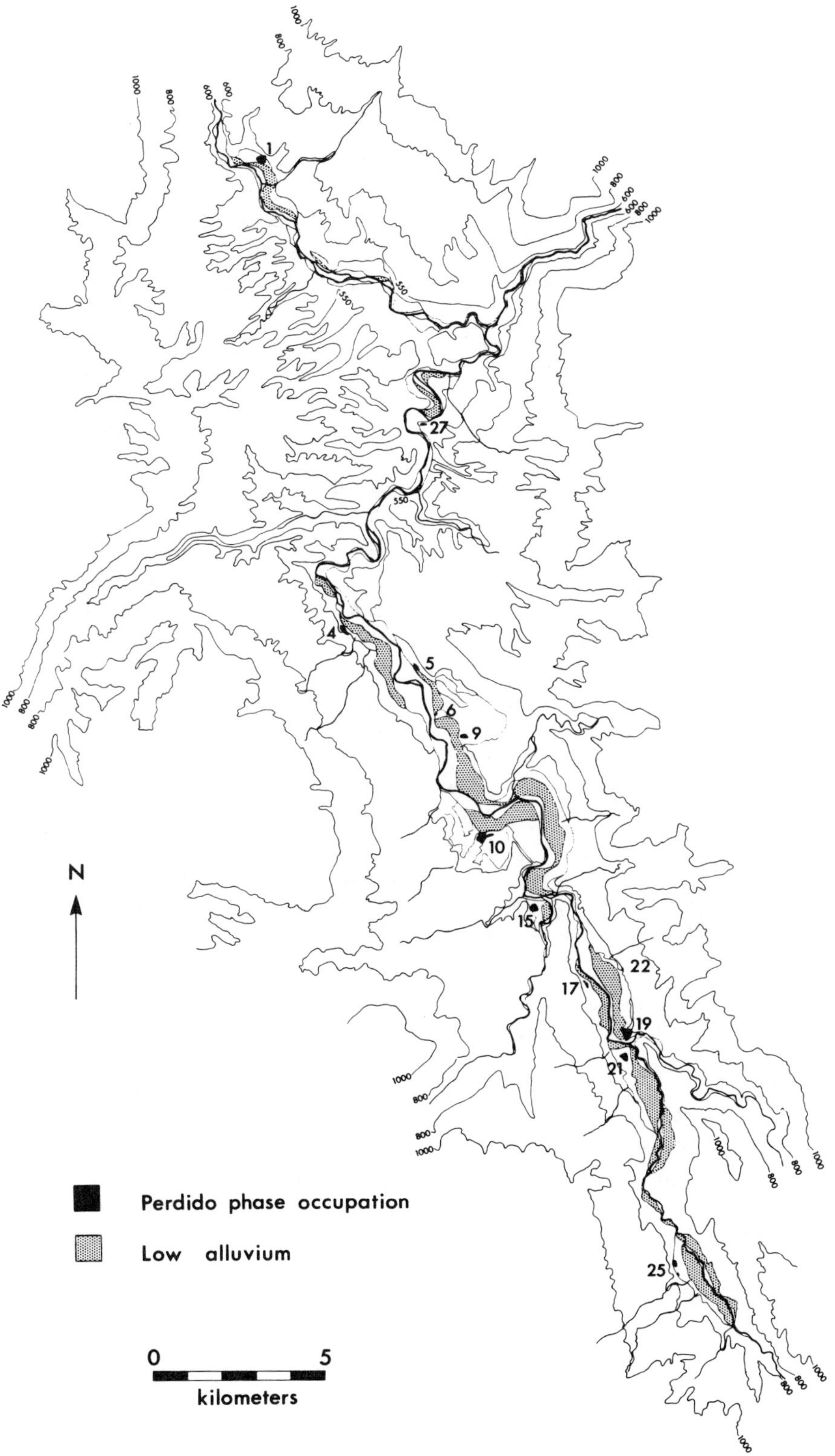

N
Perdido phase occupation
Low alluvium
0
5
kilometers
1
4
5
6
9
10
15
17
19
21
22
25
27
550
600
800
1000

emerged in the Cañada during the Middle Formative period. Their paramount centers were located on the region's central and largest alluvial fans, some 8 km apart. Smaller villages such as Cs 25 were probably headed by local chiefs, who were allied with the paramount chiefs at the nearest chiefly center. Such a two-level regional settlement and administrative hierarchy is consistent with the patterns expected for chiefdoms (Johnson 1973; Peebles and Kus 1977; Wright 1977).

All habitation in the Cañada is confined to areas where the canyon floor widens and where major tributaries join the Río Grande and produce farmable alluvial fans. In the sixteenth century, the political boundaries of the region's *cacicazgos* coincided with irrigable stretches of alluvium on the Cañada's floor, in spite of the fact that marginal lands in the surrounding uplands were exploited for firewood and other wild products (Hunt 1972:168, 234). Accordingly, we can generate conservative estimates of the territory sizes of the Middle Formative period chiefdoms in the Cañada by measuring the areas of their associated alluvial fans, which are so clearly delimited. We estimate that the chiefdom centered at Cs 10 had a territory of minimally 10.38 km^2 and the neighboring chiefdom centered at Cs 19 extended over at least 6.17 km^2 (Table 10.6). Relationships between the Cañada's chiefdoms appear to have been peaceful and to have been marked by alliance and exchange (Redmond 1983:63–81; Spencer 1982:79–149). Should excavations be carried out some day at the region's chiefly centers they will almost certainly clarify our findings in this regard, which were based on regional survey and excavations at Cs 25.

The Cañada's Middle Formative period chiefdoms were interacting with chiefly polities in neighboring mountain valleys by means of interregional exchange networks, especially with chiefdoms in the Valley of Oaxaca to the south, from whom they received painted ceramics, obsidian, and marine shell, among other prestige goods (Spencer 1982:151–97). That raiding might have been another form of interpolity interaction is suggested by the carved stone depictions of slain captives associated with public buildings at the Middle Formative centers of San José Mogote and Monte Albán in the Oaxaca Valley (Marcus 1974, 1980, 1991).

We do know that during the succeeding Late Formative period (ca. 300 B.C.-A.D. 200) the polity centered at Monte Albán in the Oaxaca Valley launched a campaign of military conquest against neighboring regions, including the Cuicatlán Cañada, as recorded on the inscribed stone slabs of Building J in the Main Plaza of Monte Albán (Caso 1947; Marcus 1980, 1983). Some of the clearest supporting evidence for this conquest hypothesis comes from the Cañada. The burgeoning chiefdoms there were brutally subjugated by the Valley Zapotec and the Cañada's native political institutions were replaced by the imperial administration of the nascent Zapotec state. The transformation of the Cañada into a tributary frontier zone is reflected in part by abrupt changes in the region's settlement patterns, local economy, and public architecture, a reflection of the Valley Zapotec's direct military control over the Cañada's subjugated peoples (Redmond 1983; Spencer 1982).

TABLE 10.5
Territorial Extent of Taíno Provinces

Province	Length (km)	Width (km)	Area (km^2)
1. Bainoa	151.25	74.25	11,230.31
2. Guahaba	151.25	74.25	11,230.31
6. Cubao	96.25	49.50	4,764.38
8. Higüey	261.25	165.00	43,106.25
10. Azúa	165.00	68.75	11,343.75
11. Baoruco	151.25	110.00	16,637.50
12. Yaquimo	192.50	74.25	14,293.13
13. Haniguayagua	137.50	74.25	10,209.38
16. Hatiey	123.75	82.50	10,209.38
19. Xaraguá	220.00	220.00	38,013.27
21. Cibao	192.50	123.75	23,821.88
22. Maguana	165.00	123.75	20,418.75
26. Maguá	440.00	74.25	32,670.00

SOURCE: Las Casas 1967, I:15-47, see Table 10.3.

TABLE 10.6
Cañada's Sixteenth-Century Cacicazgos and Their Territories

Alluvial Fan	Territory (km^2)
Quiotepec	0.92
Cuicatlán	10.38
Dominguillo	6.17

In the succeeding Classic period (ca. A.D. 200–1000), however, the Valley Zapotec appear to have withdrawn from the Cuicatlán Cañada, probably in response to the emergence of a powerful state centered at Teotihuacán in the Basin of Mexico, whose impact was felt as far away as the Maya lowlands. Instead of the unimodal distribution of settlement sizes that had characterized the Cañada's subjugation and imperial administration by Monte Albán (Redmond 1983:84), a clear hierarchy of settlement sizes now appeared in the region (Fig. 10.5). Although the majority of the 26 Classic period settlements ranged up to 4 ha in size, four hilltop settlements were several times larger; they reflect the existence of a two- or three-level hierarchy of settlement sizes in the Cañada. Each of the four large hilltop settlements (Cs 2, Cs 14, Cs 16/18, Cs 25) was associated with one of the region's four alluvial fans, and the ranking of the sizes of the four settlements agrees with the ranking of the sizes of the associated alluvial fans. As had been the case in the Middle Formative period, prior to the period of Zapotec conquest, the region's largest hilltop center (Cs 14) presided over the region's major and central alluvial fan, which supported the greatest number of satellite settlements (Redmond 1983: Table 37). Cs 14 and the other three large settlements on each of the Cañada's alluvial fans featured public sectors that consisted of one or two plazas surrounded by mound platforms and also included a ballcourt. The Cañada's settlement-size hierarchy is thus reflected in the array and volume of public architecture associated with Classic period settlements of different sizes.

During the subsequent Postclassic period (ca. A.D. 1000–1520) settlement expanded in the central and southern Cañada (Fig. 10.6). Major nucleated centers of up to 48 ha in size emerged on hilltops and ridges overlooking each alluvial fan (Cs 31, Cs 81), with impressive central plazas and public buildings, and numerous residential terraces. Secondary centers defined on the basis of their size and public architecture occurred here too (Cs 51, Cs 14, Cs 67), as did a proliferation of isolated households and hamlets. Although population grew threefold in the Cañada's heartland, we estimate that it remained well below the productive potential of the associated irrigable farmland (Redmond 1983: Table 43).

These developments in the Cañada's regional organization during the Classic and Postclassic periods as we defined them archaeologically are confirmed by the earliest ethnohistoric accounts about the Cuicatec polities in the Cañada during the Postclassic and early Colonial periods. Based largely on her study of a valuable manuscript (1562) that traces information about the region's settlements and rulers back to prehispanic times, Eva Hunt (1972) identified two Cuicatec *cacicazgos* that were associated with the Cañada's central and southernmost alluvial fans (marked by the modern towns of San Juan Bautista Cuicatlán and Santiago Dominguillo, which was formerly called Alpizagua). A minor *cacicazgo* of Mazatec speakers occupied the Quiotepec alluvial fan on the region's northern boundary (Hunt 1972:171).

Each *cacicazgo* was an autonomous polity, whose ruler or *cacique* resided at a large nucleated settlement (*cabecera*), which featured monumental public architecture—temples, ballcourts—and elaborate residential palaces for the ruling elite. Satellite villages and hamlets were located within walking distances of twelve hours or less from the *cacicazgo* center. In Hunt's words, "the pre-Hispanic settlement pattern most prevalent among the Cuicatec was one in which small hamlets were located on spurs, ridges, and flats near and above irrigated agricultural fields, in a territory partially surrounding a larger 'urbanized' settlement, or nucleus, major in population size, antiquity, and political might" (Hunt 1972:202). Hunt discovered that the smaller villages and hamlets of a *cacicazgo* had been established by inhabitants from the oldest and largest center over time, who remained politically subject to their *cacique* at the *cabecera* (Hunt 1972:201, 232, 237). Having compiled the earliest available population figures for the Cañada, Joseph

Figure 10.5 (opposite). Classic sites in the Cuicatlán Cañada.

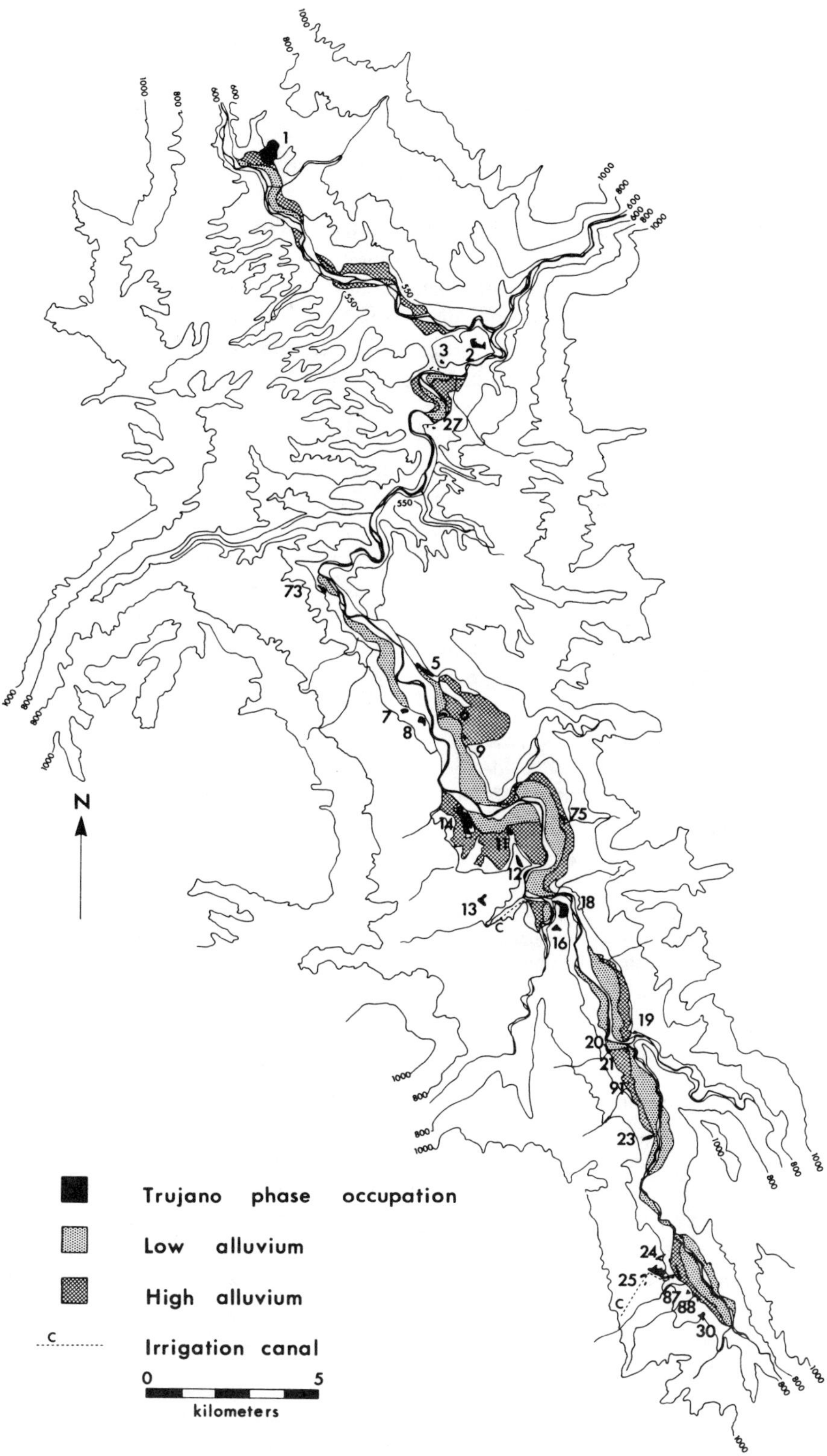

N
Trujano phase occupation
Low alluvium
High alluvium
c
Irrigation canal
0
5
kilometers

Hopkins estimates that the *cacicazgos* in the Cañada each consisted of fewer than 3,000 persons (Hopkins 1984:27–28).

The *cacicazgos* in the Cañada controlled all the land and the sources of water within their territories. As already noted, the boundaries of each *cacicazgo* usually coincided with the limits of the irrigable farmland on the alluvial fan that it occupied. In view of the Cañada's flat topography, it would have been possible for farmers to travel over considerable distances to their agricultural fields and back to their nucleated centers and villages within the work day (Hunt 1972:202). We can then generate conservative estimates of their territories by measuring the associated alluvial fans that they presided over (Table 10.6). The Cuicatec *cacicazgos* used natural features, such as streams or barrancas, or painted boulders to delimit the boundaries of their territories (Hunt 1972:171, 234).

The earliest sixteenth-century Spanish documents for the Cañada refer to the *cacique mayor,* who ruled the *cacicazgo* from his center; his title as rendered in the *Relaciones* was the Cuicatec term for "great lord" (*ditonidona* [sic]) (Hunt 1972:218). This paramount ruler had a body of retainers or kinsmen, who resided in his residential palace and served as his council of elders, including an *ayo,* who acted as the ruler's intermediary and spokesman. On the local level of the administrative hierarchy were lesser *caciques,* who were the paramount's kinsmen or affines and members of the ruling elite. Referred to by Cuicatec titles for "nobles" (*Dyille Ebe, ii'ya*), these local *caciques* administered neighborhoods (barrios) of the large centers and subject villages. Thus, on either the regional or local level there was clearly centralized political authority, but minimal internal differentiation of leadership roles (Wright 1977; Spencer 1987). The generalized nature of decision-making by the regional paramount and village *caciques* is underscored by Hunt:

> The small ruling elite as a whole controlled not only the administration of land and waters, but trade, the ritual arranged in cyclical festivities which were timed with the extraction of tribute, the administration of the native church and its dogma, and the waging of war against non-Cuicatecs. All these activities formed part of a unitary government system, without a true separation of branches. [1972:236]

These hereditary rulers and their kinsmen constituted the Cuicatec nobility. They were entitled to sumptuary privileges of housing, dress, diet, and access to as many wives as they wished. Since the Cuicatec nobility were class endogamous, they sought exogamous marriage partners among the local village elites (Hunt 1972:206). The paramount *caciques mayores,* who claimed direct descent from mythical ancestors, were considered semi-divine. Their decisions were announced by the *ayo,* the elder who served as his paramount *cacique*'s intermediary and spokesman. One Cuicatec ruler was described as a strong leader who held absolute

Figure 10.6 (opposite). Postclassic sites in the Cuicatlán Cañada.

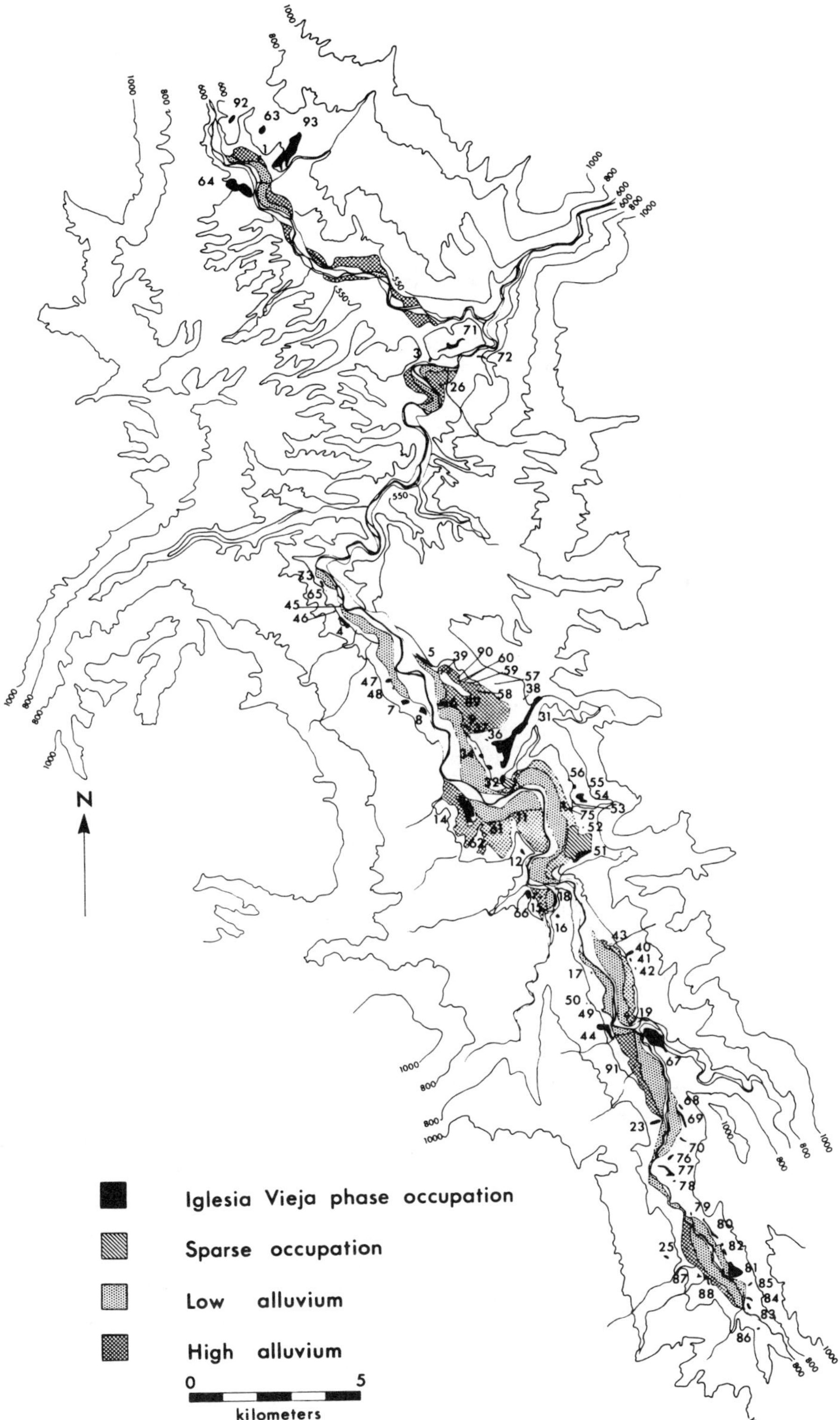
N
Iglesia Vieja phase occupation
Sparse occupation
Low alluvium
High alluvium
0
5
kilometers

power and who was treated like a god. People had to remove their shoes and lower their eyes when they entered his presence (Hunt 1972:218–20; Hopkins 1984:25–27).

The bulk of sixteenth-century Cuicatec society consisted of peasant farmers. Although they were free commoners, they cultivated the *cacique*'s fields, and rendered him tribute in mantles, cacao, maize, beans, among other products. The *Relaciones* mention individual commoners (*tequitlatoque* in Nahuatl, *nyandi* in Cuicatec) who carried out the *cacique*'s orders on the local barrio or village level (Hopkins 1984:27; Hunt 1972:204, 220). In times of war, commoners were recruited for the *cacique's* fighting force. War captives became slaves who also served their overlord as sacrificial victims (Hunt 1972:220–21; Hopkins 1984:26).

Relations between the *cacicazgos* in the Cañada were characterized by the intermarriage of their ruling elites, and by exchange. The available Cuicatec genealogies record exogamous marriages among the elite, which were often arranged by the *caciques* for political gain, to settle territorial disputes and to mitigate inter-*cacicazgo* enmities. By virtue of these intermarriages between their ruling families, the Cuicatec *cacicazgos* were closely related, and eventually the more powerful polities might have achieved greater political consolidation over the region (Hunt 1972:223–24, 218, 229, 234). Their claims to a common mythological ancestor and their intermarriages were the subject of their written codices and oral traditions. Not only did they share a common language and a body of myths, but they participated in a yearly round of ceremonies hosted by the *cacique* of each *cacicazgo*. The *Relaciones* indicated that "the different town temples were dedicated to different gods whose ceremonies were held at different times of the year" (Hunt 1972:206). In light of our understanding of indigenous Otomanguean religion, however, it is more likely that the early Spanish chroniclers mistook and anthropomorphized the supreme supernatural being, the vital forces, and the deceased ancestors revered by the Cuicatec *cacicazgos* as "gods" (Marcus 1978, 1989b).

Finally, by means of a regional exchange network, the Cañada *cacicazgos* procured salt, cotton, cacao, and other items from neighboring highland and lowland regions (Hopkins 1984:23–25). Hunt (1972:206) found no documented evidence of conflict and warfare among the Cuicatec *cacicazgos* of the Cañada, only of warfare with non-Cuicatec neighbors. The *Relaciones* indicate that the *cacicazgo* at Cuicatlán had been at war with the (Mazatec?) *cacicazgo* at Quiotepec as far back as the mid-fifteenth century A.D., and also that various Cuicatec towns were at war with their neighbors (Hopkins 1984:29). We will return to discuss the evident lack of warfare among the Cuicatec *cacicazgos* when we discuss their incorporation into the Aztec state.

The autonomous *cacicazgos* that emerged in the Cañada during the Classic period and that flourished during the Postclassic period were centralized polities that exhibited a multi-tiered settlement hierarchy and the rule of hereditary *caciques*. Although centralized politically and stratified socially, the Cañada's *caci-*

cazgos remained small in size. Their territories could be easily administered from the *cacique*'s center, for subject villages were spaced less than a half-day's walk away. The autonomous *cacicazgos* were closely bound by marriage alliances, exchange relationships, military alliances, and by a calendar of rituals celebrated at their centers. Yet the Cañada's *cacicazgos* never achieved a higher, region-wide level of political consolidation. Any tendencies toward more expansive political control were evidently counteracted by rivalries over the control of local water sources and by the rules of succession, which promoted factionalism among the *cacicazgos*' heirs. Hunt has also pointed out the logistical difficulties that would have presented themselves had a powerful *cacique* attempted to expand his administrative control over a larger territory in this broken, mountainous terrain (Hunt 1972:223, 228). Hence, each of the Cañada's *cacicazgos* remained

> a small political aggregate, extended to the viable ecological limits of expansion. The polity was economically organized on the basis of water control, irrigation agriculture, simple technology, local markets, a regional tribute network, short-lived warfare, and on absence of means of transport other than human. . . . Ecological marginality did not favor the technological expansion of irrigation . . . ; hence, the viable unit of political integration was small. That is, political centralization at a higher level of integration was apparently not viable under these technological conditions; conditions which imply instead political and territorial autonomy of relatively small and centripetally-oriented human aggregates. [Hunt 1972:234]

Possibly as early as the reign of the Aztec ruler Motecuhzoma I (ca. A.D. 1440–1469), however, the autonomous *cacicazgos* in the Cañada were conquered by the Aztec. The Cañada's *cacicazgos* became incorporated into the Aztec tributary province centered at Coixtlahuaca in the Mixteca Alta. According to the *Relaciones,* the Aztec exacted their tribute demands from the Cañada by simply tapping the region's existing administrative hierarchy; the Cuicatec *caciques* continued to administer their respective *cacicazgos* and to draw tribute from their subjects, only they were obliged to render tribute periodically in foodstuffs, fruits, cotton mantles, cochineal, gold, featherwork, hides, and green stones to Motecuhzoma's tribute collectors (Hopkins 1984:30–34). Consequently, when the Cañada's autonomous *cacicazgos* were encountered and conquered by the Spaniards around 1522, they were actually functioning under the veil of a Pax Azteca. After Spanish domination, and throughout the sixteenth century, the region's Cuicatec *cacicazgos* persisted and continued to be administered by native hereditary rulers or *caciques*. Yet, prohibited by the Spaniards from exercising their sanctifying religious institutions and their self-serving military alliances, the *caciques*' power steadily eroded. Because of these and other consequences of the Spanish conquest, the Cañada's *cacicazgos* were largely on the wane by the early seventeenth century (Hunt 1972:226–30; Hopkins 1984:39–42).

Discussion

As distant in time and space as they were, the *cacicazgos* of Hispaniola and the Cañada exhibited similarities in their regional organization and rule by *caciques* at the time of the Spanish conquest. They both had clearly defined two-level regional administrative hierarchies controlled by regional paramount *caciques* and local village *caciques*. A possible third level of administration on the local level is suggested by the as yet undetermined role of the *guaoxerí* among the Taíno and the *tequitlatoque* in the Cañada, although the latter were apparently commoners whose administrative functions seemed to have been interchangeable with those of community-level *caciques*. In both cases, there was minimal internal differentiation or specialization of administrative roles on either the community or regional levels. This is reflected in the relatively few distinct leadership titles exhibited and the generalized nature of the *caciques*' duties and responsibilities.

The centralized authority of the hereditary paramount *caciques* was legitimized by their presumed descent from mythical ruling ancestors. For example, the sixteenth-century Cuicatec *caciques* traced their lineage back almost 400 years to a single heroic ruler, "un solo casique que fue dueño de toda esta jurisdicción" (Hunt 1972:217–18, Fig. 99, Note 15). Through ritual, paramount *caciques* enjoyed privileged access to their divine ancestors, who interceded with supreme supernatural forces on their behalf. Since the ancestors of *caciques* were closely identified with the supernatural forces, they were revered by means of elaborate rituals that were performed in the inner sanctum of temples as well as in public ceremonies, like those we know the Taíno and Cuicatec *caciques* celebrated at their centers (Las Casas 1967, II:173; Roth 1887:263; Lovén 1935:581–83; Pané 1974:35, 42, 47; Marcus 1989b:148–54; Hunt 1972:206–7).

These native rulers were entitled to other privileges befitting their high rank—special insignia, dress, diet, residence, forms of transportation, and a bevy of wives. In view of their privileged access to esoteric knowledge and their ritual interaction with supernatural forces, *caciques* were considered semi-divine themselves. Thus, they spoke through intermediaries and were accorded reverential gestures by their subjects. The *caciques*' authority was sealed and sanctified in this way, and never questioned.

Local allegiance to the paramount *caciques* was sustained by actual (or fictive) kinship ties with village *caciques*. Marriage alliances between local elites did more than resolve the quest for marriage partners in these class endogamous, polygynous societies. Ethnohistorians of the fifteenth-century Taíno and the sixteenth-century Cuicatec have pointed out the important role that exogamous elite intermarriage had for the political cohesion of these hereditary *cacicazgos* (Wilson 1990a:139–140; Hunt 1972:218, 223–24). They served to strengthen their common interests apart from those of the general populace as well as to concentrate wealth, status, and political authority in fewer and fewer lineages. In return for the first fruits of the harvest, or for the rapid mobilization of warriors for a war party, paramounts rewarded their loyal followers with material and nonmaterial acts of largesse.

There were enormous differences, however, in the territorial extent of the Taíno and Cuicatec *cacicazgos,* a fact that compels us to consider the optimal territorial limits of centralized rule by *caciques* under varying socioenvironmental conditions. The smallest province on Hispaniola whose territory we can estimate, Cubao, had an areal extent several times greater than the largest *cacicazgo* in the Cuicatlán Cañada (see Tables 10.5, 10.6). Whereas the Mexican *Relaciones* indicate that the subject villages and hamlets and the farmland controlled by the Cañada's *cacicazgos* were within twelve walking hours of distance from their *caciques*' centers, the smallest of the Taíno *cacicazgos* would have required minimally seventeen hours to traverse by foot and the majority would have necessitated over two twelve-hour-days of travel to traverse.

A number of socioenvironmental conditions were undoubtedly important in the establishment and maintenance of *cacicazgo* territories of such a different order of magnitude. The Cañada is a flat river corridor through the southern Mexican highlands that is broken into discrete expanses of inhabitable alluvium, a situation that presented more limited opportunities for settlement than the vast, well-watered, intensively cultivated valleys of Hispaniola, such as the Vega Real (Dreyfus 1981:233–38; Wilson 1990a:80–81). It is not surprising that they supported populations of different sizes at the time of the Spanish conquest. A comparison of two *cacicazgo* centers will serve to illustrate this point. We have seen how the first paramount center visited by Columbus's crew on Hispaniola in 1492 consisted of 1,000 houses and an estimated population of more than 3,000 household heads and their families. The paramount center of Cuicatlán in the Cañada had 140 households and 322 household heads in 1548, with an estimated population of 1,063 persons (Colón 1945:227: Hopkins 1984: Table 2). Since this earliest available and complete population estimate for Cuicatlán falls within the estimated population range of 1,050–1,150 persons for the corresponding Late Postclassic archaeological center of Iglesia Vieja (Cs 31) (Redmond 1983:161), the differences in the size of Taíno and Cuicatec centers as reported in the early historical sources probably reflect the indigenous situation.

In spite of their size differences, the *cacicazgos* of the Cañada and Hispaniola were evidently pursuing the centralized but internally generalized administrative strategy that is characteristic of chiefdoms (Wright 1977:381). We would argue that the Cuicatec and Taíno *cacicazgos* exhibited differing degrees of political growth and consolidation, all the while remaining within the general framework of the chiefly design. Throughout their existence, the Cañada's *cacicazgos* remained small, autonomous polities, or "community kingdoms" to use Spores's characterization of the Mixtec *cacicazgos* (Spores 1967:29, 118). They never freely joined in a confederacy or in the founding of any large-scale political unit. There is no evidence that these independent *cacicazgos* "were subordinated to each other in any sort of formal ranked arrangement" (Hunt 1972:234).

It is tempting to attribute the Cuicatec *cacicazgos*' modest degree of political growth in part to the effects of their subordination, first to the Zapotec state in the Late Formative period, and later to the Aztec state in the Late Postclassic period. In the first instance of the Cañada's subjugation, the region's organization and political economy were completely refashioned to meet the Valley Zapotec's military and tribute demands. Native political institutions were invisible archaeologically, and instead, the hand of the larger Zapotec state was clearly evident in all aspects of life. Only after the Zapotec withdrew their direct control over the region in the Classic period did the native *cacicazgos* resume their development as autonomous polities. The general picture of the Cañada's incorporation into the Aztec empire is one of benign neglect, in so far as the region's *caciques* remained the nominal rulers of their *cacicazgos,* a policy that the Spaniards also adopted during the first century of their rule. Yet, there were certain limits to the *caciques*' authority under Aztec rule—and more to come under Spanish rule. Paramount and community *caciques* alike were designated lords (*tecuhtin*), and as such, they served their Aztec overlords as local administrators (and local tribute collectors) in the region (Hunt 1972:219). Since the *Relaciones* mentioned that the Aztec prohibited warfare here, the native *caciques* were limited to ruling fixed territories, in exchange for being granted their hereditary right to rule. Any attempts by the Cañada's paramount *caciques* to enlarge their territories and to achieve greater political consolidation in the region were interrupted by their subjugation to the Aztec state (Hunt 1972:229, 224; Hopkins 1984:35).

Free of such constraints, the Taíno clearly achieved effective regional consolidation under the authority of paramount chiefs (see Table 10.3). And some Taíno paramounts assumed control over extremely large, supra-regional provinces, the most extensive of which were reported to have contained up to thirty district or regional chiefs and as many as a hundred or more village chiefs (Rouse 1948:528–29; Las Casas 1967, II:309–10; Table 10.2). They had clearly reached the stage of political development that Carneiro has called the compound chiefdom—if not perhaps the fully consolidated chiefdom—in which independent chiefdoms are brought under the control of a more powerful paramount chief (Carneiro 1992:37). We have suggested that some of the larger supra-regional confederacies were probably crafted by ambitious *caciques* for the purposes of alliance, exchange, and warfare. Important as such external alliances may have been for sustaining the member *caciques*' authority at home, they were susceptible to the oscillating political fortunes of individual rulers, and therefore, usually fluid and short-lived.

A final point of comparison between the *cacicazgos* of Hispaniola and the Cuicatlán Cañada involves their external relationships. In spite of the differences in their size and political might, the native rulers of all these *cacicazgos* actively pursued interpolity marriage alliances, which helped to enhance their higher social status and legitimize their rule at the same time that they had the potential to enlarge and consolidate their territories (Hunt 1972:223–24, 229, 234; Wilson 1990a:139–40). Exchange and warfare also served these *cacicazgos* as important mechanisms for their political legitimacy and growth. Though often fluctuating and ephemeral in character, these external relationships fostered the political interests of the *caciques,* and were instrumental in the perpetuation and sometimes enlargement of their domains.

We conclude that the *cacicazgo* was a highly successful political strategy that was pursued by a great number of pre-Columbian societies under a variety of sociopolitical and environmental conditions. The centralized but generalized rule by hereditary *caciques* served to administer supra-village polities of a considerable range of sizes, and a variety of external relations reinforced the *cacique*'s authority. The persistence of the Cuicatec *cacicazgos* for nearly two centuries after the conquering Aztec forbade warfare and imposed their Pax Azteca is by itself a compelling illustration of the success of this indigenous design.

References

Arrom, José Juan
1975 Mitología y artes prehispánicas de las Antillas. México: Siglo Veintiuno Editores.

Bray, Warwick
1972 The city-state in Central Mexico at the time of the Spanish Conquest. Journal of Latin American Studies 4(2):161–85.

Brinton, Daniel G.
1871 The Arawack language of Guiana in its linguistic and ethnological relations. Transactions of the American Philosophical Society, vol. 14 n.s. part 3:427–44. Philadelphia.

Carneiro, Robert L.
1981 The chiefdom: Precursor of the state. In: The Transition to Statehood in the New World, edited by Grant D. Jones and Robert R. Kautz, pp. 37–79. Cambridge: Cambridge University Press.
1992 The Calusa and the Powhatan, native chiefdoms of North America. Reviews in Anthropology 21:27–38.

Caso, Alfonso
1947 Calendario y escritura de las antiguas culturas de Monte Albán. In: Obras Completas de Miguel Othón de Mendizábal I:115–43.

Colón, Almirante D. Cristóbal
1945 Este es el primer viage y las derrotas y camino que hizo el Almirante D. Cristóbal Colón cuando descubrió las Indias, puesto sumariamente, sin el prólogo que hizo á los Reyes, que va á la letra y comienza de esta manera. In: Colección de los viages y descubrimientos que hicieron por mar los Españoles desde fines del siglo XV, edited by Martín Fernández de Navarrete, tomo I. Buenos Aires: Editorial Guaranía.

Cook, Sherburne F., and Woodrow Borah
1971 Aboriginal population of Hispaniola. In: Essays in Population History: Mexico and the Caribbean. Berkeley: University of California Press.

Davies, Claude N. B.
1968 Los señoríos independientes del imperio Azteca. Instituto de Antropología e Historia. México.

Dreyfus, Simone
1981 Notes sur la chefferie Taino d'Aiti: Capacités productrices, ressources alimentaires, pouvoirs dans une société pré-colombienne de forêt tropicale. Journal de la Société des Américanistes LXVII:229–48.

Fewkes, Jesse W.
1907 The Aborigines of Porto Rico and the Neighboring Islands. In: Annual Report of the Bureau of American Ethnology for 1903–4, vol. 25:1–220. Smithsonian Institution, Washington, D.C. Reprint, New York: Johnson Reprint Corporation, 1970.

Flannery, Kent V.
1972 The cultural evolution of civilizations. Annual Review of Ecology and Systematics 3:399–426.

Gibson, Charles
1964 The Aztecs under Spanish rule. A History of the Indians of the Valley of Mexico, 1519–1810. Stanford, CA: Stanford University Press.

Goeje, C. H. de
1939 Nouvel examen des langues des Antilles avec notes sur les langues Arawak-Maipure et Caribes et vocabulaires Shebayo et Guayana (Guyane). Journal de la Société des Américanistes n.s. vol. XXXI:1–120.

Helms, Mary W.
1979 Ancient Panama: Chiefs in Search of Power. Austin: University of Texas Press.

Hodge, Mary G.
1984 Aztec City-States. Studies in Latin American Ethnohistory & Archaeology, vol. 3. Memoirs of the Museum of Anthropology, University of Michigan, no. 18. Ann Arbor.

Hopkins, Joseph W., III
1984 Irrigation and the Cuicatec Ecosystem: A Study of Agriculture and Civilization in North Central Oaxaca. Studies in Latin American Ethnohistory & Archaeology, vol. 2. Memoirs of the Museum of Anthropology, University of Michigan, no. 17. Ann Arbor.

Hunt, Eva
1972 Irrigation and the socio-political organization of Cuicatec cacicazgos. In: The Prehistory of the Tehuacán Valley. Vol. 4: Chronology and Irrigation, edited by Frederick Johnson. Austin: University of Texas Press.

Johnson, Gregory A.
1973 Local exchange and early state development in Southwestern Iran. Anthropological Papers of the Museum of Anthropology, University of Michigan, no. 51. Ann Arbor.
1978 Information sources and the development of decision-making organizations. In: Social Archeology: Beyond Subsistence and Dating, edited by Charles Redman et al., pp. 87–112. New York: Academic Press.

Lange, Frederick W., and Doris Z. Stone
1984 Introduction. In: The Archaeology of Lower Central America, edited by F. W. Lange and D. Z. Stone, pp. 3–12. Albuquerque: University of New Mexico Press.

Las Casas, Fr. Bartolomé de
1951 Historia de las Indias. 2 vols. México: Fondo de Cultura Económica.
1967 Apologética historia sumaria, edited by Edmundo O'Gorman. 2 vols. México: Universidad Nacional Autónoma de México, Instituto de Investigaciones Históricas.

Lovén, Sven
1935 Origins of the Tainan Culture, West Indies. Göteborg: Elanders Bokfryckeri Akfiebolag.

Marcus, Joyce
1974 The iconography of power among the Classic Maya. World Archaeology 6(1):83–94.
1978 Archaeology and religion: A comparison of the Zapotec and Maya. World Archaeology 10(2):172–91.
1980 Zapotec writing. Scientific American 242(2):50–64.
1983 The conquest slabs of Building J, Monte Albán. In: The Cloud People: Divergent Evolution of the Zapotec and Mixtec Civilizations, edited by Kent V. Flannery and Joyce Marcus, pp. 106–8. Orlando: Academic Press.
1989a From centralized systems to city-states: Possible models for the Epiclassic. In: Mesoamerica after the Decline of Teotihuacán A.D. 700–900, edited by Richard A. Diehl and Janet C. Berlo, pp. 201–10. Dumbarton Oaks Research Library and Collections, Washington, D.C.
1989b Zapotec chiefdoms and the nature of Formative religions. In: Regional Perspectives on the Olmec, edited by Robert J. Sharer and David C. Grove, pp. 148–97. Cambridge: Cambridge University Press.
1991 First dates. Natural History 4:26–29.

Mártir de Anglería, Pedro
1964 Décadas del Nuevo Mundo. 2 vols. México: José Porrúa e Hijos.

Oberg, Kalervo
1955 Types of social structure among the lowland tribes of South and Central America. American Anthropologist 57 (3):472–87.

Pané, Fr. Ramón
1974 Relación acerca de las antigüedades de los Indios, edited by José Juan Arrom. México: Siglo Veintiuno editores.

Peebles, Christopher S., and Susan M. Kus
1977 Some archaeological correlates of ranked societies. American Antiquity 42(3):421–48.

Pozorski, Thomas
1980 The Early Horizon site of Huaca de los Reyes: Societal implications. American Antiquity 45(1):100–10.

Redmond, Elsa M.
1983 A Fuego y Sangre: Early Zapotec Imperialism in the Cuicatlán Cañada, Oaxaca. Studies in Latin American Ethnohistory & Archaeology, vol. 1. Memoirs of the Museum of Anthropology, University of Michigan, no. 16. Ann Arbor.

Roth, Hy. Ling
1887 The aborigines of Hispaniola. The Journal of the Anthropological Institute of Great Britain and Ireland 16:247–86.

Rouse, Irving
1948 The Arawak. In: Handbook of South American Indians. Vol. 4: The Circum-Caribbean Tribes, edited by Julian H. Steward, pp. 507–46. Bureau of American Ethnology, Bulletin no. 143. Washington, D.C.
1982 Ceramic and religious development in the Greater Antilles. Journal of New World Archaeology 5(2):45–52. University of California, Los Angeles.
1992 The Tainos: Rise and Decline of the People who Greeted Columbus. New Haven: Yale University Press.

Roys, Ralph L.
1943 The Indian Background of Colonial Yucatán. Carnegie Institution of Washington, Publication no. 548. Washington, D.C.
1957 The Political Geography of the Yucatán Maya. Carnegie Institution of Washington, Publication no. 613. Washington, D.C.

Sahlins, Marshall
1968 Tribesmen. Englewood Cliffs, New Jersey: Prentice-Hall, Inc.

Salomon, Frank
1986 Native Lords of Quito in the Age of the Incas. Cambridge: Cambridge University Press.

Sauer, Carl O.
1966 The Early Spanish Main. Berkeley and Los Angeles: University of California Press.

Spencer, Charles S.
1982 The Cuicatlán Cañada and Monte Albán: A Study of Primary State Formation. New York: Academic Press.
1987 Rethinking the chiefdom. In: Chiefdoms in the Americas, edited by Robert D. Drennan and Carlos A. Uribe, pp. 369–89. Lanham, Maryland: University Press of America.
1990 On the tempo and mode of state formation: Neoevolutionism reconsidered. Journal of Anthropological Archaeology 9:1–30.

Spencer, Charles S., and Elsa M. Redmond
1992 Prehispanic Chiefdoms of the Western Venezuelan *llanos*. World Archaeology 24(1):134–57.

Spores, Ronald
1967 The Mixtec Kings and Their People. Norman: University of Oklahoma Press.

Steward, Julian H., and Louis C. Faron
1959 Native peoples of South America. New York: McGraw-Hill Book Company, Inc.

Taylor, Douglas
1960 Some remarks on the spelling and formation of Taino words. International Journal of American Linguistics 26 (4):345–48.

Vega, Bernardo
1980 Los cacicazgos de la Hispaniola. Ediciones Museo del Hombre Dominicano, Serie: Investigaciones Antropológicas, no. 13. Santo Domingo, República Dominicana.

Wilson, Samuel M.
1990a Caribbean Chiefdoms in the Age of Columbus. Tuscaloosa: The University of Alabama Press.
1990b Columbus, my enemy. Natural History 12:44–49.

Wright, Henry T.
1977 Recent research on the origin of the state. Annual Review of Anthropology 6:379–97.
1986 The evolution of civilizations. In: American Archaeology Past and Future, edited by David J. Meltzer, Don D. Fowler, and Jeremy A. Sabloff, pp. 323–65. Washington, D.C.: Smithsonian Institution Press.

CHAPTER 11

Indigenous Mentality and Spanish Power

The Conquest in Oaxaca

María de los Angeles Romero Frizzi

Centro Regional de Oaxaca, INAH, Mexico

At the end of the fifteenth century and in the first decades of the sixteenth century, Spain instigated expeditions of geographic discovery that culminated in the establishment of a vast empire in America. As part of this process of expansion into the New World, Spaniards brought with them essential aspects of their own culture and social organization. With amazing success, they managed, in just a few decades, to conquer the native societies of Mesoamerica, to found the viceroyalty of New Spain, and to organize a new society along the lines of their own peninsular world.[1]

Traditionally, the conquest of Mesoamerica has been explained in terms of three principal causes: (1) the greater technological development of the conquerors, (2) the enormous political divisions among the indigenous societies, and (3) the lack of concepts in the indigenous mentality that would have permitted a full understanding of the nature of the Spanish presence. Beyond these substantial factors, interpretations of the conquest and later consolidation of the colonial system have often turned to absurd simplifications. It is not unusual to find history texts that explain the whole process of conquest and the imposition of Spanish culture and institutions as a result of the brutality and barbarity of the conquerors, and the missionaries and Spanish officials who followed them.

A quick look at the sixteenth century seems to support this impression of devastation. Before the century concluded, there were already Indian communities laid out according to Hispanic convention, Renaissance convents constructed on top of ancient temples, native town councils, and Indian nobles who wore European dress and displayed the Spanish titles of *alcalde* and *regidor*. Other indigenous elite concealed the images of what had in the past been their feared gods, only to later make generous land donations to the monasteries of the imposed religion.[2] For centuries, the native peasants had to pay tribute and labor service to the conqueror as a persistent reminder of Spanish domination. But it is in those enigmatic early years of contact that we are confronted with seemingly incomprehensible evidence for the ease with which this domination was effected. Time after time the Spanish captains and their soldiers, in view of thousands of stunned Indians, hurled the statues of native deities down from their temples amd replaced them with images of the Virgin and the saints.[3] Frequently, just two or three missionaries, accompanied by their servants, went into a native kingdom where they might whip and humiliate its leaders, sometimes for unimportant matters.[4] These stories, although distorted by the Spanish desire to exaggerate their achievements and by the native desire to obtain justice, make the Spaniard appear all-powerful while reducing the natives to tolerant victims of these and many other abuses. We know that there were armed confrontations and other forms of resistance against the recent arrivals, but alongside them we find seemingly inexplicable instances of Indian submission.

Despite all that has been written about these years, despite the plethora of documents attesting to cruel or capricious Spanish behavior, it is still difficult to believe that the Indians were incapable of offering a response, a response that should have occurred not only in the form of battles and rebellions, but in the actions of daily life and in the decision-making of those in power. Indians were not a *tabula rasa* on which the conquerors wrote their history, nor were they passive spectators to the destruction of their world. The Nahua, the Mixtec, the Zapotec, and other groups were actors in that epic saga. The Indian response, however, depended on ideas and concepts evoked from their own prehispanic culture. Based on data drawn from the Oaxaca region in southern Mexico, in particular from the Mixteca and from Zapotec-speaking areas of the Valley of Oaxaca, I will try to suggest some avenues for determining this response.

The Battles and the Ideas

The first contact between the indigenous groups of Oaxaca and the Spanish armies took place in 1519; by 1530, the principal kingdoms of the Mixtec and the Oaxaca Valley Zapotec had given their recognition to Cortés's captains.[5] Before 1540, there were already Spanish judges charged with enforcing the orders of the Audiencia of Mexico in many of the more important native kingdoms such as Coixtlahuaca, Teozacoalco, Tejupan, and others (Gerhard 1972); and around 1550 many impressive churches and convents were under construction in Teposcolula, Coixtlahuaca, Yanhuitlán, and other towns (Mullen 1975). Nonetheless, the city of Antequera could have barely numbered 1,000 inhabitants in 1569 (Chance 1978:73). In spite of having a low population of Spaniards in Oaxaca in contrast with the large indigenous population, Spanish power had been consolidated in these regions by the middle of the sixteenth century.[6] What was it besides arms, gunpowder, and cruelty that contributed to the conquest of these lands? What ancestral ideas favored the Spaniards?

The conquest of Oaxaca, like that of the rest of Mesoamerica, can be analyzed in terms of relationships of power, not just material power—the number of armed men or the quantity and efficacy of weapons—but also the ideas that Mesoamericans would have held about the power of their opponents. To understand native thought in this sense is a complex process. It has been said that, faced with the strangeness of the Spaniards, the native lords confused them with Quetzalcoatl, who was supposed to return from the east. This argument has been used to explain the passive attitude of the Aztec ruler, the rationale for some native alliances with the Spaniards, and much of their attitude during the early colonial era. We will try to see something more in these ideas.

Certainly the indigenous rulers sought the help of the recent arrivals because they considered them embued with a superior power. The Indians, and especially their lords, must have believed that something special could be expected or feared from these strangers, and for this reason they made them allies. The case of the Tlaxcaltecans is well known, but there are many other examples. In Oaxaca the lord of Tehuantepec allied himself from the very beginning with the conquerors against the Mixtec of Tututepec (Cervantes de Salazar 1934:154); the same Mixtec lord of Tututepec, after several confrontations, made use of his relationship with the Spaniards to fight against Nopala and to control the Chatino community of Yaitepec.[7] And searching the documents of that era, we continue to find similar stories.[8] Consequently, it is difficult to believe that they would have set up these alliances if they had thought of the Spaniards as a few poor peasant cultivators of olives and grapevines or as vile, adventuring fortune-hunters. They sided with the conquerors because they must have thought that such alliances were inevitable or that they might be useful, given that the Spaniards possessed something that they valued. Of course, the fact that the *peninsulares* brought iron tools and artifacts, arms, gunpowder, and boats helped.

The existing rivalries between the Indian kingdoms, with their ancestral battles for the control of the best lands and the men that worked them, have long been considered one of the principal factors clearing the way for the Spaniard. And it is certain that the Spaniards, in turn, knew how to take good advantage of these native conflicts over regional power, and that such divisions were an integral part of the conqueror's success, a success that could not have happened without some 20,000 or 30,000 Indian allies on the side of the 300 Spaniards. But because traditional history has placed so much emphasis on these terrible native struggles, the no less serious conflicts among the Spaniards have been overlooked. This silence has helped to forge an image of a completely fragmented indigenous society in contrast to a unified and well organized group of Spaniards, but nothing could be farther from the truth. The Spaniards also were divided and constantly fighting among themselves. We recall the quarrels between Cortés and Pedro de Alvarado, the difficulties with Pánfilo de Narváez, the jealousies of Cortés himself and the innumerable disputes among *encomenderos* over the control of a town, disputes which at times lasted for more than ten years.[9] If, then, both sides were divided, why did the advantage fall on the Spanish side?

The manner in which native society viewed the Spaniards has to have been the determining factor, and this perception was strongly influenced by the Indians' own idea of power, an idea decisive not only in the shocking first days of contact but in the unfolding of the first century of colonial rule, and possibly even later. If the native elites aligned themselves with the Spaniards, they must have done so because they expected to be able to use them for their own advantage. If they tolerated so many abuses, it is because, in turn, the Indians feared them. A mixture of hope to manipulate the Spanish presence for their own benefit blended together with a good dose of fear in those early years. Before continuing to investigate the indigenous mind, we will review cautiously a few details of those moments of conquest.

Rethinking the Conquest of Oaxaca

The conquest and especially the later consolidation of Spanish institutions in these lands was not as straightforward a deed as it sometimes has been made to appear. The conquest was not a well orchestrated war in which the Spanish army advanced, subduing the defenseless Indians. It is better understood as a series of military and exploratory expeditions in which small forces of Spaniards, guided and accompanied by Indian allies, passed through mountainous areas and extensive regions of dense population. Starting out from the center of Mexico, Pedro de Alvarado, the conqueror of the coast and southern highlands of Oaxaca, in the space of three years between 1523 and 1526, crossed the entire Mixteca Alta, the coast of Oaxaca, a great part of the Zapotec kingdoms of the *sierra,* and went on to effect the conquest of Guatemala. In these years, he waged war continuously, remaining only a few months among the populations he subdued before moving on to the next kingdom. He did not meet hostile opposition in all the villages. In some villages, he was well received, and others he did not even visit.[10]

Alvarado's passage through the *sierra* must have caused a commotion, if only because in many of these mountain pockets word of his journey arrived through Indian messengers, interpreted according to their own cultural view. The image that the Zapotec forged of the conquerors was one received from other Indians, thereby ensuring their culturally distinctive interpretation of what was happening. Given the fact that this expedition remained just a few months in some kingdoms and never reached others, nothing would have obligated the indigenous lords to pay tribute to Alvarado or to any other conqueror, if they had not consented to do so. Alternatively, it could be argued that after the first contact there was always the possibility that the conquerors would return with new armies of Indian allies, as had happened before in the Basin of Mexico. But the mention of Indian allies disappears relatively quickly from the documents and this seems to suggest that, for much of Oaxaca, their influence and their importance in these events diminished after the first few encounters.[11]

In the late 1520s and early 1530s, despite the absence of Indian allies, the *encomenderos* and their servants collected a considerable quantity of gold coins, jewels, supplies, and slaves in most of the Mixteca and other zones of Oaxaca, even though their power appears to us to have rested on a very weak foundation. For example, beginning around 1526, Tlaxiaco—a Mixtec kingdom composed of four *cabeceras* with around 80 subject hamlets and a population of about 8,000 married men (plus children under seventeen and women)—regularly delivered tribute to its *encomenderos,* whose only contact with the town was an occasional visit.[12] Some *encomenderos* continued living in Mexico City or Antequera and were out of contact with the town for eight or ten months. Nonetheless, on their return they demanded gold, supplies, and slaves, which the Indians brought to them in the *cabecera* or delivered to their homes in the city. Gregorio de Monjaráz declared in 1529 that neither he nor his servants had gone to the town for more than eight months; still, at the end of that time, he succeeded in collecting 600 pesos of gold.[13]

In other cases the *encomenderos* barely knew the kingdoms that were supposed to pay them tribute, let alone which ones were their subject *estancias,* as seen in the suit between Francisco Maldonado and Martín Vázquez. The two *encomenderos* shared the tribute from five *cabeceras* in the Mixteca Alta: Tlaxiaco, Achiutla, Chalcatongo, Mitlatongo, and Tlacahuastepec. As the questioning in the suit revealed, they were unfamiliar with the region, arguing about where some of the *estancias* were located or what they were called.[14] Despite this, the Mixtec paid them tribute, "conociéndoles por señor todo el tiempo." Those years are famous for the numerous abuses by Spaniards and for the suits among them to take control of tribute. It was the time when the amount of tribute exacted was the greatest, and the cruelties of the conquerors innumerable: they burned the indigenous nobility, they cut off men's genitals and women's breasts, they whipped and enslaved them, branding their faces with red-hot irons to disfigure their appearance. Yet despite such cruelties the documents only say: "los dichos indios no hacían más de lo que les mandaba [su encomendero]."[15] We must bear in mind that all this happened while the native kingdoms retained the most power and the Spaniards were the most disorganized.[16]

It should be acknowledged that the Spanish penetration in the mountains of Oaxaca was not entirely based on violence or "los temores" that the conquerors instilled in the local population.[17] The alliances between native lords and the Spaniards was not based only on the battles of early days, for there existed another relationship between them. Indian nobles sought out this union with the Spaniards for another reason: to acquire the foreign goods that the Spaniards brought. There are documents from the first years of the colony that relate how the Spaniards arrived in native communities and were well received by the local lords, seated at their tables, and feted with presents and food. The Indians gave them gold, jewels, and slaves in exchange for glass beads and knives. The Spaniards knew how to take good advantage of this interchange; they themselves, eager to preserve the friendship, invited the native governors to dine at their houses, and they offered them more Spanish goods.[18]

In these pacts and in the offerings that the Indians gave the Spaniards, it is possible to detect something further about native thinking. Such interaction conveyed a basic principle of indigenous culture important then and to this day; that is, the exchange of gifts implies a relationship of mutual respect and obligation. Even the tribute the Indians paid to their own rulers had been given in exchange for protection and sacred intervention. Therefore, when these native lords established similar relations with the Spaniards, they expected to get something back in return—perhaps protection or assistance with local problems. In such exchanges, the differences between the two cultures appear with clarity. The Spaniards' interest was mercantile and their ambition was to obtain gold and slaves. But if the Spanish objective, being closer to our own way of thinking, is more transparent, that of the Indians requires further explication. The jewels and other objects which the native lords gave the Spaniards were no ordinary commodities available to all members of society. They were a unique privilege of the nobility; no peasant could have possessed or used these objects. They were a symbol of the native nobility's superior status and bringing them to the conqueror was evidence of the special recognition these lords were offering, a recognition that these foreigners held a power at least equal to, if not superior, to that of the native lords themselves.

How did the Indians interpret what they received from the Spaniards? Was it only curiosity, was it a practical measure, or, when they exchanged rich feathers and cloth for horses and scissors, did they not also do so with the desire to emulate the Spaniards at least in external form? The new goods, just like luxurious cloaks or jewels, emphasized superior rank, only now these symbols of social status reinforced the position of the Spaniards. The native lords may have wanted the horses and the new weapons for their utilitarian value as well, but their interest went beyond the goods themselves. The new articles, such as scissors, combs, or candlesticks, had symbolic value as well; they called attention to the nobles' social distance from the commoners, and they were probably used as symbols of these leaders' alliance with the Spaniards. It was important to display them before their own people and before the lords of nearby towns. And, in the wide range of Indian responses to the Spanish presence, it is possible to see one common denominator: the acceptance of Spanish power, a superior power which challenged their own.

Moving on in the study of the early years of colonialism, we continue to find apparently inexplicable or even contradictory facts. On the one hand, we have an unstable Spanish government, fearful that the large indigenous population would rebel; on the other, numerous kingdoms that continued paying tribute. In 1540, the importance of the city of Antequera had weakened, many Spaniards had abandoned it, and its *vecinos* numbered only thirty.[19] Terrorized, they wrote the king asking his help, stating that there was no fort in the city to protect them and that the Indians had not cast aside their rebellious sentiments as Spain believed. Contemporary documents make clear the fear of Indian revolt; time and time again they describe how each citizen of Antequera had his servants and relatives armed and mounted for defense.[20]

Nonetheless, in Oaxaca, the rebellions were neither as large nor as frequent as these Spaniards expected.[21] A few Indian kingdoms, once having agreed to give recognition and tribute to the Spaniards, decided to stop paying them because of the crimes and abuses they committed. Such was the case in the southern highland town of Coatlán. In 1525, the village (which early on gave tribute to Pedro de Alvarado and then to Gregorio de Monjaráz) refused to pay because of the trouble that the *encomendero* was causing the native lord. After 1530, there is mention of only two major rebellions which threatened the city, and it is possible that these were part of a single movement. This revolt, which began about 1547 in Coatlán and Teitipac, grew to encompass many villages with several hundred Indians and to proclaim the return of the ancient order. The rebels first attacked Miahuatlán, where they killed a Spaniard and several Indians. From there they advanced to the center of Spanish power, the city of Antequera, arriving at Ocotlán, just five leagues away (less than 30 km), where they were stopped, practically without the Spaniards mounting any resistance.[22] What stopped them? Fear of the 30, 60, or at most 90 Spaniards, when the documents say that there were at least several hundred Indians? Why did they fear this small group or, more precisely, what kind of power could the Spaniards have had in the eyes of the rebels? Indians of other regions such as the Zapotec of the northern highlands, the Mixe, and the Chontal waged a major resistance; some places never agreed to pay tribute and resisted Spanish control forcefully and persistently. Yet we know little about the history of these regions.[23]

The consolidation of Spanish institutions is no less disconcerting. It does not seem possible, if we take into account the number of Spaniards that inhabited New Spain in the first half of the sixteenth century,[24] the expanse of the colony, the steepness of the terrain and the poor condition of communication routes, that a system of government with effective control mechanisms could have existed either before the mid-1550s or for several years later. Nor is it credible that the Spanish judges or *corregidores,* first appointed in some Indian *señoríos* between 1531 and 1535, could have imposed all their decisions or the edicts of the Audiencia with impunity on hundreds of Indians. Nor could it have been so simple for the *encomenderos,* thanks to a letter written in the hand of Cortés or Alvarado, to dispose of hundreds of workers or tribute without having to account to anyone. How could the missionaries have arrived in a Mixtec kingdom like Yanhuitlán or Coixtlahuaca, each with about 10,000 residents, and forced them to construct a church of impressive dimensions? Any one Indian kingdom would have had more inhabitants than all the residents of the city of Antequera. Away from the cities and Spanish towns, power would have remained in the hands of the descendants of the old prehispanic rulers. They continued to hold the reins that controlled the Indian masses as well as those with whom they made the decision to comply with orders emanating from the *encomenderos,* from the Audiencia, or from the missionaries.

Indigenous Power and Spanish Power: The Early Years

During the early years the Indians could only understand what was happening by reference to concepts from their own culture and prehispanic society. The Indian response depended on the framework of ideas that existed prior to the moment of contact. These ideas charted the course of those first years and possibly influenced that which followed.

At the end of the prehispanic era, despite the existence of certain differences between them, the Mixtecs and the Valley Zapotecs had both developed a highly stratified society.[25] At the apex of their social structure, a small number of individuals, sometimes with an ethnic origin distinct from that of the majority of the community, retained an enormous amount of power. During nine centuries this governing group held control over society. They imparted justice, invoked war, controlled the best lands and the men that would plant them, enjoyed tribute and exercised a power almost without limit. Many aspects of the culture of this society joined together to maintain the status of this group. The distance which separated the noble lineages from the commoner population was enormous and the difference was palpable. The lords enjoyed a lifestyle filled with the most delicate refinements; they dwelled in palaces decorated with fresco paintings and stone mosaics, carpeted with jaguar skins and mats of rabbit fur and tropical bird feathers. The populace lived in huts of wattle, reeds, and straw and slept on palm mats. Their sumptuary consumption was proof of the dominant group's superiority. Many aspects of this culture appear to have been skillfully woven together to prevent the social mobility of the lower classes. The history of the dominant group and its inscription in sacred books, their speech, and their art, all seem to have been invented to sustain the power of these persons and the structure which ruled this society.

The power of the lords had another, more relevant justification in the eyes of the people. The religion and ideology of this society were, at one time, a response to the great uncertainties of life, and they remained the basis of governing authority. The Mixtec and Zapotec, like other Mesoamerican groups, conceived of everything that surrounded them, from plants and animals to gods and rulers, as a hierarchical entity. A sacred power, residing in all beings, increased in intensity as one moved from the lowest levels to the highest, that of the ruling nobles and the deities.[26] At the highest levels of their social and ideological structure, gods and lords were interchangeable with one another. They were equated in the ideas of the populace and in the practice of daily life. In religious ceremonies, the lords wore the apparel of the gods, the masks of the gods of rain, the colors of Tezcatlipoca.[27] In the books of divination and history, gods and lords were difficult to separate. The jewels, the costumes, and even the dishes and utensils used by the rulers were decorated with sacred images and when they died their faces were covered with masks, decorated in precious stones, which represented a deity. In sum, the Indian lords were man-gods.[28]

The *yyas* or the *coquis,* as the Mixtec and Zapotec called their most powerful lords, were the repositories of much of the group's knowledge. The Mixtecs and perhaps also the Zapotecs[29] possessed exquisite books, elaborated on deerskin surfaced with lime sizing and painted with a well-executed line and fine colors. Their covers were decorated with precious stones.[30] The beauty of these books affirmed the importance of the knowledge contained within them. There were both historical and religious codices; these last were closely connected to the 260 day calendar and were used in special ceremonies to foretell the future.[31] The ritual and calendric books were part of the exclusive knowledge of the lords. They interpreted the auguries of each day: the luck of the recently born, the propitious day to contract marriage or to declare war. They alone understood these ritual codices and could speak the divine word in sacred ceremonial sites through oracles, whose interpretation made them one with the gods.[32] This knowledge was the legacy of the Indians, it was part of their most valued patrimony and was the foundation of the rulers' authority. Their power resided not only in the auguries with which they predicted events, but also in their capacity to influence the sacred forces of nature which in turn sent the rain and created the earth's fertility. In sum, the cultural and material reproduction of the community depended on them. They were its ideological support. Knowledge was a component of their power—a sacred power (López Austin 1973).

In addition to the sacred books of divination, the native communities had historical books which told of the distinct origin of the ruling castes and of their acts of war, their marriages, their genealogies. They were historical books in which the reality of wars of conquest were mixed with travels to the underworld and contact with the sacred.[33] By means of caves the lords entered the world of their ancestors to establish contact with them, the man-gods of the past. Even the pictorial style of the imagery of both historical and sacred books, drawn in two dimensions and without the appearance of movement, seems designed to transmit a history and reproduce a society in which change is reduced to a minimum. They assure an appearance of immutability for the ruling group.[34] But this structure of power, so laboriously developed over the centuries, functioned tragically to consolidate the power of the conqueror.

The hierarchization of Indian thought and society, the identification of the upper classes with sacred powers, esoteric knowledge, and sophisticated consumption, combined in the Indian mind to ensure the power of the recently arrived. It was not a simple confusion betwen Cortés and Quetzalcoatl; it was something more profound and at the same time more difficult to overcome or to understand in its complicated reality. The Indians lacked even the most minimal element that would have permitted them to understand the existence of another world on the other side of the Atlantic. According to their belief systems, the Spaniards seemed more powerful: they possessed knowledge more sophisticated than that of their own lords, they consumed more exotic goods. How could they know that the technology of the Spaniards was not a gift of the sacred forces, like the precious masks or costumes of Tlaloc? Both the paraphernalia of the Spaniards and their unexpected intrusion into an indigenous world in which change itself signified the action of cosmic forces made it inevitable that the Indians would place them on the highest plane in their hierarchical world, both in their social structure and in their system of beliefs. The Spaniards were a superior group and power, a sacred power. Thus, the native lords tried to ally themselves with the Spaniards in their battles and rivalries, they obeyed them to the extreme, they feared them or they faced them with courage, like other man-gods.

The enigma of the conquest of Mesoamerica is born of our inability to penetrate indigenous concepts and values. What the Indians thought about the Spaniards is reflected in their actions and attitudes, not only those which operated in the first moments, when Cortés was confused with Quetzalcoatl, but also those which, as a structural component of their thinking, continued to play an active role in the years that followed. This native mode of thought can explain, at least in part, their respect not only towards the first *encomenderos* but particularly towards the missionaries and perhaps other Spanish authorities. How much longer would this Indian idea of Spanish power last?

Spanish Power in the Mid-Sixteenth Century

By 1560, it would be difficult for anyone to question the reality of New Spain. The institutions brought to these lands continued to grow stronger and political control in the region had been consolidated. At that time the second viceroy, Don Luis de Velasco, governed New Spain and the *encomenderos* had lost much land to royal power. Tribute paid by the Indian populace to the descendants of the first *encomenderos* was strictly assessed and regulated by the Spanish Crown.

The changes experienced by the indigenous populations of Oaxaca were many: celebrations were organized for the Catholic saints, the *caciques* dressed in Spanish clothing and rode horses.[35] They and their villages held small livestock *estancias* and raised silkworms which they sold in Puebla and Mexico City (Romero Frizzi 1985). Most of the Indians who had lived through the conquest had died. Nonetheless, behind these many changes in economic life and in Spanish forms, much of the old indigenous culture survived. It survived in the daily teachings which parents gave their children. The nobles continued celebrating ceremonies to the prehispanic deities, but now they did so hidden from the Spaniards, quietly in their living rooms, in the cemeteries, or in mountain caves. What did the Indians of the second half of the sixteenth century think of the Spaniards? It is always difficult to penetrate the ideas of a society, particularly an Indian society which took care to hide many of its activities, and still more its thoughts, from the dominant group. By 1560, the Spaniards were no longer strange beings come from the sea, incomprehensible and cruel. Now they were the *mayordomos* of neighboring herds of goats and sheep, they were the muleteers of the packteams, or the residents of the city—small businessmen or bureaucrats, priests that arrived occasionally to celebrate the saint's mass. They were common people, people apparently without power.

One event that took place in the Valley of Oaxaca in 1565 can help us understand contemporary Indian thinking. In that year, the Zapotec- and Mixe-speaking priest of the village of Mitla had discovered through Indian confessions and through "palabras y astucias," that the local people were continuing to perform ancient religious ceremonies in some caves nearby. The priest, armed with divine fury and accompanied by other Spaniards, went to the cave to investigate, guided by a group of Indians. What happened appears to have been commonplace; other documents written by missionaries who entered such sacred caves tell of burning the remains of the divine ancestors, breaking the sacred images, and committing every class of atrocity in the cause of smashing these vestiges of pagan idolatry.[36] In Totolapa and Zoquitlán and in other villages belonging to the Mitla curate, the same priest had in fact used unorthodox tricks to discover a great number of idols, seashells and large obsidian blades with which the Indians continued to perform sacrifices.[37] The account from Mitla is different, thanks to the details provided by a Spanish witness. This witness declared that in the cave, which they found on a high mountain some seven leagues from Mitla, they discovered a very large idol which "they called El Corazón del Pueblo, which generally all the Indians of those villages worshipped, with the head of a person whom they said was Spanish, all encrusted with stonework and along with it other very elegant masks of the same type." As the questioning progressed, new details came to light: in the cave they had found more than 300 sacred bundles, many idols, feathers and other recent sacrifices which had been made by the Indians of these villages.

Discoveries such as this were not so unusual, for the Indians' fear of the priests caused them to reveal many secrets. What makes this event so exceptional is the testimony of the Spaniard who described the skull covered with mosaic. It may be that he was mistaken and that it was not the head of a Spaniard but of an Indian noble, but the simple fact that one of the several Indians who guided them to the cave told him that it belonged to a Spaniard indicates a much more profound significance: Why the head of a Spaniard covered with mosaics in the center of the Zapotec religious world? Mitla was not only a political kingdom, but the burial place of the Zapotec lords; it was the place where the man-gods of these lands were laid to rest, the sacred place of contact with the ancestors (Burgoa 1934, II:120–21). These caves were not merely a simple refuge, sufficiently remote for maintaining outlawed religious practices and sacred objects hidden from Spanish eyes. On the contrary, they were important because of the essential role caves played in Mesoamerican history and religion.[38] We know that various groups of central Mexico placed their mythic origins in caves and, according to the Mixtec codices, caves were considered to be the path to the underworld. The man-gods entered them to establish contact with the ancestors before effecting any important activity in this world.[39]

The cave near Mitla encompasses a long history. Geological processes have produced many caves and rockshelters in the hills and mountains around Tlacolula, Mitla, and Matatlán. Thousands of years before our era, a number of them were occupied by human groups, perhaps the ancestors of the sixteenth-century Zapotec (Flannery 1986). In one field project (1966–67) conducted by a team of archaeologists from the University of Michigan,[40] some of these caves and rockshelters yielded stone tools and pottery types spanning the prehistoric phases from Monte Albán II (100 B.C. to A.D. 200) until Monte Albán V (A.D. 1000–1521). One cave in particular, called Cueva del Diablo or Biliyar Benjab in Zapotec, was occupied as a sacred site from the time of Monte Albán II until the arrival of the Spaniards. The cave measures approximately 20 m in length by 8 m in width; for a distance of some 50 m in front of the cave's entrance the whole mountainside is covered with potsherds and incense burners dating from Monte Albán II to V. Continuing this ancient pattern of use, the skull of a foreign man-god was carefully placed in this sacred site, which had a history of use of more than one thousand years and which the Zapotec connected to their distant places of origin. Moreover, several springs are found in the interior of this cave, most importantly that of the Río Grande, the principal river which waters the lands of Mitla and continues on to the Tlacolula Valley. Its association with this river gives the Cueva del Diablo an even more sacred character: it was the place of contact with the past, with the ancestors that maintained the spring which made cultivation and life itself possible in this part of the valley. As such it was the focal point of cosmologically significant associations between rain, springs, the fertility of the earth and the role of native lords. These were the associations that led them to sanctify this cave with the sacred bundles of their deceased rulers' remains and relics, the mosaic masks, and the idol who was the "Corazón del Pueblo." The objects placed in the cave leave no room for doubt: it was a sacred place of the highest magnitude.

The Indians thought that the sacred power of their great rulers resided in a few special parts of the body. The importance of the heart is well known, for it was excised from the sacrificial victim's body. The human head was another part of the body in which the dead person's power was concentrated. Decapitation ceremonies were widespread in Mesoamerica and were also an important part of native ritual. Prehispanic art gives numerous examples of decapitated heads displayed as trophies by priests and rulers (Moser 1973). But few mosaic-decorated skulls are found in archaeological excavations. In fact, there are only three known examples: two are now in European museums, those of Berlin and London. The other skull is preserved in the museum of Oaxaca City and was found by Alfonso Caso in Tomb 7 at Monte Albán. Caso thought, in keeping with studies in vogue in those years, that these skulls represented indigenous deities. We now think that they belonged to deified ancestors or, to use López Austin's term, "man-gods." If not the ancestors themselves, these men could have been surrogates, sacrificed and adorned with the colors of deities in place of the local lord. The skull in the London museum is covered with black and yellow stripes, which were the colors associated with Tezcatlipoca. Those of the museums of Berlin and Oaxaca are covered with turquoise mosaics and may have been associated with diurnal celestial deities (Caso 1969).

Why, some forty-five years after the conquest, did the people of Mitla worship the skull of a Spaniard (or someone regarded as a Spaniard) covered with the attributes of a Precolumbian god? Was it simply reuse of a skull, just as they could have used any other, or is it not possible that the Indians viewed the Spaniards, or at least one of them, as some higher-rank captain or priest, in terms similar to that of their own lords, and thus full of sacred power, or at least a different, foreign power? For such a reason they might have worshipped him; at least we know they honored him and tried to keep him or use him for their own ends. Given the importance of the cave, we are dealing with no ordinary person and it is likely that he suffered no ordinary death, but may have been sacrificed by decapitation.

Sometimes it seems that the ceremony of human sacrifice was so frequent among Mesoamerican societies that it lost its particular solemnity. Perhaps sacrifices of human beings were more numerous among the Mexica of Central Mexico, but in Oaxaca, according to the Mixtec codices, human sacrifice was unusual in prehispanic times. It occurred primarily in the religious ceremony following the defeat of an enemy lord in war;[41] by sacrificing the political enemy, his supernatural power was also appropriated. The Spaniards were sacrificed, probably with the same logic, from the very first battles (Gay 1991, II:241). Apparently this sentiment did not disappear over time, but persisted well into the sixteenth century.

Conclusions

Given the importance of religion in prehispanic thought and its central place in Mesoamerican political organization, the Spanish presence was inevitably understood in sacred terms. The ideas and concepts which had sustained the power of the man-gods were applied to the conquerors. More than just the men themselves, Spanish technological acumen and its products, from humble scissors to cannons and the ability to construct convents with arches and vaults, all favored the idea of the superiority of Spanish power, a power that for being alien, strange, and unknown was more feared. Native thought, combined with other factors, facilitated the conquest and made possible the establishment of Spanish culture and institutions.

Of course these initial conceptions underwent change as the Spaniards were transformed into common individuals, as European knowledge came to be more widely diffused and the Indians themselves tried to understand Spanish culture and incorporate it into their own world, seeking convents for their churches, exchanging gold for scissors and candlesticks, or establishing livestock ranches for their communities. Nonetheless something of these early ideas regarding the superiority of Spanish power survived well into the sixteenth century. They were, most likely, the ideas that encouraged the Indians from a very early date to fill the chambers of the Audiencia seeking not only justice before the abuses of the Spaniards, but a solution to their own problems. It has been said that the colonial regime was able to consolidate its hold because the Spaniards respected the native nobility, incorporating them into their administrative structure. While true in the formal sense, at a deeper level the colonial system managed to establish itself because the Indians themselves esteemed the Spaniards and their institutions of power. Behind the Renaissance monasteries and the apparently hispanicized *cabildos* and economy, there survived a distinctly Mesoamerican mode of thought which valued and interpreted what natives saw of the colonists' world.

Notes

1. This work is part of the research project "Acculturation and Conquest: Oaxaca in the Sixteenth Century," which I am conducting as a member of the Instituto Nacional de Antropología e Historia, Mexico, with the support of a grant from the John Simon Guggenheim Foundation. I am very grateful to Dr. Judith Zeitlin for her translation of this paper, and to Drs. Nancy M. Farriss and Joyce Marcus for their help and encouragement.
2. Donation made by the *cacique* of Tamazulapan to the monastery, 1585, AJT leg. 10, exp. 1, of the old catalogue. Legal proceedings against the *cacique* of Yanhuitlán, 1544–1547, AGN Inquisición tomo 37, exps. 6 and 7. The Indians continued hiding their ancient religious rituals during the whole colonial era, but the tribunal of the Inquisition stopped its jurisdiction over the Indians in 1571.

3. Residencia of Hernan Cortés, general interrogation, AGI Justicia 224, pieza 5, ff. 202 and following.
4. Case against certain members of the regular clergy for mistreatment of the Indians, Tetiquipa, 1561, AGI Justicia 279.
5. For the history of the conquest in Oaxaca, see Gay 1881, chapter 10. Various documents in AGI Justicia record the ceding of tribute rights to the Spaniards. Some of these are: Gregorio de Monjaráz concerning certain towns, 1529, Justicia 112; Francisco de Morcillo concerning the town of Tututepec, 1530, Justicia 113; Martín Vázquez concerning the town of Tlaxiaco, 1531, Justicia 115.
6. Even though several *sierra* groups, like the Zapotec of the northern mountains, the Mixe and the Chontal in the south, were still hostile at mid-sixteenth century. See Chance 1989:23.
7. Don Luis de Castillo and the *cacique* Don Pedro against the *cacique* of Yaitepec, 1535, AGI Justicia 126.
8. The town of Ayoquesco with the Marqués against the town of Tlapacoya, 1556, AGI Justicia 204.
9. Suit over the *encomienda* of Coatlán, 1529 to 1542, AGI Justicia 112; testimony against Martín Vásquez, 1532, AGI Justicia 115, no. 3; protection authorized for Martín Rodríguez, 1531, AGI Justicia 114, no. 2; testimony against Francisco Maldonado, 1541, AGI Justicia 134, no. 2; and many other files in the Justicia branch of the Archivo General de las Indias.
10. *Relación hecha por Pedro de Alvarado a Hernan Cortés,* José Porrúa 1954. See also the 1580 *Relaciones geográficas of Amatlán, Coatlán, Miahuatlán, and Chichicapa, Papeles de la Nueva España,* vol. IV, second series, Mexico, 1905–48; and the petition of Juan de Mansilla, 1525–26, AGI Mexico 95, cuaderno 3.
11. By 1530, barrios of the Indian allies that came in those first years remained near the city of Antequera and one, that of Analco, was located on the edge of Villa Alta in the northern *sierra*. Although it is possible that the importance of these allies is downplayed in the documents due to the Spaniards' desire to extol their own accomplishments, neither were they mentioned by the Indians, who did not share the same interests.
12. Suit of the town of Tlaxiaco, 1536, AGI Justicia 134.
13. Gregorio Monjaráz concerning half of the town of Coatlán, 1531, AGI Justicia 112.
14. Martín Vázquez versus Francisco Maldonado concerning the *estancia* of Atoyaque in the province of Tlaxiaco, 1531 to 1533, AGI Justicia 115 and AGI Justicia 134.
15. Martín Vázquez versus Francisco Maldonado, 1531 to 1533, AGI Justicia 115.
16. In these years the epidemics had affected fewer towns and their social organization was less affected.
17. Francisco de las Casas versus Peláez de Berrio, 1532, AGI Justicia 117.
18. *Residencia* proceedings against Juan Peláez de Berrio, 1531, AGI Justicia 231.
19. *Colección de documentos inéditos* . . . Madrid, 1867, vol. VII, pp. 542 ff.
20. Different *Relaciones* of the deeds and services of the conquerors, AGI Justicia, for example AGI Mexico 98, cuaderno 3.
21. Oaxaca is different in this respect from the Maya region. For sixteenth-century Oaxaca we have four documented rebellions, but there are twice as many known for the Maya region. See Alicia M. Barabas, *Utopias Indias,* Mexico, Ed. Grijalba, 1989.
22. Information concerning the deeds and services of Tristán de Luna y Arellano, 1561, AGI Mexico 97.
23. The exception is John K. Chance's 1989 book.
24. In the diocese of Mexico, Tlaxcala, and Oaxaca there were 47,000 Spaniards and 2,250,000 Indians in 1568–70, Sherburne F. Cook and Woodrow Borah 1978, p. 199.

25. For the study of Mixtec and Zapotec society during the prehispanic era see Flannery and Marcus 1983; Whitecotton 1977; Spores 1967.
26. Commentary made by Prof. Raul Alvarez during the "Curso de Códices Mixtecos," organized by CIESAS, Oaxaca, 1989. See also the work of Victor de la Cruz, *La rebelión de Tehuantepec,* edition published by the H. Ayuntamiento Popular of Juchitán, 1982, where he explains the different Zapotec lineages as distinguished in the *Vocabulario en lengua zapoteca* of Fray Juan de Córdova. The idea of a hierarchy of sacred power is mine, based on observations made from ethnography and from a few documents concerning the attitude of Indians towards plants, animals, and their rulers. The documents with this type of detailed information are from the Archivo Judicial of Villa Alta, Oaxaca.
27. Codex Vindobonensis, various pages of the obverse side, 26, 31, 35, and others.
28. The concept of man-gods has been developed in the fine book by Alfredo López Austin 1973. It has been further elaborated for the colonial period by Serge Gruzinski in *El poder sin límites,* Mexico, INAH, 1988.
29. The prehispanic codices which have survived in Oaxaca are Mixtec, but it is very likely that all the towns had at least one historical and one religious codex. Personal communication, Maarten E.R.G.N. Jansen.
30. For example, the Codex Vaticanus 3773 still shows traces of having originally had decorations in turquoise, *Codex Vaticanus 3773* (or Codex Vaticanus B), Akademische Druck u Verlagsanstalt, Graz, 1972.
31. The Nuttall and Colombino codices are examples of historical books; those of the Borgia group are ritual and calendric.
32. One instance of an oracle can be seen in the Selden Roll, a codex finished during the colonial era, presently located at the Bodleian Library, Oxford.
33. Examples of the passage into the underworld are seen in *Códice Selden,* pp. 5 and 6, *Rollo Selden, Códice Becker,* p. 9.
34. Miller's introduction to Codex Nuttall, 1975.
35. *Códice Sierra,* 1550 to 1564. This codex contains information about the expenses incurred in Tejupan for the fiesta of Santa Catalina. Although most of the permits authorizing *caciques* to wear Spanish dress and ride horseback date to the 1590s, the same *Códice Sierra* shows the native authorities of the town dressing in Spanish costume.
36. The best known case is that of Fr. Benito Hernández, who entered the cave of Achiutla; Burgoa 1934, vol. I, p. 318.
37. Information concerning the good deeds of Diego Cano de Ojeda in his petition for clerical promotion, Antequera, 1565, AGI Mexico 208, ramo 2, January-February 1565, nos. 28 to 31.
38. Burgoa, 1934, vol. I, p. 318. Other examples can be found in Marcello Carmagnani, *El regreso de los dioses: El proceso de reconstitución de la identidad étnica en Oaxaca,* Fondo de Cultural Económica, Mexico, 1988, pp. 28 and 29.
39. Interpretation of pages 5 and 6 of the Selden Codex in Maarten Jansen and Gabina Aurora Pérez, "Iyadzehe Añute: valor literario de los códices mixtecos," in Alicia Barabas and Miguel Bartolomé, *Etnicidad y pluralismo cultural: La dinámica étnica en Oaxaca,* INAH, Mexico, 1986.
40. Laura Finsten, Kent V. Flannery, and Barbara Macnider, "Preceramic and cave occupations," in Kowalewski et al. 1989.
41. Comments of Maarten Jansen based on a reading of the Mixtec codices.

References Cited

Abbreviations

AGN. Archivo General de la Nación, Mexico.

AJT. Archivo Judicial de Teposcolula, Oaxaca, Mexico.

AGI. Archivo General de Indias, Seville, Spain.

Burgoa, Fray Francisco de
1964 Geográfica descripción. 2 vols. 1934 edition published by Talleres Gráficos de la Nación, Mexico.

Cervantes de Salazar, Francisco
1934 Crónica de la Nueva España. Compiled by Francisco del Paso y Troncoso in his Papeles de la Nueva España, 3rd series, vols. 2 and 3. Museo Nacional de Arqueología, Historia y Etnografía. Mexico.

Chance, John K.
1978 Race and Class in Colonial Oaxaca. Stanford: Stanford University Press.
1989 Conquest of the Sierra: Spaniards and Indians in Colonial Oaxaca. Norman: University of Oklahoma Press.

Colección de documentos
1867 Colección de documentos inéditos relativos al descubrimiento, conquista y organización de las antiguas posesiones de América y Oceania. 42 vols. Madrid.

Cook, Sherburne F., and Woodrow Borah
1978 Ensayos sobre la Historia de la Población: México y el Cariba. 3 vols. Mexico: Siglo XXI.

del Paso y Troncoso, Francisco, ed.
1939 Epistolario de la Nueva España: 1505–1818. 16 vols. Mexico: Antigua Librería Robredo de Jose Porrúa e Hijos.

Flannery, Kent V., and Joyce Marcus
1983 The Cloud People: Divergent Evolution of the Zapotec and Mixtec Civilizations. New York: Academic Press.

Gay, José Antonio
1881 Historia de Oaxaca. Mexico: Imprenta del Comercio de Dublán.

Gerhard, Peter A.
1972 Guide to the Historical Geography of New Spain. Cambridge: Cambridge University Press.

López Austin, Alfredo
1973 Hombre-dios: Religión y política en el mundo náhuatl. Mexico: UNAM.

Miller, Arthur
1975 Introduction to the edition of the Codex Nuttall. Dover Publications.

Mullen, Robert J.
1975 Dominican Architecture in Sixteenth Century Oaxaca. Arizona State University and Friends of Mexican Art, Phoenix.

Romero Frizzi, María de los Angeles
1985 Economía y Vida de los Españoles en la Mixteca Alta: 1519–1720. Ph.D. dissertation, Universidad Iberoamericana, Mexico.

Spores, Ronald
1967 The Mixtec Kings and Their People. Norman: University of Oklahoma Press.

Whitecotton, Joseph
1977 The Zapotecs: Princes, Priests, and Peasants. Norman: University of Oklahoma Press.

CHAPTER 12

A Zapotec Inauguration in Comparative Perspective

Joyce Marcus

University of Michigan

Some time during the period called Monte Albán IIIa (A.D. 150–450), a Zapotec ruler named 12 Jaguar was inaugurated at Monte Albán. His inauguration was attended by eight noble visitors from Teotihuacán, a metropolis in the Basin of Mexico. Part of his inauguration ritual involved the dedication of a massive pyramidal structure, the South Platform at Monte Albán, for whose construction (or enlargement) the ruler wanted to take credit. In preparation for his inauguration, 12 Jaguar had taken a number of captives for sacrifice; six of them were depicted on carved stone monuments set in the building to be dedicated. Another monument set into the platform depicts a noble named 8 Deer (perhaps an ancestor claimed by 12 Jaguar) achieving military conquest.

Although this particular inauguration is unusually well-documented in a series of stone monuments, its details are in no way unusual. Claims of descent from royal ancestors, demonstrations of military prowess through captive-taking, the taking of credit for monumental public works, and testimonials of political support from foreign rulers were all typical rituals of Mesoamerican inaugurations. It should be added that these rituals were often most spectacular when the inauguree was overcompensating for not being in direct line to accede to the throne (Marcus 1992:306, 350–51).

In this paper I look first at anthropological theories of inauguration, then at examples of inaugurations in various Mesoamerican cultures, all with the intent of placing 12 Jaguar's inaugural rites in perspective.

Past Studies on Inauguration

Since the beginning of this century, scholars have focused particular attention on inaugurations—examples include Sir James Frazer's *Lectures on the Early*

History of Kingship (1905), Arthur M. Hocart's *Kingship* (1927), Henri Frankfort's *Kingship and the Gods* (1948), Robert Heine-Geldern's *Concepts of State and Kingship in Southeast Asia* (1956), David Howard Smith's *Divine Kingship in Ancient China* (1957), Charles Drekmeier's *Kingship and Community in Early India* (1962), Jeremy Kemp's *Aspects of Siamese Kingship in the Seventeenth Century* (1969), Robert S. Ellwood's *The Feast of Kingship: Accession Ceremonies in Ancient Japan* (1973), and more recently Valerio Valeri's *Kingship and Sacrifice* (1985). Some writers have emphasized general similarities among accession rites in diverse cultures (Hocart 1927; Gesick [ed.] 1983), while others documented fundamental contrasts (Frankfort 1948). In this paper I will pay attention both to the widely shared patterns and to some differences displayed by individual cultures.

At their heart, inaugurations involve the transfer of power. Although we have known for some time that the transfer of power in chiefdoms can involve competition and conflict between claimants and pretenders (Goldman 1970:24–26; Helms 1979:24–29), many scholars have contrasted chiefly competition with the supposedly smooth and peaceful transfer of power in states. From different parts of the world, however, we have indications that the transfer of power in states is not always that smooth and peaceful (Gesick [ed.] 1983; Drekmeier 1962; Kemp 1969:43). Ellwood (1973:34) notes that "the death of a king puts society into chaos, if only a ritual chaos. But it is an *occasional* rather than an annual return to chaos which the institution of kingship at once creates and seeks to alleviate."

In some ancient states, recent research shows that usurpers (those not in direct line of royal descent) more often than not ended up as rulers (Aung-Thwin 1983; Kemp 1969). In Burma, for example, at least eight of the nine kings of the Pagan Dynasty (A.D. 1000–1200) were not in the immediate line of royal descent; of the fourteen kings of the Taung-ngu Dynasty (which ruled for 250 years) perhaps no more than six were in line; and of the eleven rulers of the Konbang Dynasty, only three were direct-line heirs (Aung-Thwin 1983:81–85). Such usurpers often compensate for their lack of credentials by staging spectacular rituals.

Stages in an Inauguration

The inauguration process actually begins with the selection of a successor to the previous ruler. In between that selection and the actual taking of office, there is a period of elapsed time that may amount to days, months, or even years. During this elapsed time, the designated successor may engage in a series of prescribed activities that could themselves be considered rituals. For example, he or she may travel to consult various leaders of other ethnic groups; raid communities and take prisoners; mark off the boundaries of the polity (sometimes called "ritual circumambulation"); and/or visit sacred natural landmarks and shrines.

In various societies, the taking of office is also linked to a range of cosmological transitions such as agricultural renewal and rebirth; the re-establishment of order out of the chaos following the death of the previous ruler; and the transformation of the ruler into a god on earth. These transitions may require rites such as bathing and ritual purification; sacrifices at the inauguration to re-establish communication with the gods; and the demonstration of military prowess to show that the realm will be secure.

Hocart (1927) analyzed a series of societies (including India, Rome, and Egypt) and then isolated twenty-six shared patterns at coronations. While emphasizing that no single society displays all twenty-six—and that some patterns persist, some expand, some shrink, some lose their function, and some acquire new meaning over time—he offered them as a framework by which coronations can be compared:

A. Succession is viewed as a process by which one king dies; he is reborn as the new king; the new king is now a god.
B. By way of preparation, the successor fasts and practices other austerities.
C. Persons not admissible to the sacrifice, such as strangers, sinners, women, and children, are kept away, and are not allowed to know anything; an armed guard prevents prying eyes.
D. A kind of sabbath is observed; the people are silent and lie quiet, as at a death.
E. The new king must fight a ritual combat by arms or by ceremonies, and come out victorious.
F. The new king is admonished to rule justly and promises to do so.
G. He receives communion in one or two kinds.
H. The common people indulge at one point in obscenities or buffoonery.
I. The new king is invested with special garments.
J. He is baptized with water,
K. and anointed with oil;
L. a human victim is killed;
M. the people rejoice with noise and acclamations,
N. and a feast is given.
O. The new king is crowned,
P. puts on shoes,
Q. receives other regalia, such as a sword, a sceptre, a ring, and so forth,
R. and sits upon a throne.
S. The new king takes three ceremonial steps in imitation of the rising sun.
T. At the conclusion of the ceremonies, he makes the rounds of his dominions and receives the homage of his vassals.
U. He receives a new name.
V. A new queen is consecrated with the king,
W. and so are the vassals or officials, either at the coronation ceremony or in the course of the king's tour.
X. Those who take part in the rites are dressed up as gods, sometimes with masks,
Y. which may be those of animals, thus identifying the wearer with some kind of beast.
Z. A king may be consecrated several times, going up each time one step on the scale of kingship.

In spite of the fact that this list of twenty-six patterns was derived from non-Mesoamerican coronations, such is their universality that at least half the list can be found in ancient Mesoamerica. Let us look now at a sample of inaugurations from among the Aztec, Mixtec, Maya, and ancient Teotihuacanos.

Aztec Inaugurations

The Aztec had a particularly long process of succession, which included pre-inaugural, inaugural, and post-inaugural rites. These rites are documented in Alvarado Tezozomoc (1944), Durán (1967), Mendieta (1971), and Sahagún's Book 8 (Anderson and Dibble 1954). Richard Townsend (1987:391) has divided the inaugural process into four stages: (1) Separation and Retreat; (2) Investiture and Coronation; (3) Coronation War; and (4) Confirmation.

As part of "Separation and Retreat," the Aztec ruler-elect was taken to the base of the stairway of the Temple of Huitzilopochtli (Sahagún, Book 8, p. 61). In one account, he wore only a loincloth for this rite (Mendieta 1971:154), while in another account "he went bare" (Sahagún, Book 8, p. 62). In other words, he had been stripped of all paraphernalia that signaled his prior status and position as a noble. At the temple, however, the ruler-elect received new clothing and ritual paraphernalia: a sleeveless green jacket, a gourd with green tassels to hold his tobacco, a veil to cover his face, a cape that bore a design of bones, new sandals with green toes, and a green cotton bag decorated with bones and filled with incense. A new incense burner, painted with skulls, was placed in his hand.

After having been dressed in his new clothes and having received his new insignia of office, the ruler-elect presented himself in front of an effigy of Huitzilopochtli and burned incense in front of it. Shell trumpets were blown. The ruler-elect and similarly attired nobles then proceeded to the *tlacochcalco* or "armory" where military weapons were housed. Here the ruler-elect and his noble companions began a four-day fast, burning incense and letting their own blood with maguey spines. Afterwards, they bathed as a rite of purification. During this retreat a series of speeches was made by the ruler-elect, requesting the divine help of Tezcatlipoca and others.

"Investiture and Coronation," the second stage isolated by Townsend, began at the palace with a new ruler's enthronement. The coronation involved the placing of a special headdress on his head, and the piercing of his septum for the insertion of a new nose ornament. This ritual required the direct participation of another member of the highest nobility, such as a neighboring ruler.

> The king of Tetzcoco took the crown of green stones, all worked in gold, and placed it upon his [the Tenochtitlán ruler-elect's head], and piercing the septum of his nose he inserted a green stone as thick as a quill pen, and in his ears two round greenstone

> earplugs in gold settings, and on his arms from elbow to shoulder two very resplendent gold bracelets, and on his ankles, anklets with dangling gold belts, and the Tetzcocan ruler shod him with jaguar-skin sandals all elegantly gilded and clad him with a precious mantle of henequen-like fiber, very thin and shining, all gilded and painted with elegant pictures, and he put a waistband around him of the same, and taking him by the hand he led him to a throne that they called *cuauhicpalli,* meaning eagle-seat, also named ocelot-seat, for it was decorated with eagle feathers and ocelot hides. [Durán 1967, Vol. 2:301]

The new ruler then was transported to the main Aztec temple while sitting on his new eagle/ocelot throne.

Following the coronation rite came a series of sacrifices at the Temple of Huitzilopochtli, in front of stone sculptures at the Coateocalli (the temple of foreign gods, where the captured effigies of tribute-paying groups were kept), and at the temple of Yopico. The new ruler ascended the pyramid and entered the Temple of Huitzilopochtli; once inside, he used a jaguar's claw to let blood from his legs and ears. The ruler-elect presented as offerings both sacrificed quail and his own blood. He then descended to the base of the pyramid, where he stood next to the *cuauhxicalli* (eagle vessel), into which he made additional offerings of his own blood and sacrificed quail. He was then carried to the final two temples—Coateocalli and Yopico—where he made offerings of incense, his own blood, and sacrificed quail.

Following this round of sacrifices, the ruler was taken to the palace and seated on the throne, where he listened to speeches made by many individuals, including the rulers of Texcoco and Tacuba, his partners in the Triple Alliance. Part of one speech addressed to the new ruler was as follows:

> Although the common folk have gladdened thee, and although thy younger brother, thy older brother have put their trust in thee, now thou art deified. Although thou art human, as are we, although thou art our son, our younger brother, no more art thou human, as are we: we do not look to thee as human.
>
> thou speakest in a strange tongue to the god . . . he is within thee; he speaketh forth from thy mouth. Thou art his lips, thou art his jaw, thou art his tongue, thou art his eyes, thou art his ears. He hath given thee honor, he hath provided thee thy fangs, thy claws. [Sahagún, Book 6, pp. 52–53]

The third stage identified by Townsend—the "Coronation War"—entailed military expeditions led by the new ruler. Before he could be considered fully in command, he had to demonstrate military prowess and leadership, ability to win battles, and effectiveness in obtaining tribute and prisoners for sacrifice at his forthcoming confirmation rites.

These battles often involved reconquering rebellious towns that had refused to pay the required tribute. For example, Ahuitzotl's initial pre-confirmation campaign was directed against rebellious towns such as Chillocan, Chiapan, Xilotepec,

Cillan, Xocotitlán, and Xiquipilco, all located northwest of Tenochtitlán. Ahuitzotl directed his second expedition (A.D. 1487–1488) toward the Huasteca, another rebellious region. He subdued several towns there and took captives who would be sacrificed at the dedication of the Temple of Huitzilopochtli in Tenochtitlán (a temple whose construction was begun by his predecessor, Tizoc). The dedication of the Temple of Huitzilopochtli in Tenochtitlán was ostensibly a religious ceremony, but it really served as a pretext for the exercise of military power, as Hassig (1988:205) has noted. Not only were resubjugated rulers required to attend the upcoming confirmation ceremony and temple dedication, so, too, were enemy rulers from Huexotzinco, Tlaxcallan, Michhuacan, Zacatlán, Chalollan, and Metztitlán.

This dedication of the renovated Temple of Huitzilopochtli was considered to be the final component of the new ruler's inaugural rites (Alvarado Tezozomoc 1944:330; Umberger 1987:422). Ahuitzotl commemorated this final component by having a stone carved with the date of that dedication (A.D. 1487).

On the Dedication Stone (Fig. 12.1) we see Ahuitzotl (upper right) and his predecessor, the deceased Tizoc (upper left). Both are performing autosacrifice; each passes a sharp implement through his ear to get a flow of blood going. The two streams of blood flow to a central pit—the open jaw of the earth—located between two incense burners. The legs of Tizoc and Ahuitzotl also show evidence of having been pierced to let blood. Although the date 7 Reed appears at the top, the huge date 8 Reed (occupying the lower half of the stone) appears to be the featured date. This date, 8 Reed (A.D. 1487), commemorates both the dedication of the rebuilt Temple of Huitzilopochtli and the end of Ahuitzotl's inaugural rites.

Cecelia Klein (1987:320) argues persuasively that this bloodletting rite took place when Ahuitzotl was the ruler-elect. She suggests that the depiction of his deceased brother, Tizoc, was included to legitimize Ahuitzotl's claim to office. Since Ahuitzotl was just a child when selected, and lacked the military experience required of a new ruler, he was not favored by all factions (Durán 1964:183–186). In fact, the *cihuacoatl* (a high-ranking Aztec official) intervened on Ahuitzotl's behalf, saying that he should follow Tizoc, since "brother should follow brother."

The later Aztec ruler Motecuhzoma Xocoyotl (inaugurated in A.D. 1502) also conducted a set of pre-inaugural military campaigns, for which we have different versions. For example, Torquemada (1975–1983, 1:269–70) says that Motecuhzoma successfully attacked Atlixco, that he took prisoners, and that many warriors and captains died. Both the *Crónica Mexicana* (Chaps. 83, 84) and Durán (1967, Ch. 53) present a different account, stating that Motecuhzoma's targets were Nopallan and Icpatepec, because those two towns had refused to pay tribute to the Aztec rulers; Motecuhzoma is said to have reconquered them and taken captives for sacrifice at his inauguration.

Ethnohistoric accounts show us that captive taking was an important rite. But they also reveal other, more important reasons for pre-inaugural battles, including

Figure 12.1. The Dedication Stone shows the Aztec ruler-elect Ahuitzotl (at right) letting his own blood. Participating in the same rite is Ahuitzotl's deceased predecessor, Tizoc (at left). Below is the date 8 Reed (A.D. 1487) which commemorates both the dedication of the rebuilt temple and the end of Ahuitzotl's inaugural rites (drawn by Kay Clahassey from Klein 1987: Fig. 15).

the opportunity for the ruler-elect to demonstrate his military prowess, as well as the need to punish rebellious rulers who refused to meet tribute demands, thereby using them as an example to other groups. The latter need helps to explain why certain groups were selected for conquest while others were left alone.

The Confirmation Ceremony itself lasted four days and required that all subject provinces send provisions to the capital; porters wearing tumplines brought corn, cacao, fruit, turkeys, deer, quail, fish, feathers, cloth, and jewelry (Durán 1967, 2:323–24). Masons were set to work refurbishing old structures and building new ones. They also decorated causeways and buildings with flowers.

One of the essential parts of the Confirmation Ceremony was a reaffirmation of the political hierarchy. This was done by having the new ruler present appropriate paraphernalia to each official according to his office, rank, and position. For example, he might first present special items to the rulers of Texcoco and Tacuba, his highest ranking contemporaries. Next, high officials within Tenochtitlán, then provincial rulers, and then collectors of tribute might receive special items from the ruler. The final rite involved the sacrifice of captives taken during the "coronation wars."

Mixtec Inaugurations

Unlike Aztec documents, the Mixtec codices do not seem to display a separate iconographic convention for the inauguration of a new ruler. What they do depict are the rites that constituted components of an inauguration. For example, the codices show royal marriages that linked two royal "houses" or lineages; many of these show a Mixtec lord and his bride seated on mats, set above the place names of the town(s) they would subsequently rule or co-rule. They also show Mixtec lords getting their nasal septum pierced for a stone ornament like that received by recently inaugurated Aztec lords. Other scenes show the inauguree receiving special clothing or paraphernalia to be worn when he assumes office.

Once in office the Mixtec ruler is shown seated, either on a mat or on a cushion covered with a jaguar pelt. These two kinds of "seats" are pan-Mesoamerican symbols of rulership and authority, and they find their counterparts in other cultures. For example, in India a tiger skin was often spread out on the throne as a symbol of omnipotence (Drekmeier 1962:21). In that region, the king was not allowed to stand on the earth with his bare feet because it was thought that powerful persons and objects would lose their power if they came into direct contact with the earth (Gonda 1956:56). Among the Ashanti of West Africa, there was a similar belief that neither the ruler's bare foot nor any other body part was to touch the ground; neither was his Golden Stool (a symbol of office), so the latter was set on an elephant skin (Parrinder 1956:112). In many other cultures the rulers' palaces and courts were covered with mats, so that the ruler could walk around without his feet ever touching the ground (Kemp 1969:13).

Mixtec inaugural rites involved a protracted series of events, similar to the multi-stage sequence outlined by Townsend for the Aztec. The Mixtec sequence consisted of (1) being named/selected as the next ruler; (2) setting out to conquer new towns, or reconquer rebellious towns; (3) having one's nasal septum pierced for a noseplug; and (4) being enthroned, which was part of the actual confirmation ceremony.

Days of the 260-day calendar bearing the number 1 were favored, both for naming the next Mixtec ruler and for the confirmation ceremony itself. (This was similar to the Aztec, who also preferred days beginning with the coefficient 1, especially the day 1 Cipactli [1 Crocodile].)

A day beginning with the coefficient 1 might also be selected for the nose-piercing rite (Figs. 12.2–12.4). For example, the Mixtec ruler 8 Deer "Tiger Claw," ruler of Tututepec, prepared himself for nose-piercing by taking the lords of several rival towns as his prisoners. Following the capture of one particularly prized captive, the lord of Acatepec, 8 Deer received a special noseplug on the day named 1 Wind. This nose-piercing rite is depicted in three separate codices—the Nuttall, Bodley, and Colombino (M. E. Smith 1973:71–72, Figs. 55, 60, 61). Three days later, 8 Deer (along with other lords) sacrificed quail and set out to conquer still other places.

Three years later, following the death of his older half-brother, 8 Deer acceded to the throne of Tilantongo in the Mixteca Alta. He, thus, was inaugurated in two different *señoríos,* one to which he was entitled through his mother (Tututepec), and one to which he was entitled through his father and half-brother (Tilantongo).

Maya Inaugurations

Maya inaugurations were also accompanied by numerous rites. Included were (1) human sacrifice at the base of the stairway leading to a temple; (2) the acquisition of new paraphernalia (headdress, shield, spear, staff) associated with the office of ruler; (3) the dedication of a new building (or specially renovated structure); and (4) rituals linking the new ruler to a past ruler (or divine ancestor) in order to establish continuity. Maya monuments depicted the latter ritual—the transfer of power from old ruler to new—either by showing the ruler-elect's deceased predecessor/ancestor in the act of handing him the regalia associated with the office, or by showing the ruler-elect's footprints ascending a ladder or stairway, leading to a temple where he sat "on high" on a jaguar-pelt cushion (Spinden 1913; Proskouriakoff 1960).

The first of these two depictions, which we might call "the presentation of a ruler's regalia," can be illustrated with monuments from Palenque and Copán. The Oval Tablet from Palace E at Palenque shows (at left) a woman—Lady White Parrot—who apparently held office at Palenque from ca. A.D. 612 to 615. She is

Figure 12.2. The Mixtec ruler 8 Deer "Tiger Claw" is shown at his nose-piercing rite. At left is an individual perforating 8 Deer's nose, while another participant (at right) watches. Above is the hieroglyphic sign 1 Wind, the day on which this event took place (drawn by John Klausmeyer from Codex Colombino XIII).

handing the headdress associated with that office to a young male, evidently her son—Lord Shield (Pacal)—shown seated on a two-headed jaguar throne (Fig. 12.5). Lord Shield (Pacal) claims that he acceded to the Palenque throne in A.D. 615 when he was twelve years of age (Kubler 1969; Lounsbury 1974, Marcus 1976; Schele and Freidel 1990). His mother was evidently his regent. There is no evidence his father ever ruled.

Around the four sides of Altar Q at Copán we see a scene depicting a sequence of sixteen rulers. The *sixteenth* ruler is being handed the staff of office by the

Figure 12.3. The Mixtec ruler 8 Deer "Tiger Claw" is shown after his new nose ornament has been inserted by the black-painted figure at right (drawn by John Klausmeyer from Codex Bodley 9).

Figure 12.4. At left is 8 Death "Masked Vulture" who performs the nose-piercing operation on 8 Deer "Tiger Claw," shown leaning back on his throne. This event occurs on the day 1 Wind, painted above 8 Deer's head (drawn by John Klausmeyer from Codex Nuttall 52).

Figure 12.5. Oval Tablet from the Palace at Palenque showing the inauguration of a Maya ruler named Lord Shield (Pacal). At left, his mother, his apparent predecessor in office, holds his inaugural headdress (drawn by John Klausmeyer from Maudslay 1889–1902, 4: Plate 44).

"founding ruler," the *first* in the Copán dynastic sequence (Maudslay 1889–1902, 1: Plate 92; Marcus 1976:141–43; Fash 1991:79–81; Fash and Sharer 1991:181). The lives and reigns of the first and sixteenth rulers were separated by 300 years, so this act could never actually have taken place. Nevertheless, the sixteenth ruler evidently commissioned the carving of an altar or bench to show that the staff of office had been passed to him directly from the dynasty's founder (Fig. 12.6).

What is particularly interesting about these "presentation of regalia" scenes is that many of them juxtapose a *deceased* ruler or royal ancestor with the ruler-elect. The ruler-elect is thus arguing that his right to rule has been passed in a *direct, unbroken* line by having himself placed in a scene with long-dead but venerated rulers, receiving the staff of office directly from their hands.

The second of our two inaugural depictions, "the ascension motif," usually shows the new ruler seated cross-legged on a jaguar cushion inside the canopied doorway of a temple. Footprints and a ladder usually lead up to his throne (Fig. 12.7). A good example of this "ascension motif" is on Stela 11 from Piedras Negras, which also shows a human sacrifice (another inaugural rite) at the base of the pyramid (Proskouriakoff 1960).

Some Late Classic Maya rulers, such as Bird Jaguar of Yaxchilán, conducted military expeditions like those of the Aztec and Mixtec prior to being confirmed in office. Presumably this happened because they needed to show military prowess, gain access to labor and lands, quell rebellions of formerly subjugated polities, and acquire captives to be sacrificed at the final inaugural rite.

A Teotihuacán Inauguration and Temple Dedication

Recent archaeological evidence suggests that the Classic civilizations of the Mexican Plateau carried out elaborate inaugurations and temple dedications like those described for the Aztec, Mixtec, and Maya. Around A.D. 200, a pyramid called the Old Temple of Quetzalcoatl at Teotihuacán was dedicated to the Feathered Serpent. That pyramid ranks third in volume behind the enormous Pyramids of the Sun and Moon at the same city (Cowgill 1983:322). Built in a single episode, the Old Temple was originally about 20 m high and 64 × 65 m at its base. It is flanked by two residential complexes within the architectural unit called the Ciudadela. These residential complexes are called the "North and South Palaces," and are thought to have been occupied by the rulers of the Teotihuacán state (Cowgill 1983; Cabrera Castro, Sugiyama, and Cowgill 1991:77).

Recent excavations by Cabrera, Sugiyama, and Cowgill (1991) indicate that as many as 200 persons, mostly males, were sacrificed and buried at the very beginning of the construction of the temple. At the exact center of the pyramid, a multiple burial of 20 individuals was found; 10 had their arms behind their backs, evidently tied in that position.

Figure 12.6. Altar Q at Copán shows the sixteenth ruler (second from right) receiving the staff of office from the first ruler, the proclaimed founder of the dynasty (second from left). Their reigns are separated by more than 300 years, since the founder reigned ca. A.D. 430 and the sixteenth ruler took office in A.D. 763 (drawn by Mark Orsen from Maudslay 1889–1902, 1: Plate 92).

Not only had this mass burial been put in place as a single offering at the onset of the construction, it also included the richest offerings known to date from all of Teotihuacán. At least 400 greenstone ("jade") objects were found, including noseplugs, earspools, figurines, and headdress-like plaques. Among the more than 800 obsidian objects were projectile points, perforators, bifacial knives, and many anthropomorphic and zoomorphic obsidian eccentrics. Over 3,400 pieces of shell were found along with items of wood and cloth. Some sets of artifacts were grouped in such a way to suggest that they had been stored inside bags which had since disintegrated.

The vast majority of the 200 individuals sacrificed at the Old Temple were males between the ages of 13 and 55; many were placed in a seated position with their hands tied behind their backs. Some wore necklaces of shell carved in the form of human teeth, and some were accompanied by obsidian projectile points. Many were associated with weapons, and wore real or artificial human maxillae around their necks as trophies; Sugiyama (1989) has interpreted these individuals as sacrificed warriors.

Figure 12.7 (opposite). Stela 11 from Piedras Negras shows a newly inaugurated Maya ruler seated cross-legged inside the doorway of his temple. At the base of the pyramid is the body of a sacrificial victim, stretched out over an altar; blood, depicted as feathers, surges forth from his open wound (drawn by John Klausmeyer from Marcus 1992: Figs. 10.14, 10.15).

The occasion on which these warriors were sacrificed—the dedication of the Old Temple of Quetzalcoatl—may have coincided with the inauguration of a new Teotihuacán ruler. The feathered serpents decorating the sides of the temple and wearing complex headdresses, like those shown in inauguration scenes (Sugiyama 1992, Taube n.d.), suggest this may be true. Our speculation cannot proceed further than this, however, because rulers at Teotihuacán are notoriously "nameless"; we never see them depicted or named, as were Aztec, Mixtec, Maya, and Zapotec rulers.

The Inauguration of a Zapotec Lord

Having looked at a range of inaugural rituals among other Mesoamerican peoples, we have a better idea as to what kinds of practices might be widespread within that culture area. We can now look at a Classic Zapotec inauguration to see what it shares with inaugurations elsewhere.

We might expect to find some or all of the following patterns: (1) the seeking of support from neighboring rulers; (2) the dedication of a major public work to coincide with the inauguration; (3) demonstrations of military prowess, with captives brought back for sacrifice; and (4) references to venerated noble ancestors. Depictions of the inaugurated ruler might also show him (5) seated on an elevated throne, perhaps on a mat or a jaguar-pelt cushion; (6) wearing an elaborate headdress; (7) wearing a special nose ornament; (8) wearing a cape, or some other regal clothing; (9) holding a staff or sceptre of office; or (10) equipped with military paraphernalia.

The South Platform at Monte Albán

The South Platform is a huge pyramidal structure, more than 15 m high and 100 m on a side, situated at the southern end of the Main Plaza at Monte Albán. Architectural and ceramic data suggested to Caso (1965) and Acosta (1958–1959, 1965) that the South Platform was built during one ceramic phase, Monte Albán IIIa (A.D. 150–450); however, we cannot rule out the possibility that earlier stages occur inside the platform.

At plaza level, nine huge carved stones were set into the base of the South Platform. These multi-ton stones and the dedicatory caches below three of them provide information on the inauguration of a Zapotec ruler who ruled Monte Albán some time during Period IIIa. Because of the association of these stones with dedicatory caches (see below), we suspect that the dedication of the platform coincided with his inauguration. Let us now look at the components of this inauguration as reflected in the carved stone monuments.

I. Component 1: The Zapotec Ruler

Stela 1, a 2 m × 2 m monument forming part of the northeast corner of the South Platform, shows the new ruler (at left) seated on a jaguar-pelt cushion, which in turn is set upon an immense throne (Fig. 12.8). The base of the throne displays profile heads of the important supernatural force Lightning, set back to back in such a way that they share the same large earspool. The throne is an important symbol of Zapotec rulership, and is given exaggerated height to feature it in this composition. Specifically, the sculptor allowed the throne to occupy an area as large as the ruler, suggesting that the office was at least as important as the occupant.

Such thrones have not been recovered archaeologically at Monte Albán, probably because they were of perishable materials (for example, a jaguar-skin cushion set atop an elevated wooden seat). Sixteenth-century sources (e.g., Córdova 1578) make it clear that the Zapotec did use wood to make altars, benches, and seats. In fact, the generic Zapotec expression for all three artifacts was the same (*yaga pecogo*) and includes the word for "wood" (*yaga:* wood; *pecogo:* altar, bench, seat). The specific Zapotec terms for throne or "royal seat" were *pecogonaachi* ("seat of his majesty") or *xipecogo coqui* ("the lord's seat").

The ruler on Stela 1 holds a staff of office or military lance in his left hand. He wears a jaguar costume, a large earplug, and an elaborate headdress that combines feathers with a depiction of Lightning (Marcus 1983a:138–139). His name appears to be 12 Jaguar, written with two dots and two bars and a main sign (the fourth glyph in the second column). Like many Zapotec personal names, his is free of the kind of cartouche used for dates. The associated text includes signs describing his divine descent, pilgrimages, divination, and offerings that were part of his pre-inaugural and inaugural rites (Marcus n.d.). Thus, Stela 1 includes many of the features we expected, based on inaugurations elsewhere in Mesoamerica.

II. Component 2: The Military Captives

Also set in the walls of the South Platform are Stelae 2, 3, 5, 6, 7, and 8. Each of the six stelae displays a named prisoner with arms bound behind his back. Each prisoner stands on a different place sign that supplies the name of a specific town or region. None of these regions are identifiable at present, but we presume them to be areas from which 12 Jaguar claimed to have taken captives, probably during a series of pre-inaugural military campaigns. Like other Mesoamerican rulers-elect, he presumably needed to demonstrate the ability to discourage rebellions on the part of subject towns and to bring back captives for sacrifice and labor.

While some prisoners are relatively unadorned, some (e.g., Stela 3) wear feathered headdresses indicating they may be noble officers, and others (e.g., Stela 2) wear the kinds of "full animal costumes" awarded to warriors who had distinguished themselves in battle—like the eagle and coyote warriors of central Mexico (Figs. 12.9, 12.10). Some of the dates on which these captives were taken were

Figure 12.8. Stela 1 from Monte Albán shows the Zapotec ruler 12 Jaguar, seated atop his immense throne. At right is a two-column text that records information about the inaugural rites (drawing by Mark Orsen).

placed upside-down, below the "hill sign" or place name (e.g., Stela 3). Presumably, these captives were the ones selected to be sacrificed at 12 Jaguar's inauguration.

III. Component 3: A Noble Ancestor?

Stela 4 in the South Platform may show one of 12 Jaguar's predecessors or ancestors, a man named 8 Deer (Fig. 12.11). The monument is designed to show

Figure 12.9. Stela 3 from Monte Albán shows a captive standing on the "hill sign" that signifies his place of origin. Below, shown upside down, is the date he was taken (drawing by Mark Orsen).

Figure 12.10. Stela 2, Monte Albán, shows a captive in jaguar military garb, standing on the "hill sign" that signifies his place of origin (drawing by Mark Orsen).

Figure 12.11 (opposite). Stela 4 from Monte Albán shows a Zapotec lord named 8 Deer in military garb. In his right hand this lord holds the cord to bind the arms of any captive he takes; in his left, he thrusts a lance into a "hill sign." This lord probably preceded 12 Jaguar in office; he is not the same 8 Deer who ruled in the Mixtec area centuries later (drawing by Mark Orsen).

him as someone successful in military expeditions; he is depicted conquering a place, as indicated metaphorically by the thrusting of his lance into a "hill sign" or place name. This was a convention for conquest also used in the later Mixtec codices (M. E. Smith 1973:33).

The 12 Jaguar reference to 8 Deer may be analogous to the Aztec ruler Ahuitzotl's depiction of his brother Tizoc, or the Maya ruler Chan Bahlum's depiction of his father Lord Shield (Pacal), in their respective inaugural monuments. By depicting 8 Deer, 12 Jaguar legitimizes his accession to the throne by reference to a noble ancestor or predecessor.

IV. Component 4: The Foreign Visitors

We have seen that rulers of Tenochtitlán solicited the moral/political support of the rulers of Texcoco and Tacuba when taking office. Four monuments in the South Platform suggest that 12 Jaguar's inauguration was attended by eight noble ambassadors from Teotihuacán in the Basin of Mexico. These visitors are named on the *hidden surfaces* of four stelae—Stelae 1, 7, 8, and the Estela Lisa—each of which was set in a corner of the South Platform (Fig. 12.12). Each visitor wears the "Tassel Headdress," which Clara Millon has associated with ambassadors from Teotihuacán (Fig. 12.12). Each visitor carries a bag of incense, rather than the spearthrower, darts, shields, and other weapons Teotihuacano travelers to other parts of Mesoamerica often carry (C. Millon 1973, 1988; R. Millon 1988).

One group of Teotihuacanos is mentioned on the two southern corners of the platform (Stelae 7 and 8), while the other group is mentioned on the two northern corners (Stela 1 and Estela Lisa). A detailed study of the names of these ambassadors is given elsewhere (Marcus 1983b:176–78).

The fact that the Teotihuacán ambassadors have their names carved on the *hidden surfaces* of the monuments is an important clue to their original purpose. The scenes of these noble ambassadors were treated in a manner similar to dedicatory caches. That is, the ambassadors' participation was an essential part of the dedication, and a permanent record in stone was made of it, but it was then buried and hidden from view. This suggests that its purpose was "horizontal" propaganda—information conveyed only to other nobles present at the dedication of the building—rather than "vertical" propaganda designed to be viewed in perpetuity by commoners (Marcus 1974, 1992).

V. Component 5: The Offerings Placed in the Corner Caches of the South Platform

Stone offering boxes were located directly beneath the carved underside of monuments depicting the visitors from Teotihuacán. Such offering boxes were buried half a meter below three of the four corners of the South Platform (that is, below Stelae 1 and 7 and the Estela Lisa). Each offering contained 10 spiny oyster shells (5 *Spondylus princeps, 5 Spondylus calcifer*); 10 tent olive shells (*Oliva porphyria*), 7 jade beads, and 1 pottery vessel (Acosta 1958–1959; Marcus

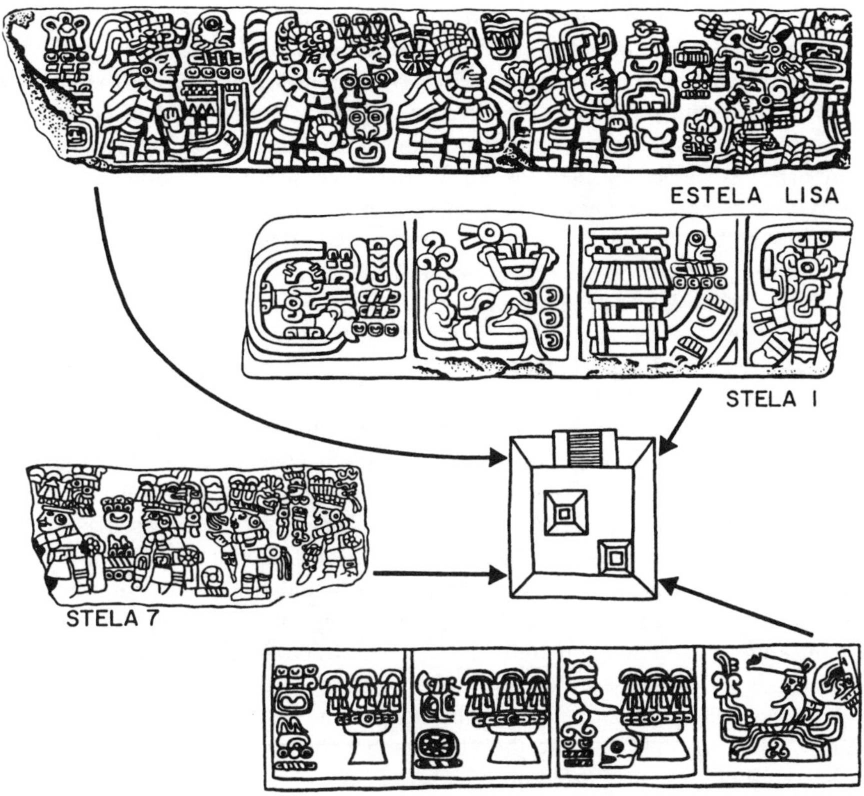

Figure 12.12. Teotihuacán visitors who attended the inauguration of 12 Jaguar and the dedication of the South Platform at Monte Albán were depicted on the hidden edges of stone monuments set in the corners of the South Platform (drawn by Kay Clahassey from Marcus 1983b: Fig. 6.5).

1983b:179). While the meaning of these offerings is unknown, it should be pointed out that in the Maya region, *Spondylus* shell was used as a receptacle for royal blood and was linked to the inauguration of a Copán ruler appropriately named Smoked Shell (Fash 1991:148–149). It may be that the ruler-elect made offerings of his own blood (such as the Aztec rulers mentioned earlier in this paper) at the time he took office.

12 Jaguar's Inauguration in Comparative Perspective

By now, it should be clear that the inauguration of 12 Jaguar at Monte Albán shared many features with the inaugurations of other Mesoamerican groups, as well as with inaugurations elsewhere in the ancient world. According to 12 Jaguar's monuments and their placement, he followed a widespread pattern of referring to an important ancestor or predecessor (Stela 4); seeking and receiving the political support of powerful neighbors (the rulers of Teotihuacán); building or enlarging a major public structure (the South Platform); demonstrating military prowess by taking captives, including members of animal-costume military orders (Stelae 2, 3, 5, 6, 7, 8); and acceding to an elevated throne in an elaborate costume, seated on a jaguar-pelt cushion and holding a staff of office (Stela 1).

Elsewhere (Marcus 1992), I have stressed that Mesoamerican monuments and hieroglyphic texts should be regarded as political propaganda, rather than objective "history." This Zapotec case is no exception; it transmits manipulative messages on several levels. Its fundamental *ideological* message is that kingship and the state will continue in a just, orderly, predictable manner by a legitimate and deserving new ruler. Since the South Platform undoubtedly supported one or more temples at that time, the *religious* message is that this ruler had the authority and manpower to raise sacred structures for the benefit of his people; some of his divine blood may even have been included in the offerings below the three corners of the Platform. The *political* messages include his claim that he was the kind of military leader who could maintain (or even expand) the boundaries of the Zapotec state, capturing and sacrificing its enemies. He also legitimized his right to rule by claiming some association with an important and militarily successful predecessor.

All of the above messages are examples of what I have called *vertical* propaganda, propaganda transmitted from the nobility to the commoners whom they ruled. We can say this because the aforementioned messages are carved on the faces of very large stelae placed at the level of the plaza. These stelae are up to 2 m high and could be seen from a distance. While Blanton's ekistic study of Monte Albán suggests that the Main Plaza was *not* an area of ready access to commoners (Blanton 1978:66), there were presumably ritual occasions when the public was brought into the plaza (Flannery and Marcus 1983:162). At such times, Zapotec scribes could have read the prominent texts to the non-literate commoners, just as Maya scribes did (Thompson 1972:5–14).

One of the messages conveyed by the monuments of 12 Jaguar's inauguration, however, was an example of a second kind of propaganda. *Horizontal* propaganda (Marcus 1992) was a message conveyed by nobles to nobles, not passed down the hierarchy for commoner consumption. I conclude that the information about the eight named visitors from Teotihuacán was propaganda of this type, since it was carved on hidden surfaces of four monuments.

Like the *Spondylus* shells deposited in caches below these monuments in the corners of the South Platform, the scenes of Teotihuacanos would have been seen by the nobles attending the dedication of the building. Once buried, however, they would never have been visible to a commoner. From this we might conclude that 12 Jaguar felt it important to let other nobles know about his political support from

Teotihuacán, but decided not to display it for his commoner subjects. This is a very interesting development.

In the Maya region, some of the most spectacular inaugural monuments were erected by rulers whose genealogical right to rule may have been questionable (Marcus 1992:306, 342–47). Those rulers sometimes referred to venerated predecessors to whom they were not related; outdid themselves dedicating temples; and made exaggerated cases for their claim to the throne. Since 12 Jaguar's monuments are among the largest and most numerous of any ruler known at Monte Albán, it is possible that he, like some important Maya rulers, was deliberately building a case for himself because he was not necessarily the person most directly in line for the throne. His reminder to his fellow nobles that he had Teotihuacán support—a reminder evidently irrelevant or undesirable for commoner consumption—may hint that he had originally been only one of several claimants for the throne. After all, Monte Albán must have had dozens of rulers during the Classic period; none of the others put on a display like 12 Jaguar.

Summary

Inaugurations are important transitional events for states, moments in which the reassuring order of society is shaken and must be restored. Societies all over the world have come up with a surprisingly similar set of rituals to make sure that the transition is smooth. The Zapotec, while not displaying all the widespread patterns, do share a great many with other cultures.

Inaugurations are also moments in which ideological, political, military, religious, and social messages are transmitted, both within the stratum of nobility and between nobles and commoners. By isolating those messages and analyzing them anthropologically in comparative perspective, we may find pathways to a better understanding of specific ancient states.

References Cited

Acosta, Jorge R.

1958–59 Exploraciones arqueológicas en Monte Albán, XVIII temporada. Revista Mexicana de Estudios Antropológicos 15:7–50.

1965 Preclassic and classic architecture of Oaxaca. In: Handbook of Middle American Indians, edited by Robert Wauchope. Vol. 3: Archaeology of Southern Mesoamerica, edited by Gordon R. Willey, pt 2, pp. 814–36. Austin: University of Texas Press.

Alvarado Tezozomoc, Hernando
1944 Crónica Mexicana, edited by Manuel Orozco y Berra. Mexico: Editorial Leyenda.

Anderson, Arthur J. O., and Charles E. Dibble
1954 Book 8–Kings and Lords, Florentine Codex. A book of Fray Bernardino de Sahagún's General History of the Things of New Spain. Monographs of the School of American Research, Santa Fe.

Aung-Thwin, Michael
1983 Divinity, spirit, and human: Conceptions of classical Burmese kingship. In: Centers, Symbols, and Hierarchies: Essays on the Classical States of Southeast Asia, edited by Lorraine Gesick, pp. 45–86. Monograph Series no. 26. Yale University Southeast Asia Studies Program, New Haven.

Blanton, Richard E.
1978 Monte Albán: Settlement Patterns at the Ancient Zapotec Capital. New York: Academic Press.

Cabrera Castro, Rubén, Saburo Sugiyama, and George L. Cowgill
1991 The Templo de Quetzalcoatl project at Teotihuacan: A preliminary report. Ancient Mesoamerica 2(1):77–92.

Caso, Alfonso
1928 Las estelas zapotecas. Monografías del Museo Nacional de Arqueología, Historia y Etnografía, Publicaciones de la Secretaría de Educación Pública. Mexico: Talleres Gráficos de la Nación.
1965 Sculpture and mural painting of Oaxaca. In: Handbook of Middle American Indians, edited by Robert Wauchope. Vol. 3: Archaeology of Southern Mesoamerica, edited by Gordon R. Willey, pt 2, pp. 849–70. Austin: University of Texas Press.

Córdova, Fray Juan de
1578 Vocabulario en Lengua Zapoteca. Mexico: Pedro Charte y Antonio Ricardo.

Cowgill, George L.
1983 Rulership and the Ciudadela: Political inferences from Teotihuacan architecture. In: Civilization in the Americas: Essays in Honor of Gordon R. Willey, edited by Richard M. Leventhal and Alan L. Kolata, pp. 313–43. Peabody Museum of Archaeology and Ethnology, Harvard University, Cambridge, Massachusetts.

Crónica Mexicana (see Alvarado Tezozomoc 1944)

Dibble, Charles E., and Arthur J. O. Anderson
1969 Book 6–Rhetoric and Moral Philosophy. A book of Fray Bernardino de Sahagún's General History of the Things of New Spain. Monographs of the School of American Research, Santa Fe.

Drekmeier, Charles
1962 Kingship and Community in Early India. Stanford: Stanford University Press.

Durán, Fray Diego
1964 The Aztecs: The History of the Indies of New Spain. Translated by Doris Heyden and Fernando Horcasitas. New York: Orion Press.
1967 Historia de las indias de Nueva España e islas de la tierra firme. 2 vols. Edited by Angel María Garibay K. Mexico: Editorial Porrúa.

Ellwood, Robert S.
1973 The Feast of Kingship: Accession Ceremonies in Ancient Japan. Sophia University, Tokyo.

Fash, William L.
1991 Scribes, Warriors and Kings: The City of Copán and the Ancient Maya. London: Thames and Hudson.

Fash, William L., and Robert J. Sharer
1991 Sociopolitical developments and methodological issues at Copán, Honduras: A conjunctive perspective. Latin American Antiquity 2(2):166–87.

Flannery, Kent V., and Joyce Marcus
1983 Monte Albán and Teotihuacán: Editors' introduction. In: The Cloud People: Divergent Evolution of the Zapotec and Mixtec Civilizations, edited by Kent V. Flannery and Joyce Marcus, pp. 161–66. New York: Academic Press.

Frankfort, Henri
1948 Kingship and the Gods. Chicago: University of Chicago Press.

Frazer, Sir James
1905 Lectures on the Early History of Kingship. London: Macmillan and Co.

Gesick, Lorraine, ed.
1983 Centers, Symbols, and Hierarchies: Essays on the Classical States of Southeast Asia. Monograph Series, no. 26. Yale University Southeast Asia Studies Program, New Haven.

Goldman, Irving
1970 Ancient Polynesian Society. Chicago: University of Chicago Press.

Gonda, J.
1956 Ancient Indian Kingship from the Religious Point of View. Numen III(1):36–71. Leiden: E. J. Brill.

Hassig, Ross
1988 Aztec Warfare: Imperial Expansion and Political Control. Norman: University of Oklahoma Press.

Heine-Geldern, Robert
1956 Conceptions of State and Kingship in Southeast Asia. South East Asia Program, Data Paper, no. 18. Cornell University, Ithaca, N. Y.

Helms, Mary W.
1979 Ancient Panama: Chiefs in Search of Power. Austin: University of Texas Press.

Hocart, Arthur Maurice
1927 Kingship. London: Oxford University Press.

Kemp, Jeremy
1969 Aspects of Siamese Kingship in the Seventeenth Century. Bangkok: Social Science Association Press of Thailand.

Klein, Cecelia F.
1987 The ideology of autosacrifice at the Templo Mayor. In: The Aztec Templo Mayor: A Symposium at Dumbarton Oaks, 8th and 9th October, 1983, edited by Elizabeth Hill Boone, pp. 293–370. Dumbarton Oaks Research Library and Collection, Washington, D.C.

Kubler, George
1969 Studies in Classic Maya Iconography. Memoirs of the Connecticut Academy of Arts & Sciences, vol 18. New Haven.

López Austin, Alfredo, Leonardo López Luján, and Saburo Sugiyama
1991 The Temple of Quetzalcoatl at Teotihuacan: Its possible ideological significance. Ancient Mesoamerica 2:93–105.

Lounsbury, Floyd
1974 The inscription of the sarcophagus lid at Palenque. In: Primera Mesa Redonda de Palenque, part 2, edited by Merle Greene Robertson, pp. 5–19. Robert Louis Stevenson School, Pebble Beach, California.

Marcus, Joyce
1974 The iconography of power among the Classic Maya. World Archaeology 6(1):83–94.
1976 Emblem and State in the Classic Maya Lowlands: An epigraphic approach to territorial organization. Center for Pre-Columbian Studies, Dumbarton Oaks, Washington, D.C.
1983a Stone monuments and tomb murals of Monte Albán IIIa. In: The Cloud People: Divergent Evolution of the Zapotec and Mixtec Civilizations, edited by Kent V. Flannery and Joyce Marcus, pp. 137–43. New York: Academic Press.
1983b Teotihuacán visitors on Monte Albán monuments and murals. In: The Cloud People: Divergent Evolution of the Zapotec and Mixtec Civilizations, edited by Kent V. Flannery and Joyce Marcus, pp. 175–81. New York: Academic Press.
1992 Mesoamerican Writing Systems: Propaganda, Myth, and History in Four Ancient Civilizations. Princeton: Princeton University Press.
n.d. Ancient Zapotec Monuments and Political History. Manuscript.

Maudslay, Alfred P.
1889–1902 Archaeology. In Biologia Centrali-Americana. 5 vols. London: R. H. Porter and Dulau & Co.

Mendieta, Gerónimo
1971 Historia Eclesiástica Indiana. 2nd ed., edited by Joaquín García Icazbalceta. Mexico: Editorial Porrúa.

Millon, Clara
1973 Painting, writing, and polity in Teotihuacan, Mexico. American Antiquity 38:294–314.
1988 A reexamination of the Teotihuacan tassel headdress insignia. In: Feathered Serpents and Flowering Trees: Reconstructing the Murals of Teotihuacan, edited by Kathleen Berrin, pp. 114–34. The Fine Arts Museum, San Francisco.

Millon, René
1988 The last years of Teotihuacan dominance. In: The Collapse of Ancient States and Civilizations, edited by Norman Yoffee and George L. Cowgill, pp. 102–64. Tucson: University of Arizona Press.

Parrinder, E. G.
1956 Divine Kingship in West Africa. Numen III(2):111–21. Leiden: E. J. Brill.

Proskouriakoff, Tatiana
1960 Historical implications of a pattern of dates at Piedras Negras, Guatemala. American Antiquity 25:454–75.

Sahagún, Bernardino de
Book 6 (see Dibble and Anderson 1969), Book 8 (see Anderson and Dibble 1954)

Schele, Linda, and David A. Freidel
1990 A Forest of Kings. New York: William Morrow and Co.

Smith, David Howard
1957 Divine Kingship in Ancient China. Numen IV(3):171–203. Leiden: E. J. Brill.

Spinden, Herbert J.
1913 A Study of Maya Art. Memoirs of the Peabody Museum of American Archaeology and Ethnology, vol. 6. Harvard University, Cambridge.

Sugiyama, Saburo
1989 Burials dedicated to the Old Temple of Quetzalcoatl at Teotihuacan. American Antiquity 54(1):8–106.
1992 Rulership, warfare, and human sacrifice at the Ciudadela: An iconographic study of feathered serpent representations. In: Art, Ideology, and the City of Teotihuacan: A Symposium at Dumbarton Oaks, 8th and 9th October, 1988, edited by Janet Catherine Berlo, pp. 205–30. Dumbarton Oaks Research Library and Collection, Washington, D.C.

Taube, Karl A.
n.d. The temple of Quetzalcoatl and the cult of sacred war at Teotihuacan. Res: Anthropology and Aesthetics (in press).

Thompson, J. Eric S.
1972 A Commentary on the Dresden Codex, a Maya Hieroglyphic Book. Memoirs of the American Philosophical Society, vol. 93. Philadelphia.

Torquemada, Fray Juan de
1975–1983 Monarquía Indiana, edited by Miguel León-Portilla. 5 vols. Mexico: Universidad Nacional Autónoma de México.

Townsend, Richard F.
1987 Coronation at Tenochtitlan. In: The Aztec Templo Mayor: A Symposium at Dumbarton Oaks, 8th and 9th October, 1983, edited by Elizabeth Hill Boone, pp. 371–409. Dumbarton Oaks Research Library and Collection, Washington, D.C.

Umberger, Emily
1987 Events commemorated by date plaques at the Templo Mayor: Further thoughts on the solar metaphor. In: The Aztec Templo Mayor: A Symposium at Dumbarton Oaks, 8th and 9th October, 1983, edited by Elizabeth Hill Boone, pp. 411–49. Dumbarton Oaks Research Library and Collection, Washington, D.C.

Valeri, Valerio
1985 Kingship and Sacrifice: Ritual and Society in Ancient Hawaii. Chicago: University of Chicago Press.

CHAPTER 13

Precolumbian Barrio Organization in Tehuantepec, Mexico

Judith Francis Zeitlin

University of Massachusetts, Boston

On the eve of the Spanish Conquest, the complex political and ethnic landscape of Oaxaca was dominated by numerous petty kingdoms. The Spaniards dubbed these political units *señoríos* or *cacicazgos* after the hereditary lords who ruled them, and it is clear that the Zapotecs themselves considered the issue of rulership to be central in defining each polity. Among Zapotec-speaking populations of sixteenth-century Oaxaca, such an entity (a head-town and its dependent hamlets) was known as a *quechecoqui,* a compound word signifying a community (*queche*) with its own ruler (*coqui*). With each ruler competing for political domination and the right to demand tribute from a conquered lesser lord, it was the strategic alliances and aggressive campaigns of a lord conqueror or *coquitao huezaquiqueche* that elevated any town to regional and interregional prominence (Córdova [1578] 1987).

In the Valley of Oaxaca, *cacicazgos* first appear archaeologically after A.D. 600, when political power shifted from Monte Albán to rival towns that controlled different sectors of the valley floor (Marcus 1989). Stone genealogical registers displayed in the royal tombs of these towns recorded important events in the lives of the ruling elite, whose preoccupation with bloodlines and marital alliances as measures of political legitimacy persisted well into the colonial era (Marcus 1983a, 1992; Whitecotton 1990). In testimony to early Spanish officials, Zapotec-speaking informants emphasized the pivotal role of hereditary rulers in maintaining the prehispanic community. Several of the communities surveyed in the *Relación geográfica* of 1580 reported that there was no law beyond that dictated by their lords (Whitecotton 1977:139; Paso y Troncoso 1905a).

In one guise or another, this form of political organization was widespread in Mesoamerica following the dissolution of Classic period centralized states. Among

Nahua cultures of Central Mexico, for example, the city-state equivalent was the *altepetl,* regarded as late as the early seventeenth century by the indigenous chronicler Chimalpahin as the key to a community's identity (Schroeder 1991). For Chimalpahin, the concept of *altepetl* not only referred to a particular physical place, but it also embodied political autonomy, personified by the successors in a long-established ruling line, whose fortunes determined the very survival of the political community (Schroeder 1991:121–31).

In these sixteenth- and seventeenth-century ascriptions of royal power among Mesoamerican *cacicazgos,* we see qualities that Marshall Sahlins (1985) attributes to "heroic polities"—hierarchically organized societies that invest in the person of a divine king and his actions the fate and structural relationships of the society as a whole. All historical accounts commissioned by royalty, whether inscribed in stone monuments or transcribed into the documentary record, present a highly centralized, idealized view of Mesoamerican *cacicazgo* organization. To understand fully the social and political structures which integrated these often populous city-states, we must look beyond the individual authority of the ruler. Such lower-level institutions would not only have been important in the functioning of the prehispanic polity, but in many instances they served to promote community survival after the demise of native rulership during the era of Spanish colonialism.

The present analysis focuses on the role that barrio or residential ward structures played in Zapotec city-state organization. It is based primarily on archaeological data collected during the course of preliminary excavations at one such barrio founded during the Late Postclassic occupation of Tehuantepec by Zapotec-speaking immigrants from the Valley of Oaxaca. In the Valley itself, late towns like Yagul and Mitla are known primarily from their restored elite and ceremonial architecture; only the earlier post-Monte Albán florescence at Lambityeco has been studied extensively (Bernal and Gamio 1974; Bernal 1966; Caso and Rubín de la Borbolla 1936; Paddock 1983a). On a broader scale, however, the settlement systems supporting these late kingdoms have been elucidated through the systematic surface surveys coordinated under the Valley of Oaxaca Settlement Pattern Project (Blanton 1978; Blanton et al. 1982; Kowalewski et al. 1989). But without considering the role of the Isthmian capital, even these studies give only a partial picture of late period population dynamics in the Valley of Oaxaca. Both its size and preeminence in protohistoric times make coastal Tehuantepec an important key to understanding Zapotec sociopolitical processes and institutions.

Archaeology of the Isthmus Zapotec

The historical circumstances that brought the Zapotecs to the Isthmus, so far from the Cloud People homeland, are colorfully detailed by Burgoa, whose fourteenth century A.D. initial migration date is further supported by glottochronological evidence (Burgoa [1674] 1989:328; Fernández, Swadesh, and Weitlaner 1960). According to Burgoa's account, the invading Zapotecs established their capital at Tehuantepec by vanquishing the indigenous Zoque and Huave populations by "fire and blood" (*a fuego y sangre*). According to the archaeological record, their presence was felt much further east along the coastal plain. The Río de los Perros, which in early colonial times formed a loose boundary between Zoque- and Zapotec-speaking communities, witnessed major disruptions in the indigenous settlement system at the onset of the Late Postclassic. Abandonment of the floodplain's regional center near Juchitán and the breakdown of the remaining settlement hierarchy into scattered small hamlets mark the intruders' presence and their political and cultural domination over the local population (Zeitlin 1978:174).

In the 1490s, when Cociyoeza, the hereditary lord of Zaachila, moved his throne to the Isthmus, Tehuantepec was the center of a vast tributary state controlling most of the coastal plain to the east and reaching back into the Sierra Madre to claim tribute rights from such distant towns as Nejapa and Ixtepeji, as well as some Valley of Oaxaca towns formerly subject to Zaachila. Tehuantepec offers us some unusual opportunities for an archaeological investigation of the institutional basis of the Zapotec *cacicazgo,* which was transplanted full-blown to the Isthmus at a relatively late date. But despite Tehuantepec's development into the preeminent Zapotec political and dynastic seat of power, for the most part, these opportunities have remain untapped. Apart from the famous mountaintop site of Guiengola, with its fortified complex of ceremonial architecture and palatial retreats for the Zapotec elite (Peterson and MacDougall 1974), very little is known about the archaeology of urban Tehuantepec and its immediate environs during the Late Postclassic. Like most prehispanic towns that continue to be occupied until the present day, Tehuantepec's past largely lies buried beneath many layers of urban growth and decay.

In the spring of 1990, supported by a grant from the Wenner-Gren Foundation, I was able to probe more deeply into the material record of late prehispanic Tehuantepec as part of a larger archaeological and ethnohistoric study of the impact of colonial period change on the region's Zapotec-speaking populations. With the assistance of Lillian Thomas, I conducted preliminary excavations and survey at the site known locally as the Panteón Antiguo, situated on the outskirts of the Tehuantepec barrio of Santa Cruz Tagolaba, overlooking the west bank of the Tehuantepec River, approximately 1.5 km southeast of the center of town. Its name derives from local lore that the small mound dominating the site houses the buried remains of Cociyopi, the last Zapotec ruler of Tehuantepec. Initial inspection, however, indicated that the mound (and partially exposed plaster-floored building nearby) were built to serve the civic and religious needs of a living community that most likely was the fifteenth- and sixteenth-century ancestor of the modern barrio of Santa Cruz Tagolaba (Fig. 13.1).

Prior earth removal operations had badly disturbed the east and south faces of

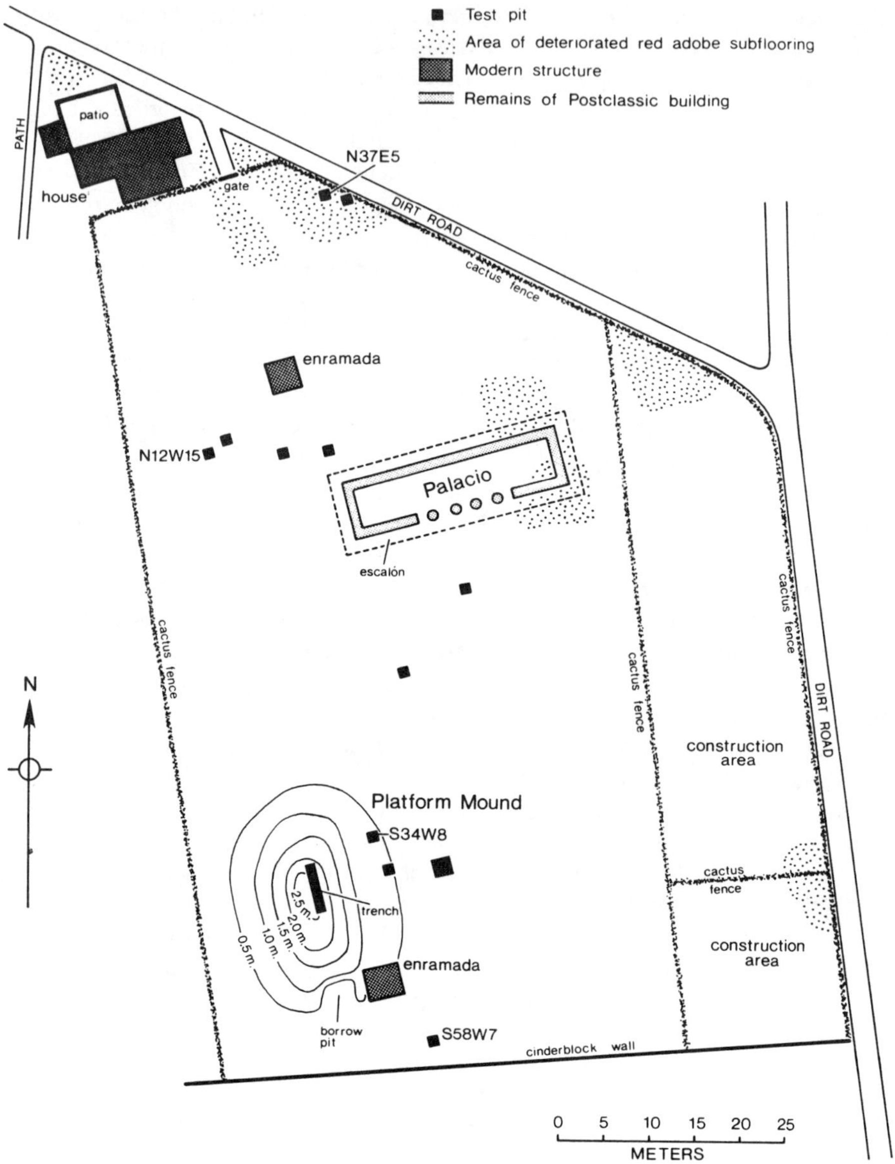

Figure 13.1. Plan of the Panteón Antiguo site, Tehuantepec, Oaxaca.

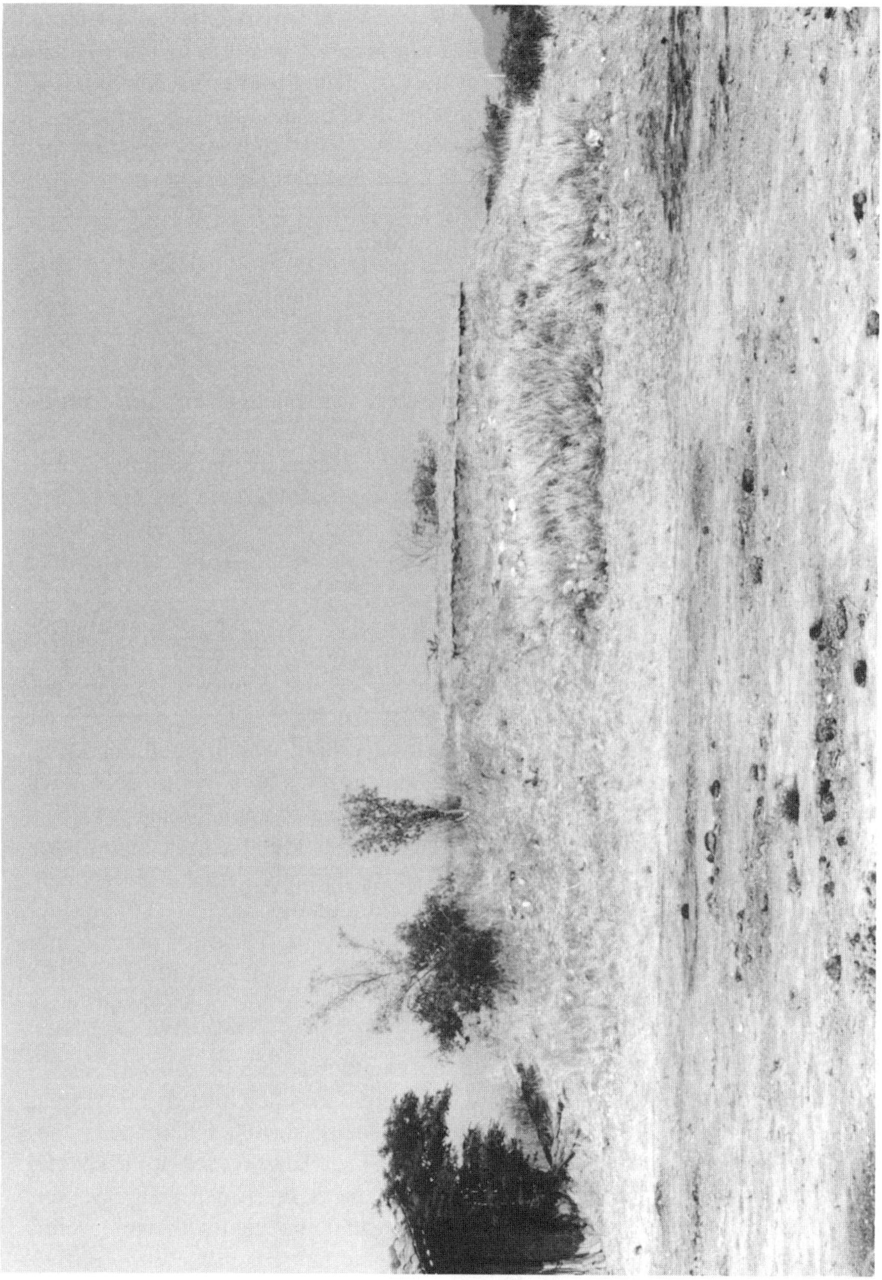

Figure 13.2. East face of the platform mound prior to excavation.

the *lomita,* so our testing operation there was mainly limited to a narrow trench dug at the top of the 2.5 m mound. A sequence of six remarkably well-preserved plaster floors associated with three separate construction phases was found before reaching rubble platform fill at a little over one meter below the summit (Fig. 13.2). Many of these floors had traces of painted decoration and one preserved a design of black triangles. Fragmentary traces of a plastered adobe interior wall found in the south trench profile suggest that the platform once supported a two-room temple, showing the continuation of a long Oaxaca tradition that first appeared by Monte Albán II times (Flannery and Marcus 1983:80).

Our major effort was centered at what we dubbed the "palacio" because of its large plaster-floor room, over 24 m long and 5 m wide. The building's orientation (16 degrees west of magnetic north) became the basis for the excavation grid used throughout the site. Excavations here were designed to expose as much architectural detail as possible and to retrieve artifacts associated with occupation surfaces inside and outside the building. A porch about one meter wide appears to have extended along the building exterior; a wide portico flanked by four columns served as the principal entrance from a large open plaza stretching between the palacio and the temple mound. A single preserved corner of a plaster-faced adobe protrusion from the north wall opposite the portico appears to be all that remains of a small, 49 cm deep, bench or raised platform (Fig. 13.3).

Searching for earlier construction phases, we took advantage of a worn path bisecting the building, and dug a small trench perpendicular to the portico entrance. Although the plaster floor was resurfaced on occasion and painted with black and specular red designs that have long since deteriorated, the palacio appears to have been built at one time. Since the building's plaster floor was in good condition, particularly where it had been protected from the elements by a fallen adobe wall, a line of three 25 cm diameter holes in the floor, spaced approximately 1.75 m apart from one another, is an intriguing anomaly. We suspect that they are postconquest postholes, cut into the floor shortly before the building's final abandonment, to secure additional posts for supporting the deteriorated roof.

Test pits were placed at several other locations as well. Traces of plaster floor were found in just the southernmost of these excavation units, but the associated structure had been badly disturbed by the modern construction of a cement block wall and plowing of the field behind it. Stippled areas shown on the site plan (Fig. 13.1) represent zones where reddish adobe subfloor is exposed, presumably associated with other habitations or ceremonial structures. Few test pits in these areas yielded occupational remains more significant than potsherds, but modern construction workers building a house foundation in the southeast corner of the site did discover large fragments of an unusual modeled mask or human effigy vessel. Charred soils, animal bone, and shell associated with a cooking area were encountered in one test pit locality, 30 m north of the palacio.

Most of the pottery found in these excavations falls into one of two ware catego-

Figure 13.3. Portico entrance to the "palacio" after excavation.

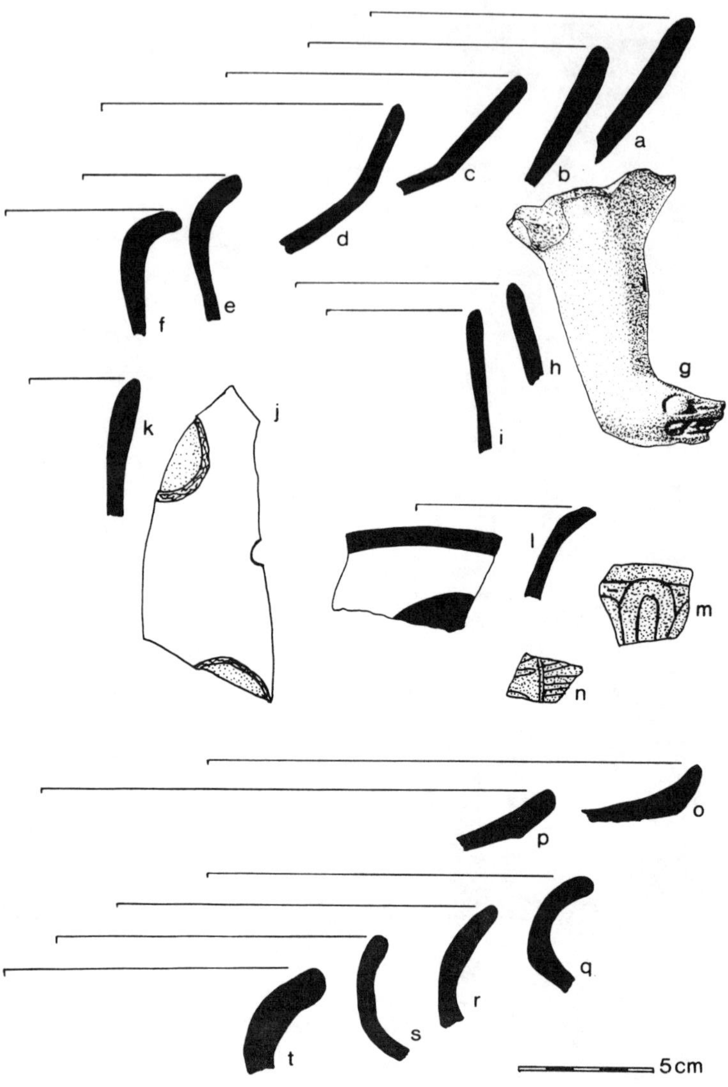

Figure 13.4. Postclassic pottery types from the Panteón Antiguo excavations and surface survey. *a-k,* Reu Silty fine gray bowls (*a-d*), strainer rims (*e-f*), serpent's head support (*g*), neckless jars (*h-i*), and incense burners with pre-fired cutouts and hollow appendage scars (*j-k*); *l-n,* Barbacana fine white, red-painted bowl (*l*), sgraffito-on-red body sherds (*m-n*); *o-t,* Orozco Coarse buff-to-orange, burnished comal rims (*o-p*), brushed olla rims (*q-t*).

ries comparable to the *café* and G-3M types typical of the Late Postclassic Valley of Oaxaca. A coarse paste, buff- to orange-firing ware was primarily fashioned into *ollas* and *comales* used for cooking and water storage. Serving dishes and containers were made of a fine paste grayware with typical forms including shallow hemispherical or composite silhouette bowls, slender *tecomates,* and everted rim *ollas* or *pichanchas* (strainers); many of these vessels rested on tripod supports, often molded into serpent or eagle heads (Fig. 13.4). Vessel surfaces tended to be badly deteriorated from the sticky clay soils of the site, but even so, there were few examples of the kind of fine orange paste that often was decorated with polychrome painting in the Late Postclassic. The indigenous Isthmian white ware tradition constitutes a minor component of the ceramic assemblage.

With a small number of distinctive colonial period imported and domestic types found in the site's shallow deposits, it is likely that some of these fine white and fine gray vessels were of postconquest manufacture. Excavations conducted during the same season at two colonial period sites disclosed many continuities in both wares during a time of vigorous local pottery innovation and the introduction of European-style glazed ceramics (Zeitlin and Thomas 1992a).

An examination of the spatial distribution of Postclassic pottery revealed one particularly striking association. Fragments of a rare grayware type, a small cylindrical incense burner, were found in some abundance in just one area, the outer porch and adjacent plaza immediately south of the palacio's columned portico. In this same area we recovered large concentrations of obsidian blades, including a few pointed bladelets probably produced on a small core. Such a core was seen in a private collection of artifacts from the site. Although both green and smoky-banded gray obsidian varieties are widely distributed at the site, both in surface collections and excavations, we found only one other locality with a comparably heavy concentration. A small zone less than 25 m west of the mound was littered with obsidian.

Kowalewski et al. (1989:357) note a similar association between outlying palace groups and areas of obsidian concentration, frequently with evidence of blade production, at Period V towns in the Oaxaca Valley. Although they conclude from this context that obsidian working may have been an activity of the lower ranking elite, the Panteón Antiguo palacio association of obsidian and incensario fragments further strengthens their other suggestion that these minor palace groups were the scene of ceremonial bloodletting.

Indeed, this particular building may have functioned within the Panteón Antiguo community primarily as a ritually consecrated hall, and secondarily, if at all, as the residence of a minor noble and his entourage.

Barrio and City Population Parameters

A much more extensive habitation zone extends beyond the site center (Fig. 13.5). Postclassic pottery is found littering the ground for a distance of about 1 km following the course of the Río Tehuantepec, and for another 500 m to the west, giving a maximum site area for the barrio of 0.5 km^2. Sherds are not scattered evenly across this residential area, but instead, display noncontiguous concentrations.

In a vacant field directly south of the plaza group, we were able to plot the distribution of these artifact concentrations on the plowed surface and found that about 40 m of unoccupied area joined what appeared to be 10 m wide house mound concentrations. If this density is typical for the site as a whole and if it was all inhabited at the same time (a likely conclusion given the brief prehispanic Zapotec occupation), then the barrio could have held as many as 200 houses.

The problem of estimating the number of people residing in those 200 houses is given some ethnographic foundation by an extraordinarily detailed census made by Baltasar de San Miguel, whose mid-sixteenth-century *visita* for the Spanish Crown affords us our first accurate native population count for the Isthmus, including the number of people of all age categories and even the number of houses, first for Tehuantepec and then all other communities taken together (Paso y Troncoso 1905b). According to his figures, there were two kinds of households on the Isthmus. In rural villages, the average house sheltered six people, or probably a single nuclear family, but in Tehuantepec, the average household size was just under fifteen and clearly represented some kind of joint family. While it seems unlikely that each of our archaeological house mounds at Panteón Antiguo was occupied by one of these large urban families, by using the more conservative rural household size of six, we still reach a total population estimate of 1,200 for this one barrio.

We know from the mid-sixteenth-century census that Tehuantepec was an unusually populous settlement, with three-quarters of the Isthmian population concentrated in 49 barrios at the urban center. How representative the Panteón Antiguo barrio may be for the Precolumbian city as a whole is a question less easily answered with archaeological or postconquest census data. Traces of extensive occupation and even another preserved barrio administrative center are still visible on the north and northwest boundaries of the modern city, although there has been no systematic settlement pattern survey of these zones.

Colonial sources indicate that a dwindling native population continued to reside in the numerous scattered barrios that defined Tehuantepec's urban plan and distinguished it from the smaller towns and villages of the province. Such a pattern was still preserved in 1580, when a map of the region was drawn by a native artist to accompany the *Relación geográfica* questionnaire (Fig. 13.6). Baltasar de San Miguel counted 11,845 men, women, and children residing in Tehuantepec in

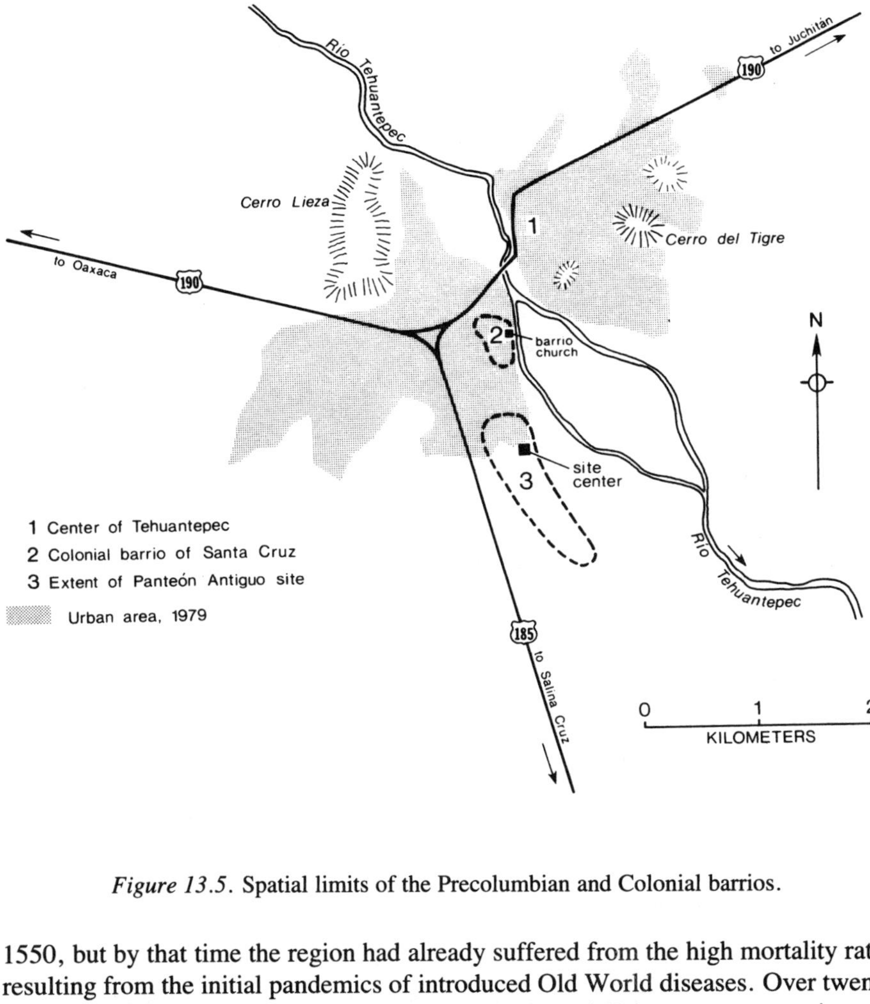

Figure 13.5. Spatial limits of the Precolumbian and Colonial barrios.

1550, but by that time the region had already suffered from the high mortality rates resulting from the initial pandemics of introduced Old World diseases. Over twenty years earlier the first recorded Spanish description of Tehuantepec was given to Gonzalo Fernández de Oviedo by a priest who accompanied the ill-fated Loaysa expedition to the Spice Islands. When their ship became separated from the others and traveled many days on meager supplies of food before making landfall off the Oaxaca coast in July of 1526, the desperate party was relieved to find themselves within a province already sworn to allegiance to the Spanish Crown. Although the priest's estimate of 100,000 inhabitants at Tehuantepec seems greatly exaggerated, Oviedo himself found the figure credible because of the practice in these parts of aggregating many large barrios close to one another (Oviedo [1544] 1959:257).

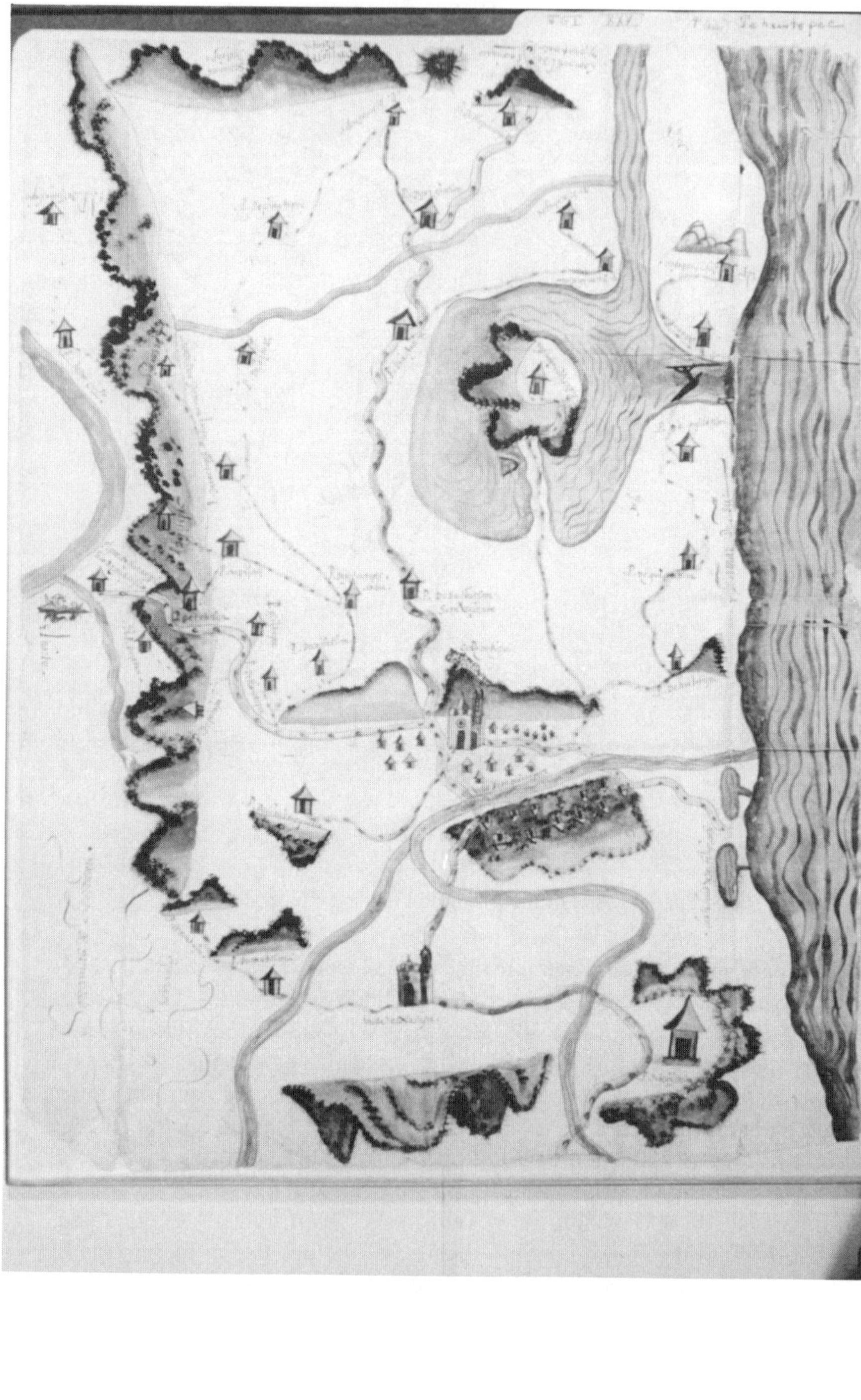

Figure 13.6. Indigenous-style map of the Tehuantepec province accompanying the 1580 *Relación geográfica*. Map reproduced courtesy of the Nettie Lee Benson Latin American Collection, University of Texas at Austin (JGI XXV-4).

If the 49 Tehuantepec barrios noted by Baltasar de San Miguel were all occupied on the eve of the Spanish Conquest and were all the same size as our site, Tehuantepec might easily have held more than 50,000 people in 1521. Using a figure of 25,000 as an extremely conservative estimate would still make Tehuantepec nearly twice as large as each of the three largest towns identified archaeologically for the Late Postclassic Oaxaca Valley. The Mixtec-speaking settlement identified as Sa'a Yucu, stretching between Cuilapan and the lower slopes of Monte Albán, is estimated to have housed 13,573 people, while Zapotec-speaking Macuilxóchitl and Mitla in the Tlacolula arm of the valley are thought to have had populations of 13,831 and 10,551 respectively (Kowalewski et al. 1989:315).

Immigration and the Establishment of Tehuantepec as an Urban Place

Given the intrusive nature of the Late Postclassic Zapotec presence on the Isthmus, it is clear that Tehuantepec's extraordinary size must be attributed primarily to immigration rather than to internal demographic growth. Since both native histories and linguistic data place the original homeland of the Tehuantepec population in the Oaxaca Valley, Postclassic archaeological evidence gathered by the Oaxaca Valley Settlement Pattern Survey should help unravel some of the processes behind this growth.

Traditional historical accounts and the probably early sixteenth-century original of the cadastral record known as the Lienzo de Guevea maintain that Cociyoeza and Cociyopi, the father and son kings of Tehuantepec, were descended from the rulers of Zaachila (Marcus 1983b; Paddock 1983b; Whitecotton 1990). Despite the rich appointments of its famous royal tomb, other archaeological data from Zaachila are at odds with that center's reputation as the paramount Zapotec polity in the Late Postclassic Oaxaca Valley. As Jill Appel points out (1982:144), even Fr. Francisco de Burgoa, who lived in Zaachila during the early 1600s, saw little in the town's archaeological zone that suggested to him substantial occupation during the immediate preconquest past. In this light she feels that the surprisingly high figure of 1,097 tributary households counted for Zaachila in the mid-sixteenth century would have been dispersed widely among outlying dependencies. No comparable concentration of people is indicated for the Late Postclassic town itself, when Zaachila had neither the architectural elaboration nor a sufficiently large population to qualify as a minor central place, according to the archaeological survey team's classification system (Kowalewski et al. 1989:329).

It may be that Zaachila's political preeminence in late prehispanic times rested more on its symbolic legacy, perhaps as heir to the grandeur of a Monte Albán now overtaken by Mixtec-speaking occupants, rather than on its actual political and economic role. Indeed, even the names of the three Zaachila kings preceding Cociyoeza, Zaachila I, II, and III, are, as Paddock (1983b) observes, curiously unspecified for a dynasty said to have been founded only a hundred years before Cociyoeza's reign. We might, in fact, be seeing in this nebulous Zaachila dynasty a Zapotec equivalent of the widespread Late Postclassic Mesoamerican practice of rulers legitimizing their authority by claiming descent from the dynasty of mythologized Tollan. That the site of Zaachila itself had lost its direct role in politics is underscored by historical accounts that Mitla, not Zaachila, was the burial place of the dynasty's kings.

Whatever the circumstances by which Zaachila rulers claimed power, seven Valley of Oaxaca towns paid them tribute in goods and services, according to the *Relaciones geográficas* (Appel 1982:144; Paso y Troncoso 1905a). Six of these (Tlacolula, Macuilxochitl, Teítipac, Tlalixtac, Teotitlán del Valle, and Mitla) are in the Tlacolula arm of the valley, and they encompass all the major *cabeceras* (head towns) known historically and archaeologically for this subregion (Kowalewski et al. 1989:317). The Valley of Oaxaca Settlement Pattern Project has identified 51 Period V sites in the Tlacolula zone as central places from their surface remains, and these have a combined population total calculated to have been 68,236; the addition of numerous smaller settlements brings the total population of the subregion to 76,040 (Kowalewski et al. 1989: Tables 10.2, 14.14).

These population estimates are based on the assumption that all Period V sites in the valley, with a few notable exceptions not in the Tlacolula subregion, were occupied for the duration of the nearly 600 year period distinguished archaeologically. That assumption is difficult to accept; certainly more transient smaller settlements might easily disappear if one or two lineages died out, and bigger towns must also have witnessed significant shifts in their population totals through such a vast span of time.

It appears that some such archaeologically imperceptible shift downward took place prior to the Conquest, for a 1548 census of Tlacolula *cabeceras* and their dependencies tallied only 2,231 tributaries, which would have represented a total population of under 9,000 for the entire subregion (Gerhard 1972:191), just 12% of the archaeological estimate for the precontact period. By contrast, Tehuantepec's midcentury population of 11,845 represents between 24% and 47% of our far less accurate high (50,000) and low (25,000) population estimates for the prehistoric city.

There is perhaps no single issue at the interface of archaeology and history in the Americas more controversial than the question of how large was the native population on the eve of the Conquest and, calculating from that base, how precipitous was the population decline after contact.[1] My interest here is not in rekindling this debate or in passing judgment on the relative accuracy of archaeological and historical demographic data, but rather, in illuminating some historical processes difficult to distinguish archaeologically. Assuming that surface survey indices yield reasonable estimates of population size, such a precipitous drop in the Tlacolula subregion population by 1548 is too great to attribute to postcontact disease and dislocation.

Such close observers of native populations in the Valley of Mexico as Alonso de Zorita and Gerónimo de Mendieta estimated that the midcentury population there had declined to as much as one-third of its 1521 levels (Gibson 1964:138). At the other extreme from these impressionistic but firsthand estimates is Sanders' conservative demographic projection based on archaeological data, which suggests that as much as 75% of the aboriginal Central Mexican population survived until 1550 (Sanders 1976: Fig. 4.4). Whatever the difficulties of reconciling archaeological and early historical demographic data may be, the scale of population loss indicated by the disparity between Late Postclassic and mid-sixteenth-century population estimates for most parts of the Valley of Oaxaca falls easily between these two extremes of two-thirds and one-quarter native decline.

For example, Gerhard's (1972:90) survey of early census data leads him to propose a Mixtec-speaking population of 8,000 tributaries, or a little over 30,000 people living at midcentury in the Marquesado's Cuatro Villas jurisdiction, which included Cuilapan, Etla, Tecuilabacoya, and their dependencies in the Valley of Oaxaca. No more than 62,606 people are estimated to have resided in the entire subregions which sustained these historically-known Mixtec communities during Period V (Kowalewski et al. 1989: Table 14.4), an aboriginal population high that would allow a maximum decline of about 50% during the first thirty years of colonial rule. An 88% decline for the Tlacolula subregion during this same period does not follow known historical patterns within the Valley of Oaxaca.

It seems then that some substantial percentage of the estimated 76,000 people residing in Tlacolula during the Late Postclassic no longer lived in this zone at the time the Spaniards arrived. Whatever more subtle internal demographic shifts may have taken place during the last six centuries of prehistory—the loss of a hamlet or small village, the realignment of settlement zones within a town—a significant amount of this decline must have resulted from the emigration of large numbers of people to the new Zapotec colony at Tehuantepec. Linguistically, it is the Tlacolula variant of Valley Zapotec to which Isthmus Zapotec is most closely related (Marcus and Flannery 1978; Aaron Broadwell 1991, pers. comm.). Politically, it was the wide recognition of Zaachila dynastic authority among Tlacolula townspeople that gave the Tehuantepec kings their legitimacy.

Zapotec and Mixtec narrative accounts give different reasons for the establishment of the Isthmus colony in the late fourteenth century and the transfer there of the Zaachila dynasty in the late fifteenth century, ranging from Zapotec irritation at the ease of access indigenous *istmeños* had given Aztec merchants, to political pressures from encroaching Mixtec settlements at home. Given the extremely high population estimates during Period V for the Tlacolula region, an area primarily suited to rainfall agriculture, one unstated motivation may well have been the need to expand food production.

Linda Nicholas (1989) has examined the relationship between human resources and agricultural potential in different sectors of the Valley of Oaxaca throughout the prehistoric settlement pattern sequence, and her figures show that the Tlacolula population came closer to reaching the subregion's agricultural carrying capacity limits than did late prehistoric communities in other zones. While the Etla subregion could have produced enough food for nearly five times its population, in years of average rainfall the Tlacolula zone would have fed just slightly more (1.1 times) than the population calculated to have lived there. All other Valley zones would have been able to feed approximately twice their estimated population (Kowalewski et al. 1989:364).

In dry years, which occur regularly but unpredictably in the Valley of Oaxaca, the Tlacolula zone's population would not have been able to meet its own food needs at Period V's high densities. In keeping with their thesis that it was increasing commercialism and the growth of market systems which led to the development of petty kingdoms in the Late Postclassic Valley of Oaxaca, Kowalewski et al. (1989:307, 364) propose that this marketing system allowed food to be moved from surplus-producing areas like Etla to needy Tlacolula communities during years of poor harvest.

However attractive the idea may be that markets were more developed and more independent of centralized authority during this period, there is in fact little ethnohistoric basis for the proposition that agricultural staples circulated freely in a regional marketing system. Even in the Valley of Mexico, where perhaps 200,000 city dwellers could not supply their own basic food needs, tribute and other nonmarket mechanisms were fundamental institutions for feeding Tenochtitlán (Parsons 1976).[2]

Late prehistoric Zapotecs had their equivalent of the Aztec *tianguez* or periodic market, which Fray Juan de Córdova glossed as *queya* or *quiya* in his sixteenth-century *Vocabulario*. While the vigor of today's Valley of Oaxaca system of periodic markets may suggest strong continuities with the Precolumbian past, there are reasons to be cautious about drawing parallels without direct evidence from the contact and early colonial periods. No Valley towns were recognized by the Aztecs as major market centers, although in the 1580 *Relaciones geográficas,* many Oaxaca communities claimed to have participated in long distance trade (Appel 1982:146f). Assuming that indigenous markets existed to serve purely regional commercial needs within the Valley, we can get an indication of how little food was offered for sale or exchange from the desperate attempts made by Antequera's early Spanish settlers to get the Crown to compel Indians to provide the few hundred townspeople with a regular supply of grain (Chance 1978:59). By the time Burgoa wrote in the late seventeenth century, periodic Indian markets were thriving in the Valley, but their establishment in important towns like Mitla as late as 1717 (Chance 1978:110) suggests that a good measure of native commerce was a response to specific colonial-period economic factors, not necessarily part of Oaxaca's Precolumbian legacy.

If surplus food production and distribution remained under political control during the Late Postclassic, then it seems all the more plausible that Tlacolula's leaders would have sought new arable land to maintain polity self-sufficiency in a time of population growth. Tehuantepec provided both the needed agricultural margin and the power base for a resurgent Zapotec state. It may even have been the case, although present evidence cannot confirm such a conjecture, that the Isthmian town's discrete barrios originated during colonization, perhaps as residential territories claimed by particular groups migrating from communities in the Tlacolula zone. In any case, the Tehuantepec barrios follow a pattern identified for the Late Postclassic Valley of Oaxaca, where occupational clusters separated by bands of unoccupied land form what Kowalewski et al. (1989:348) term the "basic building blocks of the regional system."

Role of the Barrio in Zapotec Sociopolitical Organization: Comparisons with the Nahua Calpulli

Units similar to the Zapotec barrio have been distinguished for western Morelos in surveys conducted by the Xochicalco Mapping Project (Hirth 1984) and in extensive excavations undertaken at three sites by the Postclassic Morelos Archaeological Project (Smith et al. 1989). The largest of Smith's excavated sites, Cuexcomate, appears to correspond to the *calpulli* social unit, the large Nahua residential ward or barrio, as it appears in early sixteenth-century census records completed for several towns in Morelos (Smith 1992; Carrasco 1976a). With 150 houses, Cuexcomate compares well with the average *calpulli* size in Morelos, and it contains a series of special structures historically associated with *calpulli* functions, but not found at smaller sites in the regional settlement hierarchy, including a temple, other civic buildings and higher class residential compounds, all arranged around a large public plaza (Smith 1992).

Although our Panteón Antiguo data are less complete than those for Cuexcomate, due to the absence of stone walls which would facilitate surface mapping and to our focus so far on the civic-ceremonial precinct, there are strong correspondences between the Tehuantepec barrio and the Morelos *calpulli,* both in the estimated size of the residential unit and in the nature of its plaza-centered public architecture. More than just residential neighborhoods, Zapotec barrios like Panteón Antiguo were also corporate communities, defined spatially by their physical separation from other such communities and by their religious and administrative centers.

Among Nahua urban barrios and rural villages, these corporate centers were dominated by the *tecpan,* a building which not only housed the lord in charge of the community, but also served as the locus of many community functions (Evans 1991). At the Panteón Antiguo, community-wide functions, sanctified by the traditional Mesoamerican practices of incense burning and ritual bloodletting, probably took place at the "palacio" structure, within public view from the open plaza. Private living quarters for the barrio leader were more likely housed in other rooms or nearby structures, perhaps those now indicated only by zones of reddish adobe subfloor (Fig. 13.1).

Some additional light can be shed on the corporate functions of the Tehuantepec barrios from sixteenth-century documentary and linguistic data. Córdova's *Vocabulario* gives several Zapotec glosses for "barrio," two of which reflect its functions as a landholding unit: *quiñaqueche* or *naaqueche,* a unit of community agricultural fields (*quiña, naa:* arable land, planted field; *queche:* village); *collaba* is a third term offered for barrio. The barrio was the population division from which a squadron of people was formed for public works projects ("parcialidad de gente en un pueblo para los trabajos del pueblo, o como esquadra"): *tobiquiña, tobicollaba, tobicozaana* (*tobi:* one unit). That there was a kinship component to barrio composition is indicated by this last term, because *cozaana* referred to a group of collateral kinsmen. Such a grouping would also be mobilized for war: *tobiquiñapeni, tobicollaba* ("escuadra de gente junta o como para guerra").

A 1553 complaint brought against Cociyopi (Don Juan Cortés as he was known after his baptism) gives us some additional context in which to observe how such units functioned in public works projects (AGN Hospital de Jesús, leg. 450, exp. 1). The overseer or *collabachiña* (referred to in these documents by the equivalent Hispanicized Nahuatl term *tequitlato*) for each barrio participating in the public works project—in this case, construction or maintenance of an irrigation canal—gathered together a number of men from his barrio and supervised their labor at the work site. The *collabachiña* (*chiña:* tribute or work) was also responsible for collecting the tribute owed by the barrio to the ruler and, during Tehuantepec's colonial incorporation into the Marquesado, to the Spanish alcade mayor appointed by Cortés (Zeitlin and Thomas 1992b).

So far this characterization of the Zapotec barrio community differs little from that presented for the Aztec *calpulli* by the mid-sixteenth-century Spanish *oidor* Alonso de Zorita, whose idealized view of the Mexican barrio as a democratic, kinship-based, landholding corporate entity (Zorita 1963:30) has been challenged by recent ethnohistoric research. Zorita's is a model little recognized in the urban realities of Tenochtitlán's barrio structure or kinship organization (Calnek 1976; Kellogg 1986), and perhaps it is one ill-suited to the complexities of city-state organization in general. The seventeenth-century Chalco chronicler Chimalpahin primarily used the term *calpulli* to refer to migrating groups, while reserving the equivalent terms *tlaxilacalli* and *chinamitl* to designate their settled, territorial manifestation as core subunits of the *altepetl* (Schroeder 1991:143–51).

Examining detailed Nahuatl census records from several smaller towns in Morelos, produced just twenty years after the Conquest, Carrasco (1976a, 1976b) found that kinship was not a major determinant of residence, that great disparities existed among households in the amount of agricultural land they farmed, and that wealth as well as social class were powerful determinants of social relationships within *calpulli*. Indeed, Hicks (1986:38) argues from these data and those he has analyzed from Texcoco that the Central Mexican *calpulli,* although quite variable in composition, was more typically defined as a noble "house" with its attached commoners, the commoners receiving plots of land in return for providing labor and military service for the lord who headed that particular noble lineage.

Until extensive excavations are conducted in the residential zone at Panteón Antiguo, we cannot assess the degree to which Precolumbian Zapotec barrios were internally stratified, but early colonial sources for Tehuantepec hint at economic differences among commoner households. Thirty years after the Conquest, three Zapotec commoners from one of the Tehuantepec barrios charged that their *collabachiña* Domingo Goma had taken excessive tribute payments from them, which were improperly used by the ruler, Don Juan Cortés, and his associates for their own purposes. Although the fragments of maguey paper on which these tribute payments in cash, cacao, cloth, and other goods were documented cannot be interpreted completely, they illustrate differing amounts of tribute items from individual units that probably correspond to joint households, like the one to which the three complainants themselves belonged. According to Domingo Goma's defense statement, this particular household ("Andres Tine y los dos otros yndios de su casa") had improperly hoarded a large sum of cacao that was supposed to be paid in tribute (AGN Hospital de Jesús, leg. 450, exp.1). We do not know how the household obtained this hidden reserve of cash, but usufruct rights to barrio agricultural lands alone seem an unlikely income source.

Domingo Goma insisted that he collected only that tribute which the *cacique* Don Juan and his four advisers had demanded of the barrio commoners, keeping nothing for himself, a statement consistent with other historical sources that emphasize the role of the *collabachiña* as mere agents of the ruler. Considered members of the minor nobility (*joanahuini*), they were said to have been appointees of the *cacique* (Spores 1965:967; Whitecotton 1977:144). But linguistic data indicate that this social status was inherited, as is demonstrated in the Zapotec glosses Córdova gave for a lineage of the lesser nobility, *tijajoanahuini* and *tijacollaba* (literally, lineage of the barrio). Rather than exercising personal discretion in these appointments, it is more likely that the ruler confirmed a hereditary candidate from within the barrio (Zeitlin 1984:71). Furthermore, the multiplicity of communal functions, as seen archaeologically at the Panteón Antiguo civic-ceremonial center and similar centers in the Late Postclassic Valley of Oaxaca, points to a wider-ranging political role for the barrio headman than that suggested by sixteenth-century Zapotec descriptions. Present evidence does not permit much further speculation as to the degree to which the *collabachiña* (or, alternatively, some unidentified higher status resident noble) exerted personal juridical and tributary control over barrio members.

Carrasco (1976b:63) concludes from his review of the Morelos census documents that tributary obligations may have figured as importantly in determining social relationships within the Nahua *calpulli* as did kinship ties. Although that example cautions us against presenting an idealized view of Zapotec barrio social structure, we also should not forget the complex corporate functions which bound these households together as enduring social communities. Tehuantepec's barrio organization was remarkably resistent to the postconquest forces of disease-related depopulation and Spanish-imposed *congregación*. Although the number of barrios dwindled from the 49 counted by Baltasar de San Miguel at mid-century to just 31 represented on the indigenous-style map accompanying the 1580 *Relaciones geográficas* (Fig. 13.6), there were more than 18 in the late seventeenth century (Burgoa 1989:389–90) and 16 remain today.

The colonial history of the community at Panteón Antiguo is an good illustration of the way in which successful Tehuantepec barrios persisted. Although the site itself was abandoned near the end of the sixteenth century, the small remaining population was relocated one kilometer closer to the center of Tehuantepec, where the newly erected Santa Cruz Tagolaba church (Fig. 13.5) became the ceremonial focus of a still intact barrio community. While church-sanctioned festivities assumed the public face of barrio religious and social expression, these, like other aspects of community life, were supported by a social organization with strong ties to the Precolumbian past (Münch 1989; Zeitlin 1992). It was this barrio-based organization, I contend, with its evolving *mayordomo* system, which provided both substance and continuity to social interaction in postconquest Tehuantepec. And, as they demonstrated repeatedly in petitions to the Spanish colonial authorities, townspeople counted on their barrio leaders to defend community interests rather than on the often weak or co-opted members of the Indian town council.

In conclusion, we can see that Zapotec historical sources, with their highly centralized view of the *coquitao's* political role, offer an incomplete reconstruction of Late Postclassic sociopolitical organization. Archaeological data from the Valley of Oaxaca settlement pattern surveys and from the Panteón Antiguo excavations in Tehuantepec indicate a more autonomous sociopolitical base within the barrio units administered by the *collabachiña*. Not some arbitrary political division constructed for tax collecting purposes, the barrio community, according to linguistic and documentary from the sixteenth century, was a unit held together by traditional bonds of corporate identity. In Tehuantepec, these bonds gave community institutions the remarkable resiliency with which they weathered the chaotic aftermath of colonialism and the collapse of the indigenous state.

Notes

1. The history of this controversy and many of its methodological fine points have been reviewed in Denevan (1976) and Newson (1985). While a variety of techniques, from disease mortality projections to carrying capacity calculations, have been used to estimate the size of the aboriginal population in different regions on the eve of European contact, most figures are extrapolated from postconquest census data. Only Sanders (1976), looking at the aboriginal population of the Valley of Mexico, has attempted to reconcile Late Postclassic archaeological estimates with sixteenth-century demographic data from Mesoamerica.
2. Hassig (1985:129ff) argues that late in the Aztec Empire, political constraints and territorial limitations on tribute and chinampa expansion required Tenochtitlán to improve its access to regional agricultural production by making itself the primary market for manufactured goods throughout the Valley of Mexico.

References Cited

Appel, Jill
1982 A summary of the ethnohistoric information relevant to the interpretation of Late Postclassic settlement pattern data, the Central and Valle Grande survey zones. In: Monte Albán's Hinterland, Part I: Prehispanic Settlement Patterns of the Central and Southern Parts of the Valley of Oaxaca, Mexico, edited by Richard E. Blanton, et al., pp. 139–48. Memoirs of the Museum of Anthropology, University of Michigan, no. 15. Ann Arbor.

Bernal, Ignacio
1966 The Mixtecs in the archaeology of the Valley of Oaxaca. In: Ancient Oaxaca, edited by John Paddock, pp. 345–66. Stanford: Stanford University Press.

Bernal, Ignacio, and Lorenzo Gamio
1974 Yagul, el palacio de los seis patios. Instituto de Investigaciones Antropológicas. Serie Antropológica, no. 16. Mexico: U. N. A. M.

Blanton, Richard E.
1978 Monte Albán: Settlement Patterns at the Ancient Zapotec Capital. New York: Academic Press.

Blanton, Richard E., Stephen A. Kowalewski, Gary Feinman, and Jill Appel
1982 Monte Albán's Hinterland, Part I: Prehispanic Settlement Patterns of the Central and Southern Parts of the Valley of Oaxaca, Mexico. Memoirs of the Museum of Anthropology, University of Michigan, no. 15. Ann Arbor.

Burgoa, Fray Francisco de
1989 [1674] Geográfica descripción, vol 2. Mexico: Editorial Porrúa.

Calnek, Edward E.
1976 The internal structure of Tenochtitlan. In: The Valley of Mexico: Studies in Pre-Hispanic Ecology and Society, edited by Eric R. Wolf, pp. 287–302. Albuquerque: University of New Mexico Press.

Carrasco, Pedro
1976a Estratificación social indígena en Morelos durante el siglo XVI. In: Estratificación social en la Mesoamérica prehispánica, edited by Pedro Carrasco and Johanna Broda, pp. 102–77. Instituto Nacional de Antropología e Historia. Mexico.
1976b The joint family in ancient Mexico: The case of Molotla. In: Essays on Mexican Kinship, edited by Hugo Nutini, Pedro Carrasco, and James M. Taggert, pp. 45–64. Pittsburgh: University of Pittsburgh Press.

Caso, Alfonso, ed.
1928 Descripción de Tehuantepec. Revista Mexicana de Estudios Históricos 2(5) supplement: 164–75.

Caso, Alfonso, and Daniel F. Rubín de la Borbolla
1936 Exploraciones en Mitla 1934–1935. Instituto Panamericano de Geografía e Historia, publicación 21. Mexico.

Chance, John K.
1978 Race and Class in Colonial Oaxaca. Stanford: Stanford University Press.

Córdova, Fray Juan de
1987 [1578] Vocabulario en lengua zapoteca. Mexico: Ediciones Toledo.

Denevan, William M., ed.
1976 The Native Population of the Americas in 1492. Madison: University of Wisconsin Press.

Evans, Susan T.
1991 Architecture and authority in an Aztec village: Form and function of the *tecpan*. In: Land and Politics in the Valley of Mexico: A Two Thousand Year Perspective, edited by Herbert R. Harvey, pp. 63–92. Albuquerque: University of New Mexico Press.

Fernández, María T., Maurice Swadesh, and Robert Weitlaner
1960 El panorama etnolingüístico de Oaxaca y del Istmo. Séptima Mesa Redonda de la Sociedad Mexicana de Antropología. Revista Mexicana de Estudios Antropológicos 16:137–57.

Flannery, Kent V., and Joyce Marcus
1983 The origins of the state in Oaxaca, editors' introduction. In: The Cloud People: Divergent Evolution of the Zapotec and Mixtec Civilizations, edited by Kent V. Flannery and Joyce Marcus, pp. 79–83. New York: Academic Press.

Gerhard, Peter
1972 A Guide to the Historical Geography of New Spain. Cambridge: Cambridge University Press.

Gibson, Charles
1964 The Aztecs under Spanish Rule: A History of the Indians of the Valley of Mexico, 1519–1810. Stanford: Stanford University Press.

Hassig, Ross
1985 Trade, Tribute, and Transportation: The Sixteenth-Century Political Economy of the Valley of Mexico. Norman: University of Oklahoma Press.

Hicks, Frederic
1986 Prehispanic background of colonial political and economic organization in central Mexico. In: Supplement to the Handbook of Middle American Indians, edited by Victoria R. Bricker. Vol. 4: Ethnohistory, edited by Ronald Spores, pp. 35–54. Austin: University of Texas Press.

Hirth, Kenneth G.
1984 Xochicalco: Urban growth and state formation in central Mexico. Science 225:579–86.

Kellogg, Susan M.
1986 Kinship and social organization in early colonial Tenochtitlan. In: Supplement to the Handbook of Middle American Indians, edited by Victoria R. Bricker. Vol. 4: Ethnohistory, edited by Ronald Spores, pp. 103–21. Austin: University of Texas Press.

Kowalewski, Stephen A., Gary M. Feinman, Laura Finsten, Richard E. Blanton, and Linda M. Nicholas
1989 Monte Albán's Hinterland, Part II: Prehispanic Settlement Patterns in Tlacolula, Etla, and Ocotlán, the Valley of Oaxaca, Mexico. Memoirs of the Museum of Anthropology, University of Michigan, no. 23. Ann Arbor.

Marcus, Joyce
1983a Changing patterns of stone monuments after the fall of Monte Albán, A.D. 600–900. In: The Cloud People: Divergent Evolution of the Zapotec and Mixtec Civilizations, edited by Kent V. Flannery and Joyce Marcus, pp. 191–97. New York: Academic Press.
1983b The reconstructed chronology of the later Zapotec rulers, A.D. 1415–1563. In: The Cloud People: Divergent Evolution of the Zapotec and Mixtec Civilizations, edited by Kent V. Flannery and Joyce Marcus, pp. 301–8. New York: Academic Press.
1989 From centralized systems to city-states: Possible models for the Epiclassic. In: Mesoamerica after the Decline of Teotihuacan A.D. 700–900, edited by Richard A. Diehl and Janet Catherine Berlo, pp. 201–8. Dumbarton Oaks Research Library and Collection, Washington, D.C.
1992 Mesoamerican Writing Systems: Propaganda, Myth, and History in Four Ancient Civilizations. Princeton, New Jersey: Princeton University Press.

Marcus, Joyce, and Kent V. Flannery
1978 Ethnoscience of the sixteenth-century Valley Zapotec. In: The Nature and Status of Ethnobotany, edited by Richard I. Ford, pp. 51–70. Anthropological Papers of the Museum of Anthropology, University of Michigan, no. 67. Ann Arbor.

Münch, Guido
1989 Fiestas y mayordomías en la república zapoteca de Tehuantepec: Investigación histórico-antropológico. In: Tehuantepec 1891–1991: Un siglo de fe, tomo II, pp. 11–68. Tehuantepec, Mexico: Comisión de Historia del Centenario de la Diócesis de Tehuantepec.

Newson, Linda A.
1985 Indian population patterns in colonial Spanish America. Latin American Research Review 20(3):41–75.

Nicholas, Linda M.
1989 Land use in prehispanic Oaxaca. In: Monte Alban's Hinterland, Part II, edited by Stephen A. Kowalewski et al., pp. 449–505. Memoirs of the Museum of Anthropology, University of Michigan, no. 23. Ann Arbor.

Oviedo, Gonzalo Fernández de
1959 Historia general y natural de las indias [1544], vol. 2. Biblioteca de Autores Españoles. Madrid.

Paddock, John
1983a Lambityeco. In: The Cloud People: Divergent Evolution of the Zapotec and Mixtec Civilizations, edited by Kent V. Flannery and Joyce Marcus, pp. 197–204. New York: Academic Press.
1983b Comments on the lienzos of Huilotepec and Guevea. In: The Cloud People: Divergent Evolution of the Zapotec and Mixtec Civilizations, edited by Kent V. Flannery and Joyce Marcus, pp. 308–13. New York: Academic Press.

Parsons, Jeffrey R.
1976 The role of chinampa agriculture in the food supply of Aztec Tenochtitlan. In: Cultural Change and Continuity: Essays in Honor of James Bennett Griffin, edited by Charles Cleland, pp. 223–57. New York: Academic Press.

Paso y Troncoso, Francisco del, ed.
1905a Relaciones geográficas de la diócesis de Oaxaca. Papeles de Nueva España, segunda serie, geografía y estadística, vol. 4. Madrid: Est. Tipográfico "Sucesores de Rivadeneyra."
1905b Relación de la visita que hizo Baltasar de San Miguel del pueblo de Tecoantepeque y su probincia. Papeles de Nueva España, segunda serie, geografía y estadística, vol. 1, pp. 312–14. Madrid: Est. Tipográfico "Sucesores de Rivadeneyra."

Peterson, David A., and Thomas B. MacDougall
1974 Guiengola: A Fortified Site in the Isthmus of Tehuantepec. Vanderbilt University Publications in Anthropology, no. 10. Nashville.

Sahlins, Marshall
1985 Islands of History. Chicago: University of Chicago Press.

Sanders, William T.
1976 The population of the Central Mexican Symbiotic Region, the Basin of Mexico, and the Teotihuacan Valley in the sixteenth century. In: The Native Population of the Americas in 1492, edited by William M. Denevan, pp. 77–150. Madison: University of Wisconsin Press.

Schroeder, Susan
1991 Chimalpahin and the Kingdoms of Chalco. Tucson: University of Arizona Press.

Smith, Michael E.
1992 Houses and the settlement hierarchy in Late Postclassic Morelos: A comparison of archaeology and ethnohistory. In: Prehispanic Domestic Units in Western Mesoamerica: Studies of the Household, Compound and Residence, edited by Robert S. Santley and Kenneth G. Hirth. Boca Raton: CRC Press.

Smith, Michael E., Patricia Aguirre, Cynthia Heath-Smith, Kathryn Hirst, Scott O'Mack, and Jeffrey Price
1989 Architectural patterns at three Aztec-period sites in Morelos, Mexico. Journal of Field Archaeology 16:185–203.

Spores, Ronald
1965 The Zapotec and Mixtec at Spanish contact. In: Handbook of Middle American Indians, edited by Robert Wauchope. Vol. 3: Archaeology of Southern Mesoamerica, edited by Gordon R. Willey, pt 2, pp. 962–87. Austin: University of Texas Press.

Whitecotton, Joseph W.
1977 The Zapotecs: Princes, Priests, and Peasants. Norman: University of Oklahoma Press.
1990 Zapotec Elite Ethnohistory: Pictorial Genealogies from Eastern Oaxaca. Vanderbilt University Publications in Anthropology, no. 39. Nashville.

Zeitlin, Judith Francis
1978 Changing patterns of resource exploitation, settlement distribution, and demography on the southern Isthmus of Tehuantepec, Mexico. In: Prehistoric Coastal Adaptations: The Economy and Ecology of Maritime Middle America, edited by Barbara L. Stark and Barbara Voorhies, pp. 151–77. New York: Academic Press.
1984 Colonialism and the political transformation of Isthmus Zapotec society. In: Law and Government in Central Mexico: Pre-Columbian Times to the Present, edited by Ronald Spores and Ross Hassig, pp. 65–85. Vanderbilt University Publications in Anthropology, no. 30. Nashville.
1992 La organización del barrio zapoteco en Tehuantepec y su acomodación al colonialismo: Evidencia arqueológica y etnohistórica. Paper presented at the Congreso Internacional de Antropología e Historia, Veracruz, Mexico.

Zeitlin, Judith Francis, and Lillian Thomas
1992a Archaeology and history at Santa Cruz Chihuitán, a colonial "pueblo desaparecido" on the southern Isthmus of Tehuantepec, Mexico. Paper presented at the annual meeting of the Society for Historical Archaeology, Kingston, Jamaica.
1992b Spanish justice and the Indian cacique: Disjunctive political systems in sixteenth-century Tehuantepec. Ethnohistory 39(3):285–315.

Zorita, Alonso de
1963 Breve y sumaria relación de los señores de la Nueva España. 2nd ed. Universidad Nacional Autónoma de México. Mexico.